GOD'S WAYS
WITH THE
WORLD

GOD'S WAYS
WITH THE
WORLD

Thinking and Practising Christian Faith

DANIEL W. HARDY

T & T CLARK
EDINBURGH

T&T CLARK LTD
59 GEORGE STREET
EDINBURGH EH2 2LQ
SCOTLAND

First published 1996

ISBN 0 567 08507 4

British Library Cataloguing-in-Publication Data
A catalogue record for this book is available from the British Library

Typeset by Fakenham Photosetting Ltd, Fakenham, Norfolk
Printed and bound in Great Britain by Hartnolls Ltd, Bodmin

For those in whose world of trust and thought I turn, with deepest thanks

Contents

Contents

Acknowledgements

The poems of Micheal O'Siadhail are reprinted by permission of Blood-axe Books Ltd.: 'Freedom', 'Motet', 'Out of the Blue', 'Hail! Madam Jazz', 'Perspectives', 'Cosmos', 'Disclosure', 'Rhapsody: Flow', 'Feed-back', from *Hail! Madam Jazz* by Micheal O'Siadhail (Newcastle upon Tyne: Bloodaxe Books, 1992) and 'Weaving' from *The Fragile City* by Micheal O'Siadhail (Newcastle upon Tyne: Bloodaxe Books, 1995).

Gratitude is also expressed to the editors and publishers of books and journals in which the following have appeared:

Chapter 2 in *Worship and Ethics*, ed. Oswald Bayer and Alan Suggate, Berlin: Walter de Gruyter, 1996; Chapters 3 and 5 in *Christ and Con-text*, ed. Hilary D. Regan, Edinburgh: T. & T. Clark, 1993; Chapter 6 in *Scottish Journal of Theology*, 30/2, 1977; Chapter 7 in *The Incarnation*, ed. Thomas F. Torrance, Edinburgh: The Handsel Press, 1981; Chapter 10 in *The Weight of Glory*, ed. Daniel W. Hardy and Peter H. Sedgwick, Edinburgh: T. & T. Clark, 1991; Chapter 11 in *On Being the Church*, ed. Colin E. Gunton and Daniel W. Hardy, Edinburgh: T. & T. Clark, 1989; Chapter 14 in *Keeping the Faith*, ed. Geoffrey Wainwright, Phila-delphia: The Fortress Press / London: SPCK, 1988; and Chapter 17 in *Christian Theology and Religious Education*, ed. Jeff Astley and Leslie J. Francis, London: SPCK, 1996.

I

Introduction

WHILE the essays included in this book range widely in subject-matter, style and complexity, they arise from certain convictions and concerns which need to be recognized if their significance is to be fully understood.

My most fundamental conviction is of the truth and vitality of Christian faith, one which is based in the living God and the activity of God in the world. Accordingly, these essays are attempts – originating in differing circumstances – to follow this truth and vitality by tracing the ways of God with the world. They are the product of no 'school' or pre-established way of proceeding with theology, despite the traces which they contain of the scholarship and insights of those from which I have benefited.

I am equally convinced that there is a profundity in God's ways which – despite ages of valuable contemplation and practice – has yet to be fully uncovered. The task of unearthing them is intimately associated with the exploration of the vitalities of present-day life and thought. Why those? For centuries at least, Christians have tended to divorce their attention to the character and purposes of God from other spheres in which the vitality of God is manifest, leaving those to be pursued as dissociated from the purposes of God. Even theology itself has suffered this dissociation as it has come to be confined in an academic professionalism dominated by the application of other disciplines to religion.[1] Now, as in the great eras of theological understanding in the past, the connection between God's ways and the world in which they are found must be restored in a new and deeper synthesis of faith, theology and other disciplined forms of life and thought: that is the fundamental task of theology in our time.

It is to such a synthesis that many of these essays are directed, a synthesis that makes these essays as multifaceted as the disciplined forms of life and thought with which they engage. The endeavour to understand and follow God's ways leads through a profound encounter with other forms of life and thought, for the character and purposes of God are not, in the last analysis, separable from them. The truth and purposes of God are 'refracted' – as it were spread like a band of colour – in other forms of life and thought; and the purpose of theology is to rediscover the dy-

[1] See Chapter 18.

1

namic of the God's life and work in this 'band of colour' and from it.[2] Although in many ways it is more 'comfortable' to contemplate the great statements of faith recorded from previous eras, they are inadequate except as preparatory for the task just described.

A confidence that the truth and vitality of God – inestimably greater than yet understood or followed – can be found anew in such a profound encounter with other forms of life and thought, undergirds these essays in all their variety. If it can be understood and followed, at least in some degree, the consequences for the condition and direction of life in the world, for thought and for practice, will be rich and energizing. In effect, we shall then discover again what it is to live in a Godly universe – in such a vivid way that we shall find ourselves enthralled by it.

The compass of a single book poses decided limitations for such a project, and many essays were set aside in the process of shaping the book. Even in those now included, clues must often suffice where sustained discussion would be desirable; intensely concentrated thought must displace consideration of the ramifications for practice; and there is much less of the conventional documentation than needed for a full account. The essays are, however, distillations – often written under pressure – of intensive thought and practice nourished by a lifetime of research and teaching in historical and systematic theology, interdisciplinary investigation, priestly ministry in the Church, personal engagement with those seeking to live from faith in the living triune God, and the development of institutional provision for all of these in and beyond the Church.[3] The essays are published here with little change; to edit them substantially would be impossible without encroaching on the further work which I now propose to undertake in many of these fields.

It is the task of understanding and following God's ways with the world – in all the ways offered to me – which has been at the centre of my life. Despite the modesty of the insights which have resulted, I hope that this book may be of some assistance to others in pursuit of the same task.

---

[2] This strategy for theology is considered in Chapter 18, and also in 'The Logic of Interdisciplinary Studies and the Coherence of Theology', The Director's Report for 1994, Center of Theological Inquiry, Princeton, N.J.

[3] A biographical account is included as Chapter 1 in the companion volume to this, *Essentials of Christian Community*, ed. David F. Ford and Dennis Stamps, Edinburgh: T. & T. Clark, 1996.

Part One: Orientation to God

2

The Foundation of Cognition and Ethics in Worship[1]

INTRODUCTION

WITH few exceptions, the worship of the churches today is seen as a conventional and undemanding activity whereby Christians continue the beliefs and practices of the past. In practice, it seems that worship has become 'routinized charisma'.[2] The 'conventional' position which worship occupies is symptomatic of the limitations now generally placed on its importance. Yet there is little question that worship, when fully understood, serves as the indispensable foundation for cognition and ethics.

Unfortunately, modern defences of the importance of worship do not substantially improve the situation. One such defence takes the form of establishing worship as a separate theological discipline which has to do with the texts and history of worship, liturgy, and these are thought most aptly to be approached through textual and historical methods. The practices of equating worship with liturgical history and then separating liturgy from other disciplines in theology go unquestioned; and the exclusive use of historical-textual study is not questioned either.[3] Rarely, therefore, is the nature of worship discussed. Neither is consideration given to the consequences of liturgical study for other theological disciplines, or for more general concerns with right belief and right action, whether in times contemporaneous with the liturgies studied or for today.[4]

Another more directly theological defence of the position of worship in theology brings other difficulties. Worship is seen as complementary with doctrine and life, the three 'conjoined in a common "upwards" and

---

[1] A paper written for the Durham-Tübingen Consultation, a series of meetings between members of the Department of Theology of the University of Durham and the Evangelical Faculty of Theology of the University of Tübingen.

[2] The early history of church ministry is frequently described by sociologists as the 'routinisation of charisma', but the phrase is also applicable to what has now occurred for and in worship.

[3] Often – though not always – it also presupposes the validity of directly transferring historical practices to the present.

[4] Unfortunately, at least in English universities, provision for liturgy even as a separate and developed academic discipline is rare. Where it does exist, there is little opportunity for the consideration of how it may be constitutive for right belief and practice.

"forwards" direction towards God and the achievement of his purpose, which includes human salvation'.[5] Worship is the place where this vision comes into sharp focus for the Church, and 'the theologian's thinking therefore properly draws on the worship of the Christian community and is in duty bound to contribute to it, ... aiming at a coherent intellectual expression of the Christian vision, ... to propose to the worshipping community any corrections or improvements which he judges necessary'.[6] Because liturgies for worship shape human experience and behaviour, and theology has a reflexive and critical function, the expressions of such experience and behaviour in theology can be gathered as in a 'liturgical way of doing theology' which organizes theology around worship.

Notwithstanding the seriousness with which this position takes worship, it prejudges what occurs there and also separates worship not from doctrine but from theology. In a fashion typical of post-Kantian theology, the main mediations in which the impact of worship are found are human experience and behaviour, upon which theology reflects.[7] Three consequences follow: (1) The issue of what truth is found in worship is set aside, and varieties of experience and behaviour are presented as of equal worth. (2) Closely allied to this is the problem that the dynamics of God's presence and work (and hence of his nature) in the processes of cognition and ethics as such are not considered; such ontological and epistemological matters are eschewed in favour of the discussion of religious experience theologically expressed. Correspondingly, the more demanding requirements for cognition and ethics which might follow from the presence and work of God in worship are muted. As we will see, worship is a risk which makes radical demands on cognition and ethics, because of the active presence of God manifest there; this differs from the more relative demand made by the shapes of liturgy on human experience. (3) Since it dwells on worship-focussed experience, and confines the discussion to Christian expressions of that, the consideration is – though in the broadest terms – confessional, 'from faith to faith', and does not consider God's presence and activity in the public domain within which cognition and ethics operate. With these limitations, such a defence of the importance of worship for cognition and ethics is far too limited as a

[5] Geoffrey Wainwright, *Doxology: The Praise of God in Worship, Doctrine and Life. A Systematic Theology*, New York: Oxford University Press, 1980, p. 10.
[6] *Ibid.*, p. 3.
[7] Here, following a pattern of thought very similar to that of Schleiermacher, itself a reaction to that of Kant, worship is seen as the avenue by which the absolute draws human experience and behaviour beyond its usual confinement to knowledge and ethics, which are consequently regarded as reflections on the original 'drawing up'. Cf. F. D. E. Schleiermacher, *On Religion: Speeches to Its Cultured Despisers*, trans. John Oman, New York: Harper & Row, 1958, Second Speech.

discussion both of the dynamics of God's presence and of its impact on the people and world for which it occurs.[8]

This brings us to what will be our central concerns here. What is it that occurs in worship? And how is that related to truth, as well as to those disciplines – cognition and ethics – which are occupied with ascertaining truth? How, furthermore, are these given their fullest direction in Christian worship of God?

The methods by which truth is sought nowadays have little apparent connection with worship. The main alternatives for the pursuit of truth are variants of the positivistic notion of scientific knowledge, the experience of art or the model of rhetoric.[9] By contrast, worship is seen as the most intensive expression of a faith already arrived-at, in which the issue of truth is suspended; worship is therefore regarded as the most 'confessional' aspect of Christian faith. Not surprisingly therefore, where the study of faith is assimilated to the notions of truth implicit in secular academic study, worship is the first casualty. If it receives attention at all, it is only as an interesting phenomenon, one activity alongside others in a special domain called 'religion' where questions of truth can only be raised with great difficulty. Amongst 'religious' activities, its relation to others is largely overlooked; and if the constitutive features of religion are identified as knowledge (right belief) and ethics (right action), the two comprising 'true religion', the importance of worship for these is ignored. Furthermore, its significance beyond 'religion' is forgotten. The result is fragmentation: not only the fragmentation of truth from worship, but of worship from knowledge and ethics.

This situation needs to be appreciated if we are to find the kind of connection which there is between worship, truth, knowledge, and ethics, and how that connection is formed in the Christian understanding of worship. For we shall be presenting a quite different view of their relation than this situation normally allows.

Instead of seeing worship either as the most intensive expression of a faith already arrived-at, in which the issue of truth is suspended, or as a free approach to mystery, we shall see worship as that special and primary activity which incorporates truth in its activity, and thereby defines and effects a reality which exemplifies this truth. Cognition, as we will see, finds its proper placing and methods within worship as it participates in the movement of truth and exemplifies it in the understanding of reality. Ethics likewise participates in the movement of truth, but does so through

[8] For further discussion of this position, see D. W. Hardy and D. F. Ford, *Jubilate: Theology in Praise*, London: Darton, Longman & Todd, 1984, pp. 169f.

[9] 'The post-modern – in Heideggerian terms, post-metaphysical – experience of truth is an aesthetic and rhetorical experience.' Gianni Vattimo, *The End of Modernity: Nihilism and Hermeneutics in Post-modern Culture*, London: Polity Press, 1988, p. 12.

bringing about the proper form of reality as such, particularly in the realms of nature and society. Thus, worship is the central means whereby human beings are called to their proper fullness in society and the world.

NOTIONS OF TRUTH AND THE RESTRICTION AND LIBERATION OF WORSHIP

The beginning of the fragmentation of worship and truth – as traditionally conceived – occurs when worship is seen as the intensive expression of a faith whose truth can no longer be accepted as unproblematic. And the usual result is transition to a free approach to an undefined mystery. Such a transition is described in a poem by the Irish poet Micheal O'Siadhail:

> Enough was enough. We flew
> nets of old certainties,
> all that crabbed grammar
> of the predictable. Unentangled,
> we'd soar to a language
> of our own.
>
> Freedom. We sang of freedom
> (travel lightly, anything goes)
> and somehow became strangers
> to each other, like gabblers
> at cross purposes, builders
> of Babel.
>
> Slowly I relearn a *lingua*,
> shared overlays of rule,
> lattice of memory and meaning,
> our latent images, a tongue
> at large in an endlessness
> of sentences unsaid.[10]

Here – in the first two stanzas – are two familiar views of truth. One confines truth, not only in the metaphysical but in its correspondence to reality, a correspondence which is predeterminative and therefore allows prediction. There are fixed beliefs and norms: 'nets of old certainties, all

---

[10] 'Freedom' from Micheal O'Siadhail, *The Chosen Garden*, Dublin: The Dedalus Press, 1990, p. 57.

that crabbed grammar of the predictable' – a view of truth which entangles one in convoluted fixities which include and predict all. The other idealizes freedom from such truth and the predictability which it imposes: 'unentangled we'd soar to a language of our own' – a view of truth which suggests that it lies in subscription to a minimum, which even then divides. Of course, the two views incline in opposite directions, the one toward fixed metaphysics in correspondence with reality, the self-repeating reality which such a metaphysics requires and a commonness based on standard expectations, the other toward fluidity, minimal belief, difference of expectation and change, leading to the estrangement of people (and their purposes) from each other. But both are relativized as they are made dependent on human agency: *'we* flew nets of old certainties'; *'we* sang of freedom'.

The poem, however, contrasts these views with a much less restrictive possibility for truth, that of relearning a *lingua* which is not simply based on human assertion, which has its roots in the past and its applicability in the present, and which allows people to join together in the depths of what may yet be said. At first glance, this appears to be the aesthetic and rhetorical notion of truth which is said to be characteristic of post-modernism. But it is not, simply because it is the result of a 'slow relearning', a deep sharing, of latent images, seeking a *lingua* through which an infinity of meaning can be brought to speech.

These are not simply poetic visions of truth. The same three possibilities for truth appear – in different order – in more concrete historical terms in the story of St Thomas following the Resurrection, and the ways in which that is conventionally interpreted.[11] (1) In the first place, we see in Thomas what appears to be a spirit of free inquiry, seeking to validate belief by empirical investigation unencumbered by claims from others elsewhere. When he is confronted by the fixed certainty of other disciples that Jesus has been raised from the dead, he is too fully embedded in such habits simply to accept it. It follows that he is therefore isolated, both from other disciples and from the one – the risen Jesus – around whom their community is gathered. Thomas' behaviour is commonly admired by modern people who idealize *free inquiry* and *observational evidence*, and with them the normalcy of *individualism*. In accordance with the ideals of modern thought, Thomas doubts what he does not find for himself, and does not accept general impressions or the beliefs of others; he must believe *for himself* and do so on the basis of hard, specific *evidence*. So he will not accept what he seems to think is the unconfirmed truth about Jesus rising from the dead until he himself sees the risen Jesus, and sees the specific things which show that it is Jesus that he is seeing. And even seeing is not enough for him; he must touch: 'Unless I

---

[11] John 22.24–29.

see the nail marks in his hands, and put my finger into his side, I will not have faith in it.' And, according to the Gospel accounts, the resurrected Jesus does in fact come amongst the disciples and invite Thomas to see and touch the things which show that it is the same Jesus who was crucified that now stands in front of him: 'Put your finger here; see my hands. Reach out your hand and put it into my side. Do not be faithless but faithful.' (John 20.27)

(2) But there is another side to the story, which appears to advocate *the unconditional acceptance of fixed truths*. Jesus corrects Thomas: 'Because you have seen me, have you accepted? Blessed are those who have faith even when they do not see.' This seems to suggest that it is better simply to accept given truth in faith than to raise questions about it, or to demand observational evidence. The truly faithful person simply accepts on trust what has been given him/her to accept, and lives in and from that truth. Like the other view, this notion of truth is also widespread amongst Christians. There is a 'truth given in the beginning' through revelation. This truth is theoretical in form, in the sense that it is a simple and comprehensive statement of Christian faith. And accepting it confers blessing and full community; it is the basis of full life in the Church. Correspondingly, it cannot be doubted without the withdrawal of that blessing, or without removing oneself from the Church. For those who understand Christian faith in this way, the statements of assent made by Christians are statements of simple acceptance of the truth which is 'contained in the Scriptures, set forth in the creeds, and witnessed to in the historical formularies of the Church'.[12] And they cannot subsequently question that to which they have assented without undermining their faith and its grace.

The two views just mentioned are frequently seen as unalterably opposed, as those which emphasize 'unentangled freedom' are opposed to 'nets of old certainties'. A modernity which idealizes the restless free inquiry of the isolated individual, pursued through a consistent search for hard evidence, is often set against a traditionality which idealizes the strategy of trusting acceptance of a transmitted truth, manifest in a life in that faith. The result is that the two are hardened into positions which exclude the other. On the one hand, it is said (by those committed to the fixity of truth) that free inquiry and an ongoing search for evidence, together with all the attention to reflection and empirical detail which they require, will disarm the possibility of recognizing truth; and the activity of questioning all truth can carry questioners beyond the possibility of settled or shared conviction of any kind.[13] On the other hand, it is claimed (by those committed to an adventurous freedom) that strict adherence to

---

[12] This is the affirmation required of those to be ordained in the Church of England.
[13] When seen in this way, post-modernism appears as the extreme of modernism.

traditional theories disallows the acknowledgment that any statement of faith is to some extent fluid, and therefore subject to alteration and interpretation in the light of historical understanding.[14] Proponents of each of the two views fail to understand the other, and frequently exclude the other from any kind of legitimacy. Consideration of any major issue polarizes the two and revives this misunderstanding, bringing both common understanding and common action to a standstill. Interestingly enough, the very disagreement between adherents of the two views brings constructive discussion of cognitive and ethical matters to a stop.[15]

But is either of these opposing views of truth sufficient? And is the story of St Thomas to be understood primarily in these terms, as a trial of two views of truth – one which justifies a view of truth which is minimalist, conditional and contingent upon free inquiry, and the other which presents truth in the form of fixed 'givens' to be received from authoritative sources and unconditionally accepted? And is human agency so pivotal? Or are these restricted forms of a more fundamental view of truth?

There is a third possibility to be considered, however, similar to what Micheal O'Siadhail called 'the relearning of a *lingua*'. This suggests that truth is reached and held by other means. And this option brings us closer to seeing truth as moving and – through worship – incorporating the believer's cognition and ethical awareness. How this happens in an historical situation can be seen in the story of Thomas.

On the one hand, as so often happens in the Gospels, Thomas' expectations are transformed and surpassed. Contrary to the common supposition that it is Thomas' free inquiry which brings belief, it is the *movement* of Jesus toward Thomas which elicits Thomas' *response*. Jesus presents himself to Thomas and is receptive to the kind of questions which he asks; and it is Jesus who offers the possibility for exact evidence. The result is that Thomas is called to *attend* to Jesus, and no longer persists with his desire for inquiry; in the presence of Jesus, there is no record that he does touch Jesus. How then does he respond? He does not arrive at anything so sterile as an acceptance of the 'fact' of the resurrection, but instead finds the possibility of a deep engagement with the very person whose life he had doubted. This response carries him out of his isolation and into the 'relearning of a *lingua*' in a full *affirmation of Jesus*: 'My

---

[14] This is the problem with many statements of the 'realist' position today.

[15] An interesting example of this opposition is found in the story of Martha and Mary (Luke 10.38–42), in which Martha, 'distracted by much serving' appeals to Jesus to send her sister Mary, who was sitting at his feet listening to his teaching, to help. But Jesus says to her, 'Martha, Martha, you are anxious about many things ... Mary has chosen the good portion, which shall not be taken from her.' Martha's concern for many things brings her the same distractedness and isolation which characterize the free inquirer obsessed with hard evidence, Mary's quiet listening to Jesus seems similar to simple acceptance of given truth, and there is the same misunderstanding between them.

Lord and my God!' It is this old-new language (a 'lattice of memory and meaning') employed in this affirmation which reconstitutes his belief and his action, not a successful inquiry.

On the other hand, Jesus' words to Thomas ('Blessed are those who have faith even when they do not see.') cannot be taken as a straightforward defence of the necessity of accepting fixed beliefs and norms – statements of 'old certainties ... that crabbed grammar of the predictable'. First, Jesus' words present a different *way* of faith. The inability to see does not force the sightless into accepting statements of truth from others. Rather, the inability to see confers a different way of encountering truth. For a blind person, the encounter with the world rests on its self-presentation through sound, and this means an intermittency of encounter which is not the case for a sighted person.

> The acoustic world is one in which things pass in and out of existence. This happens with surprising rapidity. There seems to be no intermediate zone of approach. There is a sudden cry from the lake, 'Hello Daddy!'; my children are there in their paddle boat. Previously, a moment ago, they were not there ... The intermittent nature of the acoustic world is one of its most striking features. In contrast, the perceived world is stable and continuous ... Acoustic space is a world of revelation.[16]

Secondly, it needs to be recognized that for the blind person, having faith is the process of orienting oneself in the presence of a truth which is otherwise present only through sound. Statements, whether from truth or from those who have witnessed it, serve as aids to its memory – and hence to self-orientation – not as substitutes for it, as if it were no longer present.[17] These are the 'memory' to which Micheal O'Siadhail refers, whose 'meaning' must be found anew by reference to the continued presence of the reality to which they refer:

> Slowly I relearn a *lingua*,
> shared overlays of rule,
> lattice of memory and meaning,
> our latent images, a tongue

---

[16] John M. Hull, *Touching the Rock: An Experience of Blindness*, London: SPCK, 1990, pp. 63f.

[17] It is sometimes said that 'When the Bible is open, God speaks; when it is shut, he stops.' This can be taken to mean that Biblical statements substitute for the constant reality of God's presence.

at large in an endlessness
of sentences unsaid.[18]

And this 'lattice of memory and meaning' gives us a tongue in which to speak, in an ongoing process of understanding never fully achieved.

In effect, then, the two views of truth which we have seen – the one emphasizing free individual inquiry and the other emphasizing trusting acceptance – are not quite what they seem. Each finds its proper placing within a dynamic of movement and response which is the heart of that activity we know as worship. Without reference to this dynamic, they become self-important and self-destructive.

THE MOVEMENT OF TRUTH AND HUMAN RESPONSE

How is it that the movement of truth – and hence the relearning of a *lingua* – occurs? We must now undertake a preliminary survey of the ontology and epistemology of worship.

As we have now seen, the proper interaction between free inquiry and accepting belief occurs within the movement of truth, in the movement of God toward human beings into which human understanding and action are incorporated. What are the circumstances in which this happens? It does not simply happen when people are 'open'; much as it is idealized today, the notion of openness is too restricted, for many of the same reasons as is free inquiry. Nor does it happen when people simply adhere to accepted statements of truth; as the old saying goes, 'I've made up my mind – don't confuse me with facts.' That is equally restricted, as we saw when we considered this notion of truth. Christian faith is neither a generalized openness to the divine nor an obedient acceptance of what is given, though both are important. Instead, it is a directed openness (or attentiveness) within the movement of truth toward human beings. The proper interaction occurs where people move in the same direction as that of the movement of truth.

When we reach this point, we find that there are three issues inextricably linked: (1) What is the movement of truth toward human beings? (2) How are people to follow this movement? (3) What are the impli-

---

[18] 'Freedom' from Micheal O'Siadhail, *The Chosen Garden*, Dublin: The Dedalus Press, 1990, p. 57.

cations for human knowledge and behaviour? We can attempt preliminary answers to the questions.

(2) If God is the primary source of all that is, the most suitable way of
following the movement of truth occurs in worship, where full attention is
given to God, moving for and in human beings in the world. Worship itself
is the recognition of ontological position and movement of that which is
worshipped, and it entails the proportioning of human knowledge and
behaviour to the being and activity of that which is recognized.[19]

(1) Such worship is based on the actual movement of the truth of God
toward human beings, whose fundamental pattern or logic can be discerned. This movement is one which energizes (enlivens) human beings
and lifts them to their proper being and activity in truth – the peace which
is their truest character. And the movement is traceable to the character of
God, in which the energy of God fulfils relationality according to the
conditions of God's own being.[20] So it is that in worship, cognition and
ethics find *their* dynamic order. Where the dynamic order of a Trinitarian
God is recognized in worship, therefore, what is occurring is more than the
acknowledgment of a static state of affairs, however ultimate, in which
principles of knowledge or morality are established and then treated as a
foundation from which other insights may be derived. Where *God* is
worshipped, knowledge is directed to the ontological recognition of a
dynamic order of indefinite depth ('God') which is directed toward us in a
particular – though comprehensive – kind of movement, a dynamic order:
it moves 'for us' and our world, exciting and sustaining the dynamic order
in which our existence and well-being consist.

(3) In directed openness to this divine dynamic order, there also occurs
an ontological movement in those who recognize it, whose existence is
totally orientated to that which is recognized, in a total alteration of
affection which brings about a habit of life.[21] In its purified form, this
ontological recognition is praise, which incorporates a purified
reorientation, in which the dynamics of human life – both individual and
social – are focused in correspondence with that which is recognized in
praise. Whatever is the dynamic order recognized in the divine is therefore realized in the arrangement of human relationships in and with the
world. And insofar as the truth of God is discovered in praise, human

[19] cf. Matthew 22.21: 'Give to Caesar what is Caesar's, and to God what is God's.'
'Honour to whom honour is due.'
[20] By thus focusing on ultimate dynamic order, I am implicitly criticizing the tradition of
monarchianism which dominates Western theology, and substituting a more dynamic form
of Trinitarianism.
[21] A homely analogy for this is the physical or bodily adaptation which occurs for a
vegetarian, when the body adapts itself to eating vegetables to such a point that it cannot
tolerate eating meat. But the notion of a total reorientation is central to the view of faith
taken, for example, by John Calvin and Jonathan Edwards.

recognition and reorientation brings truth for them; the primary marks of that divine order – such as freedom in relationship, justice and love – are realized in the human.[22]

Recapitulating these three points, we may say that it is in the movement of worship (focused in praise), together with the movement of reorientation which accompanies it, that the dynamics of divine order in human life in the world are found in most concentrated form. It is here that the dynamics of the human subject in his/her search for truth and goodness are focused. Hence, the movement of worship 'sets the direction' for cognition and ethics.[23]

It is instructive to compare this account of the appearance in worship of the dynamics of divine order in human life in the world, with the tradition of Wisdom in Judaism and Christianity. There, a wisdom purified in praise shows the dynamic order of God present for humankind, thereby illuminating and grounding all the complexities of life and knowledge. The wisdom found in praise was not limited to those who 'worshipped' in formal ways; it was closely connected with much wider human concerns, those centred on finding the 'nature of things' and thereby finding the ways to live in the world. But finding and refining wisdom through praise was the means by which human beings focussed the order and the energy of God as it appeared in the world in which they lived.

THE DYNAMICS OF DIVINE AND HUMAN ORDER

The problem, however, is that current notions of God, and hence the worship of God, are too limited for such a correlation with truth or the disciplines concerned with it. There seems to be a clear correlation between the aridity of current views of God, equally arid conceptions of

---

[22] It is very important to recognize that these primary marks of divine order are realized *together* in the human. Freedom and responsibility, justice and love, are achieved together, not in isolation from each other; and the purification of one always involves the purification of the other. It is a matter of some debate how this combination is to be achieved in human life, and each party in the debate tends to idealize its own position. The following statement idealizes one alternative: 'The model toward which the Protestant Reformation initially began to move, and which the so-called "free churches" sought to incarnate more thoroughly than official Protestantism, is the voluntary community which has about it neither the coercive givenness of establishment nor the atomistic isolation of individualism.' (J. H. Yoder, *The Priestly Kingdom*, Notre Dame: Notre Dame Press, 1984, p. 25) And even if a satisfactory combination can be achieved in the Church, it is usually a sectarian success, and there is frequently a correlative failure to bring this to the world beyond.
[23] Cf. N. Maxwell, *From Knowledge to Wisdom: A Revolution in the Aims and Methods of Science*, Oxford: Basil Blackwell, 1984.

worship, and the sterility of much current discussion of truth, human cognition and ethics.[24] Now that we have seen that worship mediates (through dynamic concentration) the dynamic order of God in the reorientation of human cognition and ethics, it is time to discuss more fully the dynamic order of God. We must now outline a view of the dynamics of God which is more adequate to the complexities of man's life in the world as we know it.

Basic to this understanding of God is the actuality of full differentiation in God, and between God and the world, while still retaining full relationality in God and between God and the world. This allows us to discern 'relativities', how there are particularities in fully dynamic exchange with each other, within God and the world, and between God and the world.

If we see this full differentiation in God – the threefoldness of God – in radically relational terms, we may see God as relationality (Father), order in relationality (Son) and energy in relationality (Spirit). If we then see this threefoldness from the vantage-point of the Spirit, the Spirit may be seen as the energy which occurs in the relational dynamics implicit in the Father and which there brings about full order in the Son, doing so through what can be called 'blessing'. This 'blessing' is a concentration of energy which 'moves' the relational dynamics (Father) and hence its order (Son). Thus, from the implicit relationality of the Father, the Spirit can be seen to generate the fullness of the Father through the Son. The Spirit can then be seen to 'unite in holiness', though doing so in the relationality of the Father and in the order of the Son, as the active agent of their unity. This uniting is the blessing of the energy of the Spirit whereby dynamic relationality is redoubled and thus fully ordered.

Though this suggests a way in which the self-structuring of God is to be seen, it is a self-structuring which occurs in an ongoing 'relation' with human life in the world. In this relation all the characteristics of the divine (as just seen) interact ongoingly with those of human life in the world. This 'interaction' is constituted by the relational dynamics of the Father and the dynamic order in this relationality is that of the Son, but the energy in the relationality is that of the Spirit. And it suffuses human participation in the interaction. The 'blessing' of the Spirit in the interaction opens and reopens human beings to the full relationality of the Father in the dynamic order of the Son, and moreover energizes them to structure themselves accordingly, within their initial conditions as finite and historical.

This can and does occur for human beings without their awareness,

---

[24] It may be the case that the post-modernist emphasis on truth as rhetoric or art derives from the substitution of human creativity for the dynamics of divine – or even natural – creativity.

preconsciously so to speak, but it occurs to best effect when, in various ways appropriate to them, human beings interact with the Spirit through their own powers. And we have already seen that this happens most importantly in the directed openness of worship – where there is a 'focusing' which both excites and directs cognition and ethics.

Just as it is in the dynamics of his order – the energizing of his re-lationality – that God reaches his fullness, and in this dynamic order interacts energetically with human beings to enable them to develop their own dynamic order, it is in their 'relativities', the energizing and ordering of their relationality, that human beings exist. This is not simply a 'fixity' about them which they can acknowledge and forget, but the condition of their existence as human beings; their self-relationality and their re-lationality to others and to the world are the matrix of their life, and their dynamic self-structuring (e.g., the ontological reorientation which occurs in worship) always occurs within this matrix. There is, in fact, no 'self' which they can be which is not also a relativity to others and the world. This is what is seen, for example, in Jesus' summary of the law, 'love thy neighbour as thyself'. But, again, this cannot be treated as an achieve-ment, as if it could be a 'fact' of their previous being which sets limits on their relationality. The quality of their life resides in the development of the dynamic order in this relationality; the goal is beyond permanent achievement, and rests on concentration and reconcentration of the energy by which they are self-structured in interaction. Such a 'wisdom' of the intersection of truth and human order in worship is fundamental to the 'moving' and 'directing' of cognition and ethics.

MISDIRECTED ONTOLOGICAL RECOGNITION AND THE PROBLEM OF POWER

Ontological recognition and reorientation may be seriously misdirected, however, and at the least the result can be distortion or trivialization, the more so where such misdirection is 'refined' through a misdirected praise. Most often, the misdirection occurs through assigning excessive im-portance to what is finite and controllable. And the result is a double displacement, as the position of the divine dynamic order and the corres-ponding positioning of the human subject (both individual and social) are misdirected.[25]

In one way, such misdirection is understandable enough. The world as we find it is a rich array of fascinating events and patterns, and humanity itself interesting enough to be its own fascination (narcissism). The very

---

[25] It will be remembered that such misdirection is the root meaning of the word 'sin', and its refinement through misdirected praise is idolatry.

fascination of such things can easily lead us to focus upon them and their inherent richness, to such a point that they are seen to be the source from which all richness is projected.[26] And there is the further attraction that concentrating on them can serve to focus the order and energy of the world in such a way as to yield benefits.[27] The fault underlying such moves is a theological one, in which the depth of the dynamic order of God is lost to such a degree that human beings confuse the fascination of the world for that of God, and confine the richness of ontological recognition to the pragmatics of knowledge or technical principles. The richness of wisdom is thereby transferred to human hands; wisdom is transferred to those capable of manipulating it for what is presumed to be the benefit of humankind. Furthermore, these displacements occur not once only, but growingly; the world in which we live is increasingly interlaced with the effects of human science, technology and manipulation. What could once have been described as 'natural' is largely a human artifact.

Perhaps unwittingly, those whose persistent searching for evidence disallows the recognition of truth, as well as those who insist on the necessity of simply accepting given beliefs, misdirect ontological recognition. For both direct attention to processes of knowledge which are under human control. The result is not simply a mistake; it is a distortion of ontological recognition and human orientation. Furthermore, the 'correct' form of ontological recognition which is offered by each to the other simply repeats the misdirection. The 'searcher' offers worship of a mysterious God, one so mysterious that his participation in the world is limited (thereby 'underdetermining' the world), while the 'accepter' offers worship of a God whose will is clear, who 'determines' (actually overdetermines) the world.[28]

THE BRIGHT MYSTERY OF FAITH

It is a very serious question how such misdirection is overcome. There is much to be learned from Job, a classic instance of misdirection.

[26] There is a negative counterpart to this fascination, when the perversities of human beings produce damage, whether in themselves or for others, and these bring a horrible fascination which perpetuates and magnifies the damage.

[27] The expansion of such fascination leads naturally to an anthropological reduction of religion, as with Ludwig Feuerbach. Karl Marx provides a 'scientific' form of this fascination, by which the order and energy of the world are focused for human benefit.

[28] There are many today who are committed to the necessity of ignorance in ontological and ethical matters, and the chief alternative seems to be a willingness to prescribe courses of action for every situation. Strangely, both lead to trivialized notions of the world and human life. Regrettably, this is very much the case with modern religious practice. It is not only Anglicans of whom it can be said, as did one professor of religion, 'Give Anglicans two things to talk about, and they will always be found talking about the more trivial of the two.' Triviality has replaced blasphemy as the main hazard of religious life.

Job seems to have claimed a knowledge of the secrets of creation, and also to have supposed that by his knowledge and power he could affect creation in its most fundamental constitution. He had in fact taken control of the richness or creativity of wisdom itself. But, in the end, he was forced to admit: 'Surely I spoke of things I did not understand, things too wonderful for me to know.' (Job 42.3) In his way, as we have already seen, Thomas was very similar. He would not accept what he was told about the risen Jesus until he knew, and he could only know by seeing and touching. He too was overwhelmed by the presence of Jesus, and he forgot about wanting to know by seeing and touching.

Both situations make it clear that the fundamental possibility of worship – true ontological recognition and human orientation – remains even where there is misdirection, and that the dynamic between this recognition and its correlative orientation may be restored even where there have been disruptions. It is simply that the dynamic order which God has introduced into the human relation with him remains itself even where the eyes of human beings are diverted to lesser (and more controllable) substitutes; and, remaining itself, it brings the possibility of ontological recognition and reorientation.[29] If, therefore, the God who is recognized in worship is a mystery, this is not the mystery of a dark and remote being; it is what we might call a 'bright' mystery. Veiled though it may be to human beings who have concentrated on mediations of it, this 'veiled wisdom' is also a shining mystery, and one which is nearby. Here again, Job's words give an important clue: 'My ears had heard of you but now my eyes have seen you. Therefore I despise myself and repent in dust and ashes.' (Job 42.5–6)

There are important lessons hidden here also for both the groups we discussed earlier. (1) For those so committed to the persistent search for evidence that they are carried beyond the possibility of recognizing truth, whose key phrase is often 'the mystery of God' (a mystery which is to be appreciated through questioning, and which always defeats the possibility of saying anything positive), the mystery of God will now be seen as a glory or richness whose recognition makes it irradiate human understanding and practice. (2) For those whose rigid adherence to traditional theories disallows fluidity, the continued nearness and brightness of God manifests a creativity which always draws human beings beyond any fixed formula. There is a creativity hidden in wisdom itself which gives it

---

[29] 'At some point along the way *I turned my back on God*. I challenged and *dared* God to prove that I was/am loved. A stubborn refusal set in to accept for myself what I preach for others, that God is love – outgoing, searching love – that moves always towards us – only we need to be facing in the right direction, to know and appreciate that. So I'm in the early stages of turning, i.e. a real repentance, but it is hard and painful and won't happen overnight.' Private Communication.

that order and energy which brings human beings to transcend their own understanding, and does so both suddenly and gradually.[30]

THE FORMATION OF WORSHIP IN CHRIST

What is the basis for the ontological recognition and reorientation we have found in worship? It is that the mystery of God is a 'bright mystery': as mystery, it is not inert but active, creative and redemptive. And to be seen fully, this ordered dynamic must be seen in Trinitarian terms, as the stirring of God by the Holy Spirit to be himself by being with humankind in Jesus Christ. This is what comes into focus in worship, as it is ontologically recognized and as human beings reorientate themselves accordingly. It is as Archbishop Michael Ramsey once said, 'The gospel of the glory of God in the face of Jesus Christ is both strange to mankind and yet nearer to mankind than the breath which they breathe. For the truth in Him is also the truth in them.'[31]

The ordered movement of God – the dynamic order of God – to humankind which occurs by the Spirit-stirred presence of Jesus becomes formative for those who recognize it in worship, the more so where this is refined in praise. The active truth which is there in him occurs for them where they recognize him (ontological recognition) and follow him (positioning their life). The truth that is in him is highly dynamic and energetic, and is so also for them.

If one speaks of this in terms of wisdom, wisdom is seen to have a creativity set within it, which is ordered there by God's command and

---

[30] Such recognition may be sudden or gradual; one need not accept the view that it must be either the one (the overdeterminist view) or the other (the underdeterminist view), for the dynamic order of God's relation to human beings includes both.
[31] Where then does wisdom come from?
Where does understanding dwell?
It is hidden from the eyes of every living thing,
concealed even from the birds of the air.
Destruction and Death say,
'Only a rumour of it has reached our ears.'
God understands the way to it
and he alone knows where it dwells, ...
When he established the force of the wind
and measured out the waters, ...
then he looked at wisdom and appraised it;
he confirmed it and tested it.
And he said to man,
'The fear of the Lord – that is wisdom,
and to shun evil is understanding.' (Job 28.20–28)

confirmation; the full shape of it is found in Jesus Christ. And this needs to be recognized through an appropriate response, what can be called creative fearfulness. The movement of God toward humankind, so near to them in love, requires that they recognize him – fear the very one who is nearest to them in love. And this fear is itself an excitement whereby they may be drawn to him. Correspondingly, the hope for God which is found in fear provides a creative spark for all human understanding and life.[32] The way to wisdom is through a proper relation (fear) to God, from which there springs a creative hope for life on earth.

THE ETHICAL CONTENT OF WORSHIP

We have seen that worship – as ontological recognition with its correlative orientation of life – is central to the human relation to God, and that such recognition takes its dynamism from the dynamic order of God which appears in worship. Now we must look more closely at the implications of what we have found for the nature of goodness and how human beings may realize it.

Corresponding to the ontological recognition which we have seen to be characteristic of worship, human beings show an instinctive yearning for fullness of life. This may take the form, for those who contemplate it, of a 'vision of life in its fullness', such as that to which Mother Julian of Norwich, the great medieval English mystic, came:

All shall be well,
and all shall be well,
and all manner of thing shall be well.

Her words speak of the goal of life as a condition of well-being for all of us and everything, where everyone and everything is in order, and all is in harmony.

Such well-being is akin to glory, but only for those who partake of it (that is, are orientated to it), even if only in anticipation. As thus seen, glory denotes not splendour or magnificence but an undistorted order

---

In that way, David Hume's explanation of religion from the human psychological experiences of fear and hope proves right, though not in the way he intended.

and harmony which pervades all.[33] And the characteristic feature of such glory is that it is 'benign' or 'right', a feature which is recognized by those who are themselves 'right'.[34] This 'rightness' is not simply the absence of disruption; it suggests more than relief that the worst will not happen – the word is most frequently used when a tumour which threatened to be cancerous is diagnosed as 'benign'. It is closer to what is suggested by the words, 'It's all right after all!' – that something is entirely 'all right', and is known as such by one for whom it is 'all right'.[35] The indefinable quality of glory or well-being, of order and harmony, the 'all-rightness' which is in the universe, whose vestiges are within the reach of human beings, is that to which everyone reaches out whenever he/she seeks for well-being – which is the most characteristic human activity. We shall need to look at this more carefully in a moment.

First, it is important to recognize that the contemplation of such well-being is a twofold activity. There is an ontological recognition of this well-being correlated to a reorientation of life by which we recognize it. Hence well-being is recognized through a correlative well-being. The same occurs where there is neither time nor inclination for contemplation, and human beings seek for fullness of life, even in the fragmented form of pragmatic behaviour.

So far as the ontological recognition of well-being is concerned, for human beings whose lives are constantly changing, 'well-being' is neces-

---

[33] I was much struck by this when, during the year of the anniversary of St Cuthbert's death, the Queen Mother visited Durham Cathedral, where Cuthbert is buried. It was not she herself who was a magnificent figure, but the grace and harmony she brought with her which was so remarkable. And, as each person was introduced to her, she surrounded him/her with her own peace and tranquillity, drawing each person into her own well-being. That was her glory, an uninterrupted order and harmony which surrounded those with whom she came in touch. She needed none of the techniques which these days are used to make people appear splendid; the well-being with which she surrounded people was her glory. And it brought amongst those who were with her that day a sense of well-being and harmony.

[34] Hence the close association of the glory of God with his righteousness, of the human anticipation of it with hope and steadfastness in hope with faith. We 'desire a better country' by hoping for it and remaining steadfast in that hope. (cf. Hebrews 11.1–16)

[35] This was shown in the film Close Encounters of the Third Kind which made such an impression a few years ago. In it, the first encounters with the visitors from other planets seem frightening, and we are inclined to regard them with suspicion as the visits of alien intruders, particularly when they seem to frighten all those with whom the space ship comes in contact, and when a young boy is taken away. But, despite the typical responses of the Americans – a huge build-up of American armed forces to deal with them, and trying to keep the whole affair hidden from the public – it becomes more and more clear that the visitors come with entirely benign intentions. All the Army takeover, and the secrecy, are shown simply to be the product of fear. But those who have been contacted by these benign beings are, quite simply, fascinated, completely preoccupied by what has happened; they are drawn into the well-being these beings create. The only problem is communication, and that is overcome by the use of musical tones.

sarily elusive; the achievement of what is thought to be well-being stimulates the vision of what might be a greater well-being.[36] And, again by the nature of the case, for human beings who are particular individuals and societies, the nature and means of well-being are matters of disagreement and competition. But the ontological recognition of well-being remains: even when they cannot envisage or achieve this well-being, or at least not as much as they would like, human beings still search for it, live for it and are relatively happy when they are more or less well. Here is the reorientation which is correlative to ontological recognition. The searching for well-being, together with the adaptation which is required to achieve it, are a constant and pervasive reorientation to anticipate well-being in the form of their lives. The undistorted order and harmony of the well-being for which they seek are anticipated even in activities which seem very different – such as struggle, for example.

It is also important to recognize that the well-being thus recognized, as well as the reorientation of life which is intrinsic to this recognition, are not abstractions. They appear in all the means by which human beings live. They are mediated in social life, as well as through human life in the world. And the supposition that one can somehow realize this well-being apart from doing so in life, with others, and in the world, provides an important and very common obstacle to full recognition of the nature of well-being. On the contrary, the glory which is sought is that which will appear in an undistorted order of life, society and world for all. That is certainly the meaning of the kingdom of God as preached by Jesus.

The ontological recognition of well-being, and the reorientation which accompanies it, are the characteristic activities which occur in worship, where well-being is ascribed to God as his perfection and human beings thereby find the possibility of well-being for themselves. As we saw earlier, the means by which such recognition is purified, and matched by a purified reorientation, is praise. Serious problems arise, however, where there are deficiencies in the understanding of God and the nature of his well-being, for then worship also legitimates forms of life which are much less than they should be.

Such deficiencies appear in a view which is found very widely today, one which is closely connected with basic features of modernity, particularly deism, analyticity and individualism.

The most fundamental feature of the view is its use of closure, whether full or 'punctuated', in relationships.[37] In the complete form of the view,

---

[36] In this way, progress is linked to utopianism.

[37] 'There are not many differences in mental habit more significant than that between the habit of thinking in discrete, well-defined class concepts, and that of thinking in terms of continuity, of infinitely delicate shadings-off of everything into everything else ... the, so to say, universal overlappingness of the real world.' (A. O. Lovejoy, *The Great Chain of Being*, New York, 1936) Punctuated relationships are those which depend on the decision of those related.

the world is closed off from God, as are items and people in the world from each other. So, in each case, existence requires distinctness, a 'being away from' others, and identity is established through differentiation: people are naturally different, 'these' different from 'those' at every point, this nation different from that nation, this class different from that class, workers different from managers, this political party different from that, this religious group distinguished from that. And as the world grows steadily more complex, particularity becomes more important.[38]

Such distinctions and differences, which have a legitimate place, become problematic when they are refined and become self-important.[39] Thus reinforced, differences are translated into sharp divisions. Thereafter, difference is shown by enhancing division by whatever means are available. Such divisions are frequently rationalized in religious terms, where the world as a whole is presented as a place divided against itself, and the universe as a place where there is a great conflict – a warfare of good and evil. God is said to have made things this way, or perhaps to have allowed them to slip into such conflict, and now gives victory to those whom he has chosen, while defeating the evil ones.

Whether seen in such religious terms or not, the view undermines all relationality. Well-being is seen as the result of standing alone and self-sufficient, impervious to the threat posed by others. The power to stand alone is supposed to derive from the intrinsic position of the strong individual, which others naturally wish to usurp in order to become strong themselves.[40] Except perhaps through (irrational) choice, it is not incumbent on such a person to engage in relationships with others, for the world is a place where everyone must struggle to improve his/her position by maximizing assets in every way.

---

[38] This is a preeminent feature of 'post-modernism', which confines all relationality to the position of forms of language by which people are constructed. 'I've been in love with you for weeks.' 'There's no such thing,' she says. 'It's a rhetorical device. It's a bourgeois fallacy.' 'Haven't you ever been in love, then?' 'When I was younger,' she says, 'I allowed myself to be constructed by the discourse of romantic love for a while, yes.' 'What the hell does that mean?' 'We aren't essences, Vic. We aren't unique individual essences existing prior to language. There is only language.' (David Lodge, *Nice Work*, London: Penguin Books, 1989, p. 293)

[39] The process by which they are refined is similar to praise. Where in Christian worship praise refines relationality, in this alternative view praise is reflexive and refines separation.

[40] The person who lives in a world which is only a place of conflict, and in which he is constantly struggling, will eventually be unable to see the world as anything else. There is a particularly striking case of this in some of the American soldiers who served for years in the Vietnam War; a good number of them have been able only to live in the wild areas of the northwestern states in a state of constant struggle with themselves. They have internalized the struggle of which they were a part for so long, and are never at peace. Hostility is a way of life for them.

THE TRUE CHARACTER OF WELL-BEING

The main issue posed for theology and ethics by such views is the true character of well-being. The most serious problems which beset the human race today arise from the distorted visions of 'well-being', and the practices accompanying them, by which people live.[41]

(a) The Nature of God's Well-Being

As recognized in worship, God is one whose *being* is *directed*, directed toward human life in the world. His well-being, therefore, is that which occurs in the direction of his being. It is, so to speak, achieved in the direction of his being. Correspondingly, human well-being in the world arises through the direction of his being toward us and our world, and as our lives are conformed to that,[42] We shall presently need to look further at the implications of these matters for the dynamics of God's well-being.

Recognizing God as one whose being is directed has important implications for the question of the nature of God. The God who is thus recognized is one who has the highest importance for explanation and valuation, for he will be that which is simultaneously the highest form of explanation and of the highest axiological importance.[43] The two are found to be interrelated in worship: where God is recognized for himself, in worship, the highest explanation is valued as such, while it also derives its explanatory importance from the value accorded it. The first priority in worship is to recognize this, but it is also important that the explanation which is thus valued should be correlated to other less wide-ranging explanations and values, and that they should be seen as proportional to it. The implication is that ontological recognition is not primarily a utilitarian matter, is not finding the highest explanation in order to translate it into useful practice, but that other forms of explanation and valuation follow naturally from the proper ontological recognition.

[41] The fact that it is found through the ontological recognition and orientation which occur in worship does not prevent human beings from posing false ideals of well-being to which they conform themselves.

[42] There are two senses in which this is so. It is the case that his being is 'toward' human beings in the world; he is 'for them'. But this is also an active movement toward them, refined in a concentration of movement. The consequence is that human beings are not only to respond to his being for them, but also to the concentration of his movement.

[43] The issue of explanation is akin to the question of being, and that of valuation allied to that of direction, for it is the nature of being which explains, and the direction which things have which constitutes their value. The claim that, at the highest level, the two are profoundly interrelated conflicts with the modern notion that factual explanation and values must be kept separate.

25

The risk of talking in these terms, of that which is highest in explanation and valuation, is that worship seems to be directed to the highest 'that which is', a static ideal of perfection to which human beings and the world need simply to conform by repeating it under the conditions of finitude. But this is a mistake, certainly as far as Christian worship is concerned.

When it is recognized in worship that God's well-being occurs in the direction of his being, it will be seen that this is not a changeless well-being, secure against the difficulties of contingency and complexity. The possibility of a changeless well-being is then seen to be an abstractive notion of well-being, abstractive because it is always distant from God's own life and the life which he confers on humankind in the world.[44] For God and humankind, harmony arises in difference (and therefore complexity), and order occurs in and through movement (where there is contingent order). This means that talking of order and harmony as 'uninterrupted' or 'static', as if order and harmony always displace movement and complexity, is untrue to God's well-being and the well-being conferred by God. Nowhere is this better seen than in worship itself, whose nature is the finding of God's own dynamic order in the dynamics of life in the world.[45]

(b) The Dynamics of God's Well-Being

As we have seen, God's well-being occurs in the direction of his being. True well-being as such is seen in the whole being and work of God, not only in himself but with us. But it is doubtful whether we can grasp this fully enough with our usual view of God's activity. We tend usually to see God as active in such a way as to have consequences for the well-being of human beings in the world rather than actively enacting his own well-being in the world. So we see God as an individual agency making a commitment for the good of his people (e.g., the covenant with the Jews), and being active in various ways to fulfil the commitment. This is similar to the way in which we see a human being who retains his/her independence while making a commitment to another and acting to fulfil the commitment; the relation begins with the commitment and ends with its withdrawal. The relationship to the other always rests on the commit-

---

[44] This is seen in many views of the kingdom of God, wherein it is a state of affairs which is reached at some point. The possibility that it always continues to be attained is thereby excluded.
[45] Correspondingly, the notion of worship as an unchanging repetition of God's changelessness, in which human beings find stillness, is to be regarded as suspect. Instead, it is properly seen as the realization of the freedom and responsibility, the justice and love, which together are the dynamic order of God, in the particular circumstances of those who worship.

ment and the actions by which it is fulfilled: the 'other' is the sphere of operation for the 'one'.[46]

This rather limited notion of relationship can be carried into the understanding of God's activity in the world. God's activity in the world is then seen to rest on the *ways* by which God is fully himself. He is himself by means of such activities as seeing, knowing, loving and judging, and these are realized in their *mediation* through speech, hearing, attention and discernment; the two sets – ways and their mediations – are inextricably bound to each other. The sheer *effecting* of God, the empowering of God to do as and what he does, occurs as the active mode (see-ing, know-ing, etc.) operative in the ways and means by which God is himself.[47] But this understanding of the Trinitarian activity of God is a complex form of individual action and commitment, and therefore fundamentally monotheistic. As with the view of individual personality which it follows, this understanding of God can be coupled with – and perhaps even leads to – a counterposed view of the freedom of human individuals.[48] When measured against another and more dynamic view, this view appears compressed and abstractive.

(c) God's Well-Being as Occurring Within Dynamic Relationality

What occurs in Christian worship, however, is an ontological recognition of a God whose well-being occurs within relationality; and this recognition confers the same relationality on those who recognize it. The point here is a simple but extremely fundamental one, that God's being includes relationality; God's relationality does not begin and end with a choice made in his independence. Hence the relationality which God confers on human beings is one which is from his own relationality; and it is this relationality which is conferred through the ontological recognition and human reorientation which we know as worship.

But the relationality of God is not an inert relationality, whose character is established once for all. It is always a dynamic relationality, comprised of a social dynamic. And the highest possibilities for relationality

---

[46] A more complex view can be produced dialectically, where the 'other' develops an independence which corrects the 'one'; but this is based on bilateral individualism.

[47] Bruce J. Malina, in *The New Testament World: Insights from Cultural Anthropology* (Philadelphia: Westminster Press, 1981), drawing on the work of Bernard de Geradon, suggests that such a 'three-zone' understanding of God mirrors the first-century view of man as comprised of zones of 'emotion-fused thought', 'self-expressive speech' and 'purposeful action', pp. 60–7. For him, this is derived from a 'dyadic' view of personality, in which the 'individual ... perceives himself and forms his self-image in terms of what others perceive and feed back to him.' (p. 55). For both man and God, therefore, the role of the other is limited to feedback.

[48] This, of course, is a plausible view of the genesis of the autonomous freedom of individuals which characterized the European Enlightenment.

are fulfilled there, moving from the love which is its character (not self-love but love *in nuce*) to the fullest expression of that love in relationality. Hence God's well-being is a fulfilment which occurs in the movement of love in his own relationality.[49] Furthermore, God expresses his own well-being by forming the well-being of his people, and by acting to maintain that where the social practices of his people are orientated to him. It is because God confers well-being in this way, that there is the possibility of well-being for his people. So it is the dynamic order in God – together with the well-being which is achieved there – which is enacted in the relationality of his people. When, for example, two people are joined in marriage, they do not simply engage in a bilateral commitment witnessed by the community, the consequence of which is mutual well-being. It is the movement of the divine relationality in them by which they receive the possibility of their sociality and the well-being in which it is fulfilled.

This is the basis for a different and fuller understanding of the activity of the trinitarian God. In this case, every aspect of God is seen as intrinsically relational and practical. Hence it becomes impossible to posit 'seeing', 'knowing', 'loving' and 'judging' as the fundamental aspects of God,[50] for these notions are inseparably connected to their corresponding dialogical relationships, 'speaking', 'hearing', 'attending', 'discerning'; and both are inseparable from those forms of energetic activity which generate and effect them. This has very far-reaching implications; it means that God's 'nature' is not comprised of 'pure' activities, but of such activities *practised* with at least one *particular* other, with the expectation that a fullness of the activities requires the contribution of this other. Each activity is therefore immediately a communicative activity:[51] seeing to seeing, knowing to knowing, loving to loving, speaking to speaking, etc. Even beyond that, each activity is also a responsibility which includes both receptiveness and conferral: seeing to speak, hearing to know, attending to love, discerning to judge. And it is always with this particular other.

(d) The Energy of Well-Being

What runs through all this relationality is a stirring ('the Spirit') which presses the activities not to some abstract perfection (perfect knowledge, love, etc.), but to the fullness of relationship with *this* one (seeing, knowing, loving, judging with *this* one). So the relationality of God is one of

---

[49] See footnote 42.
[50] Malina translates them into modern terms as the 'core personality' of God in *ibid.*, p. 61.
[51] This is what is sometimes called 'face-to-face' activity. See Emmanuel Levinas, *Totality and Infinity*, Pittsburgh: Duquesne University Press, 1969.

energetic involvement and participation, moving toward fuller and fuller relationship. And this would not be complete until all the fullness of each had enlarged the other. Even then it could not be complete, because the stirring would still continue in the vibrancy of the relationship.[52] Incidentally, such an understanding of God would not stimulate an opposing freedom; the only opposition would come through antisociality, from one who wishes to remove himself from such involvement, who would then lose the vibrancy of relationship.

Seen in such a way, it becomes clear that God is what – from the human point of view – can be called an 'energy event'[53] constituted by a concentration of well-being in relationship which is inseparable from the extending of this relationship with his people in the world, and from the expression of his well-being in that relationship. The world he has brought into being and maintained is therefore a relational one, for which he has provided the possibility of well-being. His purpose is to move toward fuller and fuller relationship with it and all that comprises it, bringing it to its fullness by sharing his own fullness with it. One way of expressing this is to say that God does not remain social within a boundedness which is himself, but is himself by enacting with us what can be called an 'ideal social community' in which it is possible for human beings to come to a full life with each other.[54] Hence his sociality is enacted with theirs; it finds its fullness where human beings are most fully social in their practice of life.[55] As God extends his sociality into relationship with a universe which is social, that sociality is ramified in an increasingly complex sociality.[56] (Hence, to talk about a substance-like

---

[52] The 'richness' of the biblical accounts of heaven is probably due to this. See Isa. 11.1–11 and Rev. 21.1–27.

[53] 'Awareness of an all-pervading mysterious energy articulated in the infinite variety of natural phenomena seems to be the primordial experience of human consciousness, awakening to an awesome universe filled with mysterious power. Not only is energy our primary experience; energy, and its multiple modes of expression, is also the primary concern of modern physics, its ultimate term of reference in describing the most fundamental reality of the universe. Physics is establishing contact with energy events rather than with substances of atomic or subatomic dimensions. These energy events extend in size all the way from subatomic particles to galactic systems. The universe can be seen as a single, if multiform, energy event, just as a particle such as the photon is itself perceived in historical reality as an energy event.' Thomas Berry, *The Dream of the Earth*, San Francisco: Sierra Club Books, 1988, p. 24.

[54] Compare Jürgen Habermas, *The Theory of Communicative Action, Vol. 2: Lifeworld and System: A Critique of Functionalist Reason*, Boston: Beacon Press, 1987, p. 2 and *passim*.

[55] And this is not to be seen in simply human terms. As we have seen previously, the ecological is not simply an environment or 'context' within which human beings are social; the ecological is necessarily implicated in their sociality and its fulfilment.

[56] And all the means by which human beings deal with their sociality politically, economically and religiously, through institutions and personally, serve further to ramify their sociality.

'relationality' or 'sociality' of the universe is to talk of an abstraction.) This increasing complexity is itself the manifestation of the ongoingly energetic involvement and participation of God, whereby he intends to move toward fuller and fuller relationship with his people and their societies, though it can also be driven by the human revolt from the responsibility which this involves.

(d) The Form of Human Well-Being

We have concentrated on the true character of well-being as that appears in worship. And we have found that Christian worship brings recognition of the dynamics of God's well-being – that God's well-being occurs in the direction of his being toward us, through the energy by which he is involved with human life in the world. It is these dynamics, and the characteristics which appear in them, which confer a proper form and energy on human relationality. In God, there is positive openness to the other by which God is *with* the other, identified with the other in whatever is his situation or need, and affirming the other there. This is what constitutes the actuality of positive openness and affirmation in our relationships, and thus breaks down the closures by which we cut ourselves off from relationship and the distortions by which we misconstrue relationships. The result is that we are opened to divine relationality in our human relationality, and thereby energized for full relationship with each other in the world.

The privilege which the ontological recognition and human reorientation of worship brings – of being thus opened and energized – permits no one to stand above the world of today, which is largely driven by the 'modern' view mentioned earlier. Instead, it confers freedom and responsibility to show the movement of God's well-being to all human beings, and only thus to partake of God's glory. This is exactly the way followed by the movement of God toward humankind in Jesus Christ, who brought benignity and well-being by undermining the hostility of the world in his death.

3

The Future of Theology in a Complex World[1]

BEING THEOLOGICALLY RESPONSIBLE

THE title I have given for this lecture is presumptuous, of course. How can I, even after many years of involvement with theology across several continents, presume myself fit to address such a topic? I promise you that I do not. Nonetheless, it is most important for the issue of the future of theology to be placed on the agenda for discussion. Each thing which will be said in such a conference as this not only implies but effects some sort of view about the future of theology. My first aim is simply to help you to recognize this.

At the same time, unless theology is simply a curious study of religious thoughts and practices, you and I and we need to be reminded that in what we say we are morally responsible for the future of theology. Not only in what we say, but in the manner in which we deal with the questions and disagreements with which we will be concerned, we are exemplifying theology and fashioning it for the future. It used to be said that theological statements are self-involving, and that is true enough. But theological statements are also God-, community- and world-involving; each statement enhances or destroys relationship to God, others and the world. It is facile – if not irresponsible – to suppose otherwise. I have always been amazed that those who engage in discussions and disputes about theological matters do not seem to recognize that the very process by which they do so is theological. It is; we here are morally and theologically responsible for the future of theology in what we do. That is one side of the issue with which we will be concerned in this Symposium.

THE PROBLEM OF COMPLEXITY AND CULTURE

The other side is what I have called the 'complex world' in which we exist as we meet to discuss. It is a complexity which reaches far into the heart

[1] Opening Address, Symposium on Christ and Context, Dunedin, New Zealand, Sunday, 12 May 1991.

31

of the issues which we will discuss, probably farther than any of us cares to admit. We are too fond of simplicities and the comfort they bring to face how deeply complexity reaches into the issues which we discuss.

Perhaps I can explain this by talking for a moment of the idea of 'context' which appears in the title of the Symposium. Through long habits instilled into western patterns of thought by figures of the past, we are inclined to think in terms of dualities. Whenever, therefore, we need to identify something, we do so by differentiating it from what it is not. We tend therefore to see everything as sharply atomized, this from that, you from me, God from the world, and so on. These differentiations quickly turn into sharp distinctions, and the distinctions into oppositions or confrontations; and it soon seems paradoxical to suppose that there is some fundamental unity between those which/who have been disjoined. And if you see this Symposium in these terms, the title 'Christ and Context' will be taken to mean that Christ and context are naturally distinct and opposed, a notion that the subtitle of the Symposium ('The Confrontation Between Gospel and Culture') reinforces. By the same token, you will see contexts primarily as distinct and disjoined, rather than related in some more fundamental unity.

CONTEXT, CULTURE AND GOD'S PRESENCE

But the notion of context needs to be looked at more closely. Etymologically, its meaning is quite different, not at all a designation for something which is divided, stands outside and confronts. The Latin verb *contexere* means to 'braid', 'weave' or 'connect'. If you understand the Symposium title in this way, 'Christ and Context' speaks of an interweaving, a braiding, of what otherwise – with our usual habits – we see as divided. And the question before us is *how* that interweaving occurs.

For what it is worth, I would add that there is a similar problem with the word 'culture'. We are accustomed to hypostatizing 'it' as something fixed and outside the Gospel, like a self-same, alien world 'into which' the Christian mission goes – like a divine intervention – in order to 'confront' and convert it by the proclamation of the Gospel. But this is fair neither to the culture nor to the place of Christ in it. Cultures are not fixed and self-enclosed; they are dynamic and intertwined with others. And yet within this intertwining, there is a braiding in which God himself may be present. And the question before us is *how*, in that intertwining, God in Christ is present, and how, by recognizing the presence of God in Christ, we may further effect the consequences of this presence. To ask such questions is not to evacuate the distinctive character of the Gospel of Christ, or to engage in some new conflation of Christ with culture, but to seek for the fundamentals of God's work in Christ in the human world. For God's identity does not rest on 'being outside' but on *who* he is in *what* he does, on his being in his acts.

Cultures and the Agenda for Theology

What makes this especially difficult is the very dynamism of particular cultures today. Across the world, the old – and by today's standards monolithic – unities, neatly demarcated as lands and nations by ancient geographical boundaries often themselves sacralized, are being called into question. And what often seems to be replacing them is chaos, not simply the chaos of groups and individuals seeking self-realization but a chaos of fundamental divisions which loses the vision of any unity at all. In view of this, in order to continue to exist, nation after nation is driven to a desperate attempt to preserve a rather low and pragmatic form of unity.

> 'Inclusivity', which ... is interpreted as amalgamation of people with vastly different beliefs and ways of life, thus becomes not only the method but also the end of authority's exercise ... [A] political version of art for art's sake, inclusion for the sake of inclusion becomes the going wisdom of the day and from this wisdom the notion of sharing and serving a common good is steadily evacuated ... [All this happens] within a society of strangers who define themselves in opposition one to another by rights, possessions, and differing 'life styles.' Within the amalgam, people increasingly define themselves by what they demand. Voluntarism defines religious as well as political communities. Within all social institutions interest groups multiply like amoebas.[2]

Such circumstances produce two very difficult questions. The first question is this: In a world where the possibility of deep unity between peoples, one based on their service of a common good, has been lost in the welter of the conflicting claims of self-interested groups, how are we to recover the intertwining of cultures and peoples? How are cultures dynamic not only in their distinction from each other but also in their intertwining? In itself, that question has nothing necessarily to do with theology. The second question, therefore, is this: How, in the braiding

---

[2] Philip Turner, 'Authority in the Church: Excavations Among the Ruins' in *First Things*, December 1990, p. 30.

together of cultures and peoples in a dynamic unity, is God himself present? How, indeed, does God's life appear in their service of a common good? And what, then, is the identity of the God who so appears? Those are the questions which are before us in this Symposium. These questions are demanding, to say the least, and require a delicacy of working together, and a willingness to go to the depths of the Christian tradition which we are not at all accustomed to.

Along with these issues comes another which can hardly be separated from them today. With the division of cultures and contexts, both from each other and from the common good or the presence of God, the territories where these cultures are found are seen to be divided also, both from each other and from the presence of God.[3] Given the human preoccupation with such divisions, it is unlikely that there can be any serious attention to ecology, in the sense of a recognition of the interrelatedness of all the natural world. Furthermore, there can be no theological ecology, in which the common good and the presence of God are found in the interrelatedness of all the natural order. In other words, seeking for the dynamic contextuality – the interwovenness – of cultures also presses us for a better understanding of 'the land', the environment with (and in) which all cultures coexist. How is God present in our contextuality with the natural world?

Even if it can easily be forgotten in a beautiful place like Dunedin where we are comfortably provided-for, the situation which we have just indicated is one of unparalleled gravity. As a Nobel prizewinner wrote recently,

Whatever our professional preoccupations may be, we cannot escape the feeling that we live in an age of transition, an age that demands constructive modification of our environment. We must find and explore new resources, must understand our environment better, and must achieve a less destructive coexistence with nature. The time scale of the qualitative modifications that are required to achieve these major goals is not comparable to the immense time spans involved in biological or geological evolution. Rather, it is of the order of the decade ... the modifications that must be made interfere with our own lives and the lives of the next generation.[4]

Can we also find God's presence in our proper interwovenness with nature? Unless we can, finding the answer to our other questions about

---

[3] It is no accident that disputes over the rights to land feature so prominently in controversies between cultures, and particularly where two groups claim rights to the same territory, for example in Palestine.

[4] G. Nicolis and I. Prigogine, *Exploring Complexity*, London: W. H. Freeman, 1989, p. 1.

the interwovenness of people and cultures in which God is present will resemble Nero fiddling while Rome burned.

If we put all these together, we have the agenda of theology for the future. (1) The first question is this: We live in a world where the possibility of deep unity between peoples, that which is based on their service of a common good, has been lost in the welter of the conflicting claims of self-interested groups. We live in a world where the proper unity or interwovenness of humanity with nature has also been lost. How then are we to recover the proper intertwining of cultures and peoples, and our proper interwovenness with nature? (2) And the second question is: How, in the braiding together of cultures and peoples and nature in a dynamic unity, is God himself present? How, indeed, does God's presence and life appear in the achievement of the common good of cultures, peoples and nature? Who is the God who so appears? Regrettably, in what follows, we must largely confine ourselves to the question of the braiding together of cultures and peoples, and leave the question of their interwovenness with nature to another time.

PRECEDENTS FOR SUCH CONCERNS

It is not that these are altogether new problems. The fact is that people in the past, when faced with these issues simultaneously, have found ways of recovering God's presence in the recovery of the intertwining of peoples and the natural world. Let me give two examples.

One is the 'dream-time' practices of the Aboriginals in Australia which are described in Bruce Chatwin's book *The Songlines*. As he says there,

> The Aboriginals had an earthbound philosophy. The earth gave life to a man; gave him his food, language and intelligence; and the earth took him back when he died ... [They] were a people who trod lightly over the earth; and the less they took from, the earth, the less they had to give in return ...

> My reason for coming to Australia [Chatwin says] was to learn for myself ... what a Songline was – and how it worked ... [As I found] Every Wallaby Man believed he was descended from a universal Wallaby Father, who was the ancestor of all other Wallaby Men and all living wallabies ... Each totemic ancestor, while traveling through the country, was thought to have scattered a trail of words and musical notes along the line of his footprints ... these Dreaming-tracks lay over the land as 'ways' of communication between the most far-flung tribes. A song ... was both map and direction-finder.

Providing you knew the song, you could always find your way across country ... as long as [a man] stuck to the track, he'd always find people who shared his Dreaming, who were, in fact, his brothers ... from whom he could expect hospitality. So song is a kind of passport and meal-ticket ... In theory, at least, the whole of Australia could be read as a musical score ... And [the Aboriginals] could sing [all the white man's gear, even] the railway back into the created world of God.[5]

Though not based on a Christian understanding of God, this shows deep similarities to Biblical faith of the sort found throughout the Old and New Testaments, where the presence of God is found in the movements of people through the lands. A particularly interesting example is found in the Wisdom Literature, which finds the presence of the divine in the right practice of human relationships. As the Book of Proverbs suggests, 'The fear of the Lord' is in 'turning your ear to wisdom and applying your heart to understanding ... For the Lord gives wisdom, and from his mouth come knowledge and understanding ... Then you will understand what is right and just and fair – every good path.'[6]

Incidentally, the understanding that God's presence is to be found in the interweaving of human beings with each other, may be far more widely appreciated by ordinary Christians than the theologians are prepared to recognize. While they, the theologians, are busy reinventing the wheel, ordinary Christians may simply be getting on with the job. On the way here, on the aeroplane from Los Angeles to Auckland, I sat next to a Bible salesman – a 'Bible Broker' he called himself – who told me an interesting statistic: if copies of the New Testament are bound with the Psalms, sales go up 10%; but if they are bound with the Psalms and Proverbs, sales go up by 50%. Perhaps ordinary people do see that God's presence is to be seen in the interweaving of human lives.

The other example of God's presence found in the interweaving of human beings is explicitly Christian, drawn from the north of England which I learned to love so much, a place in many ways very like Dunedin. There the tradition of Celtic Christianity is very much alive, not least in Durham Cathedral of which I was Residentiary Canon while I was Professor in the University. It is a form of Christianity quite unlike the pattern which dominates the West. The Celtic view of God in the world was far more dynamic than the form of Christianity which came from Rome and eventually triumphed. The Celts saw God's life and purposes intertwined with those of human beings as they are intertwined with each other and with the natural world. The well-known Irish blessing which

[5] Bruce Chatwin, *The Songlines*, London: Pan Books, 1988, pp. 14–17.
[6] Proverbs 1.7; 2.2, 6, 9.

goes 'May the road rise up to meet you' hints at the way God cooperates with the order of nature to bring goodness to human beings. In the North of England, wandering missionaries gathered communities around them who lived close to the natural world, and within their natural life together found a God who walked with them and brought them blessing. The best images of this intertwining are the interweaving tracery of Celtic art and stonecarving which mark the great Christian buildings of the North of England. Sadly, the form of Celtic Christianity was nearly lost under the weight of law-based Christianity, and the formalistic theology and practice which goes with it. It was much more dynamic than that which could be captured in the patterns of Roman law, but it was the law-based patterns which predominated in the West as a whole.

THE FAILINGS OF THEOLOGY

Such examples offer some precedents for recovering God's presence in the recovery of the intertwining of peoples. They show people whose very wandering and finding themselves one with other people and with the natural world is a creative realization of the presence of God. But the fact remains that such practices, not only the primacy given to the intertwining of peoples but also to the creative realization of God's presence there, have almost always been displaced by more formalistic practices in theology.

Perhaps, therefore, a note of caution is in order before we proceed with our task. It amounts to this: beware of habits. In my present role as Director of a new institution, the Center of Theological Inquiry, dedicated specifically to the redevelopment of theology for its future role in public life, I have learned well the habits which undermine theology in its prospects for the future. Perhaps you know Hans Christian Andersen's story, 'The Emperor's New Clothes'. Let me tell you that all human beings and institutions, including those engaged in the enterprise of theology, are always a little like the emperor (in the story) who, in his love of finery, allows himself to be deceived by his advisers into parading in an imaginary set of new clothes; and the emperor's loyal subjects are quite prepared to join in the deception.

Like the emperor in the story, theologians wish to be accepted and admired by those around them, and are easily deceived into false agendas, into – quite unintentionally – being what they are not. These days, I think it is very difficult for them not to be led astray, given that there are so many 'experts' who will see to it that theology is woven an imaginary set of new clothes (if not a new set every year!) in which to parade before the whole world. What is more, not a few of them have the influence to coax theology into the 'new clothes' which they invent, and then to parade it through the town, while at the same time convincing bystanders that these imaginary new clothes are better, and that they should applaud such wonderful new garb. Earlier today, Professor Moltmann and I were commiserating over the increasing separation of academic theology from Church life, as theologians – so anxious to be accepted as 'scientific' by their university colleagues – adopt esoteric and convoluted mental strategies. Such tactics subvert theology.

Let me be more exact. What are these bad habits? In the language of 'The Emperor's New Clothes', they are an interesting combination of 'vanity' and 'new fashions'. The vanity comes where theologians are preoccupied – like the Emperor in the story – with their position. And the means by which they do retain their position is to outdo others in their grasp of the formalisms which have dominated Christian theology in East and West. By this they perpetuate intellectual habits learned over the past centuries, as if those were the only ways suitable. The unfortunate by-product of this is the disengagement of intelligent Christian faith from the means by which truth and understanding are sought in the modern world, whether by the experts or by ordinary people. Intellectually and institutionally, therefore, faith has come to be promoted in ways that are strictly marginal to modern life.

And this, in turn, leads to a confrontational stance: having confined theology to such formalisms, they go on to say that the truth of theology can only be shown through the confrontation of all else. What they mean, however, is that theology can only be true to itself if it is seen in the formalisms of the past, with the intellectual procedures of the past; and that causes it to be marginal to, confrontational with, the methods of today. So theology itself comes to be seen as an esoteric, abstract and sectarian activity. It's a caricature of theology.

The second bad habit can be likened to the 'new fashions' in which the king's advisers outfitted him. Perhaps the most damaging of these new fashions is that faith can be – even ought to be – disengaged from its engagement with intelligent understanding. This supposition pervades places where religion and theology are taught. Where religion/theology is studied in public institutions, it is supposed that the question of the truth of faith should not be addressed; it is sufficient to catalogue the phenomena of religions, and it is supposed that these must all be equally valuable. That is supposed to be the strategy for preserving the place of religious study in public institutions, or in places where there is disagreement about the value of different traditions. Such an approach mirrors the blandness and vacuousness of much life in the West, where there is nothing but appearance and all appearances must by definition be equal. 'Plastic life' is what it's called in California.

And the study of theology by Christians has usually followed this lead, at least in the western world. If that is what is deemed academically credible for theological study, it is thought that it should be followed in theological institutions also. For this reason, 'theological' study in private institutions consists usually of ever more detailed study of the religious or theological material which is thought normative for a particular tradition, by means of the historical, phenomenological, sociological or political techniques which are found in the academic market-place. These 'new clothes' are titillating, but their freshness seems often to rely on the discovery of new data or methods. Again, questions of truth are avoided where they emerge in (or about) the material studied. Such study is sometimes accompanied by a rather un-self-critical redescription of the 'substance' of the material, frequently in terms currently popular, or by a philosophical testing of the continued viability of the tradition. But the issue of its truthfulness for today is not addressed.

Such forms of study do, in a sense, preserve the faith of previous generations, but in doing so they repeat the mistakes which led to the disengagement of faith from public life and of faith from the intelligent appropriation of faith. Assumptions about the continuing authority of the tradition replace the engagement with modern understanding and life by which the tradition must be revalidated. Acquaintance with the phenomena of faith, religion and theology replaces intensive engagement with the depth and truth of tradition. The exaltation of private or group opinion undermines the possibility of a common truth by which society may be maintained. The results are profound and many-sided: the intelligent understanding of faith (theology), and the institutions which support it, grow weaker, while the prospects for social unity grow more dim.

MOVING BEYOND OUR BAD HABITS

So we must be cautious both about the vanity by which theologians perpetuate habits learned over the past centuries, as if those were the only ways suitable, and about the new fashions which operate in most theological study today. It is the proper task of theology today to respond to the need to find the presence of God in the intertwinings of people in and with the natural world. And that will require reaching beyond the vanity which confines theology in its past, and beyond the fashions which restrict theology from the task of intelligently discerning the truth of faith. I know that is very difficult in today's world; but it always has been. That 'reaching' is the basic vitality of theological work. In religious language, it is the art of transcendence. And, as one woman put it: 'I believe that learning to admit transcendence may be one of the major undertakings of a man's life, perhaps the major undertaking, so that if it is ignored his personality may be stunted or destroyed.'[7] Nowhere is that more true than in the study of theology itself. It is part of the very purpose of theology to reach to the higher goals which it serves, and to hold fast to them even in difficult times.

This task, which we need freely to undertake, is strangely similar to those which are forced upon us by the others which we have discussed: In all the turmoil of conflicting voices and national layers of voices, can we find the presence of God in the interweaving of people and cultures? And can we do so while also finding the presence of God in a true braiding of humanity with nature which will ameliorate the frightful damage being done to the natural world? These are all 'transcending questions', which call us out of our captivity to the vanities and new fashions of theological study.

APPROACHING THE TASK OF THEOLOGY

So far, I have only identified the agenda for theology in the future, and asked you to be bound neither by the habits of the past nor by the new fashions of the present in which theology is so often confined. I want now to turn more directly to the task of theology itself in the complex world in which we live. The most apt way of turning to this is to read a poem by a fine Irish poet whom I know, Micheal O'Siadhail.

> O my white-burdened Europe, across
> so many maps greed zigzags. One voice
> and the nightmare of a dominant chord:
> defences, self-mirroring, echoings, myriad
> overtones of shame. Never again one voice.
> Out of malaise, out of need our vision cries.

> Turmoil of change, our slow renaissance.
> *All things share one breath.* We listen:
> clash and resolve, webs and layers of voices.
> And which voice dominates or is it chaos?
> My doubting earthling, tiny among the planets
> does a lover of one voice hear more or less?

> Infinities of space and time. Melody fragments;
> a music of compassion, noise of enchantment.

---

[7] Monica Furlong, *Contemplating Now*, Cambridge, Mass.: Cowley Publications, 1983, p. 50.

Among the inner parts something open,
something wild, a long rumour of wisdom
keeps winding into each tune: *cantus firmus*,
fierce vigil of contingency, love's congruence.[8]

What O'Siadhail says about the 'white-burdened Europe', its greed, defensive self-interest, divisiveness in shame (shame always divides), and loss of a common identity, could be found the world over in greater or lesser degree. In all the turmoil of conflicting voices and national layers of voices, can we find the *cantus firmus* – like the ground bass in a Bach piece – of unity? Can we find and affirm that *cantus firmus*, that '*All things share one breath*'? And what kind of spirit do they share? Those are the questions we must face – as theological questions.

Theology as Poesis

Before we do, we should look for a moment at how to approach these questions as theological questions. Implicit in O'Siadhail's poem is the purpose of poetry itself. Poetry, in its creative perception, provides a concentrated opportunity by which to 'sing reality'. As Chatwin says of the Aboriginal Creation myths,

> [They] tell of the legendary totemic beings who had wandered over the continent in the Dreamtime, singing out the name of everything that crossed their path – birds, animals, plants, rocks, waterholes – and so singing the world into existence ... By singing the world into existence, the ancestors had been poets in the original sense of poesis, meaning 'creation'.[9]

So the multistranded reality in which we live needs to be 'sung into existence'. For a Christian, this means that it needs to be sung as a hymn of praise to God the Creator. It is the task of theology to fashion the creative poesis by which it is sung as a hymn of praise to God.

In more technical terms, poetry – or theology – provides a wisdom, heuristic or direction for exploration, which serves to orientate a search, much as the Aboriginals' songlines provide a 'map and direction-finder' for travel. This is often where we are at our weakest. Our lack of orientation is what allows us to be subverted by our vanity and the new

[8] Micheal O'Siadhail, 'Motet' in *The Chosen Garden*, Dublin: The Dedalus Press, 1990, p. 82.
[9] Bruce Chatwin, *The Songlines*, London: Pan Books, 1988, pp. 2, 16.

fashions of the world. The crucial question is how we achieve the proper sense of direction.

In a much simpler time, though one not without its own complexities, Plato quotes Socrates as saying,

> This, then, every soul looks for, and for this every soul does all that it does, feeling in some way what it is, but troubled and uncertain and unable to see it clearly enough. The soul forms no fixed belief about the good as it does about the other things ... And are the best men in our state, in whose hands everything is to be placed, are they to be equally in the dark about something so important as this?[10]

The orientation point to which Socrates was referring, is that for which human beings reach in everything they know and do, though it is itself beyond their grasp. It is the orientation point by which wisdom in life is promoted, and by that means intellectual, social and moral life is brought about. As one writer summarized it recently, '[Socrates] sought to promote wisdom in life by rational means – and not mere intellectual wisdom or knowledge.'[11]

Another form of the same orientation-point was offered by the great philosopher/theologian Anselm. There is, he said, 'that than which nothing greater can be conceived', and this is God, the one to whom we should turn ourselves to do honour; for honouring this excellence is the basis of all knowledge and practice. If theology has to do with singing everything into existence as a hymn of praise to God the Creator, actually to do so – to honour God in all knowledge and practice – is the best kind of theology. It is God-focused wisdom.

THE NEW FORM OF WISDOM

Is such an orientation-point, manifest in wisdom – the creative use of our knowledge and practice – lost forever? Micheal O'Siadhail's poem suggests not.

> Infinities of space and time. Melody fragments;
> a music of compassion, noise of enchantment.

[10] Plato, *Republic*, ed. and trans. I. A. Richards, Cambridge: Cambridge University Press, 1966, p. 114 (Book 6, 505).
[11] Nicholas Maxwell, *From Wisdom to Knowledge*, Oxford: Basil Blackwell, 1984, p. 120. For a specifically theological discussion, see D. W. Hardy, 'Rationality, the Sciences and Theology' in *Keeping the Faith*, ed. G. Wainwright, Philadelphia: Fortress Press, 1988, London: SPCK, 1989, Ch. 12; Ch. 14 below.

Among the inner parts something open,
something wild, a long rumour of wisdom
keeps winding into each tune: *cantus firmus*,
fierce vigil of contingency, love's congruence.

So what has been lost is not the possibility of such wisdom, the possibility
of a direction which can be the source for creative human understanding
(poesis) and goodness, but the ancient *form* of wisdom. The form of
wisdom itself has become more complex, as one would expect in a world
grown much more complex.

It has been commonplace, if not popular, for a very long time to
abandon any explicit orientation to wisdom, or to forego the honouring
of excellence in that full sense to which Anselm was pointing. But this is
not because people have no inkling of it. They do glimpse it, but only in
fragments: 'melody fragments'. And the world in which they live is so
fragmented that they cannot have more than a glimpse of it. But that is
not to suggest that the elements of this wisdom are not all over the place.
If it isn't too odd for an American to recall an English national holiday, I
can remember some marvellous bonfires, towering eight feet high at least,
in the workers' yard of Durham Cathedral on Guy Fawkes Day. After a
while, the fire collapsed into large glowing coals, glowing embers, on the
ground. The fragments in which we experience wisdom are like those
embers. Those isolated embers, the elements of wisdom which still burn
with the heat of the fire from which they come, can still provoke great
interest, but in their separation people forget that they do derive from the
fire.

This forgetfulness is due in no small part to the simple difficulty of
conceiving this wisdom. We are simply not in the position of those who
in earlier days could speak so simply and trustfully of wisdom. It is very
difficult for us to say with the Psalmist,

[Lord], how I love your law!
I meditate on it all day long ...
How sweet are your words to my taste,
sweeter than honey to my mouth!
I gain understanding from your precepts;
therefore I hate every wrong path.[12]

Neither the Lord nor his wisdom seem so clear or sweet to us now as to
evoke such simple and trustful meditation. It is not that they are not as
much present as ever they were. But our minds are clouded by other

---

[12] Psalm 119.97, 103–104.

preoccupations, and they have become too manifold for us to trace their roots in the wisdom which is the excellence of the Lord.

But perhaps we make too much of this difficulty. The fire for which we seek is already among us, in all those isolated sparks of which I spoke, or – in O'Siadhail's words – there is music in the fragments of melody. Where these are drawn together in their interconnections, there is the 'long rumour of wisdom' of which he speaks. And that, as we saw before, is the issue – how in the interweavings of people, their cultures and nature, God is present. Where we can draw out these interconnections, we will be finding *wisdom in practice*; where our searchings converge, there will be a practical manifestation of wisdom. Wisdom will thrive amongst us where this convergence is achieved, where the bonfire, so to speak, is seen in the fire of all the sparks, or the music in the melody fragments.

I realize that such a thing is difficult to grasp. We are habituated to think of a wisdom which is compact, intense and accessible to us; and such a notion is attractive and reassuring. But, as I said, the form of wisdom seems to need to be rethought. Let me repeat the last stanza of the same poem.

> Infinities of space and time. Melody fragments;
> a music of compassion, noise of enchantment.
> Among the inner parts something open,
> something wild, a long rumour of wisdom
> keeps winding into each tune: *cantus firmus*,
> fierce vigil of contingency, love's congruence.

Wisdom appears as hints and rumours, and its form is an open one through which there runs 'something wild', an excess of life entering all the contingencies which are all we know of existence. And this winds through each of the many tunes into which the melody of existence is now fragmented. Nonetheless, in its own 'nature', it is itself a *cantus firmus*.

THE NEEDS OF A CREATIVE POESIS

But what is the character of the creative poesis which we need to find the wisdom by which people and cultures may be properly interwoven with each other and with the natural world? Micheal O'Siadhail gives a hint of it. Amongst the fragments of melody – amidst the noise of enchantment – there is 'a music of compassion', and amongst the wild openness of inner parts 'a long rumour of wisdom'. Such a thing can only be found through a risky waiting in which may be found the 'congruence' brought about by love. This is the kind of braiding together of people, cultures and nature in which we will find the wisdom – with all its excess of life – which is present amongst them.

> Infinities of space and time. Melody fragments;
> a music of compassion, noise of enchantment.
> Among the inner parts something open,
> something wild, a long rumour of wisdom
> keeps winding into each tune: *cantus firmus*,
> fierce vigil of contingency, love's congruence.

So far as it goes, this is an answer to the questions we posed earlier.

But at the same time, it leaves uncharted the kind of congruence which we should expect in love, as well as the nature of the openness and risk which are needed for the flowering of compassion and love. Does congruence mean sameness? For if so, the braiding together will sacrifice the distinctness of those so interwoven, whether they be individuals, peoples, cultures or nature. Do openness and risk mean openness to anything and everything, so that every kind of difference is legitimate? For if so, we will be back in that 'inclusion for the sake of inclusion' which we mentioned before. These are surely crucial matters if we are to find the proper braiding together of people, cultures and nature.

I suggest the fuller creative poesis which is really needed is actually to be found in the inmost structure of Christian faith, where it is seen what is the full congruence of people with each other and with nature, and how it derives from the presence and activity of God amongst them. There are many ways by which this may be shown, but I shall start from the Resurrection. For in the events following the Resurrection we can see the incorporation of Jesus' followers into an open and lifeful congruence by which they are interwoven one with another through the fulfilling presence of God amongst them.

Just how does this happen? We need to try to unravel the dynamics of the lives and relations of those who came after the Resurrection, and the dynamics of God's presence there amongst them. How was it that the Resurrection showed this new human dynamic, and led these people into the character of God's activity amongst them? And what did it show about the character of God?

A particularly interesting insight into these questions is found in the story of Philip and the Ethiopian Eunuch.[13] For there was Philip, told by an angel to go out to the Gaza Road outside of Jerusalem, and then told by the Spirit to go up to the chariot in which a Ethiopian eunuch was

[13] Acts 8.26–40.

returning from worship at Jerusalem. As it happened, the Ethiopian was perplexed about a passage from the Book of Isaiah, and Philip answered showing him that it spoke of the humiliating sacrifice of Jesus and the new life which came from it for those who followed him. The eunuch immediately asked to be baptized – and afterward 'went on his way rejoicing'.

As scanty as the story is, it is clear that God himself, the Spirit, through Philip, gives the eunuch that remarkable insight into God which is contained in the narrative of the silent suffering of Jesus, the denial of a just trial, his death and his being taken up from the earth. And what was given was not a lot of information about what had happened, and how important it was, but the *generativity* of it, the *creativity* of it. The experience of the eunuch was that what had occurred for Jesus was still happening, through the Spirit, as others were drawn into that suffering, death and resurrection. The 'generation' of the Jesus who suffered, died and was raised was those who came after and, in the Spirit, were drawn into what had happened. The baptism of the eunuch enacted, implanted, this generativity in his very being, and he went on his way in joy, the joy of Easter.

So that apparently simple story tells us how, following after the Resurrection, people are drawn into God's activity in the trial, death and resurrection of Jesus. It happens this way: through the witness of the Spirit, they – like the eunuch – are led into the suffering of Jesus, his death and his resurrection, and the activity of God's Spirit is confirmed in them so that they too may go on their way rejoicing.

Our first question is: *How did these events show a new human dynamic, the full congruence of people for which we are seeking?*

In our very individualistic society, we are well accustomed to the habit of declaring our concern for others while also withdrawing from them. In our early days in Princeton, my wife and I learned with what readiness and friendliness people would say, 'how very nice to meet you; we must get together for lunch – we'll be in touch with you this week!' The only problem is that the call never arrived, and there was no further meeting – unless we ourselves initiated it. This is not very much different from the supposition that God affirms his people with a resounding 'yes!' while at the same time staying distant from them. Nor is it far different from the idea that God sets in motion a drama of righteous love, played out in Jesus and those who follow him, while himself standing apart. But suppose God is involved in the suffering death and resurrection of Jesus in a different way.

Let me quote the words of a love poem, another of Micheal O'Siadhail's:

Nothing can explain this adventure – let's say a quirk

of fortune steered us together – we made our covenants,
began this odyssey of ours, by hunch and guesswork,
a blind date where foolish love consented in advance.
No my beloved, neither knew what lay behind the frontiers.
You told me once you hesitated: a needle can waver,
then fix on its pole; I am still after many years
baffled that the needle's gift dipped in my favour.
Should I dare to be so lucky? Is this a dream?
Suddenly in the commonplace that first amazement seizes
me all over again – a freak twist to the theme,
subtle jazz of the new familiar, trip of surprises.
Gratuitous, beyond our fathom, both binding and freeing,
this love re-invades us, shifts the boundaries of our being.[14]

The poem gives two especially important hints of the astonishing relation of two people in love. On the one hand, it gives an idea how much
such relations are – and remain – contingent and gratuitous. They occur
in the overflowing richness of a complex world where things need not
happen, but do; and where they do, they are fully graceful, drawing those
involved into a fuller kind of life, 'binding and freeing' them.

On the other hand, the poem contains a remarkable insight into the
nature of love. 'This love re-invades us, shifts the boundaries of our
being.' For us who have such love, love means that we are not selves in
the way we were before, nor need we be withdrawn and self-protective in
the way we have come to consider normal. The boundaries of our being
are shifted, and go on being shifted, as our love draws us more and more
deeply together, more and more profoundly with each other, limited only
by the quality of the love which gives us freedom to love. The boundaries
of our being, whether as individuals, peoples or cultures, are constantly
redrawn by the love shown each to the other, moment by moment. And
that in turn makes us still more free, in all the extremities of life, to love
and cherish each other. As love develops, so does freedom, the freedom
to love.

I need hardly say that this is an astonishing development of the possibilities for the interweaving of human beings. For it makes clear that the
boundaries by which cultures and contexts are divided may shift as – in
love and compassion – peoples are drawn together.

But that does not bring us far enough. The Ethiopian Eunuch was not
drawn primarily into overwhelming compassion; the 'generativity' which
he found derived from being drawn into a particular form of compassion,

[14] Micheal O'Siadhail, 'Out of the Blue' in *The Chosen Garden*, Dublin: The Dedalus Press,
1990, p. 71.

that of the Jesus who suffered, died and was raised. The content of the new life which the Eunuch found was the generativity of being drawn into the life, death and resurrection of Jesus. That tells us much more about the proper interweaving of human beings, that they find new life in their sacrifice for others, not simply in cost-free compassion.

Now, *what does this show about the dynamics of God's presence in the interweaving of peoples, and about the character of God?*

One answer is that these things of which we have been speaking, whether the compassion which 'shifts the boundaries of our being' or the generativity which comes from sacrifice for others, are simply aspects of a drama into which we enter, which shows rather indirectly the righteous love of God. There are those who would have us think that it is only this, a drama in which we – to quote one present-day theologian – 'project ourselves onto an ultimate plane that gives meaning, and thus we are given ourselves ... surrender[ing] ourselves to something that transcends and gives meaning to the limited horizon of everyday life.'[15] And in such a drama as the suffering, death and resurrection of Jesus, they see a demonstration of God's righteous love – a righteous love which somehow stands apart from the drama itself. In other words, God is the author and producer of this drama of righteous love, where we are the actors. The author and producer have gone away, leaving this powerful drama by which we may recover ourselves.

It seems to me that that considerably understates the righteous love of God, and its implications for the way in which God draws us to himself. If love does 'shift the boundaries of our being', can it be any the less so with God? Can we really suppose that the drama of the suffering, death and resurrection of Jesus into which we are brought (like the eunuch) by the Spirit is a drama from which God stands apart? The truth is that the boundaries of being between God and us shift with each new expression of his love, and do so *most* of all in the drama of the suffering death and resurrection of Jesus as we are drawn into it by the Spirit. The Holy Spirit does not simply draw us into the drama of Jesus. The Spirit draws us into the place in which God's love is most deeply present, and in which God is closest to us. The only limiting factor is the degree to which we are prepared to respond in love. It is, therefore, *we* who insist that God is distant, and *we* who erect a barrier which keeps God in heaven and leaves us alone here on earth. Far from this, God is most God where in the utmost love he enters most deeply into our life, in the suffering death and resurrection of Jesus into which we are drawn by the Holy Spirit. There, as I need hardly tell you, God lives through the extremities of our life – our sin and self-isolation, and our death – and is still most near to

---

[15] Hans Urs Von Balthasar, *Theo-Drama*, San Francisco: Ignatius Press, 1988, Vol. I, p. 309.

us. Not even the boundaries which we erect to separate ourselves from God are barriers to this love; this love shifts all such boundaries.

Strangely, *the marks of this are found in the proper interweaving of people and their cultures.*

You recall the words from the First Letter of John:

> We know that we have passed out of death into life, because we love the brethren. He who does not love abides in death. Any one who hates his brother is a murderer, and you know that no murderer has eternal life abiding in him. By this we know love, that he laid down his life for us; and we ought to lay down our lives for the brethren ... Little children, let us not love in word or speech but in deed and in truth.[16]

For those who are drawn by the Holy Spirit into the suffering death and resurrection of Jesus, and thus drawn into the love of God, the chief mark of this 'new generation' is to be found in our 'love for the brethren', a love which includes 'laying down our lives for the brethren'.

The suffering death and resurrection of Jesus are not simply the illustration of some kind of ideal which should vaguely inform our actions toward others. When we are drawn by the Spirit into the suffering death and resurrection of Jesus, we are drawn into a new kind of life with each other. That may seem scary. Sacrifice for each other usually frightens us because it seems death-like, wasting ourselves for the sake of someone else; and we usually rationalize ourselves into believing that no one else could be worth such sacrificial wasting of ourselves. And for that reason, we usually turn the suffering death of Jesus into a vague ideal for a kind of love which isn't really expected of us.

But these reactions are simply wrong. Far from being informed of a vague ideal, we are actually drawn by the Spirit into 'the truth', the awesome dynamic of God's pervasively boundary-shifting love, and it is in the dynamic of that love that we are to be interwoven with each other. Following that dynamic, we 'lay down our lives for the brethren', not in fear but in the realization that in such sacrifice God meets us most closely and – in our very loss – raises us up. As we lose ourselves for the brethren, so we will win ourselves. This is the mark that the Spirit has drawn us into the suffering death and resurrection of Jesus.

The dynamic of this love transforms the way in which we are with each other as peoples, cultures and contexts. It is 'gratuitous, beyond our fathom, both binding and freeing ... [it] re-invades us, shifts the boundaries of our being'. We can embrace others, and be embraced, in ways quite beyond our imagining – and there continue to be enlarged by the

[16] I John 3.14–18.

49

nearness of God's love. That is the fundamental pattern by which, in the interweaving of human beings and cultures, the presence of God is found. It is the way in which the love of God is continued amongst us who are so sharply separated.

CONCLUSION

We are at an end. What I have sought to show is the agenda of theology for the future – finding God's presence in the interwovenness of human beings, their cultures and the natural world. Secondly, I have suggested how this agenda is to be met in a theology which is a creative, intelligent, practical poesis by which peoples, cultures and contexts are interwoven. Thirdly, I have suggested that the fullest form of this poesis is found in the Resurrection of Jesus Christ and the generativity which followed from it. By such means, I suggest, we are led both to understand the proper form of the interwovenness of human beings and the way by which God is present in it.

To quote an American evangelist whom I hear on radio broadcasts occasionally, 'think about it'. But perhaps you should also do more, that is *be interwoven with others in the way which God has made possible*.

4

The Trinity in Language[1]

INTRODUCTION

THERE are many avenues through which the substance of Christian faith – which is Trinitarian faith – can be considered. Amongst the most central is the issue of language, what it is and how it is properly used. Most issues about the substance of faith, and about the dilemmas of faith, appear sooner or later in the form of a discussion about the nature of language and how language is properly used. That is not to say that the question of language is all there is to the question of faith, or vice versa, but only that it is central enough to manifest most of the problems – and distortions – of Christian faith.

In this talk, I hope to show the limitations of certain widespread notions of language as they are used in relation to Trinitarian faith, and then try to outline a way forward. I shall suggest that there are two prevalent notions of how language is grounded in Trinitarian faith, and that these need to be supplanted by a third, if we are to have a notion of language which is suitable to God's creative and redemptive work, or indeed appropriate to the kind of mystery which God is. The first of these two notions of language is, broadly speaking, one centred on the dynamics of language itself, in which its source in Trinitarian faith is obscured or lost altogether. The second is one centred on the way in which language is used to refer to objects, and authorized by Trinitarian faith. In preference to these two, I shall suggest that we need one focused on God's participation in the formation of language itself.

Which of the three we use has important consequences for how we use language and find God through language. Instead of seeing God as the one to whom various metaphors are applied, or as one who mandates us to refer to or describe God in particular ways authorized by the Christian tradition, it is more desirable to adopt a view of language in which God participates in the various ways by which we speak of God, and is identified through that participation. You will see that dividing the options into three is somewhat artificial, but at least this serves to clarify some of the main questions about language in theology which need to be considered.

[1] First Annual Lecture, Scholars Engaged in Anglican Doctrine, Alexandria, Virginia, 1 May 1992.

THE HISTORICAL PROBLEM WITH LANGUAGE

Before embarking on this 'trilogy', it may help to preface the discussion by describing what has been the central preoccupation in considerations of language through the centuries.

In most theories of language, words, thoughts and things have been seen as in some way parallel to each other – matching each other isomorphically (one-to-one). The following is an apt illustration:

> Consider, for example, the relationship between the notes on a sheet of music and the keys struck by a pianist playing the music. To each mark on the sheet, with its specific location (higher or lower, on this line or that), there corresponds a specific ivory key, which is struck by the pianist's finger; a specific string, which is set vibrating; a specific vibration, excited in the air; and a specific sensation, registered in the hearer. Yet the mark does not resemble the ivory key, nor the key the string, the string the vibration, the vibration the consequent sensation, or the sensation the original mark on the paper. What we observe instead is a perfect correlation: this mark paired with this key, this string, this vibration, and this sensation; another mark with another key, string, vibration, and sensation; and so on – one-to-one matching.[2]

Such a correlation between verbal signs and mental concepts and between mental signs and objects has usually been considered a required precondition for verbal or mental truth. And there have been many variations on the claim that a correlation is necessary for verbal or mental truth.[3]

The isomorphic tradition survived as late as the eighteenth century, when words and combinations of words

> were thought to be accessible because they refer to, or represent, states of affairs which one perceives, or else ideas which one grasps regardless of their linguistic embodiment ... Meaning itself was thought of as a kind of unvarying subsistent medium in which words flourish or, to change the figure, a kind of conveyor belt onto which

---

[2] Garth L. Hallett, *Language and Truth*, New Haven: Yale University Press, 1988, pp. 5f.
[3] For a description, see Hallett, *op. cit.*, Chs. 2 and 3.

words are dropped for their proper reference or destiny. Language is a fit instrument because words have stable, lexically determined meanings.[4]

So words or ideas were still isomorphic with perceived states of affairs, and for this reason they were stable, with self-same meanings; and they flourished in a subsistent medium. To use other words, *what* was experienced, and the language in which it was *expressed*, were well-matched.

Implicit in such views was the supposition that what was perceived, and the language used for it, operated under the constraints of certain universal conditions which were ultimately traceable to God. Increasingly, however, the responsibility for experience and language was devolved upon humanity. For a while, as in the philosophy of Kant, it seemed possible to specify the universal conditions for human awareness and language; even then, the conditions applied primarily to formal characteristics of perception/experience and the formal language of mathematics. But soon, even these were overtaken by the burgeoning science, history, culture and life of the nineteenth century; these simply out-flanked notions of universality and the possibility of finding their ground in God.

In general the views of language which now prevail comprise two different reactions to the loss of universality in experience and language. One view embraces this loss, while the other resists it.

EMBRACING THE LOSS: RHETORIC BEFORE (OR WITHOUT) REFERENCE

It is characteristic of much current use of language, even very well-intended, to suppose that it must follow, describe or enhance the irreducibly historical or particular character of human experience. It is said that it is no longer necessary to suppose that there are essences – whether human or otherwise – which language expresses; and it is no longer necessary to search for universal conditions of experience and language – they are false to the 'gutsiness' of particular experience. Instead, experience and language are thought to arise within what can be called the 'circle' of individual and particular culture, as people are formed by, and form, their culture; and both experience and language are as localized or transient as is their culture.

[4] Hans Frei, *The Eclipse of Biblical Narrative*, New Haven: Yale University Press, 1974, p. 109.

The extreme to which this view can be taken is beautifully sketched in an episode from a novel by David Lodge, *Nice Work*. Two of the main characters are speaking to each other:

'I've been in love with you for weeks.' [Vic says]
'There's no such thing,' she says. 'It's a rhetorical device. It's a bourgeois fallacy.'
'Haven't you ever been in love, then?' [he responds]
'When I was younger,' she says, 'I allowed myself to be constructed by the discourse of romantic love for a while, yes.'
'What the hell does that mean?' [he says]
'We aren't essences, Vic. We aren't unique individual essences existing prior to language. There is only language.'[5]

This episode is the confrontation of a naively realistic human being, speaking directly to another of a love which he thinks somehow objective, with another for whom life is formed by a sequence of linguistic constructions. For her there is nothing but what is provided by the transient forms of language, no 'subjectivity', 'objectivity' and common experience except what their joining momentarily in conversation will allow. She seems to deny both the possibility of being selves ('individual essences') apart from language, and the possibility of even having a world – whether separately or together – which is somehow self-same. Strictly speaking, it is not even legitimate to refer to one's particular experience and decisions, or to find meaning in the present.[6]

That, of course, is an extreme version, one which is founded on a well-developed theory of language. And it undercuts every form of universality, whether of experience or language, and correspondingly raises the deepest questions about a faith traditionally expressed in universal forms. Perhaps, as George Steiner argues in *Real Presences*, it is more widespread than we would like to believe. An advertisement in last week's *Church Times* reads:

Sea of Faith: A network for bringing together all those who hold or are interested in a non-supernatural idea of 'God' and who want to meet like-minded people and study the implications of religious faith as a human creation. Fifth Annual Conference 28th to 30th July at

[5] David Lodge, *Nice Work*, London: Penguin Books, 1989, p. 293.
[6] Hilary Lawson, *Reflexivity: The Post-Modern Predicament*, London: Hutchinson, 1985, p. 99.

Leicester University. Speakers: Don Cupitt, Lloyd Gearing, Ronald Nicholson.[7]

Amongst Christians, milder forms of this view of language have become very common, however. And they tend to use it not as theory but as practice, in order to achieve certain ends, usually to promote tolerance and equality for the powerless. If it were to be put in the form of an argument, the position could be stated as follows: Human perception of the world, and its basis in religious faith, is a human construction, and as such distorted. This distortion produces, and results from, a biased expression in language. Both the distorted perception and the biased language are used as a means of control exercised by those in power, who claim that their perception and their language – and indeed their power – are founded in the nature of reality as constituted by God. The best means of undermining *their* power is to recognize that their language is devoid of reference to universal reality, a purely human creation. If we return to the episode from David Lodge's novel, it is like saying that her reaction against Vic's offer of love (Why should he import her into his idea of love?) is best extended to a general denial of love ('When I was younger, I allowed myself to be constructed by the discourse of romantic love for a while, yes.')

The costs to Christian theology are large, as such views of language are applied to what is (significantly) called the 'central core symbolism of Christianity and its effects on their self-understanding and their relationship to God'.[8] What can happen is that injurious uses of language by *particular* people – or indeed whole sections of the Church – are to be combated by depriving *all* language of its possibility of referring, and nullifying the basis of referential language in God. And what follows is the loss of any way of finding the character of God's work and life, except as a human projection.

Where not taken to such extremes, embracing the loss of universality in experience and language can bring an attempt to find 'webs of meaning and language' through which knowledge, morality and faith can be sustained. But their relation to Christian faith is, if not problematic, certainly unexplicated as yet. The problems are suggested in a poem by one of the best present-day Irish poets:

> Enough was enough. We flew
> nets of old certainties,
> all that crabbed grammar

---

[7] *Church Times*, 24 April 1992, p. 14.
[8] Ann Loades, 'Feminist Theology' in David F. Ford, ed., *The Modern Theologians*, Oxford: Blackwell, 1989, Vol. II, p. 242.

of the predictable. Unentangled,
we'd soar to a language
of our own.

Freedom. We sang of freedom
(travel lightly, anything goes)
and somehow became strangers
to each other, like gabblers
at cross purposes, builders
of Babel.

Slowly I relearn a *lingua*,
shared overlays of rule,
lattice of memory and meaning,
our latent images, a tongue
at large in an endlessness
of sentences unsaid.[9]

The question, however, is whether such a 'tongue at large in an endlessness of sentences unsaid' can do more than signify the mystery of God,
and – if so – how.

RESISTING THE LOSS OF UNIVERSALITY: TRADITIONAL REFERENCE

If one turns away from the legions of people who associate the theory
and practice of the language of faith only with the theories and practices
of literary criticism, there are many who find the possibility of reliable
reference to states of affairs, and the possibility of grounding this referring in universal conditions established by God. The main difference
between them is in how they specify these 'possibilities'. It is worthwhile
outlining the main types of position which they take.

Some scientists advocate a time-neutral, unitary scientific method
which largely eliminates reference to the human knower, but nonetheless

---

[9] 'Freedom' from Micheal O'Siadhail, *The Chosen Garden*, Dublin: The Dedalus Press,
1990, p. 57. See also George Lindbeck's view of theology as intertextual (*The Nature of
Doctrine*, London: SPCK, 1985) and Rom Harré's view of scientific realism as 'semantic
networks, webs of meaning held together by ordered sequences of analogies' (*Varieties of
Realism*, Oxford: Blackwell, 1986, p. 7).

maintains the possibility of an isomorphism of words/symbols and states of affairs in the world. Others advocate a more dynamic view of human experience, finding that scientific method varies with historical locales (in what are called 'paradigms') which condition the isomorphism of words/symbols and states of affairs in the world. Either way, there is little concern with the supposition that this isomorphism or its variability is traceable to God's action.

On their side, some theologians also find a time-neutral, unitary method – which provides isomorphism of words/symbols and states of affairs in the world – which is established by the activity of God on the knower in the Trinitarian activity of revelation. Others see in God one who is involved in the dynamic of human history, and are attracted by more fluid ways of referring to God – emphasizing the place of models and paradigms in human understanding and language; they tend to replace the Trinitarian view of God's activity (as providing the isomorphism of words/symbols and states of affairs in the world) by general transcendental or metaphysical philosophies (neo-Thomism or process philosophy, for example). Whatever their difference, however, they are agreed that human experience and language derive from attending to what is real; they are not wholly confined within the transient forms of language found in varying cultures. For this reason, there can be a continuity and universality in history and its language which can be revalidated by present experience.

Against those who insist that this 'continuity' is only a persisting set of core-symbols, an ancient and threatening 'cloud of truth' which hovers over all that follows, unfairly requiring conformity to a distant and outworn set of 'truths', those who find this continuity find in it a true language which meets present-day experience and gives it the form which it needs. This is, they find, a living tradition in which one lives from and with God, much like a memory from which one derives an identity.

Within this living tradition, seen as continuing in the life of the faithful, there is a natural rational concentration which occurs (Lonergan), both in the narration of key events and in focusing on what are thought to be its major features. In either case – and the purposes of narrative history and those of systematic theology are not so far apart as people suppose – the effect is to suggest an 'economy' of history and to establish the figuration of that economy in terms of the agency of God and human beings.

It is from such 'economies' that human beings come to see themselves as the beneficiaries of the free and graceful activity of God in the history of creation and redemption. For many reasons, not least the difficulties of integrating such a singular notion of God's work with the complexity by which it occurs, the result is the ascription of triunity to God, not only in the work of God but in the very being of God. That is what is indicated in such compressed statements as 'the economic Trinity is the immanent Trinity'.[10]

There is a tendency amongst them – perhaps brought about by the 'need to know' which seizes so many amidst the uncertainties of the modern world – to leap too quickly from the possibility of establishing a pattern in natural events, an economy for human history, to grounding it in the economy of God's action and being, and seeing it in terms of direct communication or revelation. Then, all naming of God is thought to be derived from acts by which God names or interprets 'himself' for human beings, and by which 'he' also frees them to name or interpret 'him'. This self-naming of God, they say, follows the three 'arrows' of time – past, present and future. Thus, fulfilling the old covenant with the Jews, there is the fundamental self-communication of God in the world in the person of Jesus which is thereafter 'deployed in the divinization of the world in the Holy Spirit (... the creative, loving, sanctifying power of God which draws the world to God) – and in its historical and eschatological manifestation through the historical and definitive word of God.'[11]

This strategy, by which God is seen as self-naming for human beings, is sometimes also understood as authorizing very specific names for God:

> In that God has identity, he has a proper name, and one that is truly proper, that he does not 'share with another.' Later prophetic insight could summarize the whole salvation of Israel in the promise: 'They shall know that I am Jahweh and no one else ... In the Resurrection, this God publishes a new name. And here again, the risen Lord could summarize the whole mission of the church as the initiation of the disciples into that name, into 'the name Father, Son and Holy Spirit.' A faithful church would be faithful to these names ... A church ashamed of her God's name is ashamed of her God.[12]

While assuredly there is a very close connection between the economy of human history and the economy of God's action and being, or between language itself and the ontological conditions which provide for true language, there should be no such easy move from this to the supposition that human language for God is authorized by a straightforward self-naming on God's part. One can be fully Trinitarian without supposing that the 'sonship' of Jesus makes his language for God as 'father' into an unavoidable – if not the only – primary language by which God has named himself. God's ontological self-conferral in Jesus and the Spirit

[10] Karl Rahner, 'The Trinity' in *Sacramentum Mundi*, Vol. VI, p. 295.
[11] Rahner, *op. cit.* p. 299.
[12] Robert W. Jenson, 'A Call to Faithfulness', *Dialog*, Vol. 30, No. 2, p. 92.

does not necessarily imply the linguistic conferral of such particular language.

The divine 'I am', and the consequences of the Cross and Resurrection for it, needs careful reconsideration. Is the 'I am' a self-naming? Should the language of being ('I *am*') therefore be accorded preference? Is the Resurrection a new naming? And if so, should 'Father' and 'Son' be used preferentially, as distinct from the many other words which abound in the New Testament witness? Above all, perhaps, are we bound to such restricted views of God's participation in the formation of human language, as if the Spirit's place was only to bring about faithfulness to these names? Where those who embrace the loss of universality end by saying too little about the Trinitarian God (what I call *underdefinition*), those who resist the loss of universality often end by saying too much (*overdefinition*).[13] Of course, such faults eliminate neither group – the rhetoricians or the realists – from the field. They simply limit their value, particularly as regards Trinitarian language.

LANGUAGE UNDERWRITTEN BY GOD'S PRESENCE

For all its virtues, therefore, the 'isomorphic tradition' is also severely limited where a theological conception of language is concerned. And while I do not wish to undermine it, it seems to me that the tradition needs to be recast in order to take account of God's participation in language.

One important, if much disputed, attempt to do this has been made recently by George Steiner:

Any coherent understanding of what language is and how language performs, [and] any coherent account of the capacity of human speech to communicate meaning and feeling is, in the final analysis, underwritten by the assumption of God's presence. I will put forward the argument that the experience of aesthetic meaning in particular, that of literature, of the arts, of musical form, infers the necessary possibility of this 'real presence'. The seeming paradox of a 'necessary possibility' is, very precisely, that which the poem, the painting, the musical composition are at liberty to explore and to enact.

This study will contend that the wager on the meaning of mean-

[13] Cf. Daniel W. Hardy, 'Epilogue' in D. W. Hardy and P. H. Sedgwick, *The Weight of Glory*, Edinburgh: T. & T. Clark, 1991.

ing, on the potential of insight and response when one human voice addresses another, when we come face to face with the text and work of art and music, which is to say when we encounter the other in its condition of freedom, is a wager on transcendence ... The conjecture is that 'God' is, not because our grammar is outworn; but that grammar lives and generates worlds because there is the wager on God.[14]

I agree with Steiner that language is – and must be – underwritten by the assumption of God's presence. But all the difference is made by how this presence occurs. His view suggests that language rests on

a direct and immediate sense of givenness, of awareness of something Other and something More, of experience of being taken beyond oneself – not out into nothing, but deep into something which is both the basis of, and the promise and fulfillment for, the sheer and mere fact that one is there (here) and actually experiencing some possibilities both of creativity and of creation.[15]

That, of course, grounds language and creativity in the other which is present in language and frees language to explore it, which serves as a theological authorization of autonomous human creativity.

Nonetheless, it has a signal advantage: it makes the question of God central to culture without compromising the freedom of culture. To appreciate the significance of this, it must be remembered that the modern literary tradition has arisen largely outside faith, and has tended therefore towards extremes – as was evident, for example, in the case of Salman Rushdie – while faith has tended to deny the legitimacy of freely creative language.

A Trinitarian Economy of Language

That is all well and good, so far as it goes; but it is sub-Christian. I shall contend for the view that language is founded not in transcendence but in the involvement of the Trinitarian God in the dynamics of language itself. Furthermore, I shall argue that the establishment of truth in language rests on God's involvement also. For God's identity and creative and redemptive activity are not simply a 'state of affairs' to which our mental

---

[14] George Steiner, *Real Presences*, London: Faber & Faber, 1989, pp. 3f.
[15] David Jenkins, 'A Gamble on God' (Review of Real Presences) in *The Times Higher Educational Supplement*, 8 September 1989, p. 13.

concepts and language are correlated through the conferral of words – or a salvation-history by which they are embraced – by God. Instead, his identity and creative and redemptive activity occur through his participation in our language and culture. And God actively confers himself in establishing and reestablishing our language and truth as we communicate with each other. The result is the possibility of a richer and more dynamic language and truth from God and amongst us than traditional theories of isomorphic language – rooted as they were in secular (often Platonic) theories of language can allow. It is for this reason that I wish to go beyond the two theories of language which have become conventional in our day.

That means that language is not simply instrumental to God's action in bringing others to their truth, that there is a creative and redemptive work which happens independent of language – a work which is *then* spoken of. This would hold language outside the creative and redemptive work of God, as if language was extrinsic to that and invoked only to present information about what occurs. But language is in no such position in Christian faith. As evidence, consider the importance of the Last Supper, a symbolic and linguistic incorporation of the disciples into the sacrifice of Jesus; there language is shown as intrinsic to the redemptive purposes of God.[16] Language is an 'economy' in which the Trinitarian God is active.

THE ACTIVITY OF THE TRINITARIAN GOD IN LANGUAGE

The question, of course, is how the Trinitarian God is active in the 'economy' of language. Answering that question would be a very large task indeed. It must suffice here to trace some of the broad outlines of an answer. I shall begin by reminding you of two important issues, one which has to do with the 'largesse' of language in the 'hands' of God – as contrasted with the determinism which is at work in most discussions of language in relation to God, and the other which has to do with the importance for the formation of language of the fundamental content of the relation of the Trinitarian God to humanity.

(1) THE LARGESSE OF GOD IN LANGUAGE

First of all, let us take up the matter of the largesse of God as the source

---

[16] Anglicans should be especially attuned to this, since in Anglican tradition, symbols and language have been primary means for the incorporation of Christians into a common faith.

of language. Concentrating on the self-naming of God gives preference to the language of being and the terminology of Father–Son relationships. But we must recall that neither self-naming nor such language (being, father, son) have been so primary as these current preoccupations make them. Recall these words from the Book of Revelation:

> Between the throne and the four living creatures and among the elders, I saw a Lamb standing, as though it had been slain, with seven horns and with seven eyes, which are the seven spirits of God sent out into all the earth; and he went and took the scroll from the right hand of him who was seated on the throne. And when he had taken the scroll, the four living creatures and the twenty-four elders fell down before the Lamb, each holding a harp, and with golden bowls full of incense, which are the prayers of the saints; and they sang a new song, saying, 'Worthy art thou to take the scroll and to open its seals, for thou wast slain and by thy blood did ransom men for God from every tribe and tongue and people and nation, and hast made them a kingdom and priests to our God, and they shall reign on earth.' Then I looked, and I heard around the throne and the living creatures and the elders the voice of many angels, numbering myriads of myriads and thousands of thousands, saying with a loud voice, 'Worthy is the Lamb who was slain, to receive power and wealth and wisdom and might and honor and glory and blessing.'[17]

From this passage, you will quickly see how rich is speech as it is construed in the New Testament. Here, God is identified primarily as the abundant source of all. Christ opens this fullness, but does so as the 'Lamb', the sacrificial means by which the informative content of language is opened.[18] In this connection, George Caird makes a very important point:

> John undoubtedly invests Christ with the attributes of deity, but he also does something more important still: he redefines omnipotence. Omnipotence is not to be understood as the power of unlimited coercion, but as the power of infinite persuasion, the unlimited power of self-negating, self-sacrificing love.[19]

---

[17] Revelation 5.6ff.
[18] In all the Old Testament references with which this text abounds, the 'Lion' is replaced by the 'Lamb'.
[19] George Caird, *The Revelation of St. John the Divine*, New York: Harper & Row, 1966, p. 75.

Correspondingly, the Spirit radiates from the Lamb to persuade, inform and enliven all people in their particular places and thereby incorporate them into the 'river of life' – hence the mention of the seven spirits sent into all the earth, to bring about a witness which is contingent and appropriate for every place but fundamentally coordinated in the life of the Spirit.

There are two issues on which to comment. Here is a full expression of the Trinitarian life of God which does not accord with the supposedly normative conception of God as self-naming, and which shows the selectivity implicit in that conception. Furthermore, it is one which suggests a different notion of God's conferral of language than that suggested by restrictive notions of isomorphism. According to this notion, God – seen here as the scrolls of wisdom – is the source of the fundamental informative content of language itself. And Christ opens this fullness, but does so as the 'Lamb', the sacrificial means by which the informative content of language is opened. Where human language had been robbed of its source, and had therefore become closed, impoverished and unreliable, Christ reopens the connection of language with its source. But that does not establish a single preferred language. Instead, the Spirit brings about a witness which is contingent and appropriate for every place but fundamentally one in Christ. According to this view, God's conferral of language is much less restrictive than that of providing certain key names for himself.

(2) LANGUAGE AS FOLLOWING THE PATTERN OF GOD'S WORK

The second matter of which I should remind you is that the logic of God's work for humankind is in any case much fuller than a simple isomorphism would suggest. The dynamics of God's Trinitarian life and activity exceed conventional notions of self-presentation in language, even where that is conceived of as introductory ('I am'), new (the Resurrected Lord) or a summation of salvation history. In this connection, recall the parable of the Prodigal Son.

The parable needs to be read as an indication of the abundance which is characteristic of God, overflowing the bounds of what might be customary in relationships. In the behavior of the father to his returning son, we find an abundance of life which is out of all proportion to what might be expected, but one which is communicated in a *specific* way in very *particular* circumstances. It is specific but not confined to what custom might dictate – that the son, having placed himself outside the customs of the family, should reenter the household only as an hireling. Specifically, it is an unrestricted conferral of abundance. Even while the son is far away, 'his father saw him and had compassion, and ran and embraced and kissed him.'[20] That is remarkable; to have compassion is to bond oneself very deeply to another person. And here, even before he goes out, he bonds himself very deeply to his alien, wayward son; and then he passionately goes out to him and embraces and kisses him. And despite the son's cries accusing himself of sin, and denying any place which he might have in the household, the father confers all his own abundance on him. Even more, he raises this alien son to a new position of dignity. Now that he is found, his place is greater than before he was lost. What he does is truly abundant – abundant in its compassionate love, abundant in its going out, abundant in his mercy, and abundant in the place which he gives his returned son, not only welcoming him as his son but elevating him to a new honour. There is a bonding to the wayward, a willingness to join him in his dereliction, a loving and abundant conferral of new dignity which customs cannot provide or comprehend.

In telling this parable, Jesus appears to have been portraying the fundamental content of the Trinitarian life and work of God, an abundance which goes out to meet others, to embrace and raise them. This is the means by which they are met and raised to their truth by the 'king of truth' – which is the place which Jesus is given in John's Gospel. What the king of truth does is to establish the truth of each and every person and society. Jesus had always tried to show that the way by which truth was made in another person was not by condemnation and force administered from afar, but through a deep bonding (compassion) to another person, going out to meet him, embracing him and raising him to new truth and dignity. But in his compassionate goodness on the Cross, Jesus himself became the alien one, identical with the lost and dying, thereby to make anew the truth of humankind. 'By a single offering he has perfected for all time those who are sanctified.'[21] On the Cross, the truth of humankind was restored.

If we ask what are the implications of this for language, the parable – and Christ's life – suggest how language is to be redemptive. It is addressed to others (in their otherness) as the means by which they are met, responded-to, bonded-to and raised to their truth. By comparison, a view which requires that all language be determined by its source – seeing certain language as conferred 'from above' – seems formalistic, ignoring the dynamics through which others can be met, heard, and abundantly raised to their own truth. A truer view of language will enable it to reach out to the other in his/her otherness and particularity.

[20] Luke 15.20.
[21] Hebrews 10.14.

The 'logic' of the Trinitarian life and work of God – hence the logic of God's activity in language – is that of the most radical form of gift. That requires an enlargement of our conventional notions of isomorphism and of our preferred language for God, whether existence (being) or any conventional notions of father and son:

> Because God does not fall within the domain of Being, he comes to us in and as a gift ... the gift does not have first to be, but to pour out in an abandon that, alone, causes it to be; God saves the gift in giving it before being.[22]

Language in which the Trinitarian God is active is such a gift, and occurs where human speakers reach out to others in their particularity and speak lovingly.

By now, we have seen that the activity of the Trinitarian God in the 'economy' of language is of such a kind as to enlarge or enrich the dynamics of language in accordance with the richness of God, and to make it intrinsic to the redemption whereby the other – in otherness – is restored to true being. In these respects, the fundamental content of the Trinitarian God forms the economy of language itself.

CONCLUSION: LANGUAGE IN THE AGE OF DIVERSITY

These insights are particularly important in an age where the diversity of language overwhelms theology, and where people argue over how their special interests may be adequately maintained through language – to the exclusion of questions of the truth of God. For through the richness of God's conferral of language in the economy of human language, we see that God is active in developing this diversity and complexity and yet resolving the tensions which emerge in such diversity.

If the coherence of theology is to survive in an age where there is such diversity, individuals and groups must be able to rejoice in particularity while at the same time recognizing each other with compassion. The issue is well captured in this poem:

> Worship, hold her a moment in thought.
> *Femme fatale*, she shapes another face,
> unveils an idol. O Never-To-Be-Caught,

[22] Jean-Luc Marion, *God Without Being*, Chicago: University of Chicago Press, 1991, p. 3.

O Minx beyond this mind's embrace,
Hider-Go-Seeker, Miss Unfathomable,
Demurring Lady playing at the chase.

As stars or atoms we turn, fall
towards each other's gravity. I spin
in you, love's nexus, Mistress All.

Once a child of Newton's fallen
apple, I'd be the measure of your ways.
My stars, my atoms, are we one?

Mischievous Strategy, Madam Jazz!
old tunes die in metamorphosis.
Rise, fall, reawakening. I praise.[23]

It is possible – more than that, necessary – to have language which is particularizing, which is adequate for reference to particular objects according to their proper character, without feeling constrained to collapse all these particular differences into universals. And the abundance of God present in language enables each thing or person to be different in its particularity, and yet capable of achieving unity through reference to the common source of particularities which/who is present in the dynamics of mutual engagement.

That is astonishingly liberating. There is no need to collapse differences in order to achieve unity. Accordingly, the Trinitarian God can be seen to participate in any identification of a thing in its particular truth, and to participate in their relation.

That is not to suggest that difference or particularity in itself constitutes truth. There are different kinds of differentiation. An absolute differentiation, which detaches an individual or social group – like an atom – from all around it, and makes every relationship extrinsic and contingent, if not self-serving, is quite unlike a relative differentiation in an intrinsic relatedness. The one is a misuse of freedom, while the other is a legitimate freedom in responsibility. The one is the preparation for waywardness; the other is not. The creative Trinitarian activity of God allows both but promotes a language in which there is true – that is relative – differentiation, a differentiation in free mutual responsibility.

The true language of such free mutual responsibility is a language which arises in the inner life of God himself.

[23] Micheal O'Siadhail, 'Hail! Madam Jazz' in *The Chosen Garden*, Dublin: The Dedalus Press, 1990, p. 90.

The essence of the Christian God is love in eternal process. It is the Trinitarian history of love. It is the Trinity as the eternal history of love which sets in motion, assumes and pervades the history of the world, the object of his pure love.[24]

And this history is everywhere in motion through language itself.

[24] Bruno Forte, *The Trinity as History*, New York: Alba House, 1989, pp. 149f.

5

The Spirit of God in Creation and Reconciliation[1]

INTRODUCTION: CONTEXTUALITY AND THE TRINITARIAN GOD

IT may seem surprising for a paper on 'The Spirit of God in Creation and Reconciliation' to be offered to a Symposium on Christ and Context. The title is a rather coded one, indicating that I propose to discuss the relation of the Trinitarian God to the dynamics of humanity and nature. The paper will attempt to deepen the discussion of 'Christ and Context' by relating it to the Trinitarian God, to the nature of contextuality and to the dynamic relation between them. It may be best to start by suggesting why these issues are important.

Contrary to our usual suppositions, 'context' does not indicate that which surrounds us, as if that were distinct from us, as if it were an envelope in which we are contained. Nor, much as we might suppose otherwise, are 'contexts' clearly distinct or disjoined from each other. This is true both conceptually and in actuality. Conceptually, the notion of context derives its original meaning from the Latin word *contexere*, which designates the interweaving or braiding together of what might otherwise be considered distinct. So contextuality designates the interweaving of human subjects with their cultures and the natural world, and of cultures with each other and the natural world. In actuality also, it needs to be recognized that 'context' is a mental, if not also a cultural, construct, one which serves to tidy up the often confusing mixture of situations in which we find ourselves. There is some danger in this tidying up that we lose the vibrancy of the very mixture which we seek to clarify – that we 'murder in order to dissect'.

It also needs to be understood that the Trinitarian God does not designate one alien to this world, the world in which human beings and cultures and the natural world are interwoven. It often seems to be thought nowadays that, as a matter of principle, Christian speaking about God must somehow be alien to the wide multicultural, multi-religious world which we inhabit. That is not necessarily the case; whether it is has still to be decided. It is that issue to which this paper is

[1] An Address to the Symposium on Christ and Context, Dunedin, New Zealand, 15 May 1991.

addressed. We shall attempt to find how the Trinitarian God is present in the interweaving of human subjects with each other, their culture and the natural world.

ON POESIS, THEORY AND TRUTH-TELLING

If contextuality is itself a dynamic, and if the Trinitarian God is to be sought in the braiding together of human beings, their cultures and the natural world, we will need to approach these issues by means of a dynamic of thought which transcends the limitations of our usual habits.[2] To put this very succinctly, we will need to develop a creative perception by which to sing our world as a hymn of praise to God; fashioning such a song is actually the task of theology.[3]

Attractive and valuable though it might be, such a creative perception cannot simply be 'poetic' in the normal sense, providing an explicitly poetic concentration of the nature of God's presence in our interwovenness. To be sure, such a thing has the advantage of freeing itself from the norms which often operate in analytical-empirical 'science'.[4] But if we

---

[2] 'I believe that learning to admit transcendence may be one of the major undertakings of a man's life, perhaps the major undertaking, so that if it is ignored his personality may be stunted or destroyed.' Monica Furlong, *Contemplating Now*, Cambridge: Cowley Publications, 1983, p. 50.

[3] Poetry, in its creative perception, provides a concentrated opportunity by which to 'sing reality'. Bruce Chatwin, in *The Songlines* [London: Pan Books, 1987], says of the Aboriginal Creation myths,

> [They] tell of the legendary totemic beings who had wandered over the continent in the Dreamtime, singing out the name of everything that crossed their path – birds, animals, plants, rocks, waterholes – and so singing the world into existence ... By singing the world into existence, the ancestors had been poets in the original sense of poesis, meaning 'creation'.

So the multistranded reality in which we live needs to be 'sung into existence'. For a Christian, this means that it needs to be sung as a hymn of praise to God the Creator. It is the task of theology to fashion the creative poesis by which it is sung as a hymn of praise to God. In more technical terms, poetry – or theology – provides a wisdom, heuristic or direction for exploration, which serves to orientate a search, much as the Aboriginals' songlines provide a 'map and direction-finder' for travel.

[4] To the consternation of many in the literary community, George Steiner has suggested that 'there is some fundamental encounter with transcendence in the creation of art and in its experiencing', and that works of art manifest 'a root impulse of the human spirit to explore possibilities of meaning and of truth that lie outside empirical seizure or proof ... '; they constitute a 'wager on survivance, [and] are refusals of analytic-empirical criteria of constraint.' *Real Presences*, London: Faber & Faber, 1989, pp. 228, 225f. While this view is helpful, it is an overstatement to claim that 'it is ... poetry, art and music which relate us *most directly* to that in being which is not ours' (p. 226, emphasis mine).

are to remain in touch with the factors which are formative of modern life and understanding, we cannot so easily distance ourselves from the the empirical and theoretical considerations of other disciplines and of theology; we must probe and test them. But the theoretical character of what follows should not obscure its place in the task of building a creative poesis or heuristic. And, as a poesis, it starts within – and remains within – the field which it explores; it does not stand outside, in a position of supposed neutrality.

Hence, as we speak of our contextuality and the presence there of the Trinitarian God, we shall be doing so from the position of those in whom they intersect, as those for whom God is present in our interweaving. To use more poetic images, we shall be engaging in a concentrated 'song of reality' even as we attempt to find better ways of following the line of the melody; and the song will draw its inspiration – and I use that word advisedly – from the very reality which is sung.

Such a thing is far more important than it may seem. For what we seek are the intellectual conditions for a true poesis, by which we may fully participate in the work of the Trinitarian God in our interweaving. They are the intellectual conditions for truth-telling about God's presence in our interweaving, the intellectual conditions for what John de Gruchy called the 'promised land', for what Jürgen Moltmann called the 'mutual indwelling of humanity and nature'.

A true poesis – in which we participate more fully in the presence of the Trinitarian God in our interweaving – is not a field which (more or less) approximates to a truth somehow independent of God. Its truth is God's; and our seeking for it is an activity in which the Trinitarian God participates. The truth of this poesis is God's performance of the truth. This makes truth somewhat different from what we usually expect. It is not something fixed, like a fixed star which is near or far away, which serves as a simple point by which we can check the position of everything else. Rather it is an active truth, active everywhere, working to bring all things, including our understanding and actions, into its movement. The inner pattern of this truth is Trinitarian, active and lifting and livening. But that is a discussion for some other time.

At the same time, we are in the position of those who think and live in a contextuality of falsehoods, one in which – in thought and deed – we suffer from the illegitimate divisions into which our contextuality is now divided, and in turn enhance them. Finding the intellectual conditions for truth-telling about God's presence in our interweaving will give us a means of combating the illegitimate division of human thought, of human beings and cultures, as well as the illegitimate separation of human beings from nature, by discovering the way in which God is present through the interweaving of human beings, cultures and nature. But, as I have already implied, the search will take us into Trinitarian, as well as other, ontology. In good English fashion, I was going to say, 'Sorry about that!'; but I'm really not, because the difficulties start as far back as that.

The results of such an inquiry have a peculiar position. I am sure that if theological work is to have maximum impact upon today's world, it cannot simply be evocative and exhortation; it must be explanatory, and as such interact with the means by which people in other disciplines explain the world. That is the modern, as well as the ancient, form of prophecy. That is not to say that theological explanations should be *identical* to the explanations by other disciplines, only that they should *interact* with them. For theological explanations are concerned with what ought to be, and its contrast with what is. This explanation of 'what ought to be' can be placed either historically – as protology or eschatology, or naturally – as transcendental; but in either case, it is interactive/interwoven with what is, as a form contrasting to what is. However, affirming this 'what ought to be' and bringing it about in historical-natural life, are the only ways by which it may be understood and effected. This is always costly, both to the understanding and to the actual living of life in history and nature. In other words, reconciling the two is always affirmative but costly.

Let me put the same point differently. The rather theoretical form of what follows may lead you to suppose that it is impractical. I assure you that it is not. No, it is not 'reflecting from the garbage-heap or dung-hill', in the fashion mentioned by Professor Gutierrez, though I would be far from denying the value of that. But – like reflecting from the dung-hill – it does suppose that visions are influential and capable of changing practice. This is not only true of evocative language, but also of the much more empirical and theoretical language of the disciplines which form modern understanding and life. An explanatory description of what is the state of affairs has a normative effect, influencing performance. What is believed about God's presence in the world and human life forms what is done by human beings; and good practice rests on good belief (and vice-versa). What, therefore, I am attempting here is a critical realignment of the explanations we use for God and the world, supposing that the very act of doing so will bring about a change in our practice.

Two last preliminary comments. The first is that my allusions to the 'song of reality' in which we are engaged are both epistemological comments and more. They free us from the supposition that our apprehension of reality is based in certain axioms, and that reality is fact-like, consisting of fixed states of being for God, us and the natural world, fixed orders of being. As we will see, many of our habits of thought are still based on such assumptions.

It is a strange irony that theology has been only half-purged of the notion of fixed orders of being which arise from God's creation. At least by those whose 'order of being' was relativized by the person and work of Christ, these 'orders' were seen to result in the assignment of superior and inferior status in Nazi Germany, hence they were expunged from the doctrine of creation. But the notion of orders has been retained through the persistence of the supposition that there are fixities which pertain to God's being, ours and that of the natural world. The allusions to the song of reality suggest a purging of these orders of being from theology itself, and their replacement by *dynamics* of different kinds within a harmony of being. They open us to the possibility that God, human beings and nature interact *dynamically* in ways to which our habits of thought blind us.

This is not to say that the 'fixities' which we habitually prefer are not important. But they are to be seen more like the capturing of the rhythms of movement in static forms than as the primary characteristic of the 'nature' and interrelation of God, human beings and nature. A suitable analogy is the position of individuals in the interwovenness of human beings: the fact that human beings are interwoven does not preclude individuality – only individualism; there is still 'space' for individuals to be, and to move to other relationships, while carrying the benefits (or the harm) of the previous relationships there. Likewise, the locating of the patterns in which the rhythms of movement consist is a means by which they can be found and seen elsewhere.

The second of these last preliminary comments is this. By encouraging you to think in dynamic terms, I do not wish simply to set up 'dynamic movement' as a mediating category, and to collapse theology, and indeed the understanding of humanity and nature, into a philosophical or quasi-theological middle-ground which does justice to none of them. That may be very attractive, particularly where it seems to provide a thematic place in which different religious traditions may meet. This seems to me to be the fallacy into which the now famous address by Chung Hyun-Kyung at the Canberra Assembly of the World Council of Churches fell. It is also the kind of strategy which is the most common fault of current discussions of theology and science.

The dynamics on which I wish to focus are no such middle-ground, but a category which will need to be developed in various ways according to the ontological domain being discussed, whether God, humanity or the world. At this point, I am simply signalling a change needed for present-day understanding of theology, humanity and the natural world, one which may move us beyond the static ontology which predominates, at least in theology; and it is the development of a dynamic ontology which is suitable to theology, humanity and the natural world which concerns us here.

THE MODES AND OPERATION OF CONTEXTUALITY

It will be well now to specify the range of issues which we are to discuss. I can do that by resuming the discussion of the nature of contextuality. As I have already mentioned, contexts are not so clearly distinct – either from us or from each other – as we normally assume. Neither conceptually nor actually are contexts so distinct; they indicate an inter-wovenness or braiding. A conference on Christ and Context is therefore concerned with the question of how God is present in our interweaving.

But there is a vast variety of modes of contextuality, of those elements which are interwoven in us and for us; and we cannot proceed without identifying them, at least in a rudimentary fashion. Our contextuality is the presence in/for us of those factors by which we are constituted. There seem to be two sets of such constituting factors. For human beings, one set is *social*: symbolic signification (linguistic and cultural procedures), political order (the distribution of responsibilities), economic order (the distribution of benefits) and customary/legal structures (the regulation of practices). These, whether formal or informal, are the social elements which constitute our contextuality. The other set of factors is *natural*: cosmic order (comprised of elements both spatial and temporal), and the order and distribution of animate beings and of human beings. Again, these factors constitute our contextuality. Taken together, social and natural factors meet in us, and provide the fields in which we interact with others.

'What about me as an individual?' you may ask. I will only repeat what I have already said, though in slightly different terms. The fact that human beings are interwoven in a full contextuality through the meeting of social and natural factors does not preclude individuality, together with a sense of meaning (symbolically expressed), individual responsi-bility (manifested politically), benefits (arranged economically) and rights (either customary or legal). Furthermore, such individuality is based on the possibility of occupying a place, being an undamaged human being and having access to suitable resources. To have all these, however, is a *privilege*, and can only be attained if social and natural circumstances permit. And they often do not, whether by accident of circumstance or design of other people.

It is well to recognize how fragile is this interweaving of factors in our contextuality. Natural and social circumstances, separately or together, can savagely undermine the contextuality – the interweaving of factors – which is necessary for the well-being of individuals or social units. We see this increasingly in the world today.

But there is a further issue which needs much more recognition than it receives, the creativity with which human beings use their contextuality. For the interweaving of these factors in contextuality is not fixed, and human beings creatively develop their own contextuality. As one scientist said recently,

> Human thought and action are the most prolific sources of order in the world as we know it. Speech, writing, music, painting and sculpture, dance, and the ordinary activities of everyday life are at once the most familiar and the most mysterious of all order-generating processes.[5]

The items listed, to which one should add the humanities, science and technology, and all institutions, are the means by which human beings and their societies not only understand their contextuality more deeply, but also readjust it. And the effects of this readjusting ripple through the contextuality. The major question is not in whether the rebalancing does or does not affect others, but how far it does so, and how far it harms the contextuality – impoverishing others or nature. For this reason, the human creative reordering of contextuality provides one of the most basic moral and theological questions. For it can be a prime means of securing and enhancing privilege – precisely by manipulating social and natural contextuality (so far as it is possible to do so) for the benefit of some. As one sees in Church of England debates about women's ordination, or in the politics of South Africa, the room for protecting privilege through creatively readjusting contextuality is very great.[6]

By now, you may see that talking of the modes and operation of our contextuality is a way by which to identify the issues with which we must be concerned in discussing creation and reconciliation. The factors which meet us in our contextuality are interwoven in our very being. They are intrinsic to us, and it is a strange act by which we externalize them, as if they could be treated as extrinsic, even incidental, to us.

Let me make three comments about these externalizings. Firstly, the idea that we are actually autonomous, and everything else – God, others, world – external, is based on privileging ourselves within a contextuality, supposing that everything else will 'hold still and behave itself' while *we* see and use it. The notion of human autonomy is based on a very limited

---

[5] David Layzer, *Cosmogenesis*, New York: Oxford University Press, 1990, p. 16.
[6] The debate about women's ordination in the Church of England provides an instructive example, where convictions about the necessity of a male priesthood are perpetuated by appeals to the symbolic necessity of such a priesthood, and by political, economic and legal means.

notion of contextuality, an essentially separatist and instrumental view of others and the social and natural worlds.[7]

Secondly, the same holds true for other factors in the contextuality. It is a mistake to suppose that any of the issues which we listed before – social and natural – can be isolated from each other. Yes, of course, they can be separated temporarily for purposes of study. And much of the success of modern academic understanding rests on such separations. But such separation is a privileging of a particular subject-matter which rests on its interconnection with all the others.

Thirdly, the supposition that God is fundamentally isolated from the contextuality is also highly questionable. Powerful as this supposition is in the Christian tradition, and richly suggestive as it is for the richness of the Divine Being, we only know God through his relation to the contextuality which is ours. Karl Rahner's famous dictum, 'the immanent Trinity is the economic Trinity', expresses this, albeit in very formulaic terms. The *economy* through which the Trinitarian God is *himself* is our contextuality, that rich interweaving of all the social and natural factors which we have seen. The question is *how* he is himself in this economy, or – as we have posed the question previously – how he is present in our contextuality.

That is the heart of the issue before us, and to it we must now turn.

THE DYNAMICS OF CONTEXTUALITY

The first question to which we must address ourselves is, 'what are the dynamics of contextuality?' It is at least possible to answer the question in general terms, by looking more closely at the evidence of life in the world. That will at least provide us with an 'arena' in which we might identify the economy through which the Trinitarian God is himself.

If we confine ourselves to animate creatures, the evidence of life in the world suggests a diversity in a complex contextuality (interwovenness). Central to this is the fact that life manifests itself

> through a closed organization of production processes such that (a) the same organization of processes is generated through the interaction of their own products (components), and (b) a topological boundary emerges as a result of the same constitutive processes.[8]

[7] See D. W. Hardy, 'God and the Form of Society', in *The Weight of Glory*, ed. D. W. Hardy and P. H. Sedgwick, Edinburgh: T. & T. Clark, 1991; Ch. 10 below.

[8] M. Zeleny, ed., *Autopoesis: A Theory of Living Organization*, New York: North Holland, 1981, p. 6.

In other words, the organization of production processes for life is a closed one, yet generates self-same processes in the interaction of the components of particular life-forms; thereby emerge boundaries by which they are distinct from, and yet related to, what is not themselves. If we take human beings, the overall organization of life-processes is such that each human being manifests the same organization of interactive processes, and from these develops its distinction and relation to others.

An interesting human example appears in Shakespeare's *Merchant of Venice*. There, Shylock seeks acceptance by pointing to the self-same interactive processes by which human beings are constituted, following the closed organization of the production processes of life. He cries: 'when I am cut, do I not bleed?' But later he does something different. He turns such interactive processes into a device for structuring his relations to another man; he asks for a 'pound of your flesh' as security for a loan. When the loan cannot be repaid and he claims his bond, however, the claim is disallowed because he had made no mention of the blood to be shed in taking the pound of flesh. Ironically, for one who had appealed to a common humanity on the basis of interactive processes ('when I am cut, do I not bleed?'), he had overlooked the same interactive process, that cutting out flesh means the loss of blood.

Following the same closed organization of production processes for life, any life-form is itself through its interactions in its place, two aspects of its contextuality:

> This structure conditions the course of its interactions and restricts the structural changes that the interactions may trigger in it. At the same time, it is born in a particular place, in a medium that constitutes the ambience in which it emerges and in which it interacts. This ambience appears to have a structural dynamics of its own, *operationally distinct* from the living being.[9]

Between the living being and its ambience (what is often – in the more common sense of the term – called its 'context'), there is a structured relation, a structural congruence. And within this, there are undetermined interactions – perturbations – which 'trigger' changes for both. The interactions produce changes which serve to preserve or destroy the organization (and hence the identity) of either living being or environment. These may be summarized as four domains:

a. Domain of changes of state: viz., all those structural changes that a

[9] H. R. Maturana & F. J. Varela, *The Tree of Knowledge*, Boston: Shambhala, 1988, p. 95.

unity can undergo without a change in its organization, i.e., with conservation of class identity

b. Domain of destructive changes: all those structural changes that a unity can undergo with loss of organization and therefore with loss of class identity

c. Domain of perturbations: all those interactions that trigger changes of state

d. Domain of destructive interactions: all those perturbations that result in destructive change.[10]

At first, this appears to be a very bare catalogue, including only those interactions (c) which trigger the structural changes which would be considered normal to a living being (a), and all those destructive interactions (d) which would trigger structural loss incompatible with its identity as a living being (b).

But the list may be more inclusive than it first appears, especially if the various domains are understood with sufficient sophistication. For example, the domains of destructive changes and interactions go a long way toward providing the possibility for understanding contextual imbalance and damage. It ought also to be recognized that domains may have a recursive dynamic, through which the effect of a damaging perturbation may be 'doubled' by repetitions or by being internalized in the structure of a living being. A contextuality may become so asymmetrical that contextual interweaving becomes the domination of a living unit by external forces. In this case, the external forces '[becomes] *domination*, [and] the internalization of shame *legitimates* the system of domination ... The more shame is internalized, the less is brutal force needed in order to integrate a social structure.'[11] Hence, through domination the structure of a living being can be changed to undermine itself. That, by the way, accounts for the power with which poverty undermines the structure of a living being.

This is a very basic picture which requires supplementation in two ways. One is the recognition of interaction with the natural factors which also figure in the contextuality of a living being.

The most dangerous tendency in modern society, now rapidly emerging as a scientific-industrial ambition, is the tendency toward encapsulation of human order – the severance, once and for all, of the umbilical cord fastening us to the wilderness or the Creation. The threat is not only in the totalitarian desire for absolute control. It lies in the willingness to ignore an essential paradox: the natural

---

[10] *Ibid.*, pp. 97f.
[11] Agnes Heller, *The Power of Shame*, London: Routledge & Kegan Paul, 1985, p. 40.

forces that so threaten us are the same forces that preserve and renew us.[12]

For if living beings structure themselves through interaction with each other in constructive and destructive ways, they also do so in interaction with nature in constructive and destructive ways. And the logic of the self-structuring of human beings is to get bigger and more elaborate, which requires that they develop an increasing asymmetry in their interaction with the environment: nature becomes simply a resource for the self-structuring of human beings or a receptacle for their waste.

The other is to recognize that the basic picture presented is more appropriate to primitive situations than to well-developed ones. As Habermas observes of cultural anthropology, 'primitive societies ... have the advantage of being units that are relatively easy to delimit and relatively static.'[13] Where more developed situations are involved, societies and their norms must be taken into account as maintaining themselves through self-structuring in interaction with wider social environments, and individuals seen as interacting with such societies. And the codes through which societies structure themselves can become indistinguishable from the societies themselves. A notable example is the patriarchal code by which most societies are structured, which identifies the position of women in society as the position in which they *are put* by men.

Such an explanation provides a general account of the dynamics of contextual interweaving. It shows the possibility of innovative change or destruction, whether in living being or nature or their interaction, albeit constrained by the previous structuring of the living being and its congruence with its environment. Furthermore, it maintains a complex view of self-maintenance through turbulent interactions. Boundaries, which are relative not absolute, are a natural counterpart of the self-structuring by which this self-maintenance occurs. The result is a picture of ongoing generativity (or diminishment) in all the elements of the picture (structured living being, interaction and nature) which may be doubled through the restructuring of them.

In sum, the advantage of this form of explanation is the explanatory diversity which it incorporates. It opens a vision of ontological diversity, which is very important for survival in a changing world.

Social diversity works to preserve the system's personal, psychological, and economic flexibility, and thus helps to maintain the single

[12] Wendell Berry, *The Unsettling of America: Culture and Agriculture*, San Francisco: Sierra Club Books, 1977, p. 130.
[13] Jürgen Habermas, *On the Logic of the Social Sciences*, Cambridge: MIT Press, 1988, p. 78.

most important condition for long-range survival in relation to the environment, which is of course all the more significant if the environment is changing or being changed (by society): what Gregory Bateson called our 'uncommitted potential for future change'.[14]

In this form of explanation, both self-structuring and the boundaries which it brings are both relatively open and contingent, in the sense that they require constructive response to interaction. The perturbations in these interactions are then possibilities for constructive change. The implications of this form of explanation for behaviour are also advantageous. For the world is seen as a place of diversity which invites freedom in self-structuring through interactions, yet a freedom constrained by the conditions of previous structures.

These constraints guide what may happen, but their open texture allows far greater freedom for diversity. Neither these constraints upon behaviour, nor the explanation in which they figure, are overdeterminative. Instead, there is what could be called 'affirmative underdetermination'.

There is a rich and fascinating poem by the Irish poet Micheal O'Siadhail which gives some indication of such affirmative underdetermination.

> O my white-burdened Europe, across
> so many maps greed zigzags. One voice
> and the nightmare of a dominant chord:
> defences, self-mirroring, echoings, myriad
> overtones of shame. Never again one voice.
> Out of malaise, out of need our vision cries.
>
> Turmoil of change, our slow renaissance.
> *All things share one breath.* We listen:
> clash and resolve, webs and layers of voices.
> And which voice dominates or is it chaos?
> My doubting earthling, tiny among the planets
> does a lover of one voice hear more or less?
>
> Infinities of space and time. Melody fragments;
> a music of compassion, noise of enchantment.
> Among the inner parts something open,
> something wild, a long rumour of wisdom
> keeps winding into each tune: *cantus firmus,*

[14] Anthony Wilden, *The Rules Are No Game: The Strategy of Communication*, London: Routledge & Kegan Paul, 1987, p. 105.

fierce vigil of contingency, love's congruence.[15]

Despite the 'dominant nightmare' of defensive, reflexive, shameful, changeful, perhaps even chaotic, contexts interwoven in us, what we have called an 'affirmatively underdetermined' world has two outstanding features which suggest the possibility of the presence of God. One is the vitality present in the 'turmoil of change' itself, the 'slow renaissance' of the realization that 'All things share one breath.' The other is the presence of an open structure: 'among the inner parts something open, something wild, a long rumour of wisdom [which] keeps winding into each tune' as a 'fierce vigil of contingency'.

These features of the interweaving which occurs in our contextuality enable us, at least in some degree, to identify the economy of the Trinitarian God. As we do so, however, we will need to locate substitutes with which these – both our contextuality and the economy of the Trinitarian God – have been confused. We shall hope to rediscover the proper form of contextuality by reference to specifically Christian (Trinitarian) understanding, while disengaging them from sub-contextual and sub-Christian forms of understanding. In more familiar categories, this will be an attempt to find the impact of the presence of God (Revelation or Grace) on the forms of our contextuality (Nature).

'A LONG RUMOUR OF WISDOM . . . FIERCE VIGIL OF CONTINGENCY, LOVE'S CONGRUENCE . . .'

We have been attempting to provide an account of the dynamics of contextuality. Furthermore, we have been able to identify two primary aspects of these dynamics, 'all things share one breath' and the open structure of contingency. If the possibilities latent in such accounts of the dynamics of contextuality are carried into theology, the activity of God is also seen quite differently. As you will quickly see, while we can make a notional distinction between the immanent and the economic Trinity, this should not be turned into a division between the two.

First, as regards the economic Trinity, and employing the kind of explanation which we have been using for worldly contextuality, we find a Trinitarian God who is himself by the economy of his presence in the

[15] Micheal O'Siadhail, 'Motet' in *The Chosen Garden*, Dublin: The Dedalus Press, 1990, p. 82.

world. He is himself in maintaining the consistency of his life in an ordered but energetic congruence with his world; he is capable of self-restructuring in a controlled response to the perturbations (constructive or destructive) which occur in that interaction and in those with whom he interacts.

As regards the immanent Trinity, his own unity is that of a dynamic consistency, not inert but energetic in the consistency of his self-structuring in self-sameness. Such an explanation of the immanent Trinity provides for an energetic (Spirit-driven) unity in the Godhead which is yet true to its own initial conditions (what we designate by the word 'Father') and ordered in its interactions (that which we call 'the Son' or the 'Logos'). But this is not so much an explanation of a 'state of affairs' in God as it is an explanation of the energetically consistent congruence with the world by which he remains himself. 'Energetic' refers to the operation of the Holy Spirit, 'consistency in following initial conditions' refers to the Father and 'congruence with the world' refers to the Son. This is the 'fierce and excited contingency' of which Micheal O'Siadhail speaks, the Spirit 'exciting' the fulfilment of initial conditions through an ongoing self-structuring in which there arises a true congruence with the world in love. To use more formal words, God is a dynamic structured relationality in whom there is an infinite possibility of life.

But more needs to be said about the life of this Trinitarian God and its presence in the contextuality of the world, and what form it takes. I propose to discuss this a little because of the paucity in the Symposium so far of reference both to the Father and to the Holy Spirit, but I do not wish thereby to abandon the discussion of Christ. The activity of God in the contextuality of the world is not to be confined to the presence of Christ, but it is not simply to be identified with the Holy Spirit either. The activity of God in the contextuality of the world requires recognition that the operation of the Holy Spirit achieves its consistency by following the initial conditions which we conventionally identify as the 'Father' and the congruence with the world which we identify as the 'Son'.

What occurs in the life of the Trinitarian God is an outpouring of energy through which the initial conditions of God are fulfilled, and this fulfilment is in God, but occurs also through the congruence of God with the world by which God is himself. What occurs in God, therefore, is a self-enhancement, but this occurs also in both his constitution and active sustenance of the contextuality of the world. Words for this are difficult, but the language of 'blessing' and 'glorifying' may be best, for they signify the intensification of *ordered life* (the combination of words is significant) which occurs in God and from God in the contextuality of the world. So far as God himself is concerned, it brings a concentration of energy in the initial conditions by which God is himself and which are manifest in the fullness of ordered relationality in God, and also with the world in the Logos. Thus, from the implicit relationality of 'the Father', the Spirit can be seen to generate the fullness of the Father through the Son and through the Son's work in the world.

What are the *marks* of the activity of the Trinitarian God in the contextuality of the world? It is the active source of contextual inter-weaving, constituting and sustaining this contextuality. I agree with Pro-fessor Moltmann's remarks elsewhere in this Symposium that there is a transcendent unity which arises through God's creation, but I disagree that it 'precedes' the diversity of all things. There is, as he says, an immanent unity, but it is an active unity which arises in their diversity, rather than preceding it; it is therefore more correctly called an active contextuality/interweaving, and should be attributed to the Trinitarian activity of God by which God is one. By the way, this changes the character of universality, and avoids the monistic tendencies – whether logocentrist or phallogocentrist – against which the post-modernists rightly protest.

At the same time, with this contextuality, the Trinitarian activity of God sustains a complexity of particularities, establishing 'relativities' with their own integrity in fully contextual interweaving. This is to be sharply distinguished from the post-modernists' notion of particularism, which opposes a false universalism by a false particularism. Their notion of particulars rests on privileging, and the supposition of the inaccessi-bility of others with whom we are interwoven/contextually related. The active sustenance by the Trinitarian God of a complexity of particulari-ties is also to be distinguished, if I may say so, from those who suppose that becoming indigenous requires severance from others, especially those considered outsiders. These are over-statements, understandable for those who need to recover their particularity from submersion in a monolithic world, but fundamentally a denial of the wider interweaving which contextuality involves.

And the 'relativities' or 'particularities' are linked into active and con-tingent ways, in the fashion appropriate to an actively self-ordering God. Perhaps two stanzas of another poem by Micheal O'Siadhail may lighten this 'heavy' discussion while also showing the character of the network of particularities which is sustained through the activity of the Trinitarian God. The first recalls the task given to children by their knitting mothers.

> Like pegs, our forearms held the skein's coil.
> Arcs of the knitter's hand unloop
> and ball by turn. Sweep and detail.
> A feeling of beginning in childhood's wind-up
> I keep on recalling. Somehow I'm between
> a yarn uncoiling to a tight ball of destiny,
> a ball unravelling back the promise of a skein.

Plain stitch and design; point and infinity.
Who changes the world? Oh, this and that,
strands as they happen to fall, tiny ligatures,
particular here and nows, vast loopings
of pattern, the ties and let-gos of a knot,
small X-shapes of history; our spoor and signature
a gauze of junctures, a nettedness of things.

Whose music? A quiver enters like a spirit,
a murmur of tension from and back
into space. A tune of trembles in catgut.
The pride of an instrument as at its beck
and call the heart vibrates: pulse-sway,
dominion of rhythm, power before the slack
and silence. 'Pride before a fall' we say,
sic transit .... Should we've been puritans,
taut, untouchable, our unshakeable self-mastery
a vacuum of muteness? O noise of existence
shake in me a tone you need; sweet
friction of rosin, play me limp or tense.
Possessor of everything, owner of nothing.
Whose bow shivers its music in my string?[16]

The poem makes clear the active bestowal, by its source, of the highly contingent complexity of the contextuality of our being and activity, in which are interwoven nature, sociality and God. It is that very contingency which 'opens' our freedom, while also providing the scope and parameters within which it may operate. At the same time, this freedom in our contextuality is activated and energized by the free ordering of God, by which it is blessed/enriched.

But the proper use of our freedom-in-contextuality follows the pathway followed by God's Spirit, the pathway constituted by the initial conditions of 'the Father' and fulfilled in the ordering of the Logos. This means that the right use of our freedom is ex-centric, outward turning, conferring the benefits of our particularity upon those with whom we are interwoven. Our freedom confers freedom through our love.

It seems, therefore, the relatedness of God to the contextuality of our life and activity is far more complex than it is generally thought. God's ongoingly active/energetic self-structuring in the bestowal and sustenance of the highly contingent complexity in which our contextual being-in-freedom consists, provides a far more complex and contingent relation

---

[16] Micheal O'Siadhail, 'Perspectives', *The Chosen Garden*, Dublin: The Dedalus Press, 1990, p. 86.

between him and our contextual being. That is not to say that the marks of God's presence in our contextuality cannot be found, preeminently in the ordered energy which activates our freedom to love and therein to confer freedom upon others. This is no 'heroic' freedom which magically transforms all in sight. Much as we might wish for the capacity to work an overnight transformation, without having to attend to all the factors by which we and others are shaped as we are, our freedom to confer love and freedom is itself contextual, mediated through all the factors – natural, biological, social – which locate us and render us finite there. The sign of the blessing which God confers is in our conferral of such blessing on others, with all the natural and social modifications that may require, and even the creativity by which to fashion new and more humane contextual interweavings.

THE CONTEXTUAL LOSS OF GOD

The active achievement of such fullness within the contextuality of life rests on the ongoing participation in the blessing which God confers, the God who reaches 'his' fullness through the energizing of his loving congruence with natural and human contextuality. In that sense, the natural-human contextuality is a radically contingent one. Insofar as it structures itself in accordance with God's actively benevolent presence, it is blessed, energized for its proper order. That is, it moves towards an interweaving which is just towards all, where benefits and responsibilities are fully shared.

So it can be said that the conditions for the full contextual interweaving of human beings and other animate creatures, as well as nature itself, are already actively present in the contextuality of human life, and that we here are simply uncovering what already is by God's grace, so that it may be seen and performed more fully. But in another sense, it is also accurate to say that it is not actively present there. This is because there are those in a contextuality who fail to orientate their interweaving with others to the active presence of God and the energetic order which that provides. The consequences are seen in the impoverishment of contextual relationships. These are the contextual counterpart of sin, 'missing the mark', with the loss of energy and order which that involves. The evidences are readily seen. Let me take some examples from the social sphere.

One is what can be called 'social narcissism', where society develops its interrelations while at the same time supposing that it is itself encapsulated from the natural world. This is a certain kind of self-structuring by society of its dynamic relations with the natural world. As the dynamic self-structuring of human beings and societies has led them to greater and greater complexity, they have structured their relation with nature as one of use or domination; the 'guest who came to dinner' gradually centred the household on himself. This structuring has led human beings to see the natural world as 'only a resource' upon which human society may endlessly draw, or a 'receptacle' into which the waste-products of society are discharged. The same structuring, though in a different form, is present where it is said that nature has its 'limits' beyond which it cannot be imposed upon.

In other forms of 'social narcissism', society structures its interrelations in 'totalities', thereby encapsulating them from smaller social groupings; the result is – in the name of ideals of 'purity' – to eliminate the very social diversity by which society preserves its flexibility and long-term survival. The reverse form of the problem arises where society structures its interrelations in 'localities' or 'individualities', thereby encapsulating them from wider social contexts. Still another form of the problem is seen where society structures its interrelations as encapsulated within a 'present' which bears no relation to its past or future, thereby losing sight of the sources and effects of its own structured dynamics.

From a theological viewpoint, all these are 'missing the mark' in that they show society as structuring its dynamic relations in self-encapsulation from God. The social universe is 'simplified' by reducing its dynamics to those of human autonomy, whether social or individual. And God is seen to have been the false projection (self-alienation) of ideal human attributes, whether those of individuals or societies. It is then thought to be an act of human responsibility to end this alienation:

> The madman jumped into their midst and pierced them with his glances. 'Whither is God?' he cried. 'I shall tell you. *We have killed him* – you and I. All of us are his murderers.'[17]

The self-structuring of the dynamics of society by such means are the products of social power seeking to consolidate or expand its position by disadvantaging others, not to mention nature itself.

RECONCILIATION IN CONTEXTUALITY

Much of this is the result of human anxiety, and the desire to compensate for what is not – by blindness – found in a God understood as barren.

---

[17] Friedrich Nietzsche, *The Gay Science*, trans. Walter Kaufmann, quoted in Anthony Flew, *An Introduction to Western Philosophy*, London: Thames & Hudson, 1971, p. 468.

The growing complexity of contextuality is not in itself a problem, so long as it is accompanied by the realization that there are resources with which to develop an active and ordering love, both amongst cultures and societies and between them and the natural world. But it may easily be seen as a deficiency (an emptiness where there should be a fullness), and therefore a cause for anxiety.

The response is typically to meet the sense of emptiness occasioned by the growth in this complexity by consuming energy for self-structuring from elements beyond and within ourselves. We take action to remedy the deficiency (fill the emptiness), and do so by fundamental strategies of isolation, self-love and domination; by these means, the 'originative' or 'fundamental' sin becomes actual, whether for individuals as societies. The effect is to exteriorize (alienate), reconceive and instrumentalize (dominate) those sources upon which I/we draw our energy. These we may do to ourselves, our fellow human beings and our environment ('the context'). This is a deception which 'builds our being' (fills our emptiness) by diminishing others to 'non-being' (no value) or a 'supply' (limited value).

Underlying the conception of human being as emptiness, and also the stratagems by which we attempt to overcome it, is a key question about the nature and supply of energy for the development of new forms of unity and reconciliation in contextuality. What is available, and how? It is commonly assumed that dynamic order is derivable only from what is available through human life in the world, that is in the bounded situation of an ecosystem; only such energy as can arise within this context will count as 'kinetic energy' usable for work. Since the supply is limited by this limited context, human life will become a competitive struggle for the available supply of energy.

But this is a reductionist account of the energy available for the development of relationality, and will serve as grounds for human beings to distort the dynamic order of their social and ecological environment, and to refuse to develop the necessary kind of contextuality. There is, of course, a sense in which the ecosystem must be taken as limiting the energy available, and therefore requiring an appropriate balance within it; the material resources of the ecosystem are, for practical purposes, limited, and the balance of these resources (their diversity-in-unity) cannot be damaged without dire consequences. But in a still more fundamental sense even this ecosystem operates within and from a fuller dynamic order, and without reference to this dynamic order, treating the ecosystem as a limited source of energy is reductionistic.

The fuller dynamic order from which the ecosystem operates, by which it is energized for its unity and reconciliation, is the dynamic order of God himself which he confers on human beings in and through their world. This confers not only a richer source of energy on the world than that which is available simply by reference to the ecosystem itself, but a higher quality of relationality than is available therein; taken together, these provide a higher order of dynamic order than that available by reference to the world alone.

The act of God's reconciliation is the renewal of his presence in the contextualities of existence, whereby he provides the ordered energy of his own being as the means by which is restored the full contextuality of human beings with each other, with the animate and with the natural order. This is not simply an illuminist view of the act of reconciliation, for the principal means by which God reconciles is to be interwoven in the lives of those most 'decontextualized', those most diminished in their contextuality, providing new life for them in their abandonment – and for those who meet them in the gift of love by which they and their contextuality are restored.

CONCLUSION

In this discussion, we have followed a difficult path. But nothing less is necessary if we are to answer the question of how God is present in our contextuality. What I have sought to show is the kind of interweaving which occurs in our contextuality, and therein to show the economy of the life which derives from the immanent Trinity of God and from the reconciliation which is brought by this same God in our loss of contextuality.

Part Two: Creation

6

The Human Being as Creature[1]

IT is, of course, no secret that theology is a tissue of many things in interrelation. Begin at any point in it, and you will quickly be led to all the others – or at least the need for all the others. Eschatology requires one to talk about judgment and reconciliation, and they require talking about covenant, but discussion of the covenant requires finding the circumstances or context of the covenant, fallen creatures; and 'fallen creatures' brings one to talk about the creature, and in turn to treat his context, creation; and any elucidation of creation requires discussion of the action of God. So it may be seen that each notion demands another as an immediate context, and others as an ultimate context.

CREATION AS AN EXTENSION OF COVENANT

Thus it is no surprise that the historical origin of ideas of creation and creature was in Israel's awareness of her election into covenantal relationship with God: creation is in fact an extension of belief in election and salvation to the beginning or origin of history, to which God is antecedent or transcendent, whereby it is suggested that the God who elected Israel is also God over all the whole world. From the vantage-point of covenant-awareness, creation and creatures are the context for election, to which awareness of election points. Similarly, one might be driven, from the foreground of consideration of any basic idea in the list given above, to the background of another whose consideration would require attention to its background, etc. Each 'foreground' has a 'background', as we have already said.

But it is one thing to point to a background or context from the vantage-point of the foreground or content, and quite another to detail it fully. And one can say that it is impossible to start anywhere or within the foreground and by elucidation of that alone specify adequately the background or context. If one tries to do so, the background will simply be an extension of the foreground or an elaboration of it – just as for Israel creation and creatures are a universalizing background to saving history, or at least would be so if purged of left-overs from other sources

---

[1] This paper was originally presented at the Annual Conference of the Society for the Study of Theology in Edinburgh, 8–11 April 1975; the last four parts were not included in the original. It appeared in *Scottish Journal of Theology*, 30.2 (1977), 111–136.

(e.g. old mythological ideas). Hence those who worked back from the covenant to creation, showed the creative process resulting in 'a lofty teleology in the Creation of man, who alone in this world is able to be the partner of the God of the covenant'.[2]

THE INADEQUACY OF ANY VANTAGE-POINT

More is required to be said about creation and creature, however; and such, we would maintain, requires more than doing better what has been done – doing more than a particular starting-point within the salvific process will allow. Only doing this, presumably from other 'starting-points', will give the full context or background required for understanding the foreground. Presumably the most adequate way of using other starting-points is to adopt from each a 'moving viewpoint' from which a coherent sequence of sets of statements will result, reflectingly improving the viewpoint as one goes along. But that is still doing the job from one direction, from the 'inside' outwards, or from content to context, as from the particular to the general – however multifarious may be the moving viewpoint, or the 'content' arrived at, the 'particular' vantage-point employed. One can, by persistent movement and questioning, start from a starting-point within a limited context and go beyond it, enlarging the starting-point and the context, and from that enlarged position and context carry the enlargement further and further, step-by-step, even to a universal viewpoint and context. But even that 'completes' neither the vantage-point nor the context. And these are not 'completed' even by assembling many enlarged starting-points each with its own moving horizon. Every one of the starting-points and its context, no matter how far taken, is essentially incomplete, as Godel's proof shows for arithmetic. The vantage-point is incomplete without the context, and the context cannot be fully specified without reference to another context beyond.

There is a peculiar kind of comfort in this. Creation and creature need more said about them than can be said from any or all of the starting-points, however extended through movement and enlargement, which are available within them. And we shall see later how persistent are the claims to be able to say all that needs to be said from one vantage-point or another, suitably extended, from the sciences, religion, etc. But they are not capable of saying what needs to be said, and end by elaborating their starting-point; this we shall also see. The very fact that they are not capable of doing more is a comfort, not because it gives anyone a privi-

[2] L. Scheffczyk, *Creation and Providence*, London: Herder & Herder, 1972, pp. 9f.

leged position, but because it radically alters the character of the boundaries which are implied and searched for in any discussion about the basic character of creation and creature, as though they are contained entities whose nature we can fully discover. In thinking about covenant (for example) we often find ourselves thinking of the beginning of the world or man as though that was the passing across a boundary from a not-being to a being. Since we cannot find these boundaries, it follows that all the boundaries and all the relationships within existence are altered as well.

EVERYTHING IN MOTION AND NOTHING CLOSED: OPENNESS AND RELATIVE CLOSURE

The implication of the insufficiency of extended vantage-points can be put very starkly: when everything is in motion, nothing is closed. That does not, of course, mean that there are no boundaries and that it is possible that there can be a 'signification without a context',[3] but neither does it mean that we can talk of nature as a 'nest of boxes' (John Donne) – of the boundaries as barriers enclosing totalities in whose terms the individuals within them find or can be assigned meaning. The one idealizes openness into an infinity which overflows every thought – making God 'by definition the One who stands outside of system as the Absolutely Other';[4] the other erects rigid barriers defining what is inside by the fact of its exclusion of what is outside – an arrogance which invites warfare, as Rosenzweig and Levinas have shown.[5] In particular, the radical alteration of boundaries 'when everything is in motion' and 'nothing is closed' does not mean that there is no distinguishing of creation and creature from each other (panphysicalism or panevolutionism) and from God (pantheism); and it does not mean that in talking about creation and creature we are speaking of enclosed spheres which are distanced from each other by their boundedness, their distinction. Of course, it would be simpler to have bounded spheres for talking about creation, creatures and God: (1) they make possible for each a comprehensive, integrated, closed-off theorizing which holds for all time – we may say what each is and always will be in all its complexity, even if there is still uncertainty about how such theorizing applies to the world of

[3] E. Levinas, *Totality and Infinity*, Pittsburgh: Duquesne University Press, 1969, p. 23.
[4] A. A. Vogel, *Body Theology*, New York: Harper & Row, 1973, p. 50.
[5] F. Rosenzweig, *The Star of Redemption*, London: Routledge & Kegan Paul, 1971; E. Levinas, *Totality and Infinity*, Pittsburgh: Duquesne University Press, 1969.

experiences; and (2) since almost all conceptualizing to date has relied on such bounded spheres, it would be easier to integrate our present thinking to that of the past if we were to continue in this pattern.

But the 'blooming, buzzing confusion' – everything in motion – eradicates the possibility of boundaries and the paradoxes which they produce (Kierkegaard's 'infinite qualitative distinction' and 'absolute paradox' are obvious examples): nothing is closed.

UNIQUENESS AS SELECTIVE EXCHANGE WITH ENVIRONMENT

What does this mean, however? (Definition is a problem – how can one avoid de-fining, setting boundaries which close what we have just said is open?) A negative reply is to say that any thing exists only in a relative distinction from any other thing (or its environment); distinction arises only insofar as they are capable of distinguishing themselves. Hence a continuum is open and undistinguished except insofar as a 'punctuation' arises within it; and this punctuation is only temporary. 'Dust thou art, and to dust thou shalt return.'[6] It is also relative and a process: human self-identifying is a process 'always changing and developing': at its best it is a process of increasing differentiation, and it becomes ever more inclusive as the individual grows aware of a widening circle of others significant to him, from the maternal person to 'mankind'.[7]

This 'punctuation', temporary and relative as it is, is a kind of closure, but it is not fixed or exactly locatable, and it permits a selective relation between the differentiated item and its environment. The closure is more like a permeable membrane, and the differentiated item is never stable so long as that selective relation with the environment which is allowed by the permeable membrane continues. ('Any man's death diminishes me, because I am involved in Mankinde.' John Donne) In fact, the uniqueness of the item is constituted by the kind of exchange – input from and output to – it enjoys with its environment; and this is itself continuously variable, ranging from rest (a decrease of input below the threshold required to occasion output) to extreme activity. Each exchange affects the permeable membrane, varying its permeability, which has consequences for further exchanges.

Thus 'everything in motion and nothing is closed' means that any 'thing' is an open system which is within an open environment. It stands out by virtue of the selective relationship it enjoys with its environment,

---

[6] Genesis 3.19.
[7] E. Erickson, *Identity: Youth and Crisis*, London: Faber & Faber, 1968, p. 23.

which itself is punctuated or differentiated. But this punctuation or 'standing out' is a matter of degree; how much it results in what we would call 'being whole' as a 'unity', identified and integrated as a unity, depends on the kind of exchange it undertakes with its environment. One measure of this is its organization. If the closure is complete and the thing is differentiated completely, it is stable and becomes stagnant; any intrusion from 'outside' is extremely disruptive and dis-organizing. Such a thing is a whole which tends to run down in an increase of 'entropy'. But if the closure is only partial, if the thing is constituted by a selective relationship with its environment, it tends to respond to the environment by adapting its structure, changing it to a higher or more complex level; as a 'whole' it tends to 'wind up', to elaborate structure or to decrease in 'entropy'. (In the one case, only marginal stress, or in human terms anxiety or doubt, is tolerated because the closure and self-organizing are not complete; in the other case, they are selectively welcomed as stimulants, as an intake of energy which may be productive.) In the course of this 'wind up' the punctuation which differentiates or identifies the thing takes on 'character' by the development of a mapped relationship with its environment and a self-correcting tendency which keeps it within tolerable proximity to its established character; but the exchange between the thing and its cnvironment continues. It is almost impossible, however, to chart all the ways in which the exchange may occur or even the ways in which the 'mapped relationship' of a thing to its environment selects for it to occur. In the broadest sense of the term, it is all 'information', but that may include everything from chemical signals between cells in the nervous system to food to sympathy.

They *knew* that to *Praise*, as mere Praise, I was characteristically, almost constitutionally indifferent. In Sympathy alone I found at once Nourishment and Stimulus; and for Sympathy alone did my heart crave.[8]

SELF-DIFFERENTIATION THROUGH ATTENTION

So far we have been talking about the relative distinctions from an open environment which constitute open, self-organizing items in the environment. We have suggested that this is the proper way of understanding them rather than speaking of them in terms of bounded, enclosed

[8] S. T. Coleridge, *Selected Letters*, London: Oxford University Press, 1959, Vol. IV, p. 888.

spheres. We have made no attempt to differentiate between kinds of 'item', nor have we examined the background conditions for this open environment and these relative distinctions.

When I sit in a railway train passing rapidly through the countryside, my whole environment (train and countryside) is undifferentiated for me until I fasten my attention on something. When I do, the 'something' suddenly becomes a foreground against a background; fastening attention on it forms a distinction (a relative closure) between that 'figure' and its 'ground'. But this opening of myself to my environment, this act of attending, also constitutes me as distinct from the environment and as engaging in a selective relationship with it: in order to accomplish this opening, I must be differentiated from the environment so as to select from within it. Again this is a relative closure or punctuation, a 'distancing' which is correlative with opening, a self-identifying which is correlative with selective attention to the environment.

But I can also alter the direction of my attention from the countryside to the task which I must perform when I have arrived at my destination. This has the effect of 'cancelling out' (partly or completely) the countryside for me, detaching me from it in order to allow me to attend to anticipations about my task. Going one step further, I can turn my attention on myself as the one who is travelling toward the task, and in this case both countryside and task are left behind. Still beyond this, I can begin to think about what it is that enables human beings to direct their attention in such diverse ways, and even hypostatize an essential 'human nature' with these capacities. But in all these cases, the giving of attention is an opening which is correlative with a relative closure by which I am constituted as distinct from that to which I attend. Furthermore, the attention is a selective relationship, and that selection is correlative with my character, which has arisen as a mapping of the kinds of exchange in which I engage.

The two-sided effect of attention-giving must be taken seriously. One side is that, while it distances the questioner from that which he experiences, it does not altogether separate him from it. It 'opens' that which he experiences, so that the character of the thing to which he attends may emerge afresh, against its background. This is in fact a 'dignifying' of that to which attention is given. The other side is that the attending 'dignifies' the one who attends, giving him importance as an active subject so that he is not simply a passive recipient of his experience. If and when the truth emerges from his attending, it is truth for him – within, not only external to him; and he is capacitated by it – he is not as he was before. This is what Coleridge meant in saying that

WE (that is the human race) LIVE BY FAITH. Whatever we do or know, that is in kind different from the brute creation, has its origin in a determination of the reason to have faith and trust in itself. This, its first act of faith is scarcely less than identical with its own being. *Implicite*, it is the COPULA – it contains the possibility of every position, to which there exists any correspondence in reality.[9]

It should also be seen that this process of attending is not simply intellectual, it is an active proceeding along paths chosen, though this may sometimes be attenuated into an imaginative movement in which the proceeding is by projective anticipation. So far as it assumes a determinate direction, it becomes a 'discipleship' in which the attention-giving is a self-involving proceeding, a selective relationship with the environment which is correlative with the character of the one who gives attention, an active going in a chosen direction.

RELATIVE DIFFERENTIATION OF THE HUMAN FROM OTHER SPECIES

Since this picture of human activity as self-organizing and self-differentiating is basically so similar to all open, self-organizing systems, we cannot introduce a stratification of species which suggests that there is an absolute differentiation between human beings and other species, a series of boundaries between species. It is in good part the supposition of such differentiation that causes such trouble in considering the human being's place in relation to nature, whether inanimate, animate, or his own nature. For example, supposing that the human is ideally a spiritual dimension meeting and controlling a natural one has frequently led to alienation from the body, the refusal to be 'there in the body', a situation which D. H. Lawrence stressed in describing the sexual act: 'she lay with her hands inert on his striving body, and do what she might, her spirit seemed to look on from the top of her head'.[10] Equally, the command 'Be fruitful and multiply, and replenish the earth, and subdue it, and have dominion ... over every living thing' (Gen. 1.28) has resulted in a false 'humanizing' of nature whereby the human being is taken as the inclusive purpose of creation whose right it is to 'ingest' nature. These views are based on the supposition of an absolute demarcation between humankind and nature, in which the spirit should subdue nature, and manifest the human being's refusal to be 'there' in nature, in an exchange with it.

But there is obviously a relative distinction between the human, other creatures and creation, and it appears to involve all of the means by

[9] S. T. Coleridge, *Lay Sermons*, London: Routledge & Kegan Paul, 1972, p. 18.
[10] D. H. Lawrence, *Lady Chatterley's Lover*, New York: Grove Books, 1959, p. 205.

which exchange between them takes place – all the means by which he and they are related to the natural world and also those by which he alone is related to other creatures and the natural world. Looking at this exchange in terms of the 'measure' we mentioned earlier, organization, the human being is characterized, more so than other creatures and in contrast to the natural world, by increasing organizational complexity (negentropy): the living world increases in orderliness, and the human most so, while the inanimate world moves to disorderliness (entropy).

There is, of course, much disagreement at this point, for this distinction opposes the widespread claim that all reality is explainable in terms of physical laws, a view which has recently been given support by the dramatic advance in biochemistry ('cracking the genetic code'), and also the claim that all animate beings are explainable in terms of the theory of evolution. And indirectly it raises the general question whether any set of principles which can function perfectly well in restricted investigations ('critical monism'), can be extended to universal applicability ('transcendental monism').[11] We must now examine first this general question and then the claims that physical laws and the theory of evolution are universally applicable.

Transcendental Explanation

We can observe a pattern followed by transitions from critical to transcendental monism. What occurs is that a base consisting of some line of questioning is chosen, at first by a random guessing procedure; this is not, of course, independent – but presupposes much which it does not recognize. With experimenting and clarifying, this takes on the character of 'self-sustaining' principles, and the application continues more and more widely. As it continues, particular interpretations of the principles which do not fit the wider uses to which they are now put are consigned to the place of 'interpretations', while the principles are considered more 'general'. Thus, what began as 'one-level theorizing' takes on a more elaborate theoretical structure: a distinction is made between several levels of theory, varying in generality, and those levels are related through 'translation', 'interpretation' or some kind of 'passage' from one to the other such as that contained in the notion of 'hierarchies'.

This understanding of theories as distinguished or 'typed' by the level of their generality has an important consequence: it 'protects' the basic principles being advanced as universally applicable by subordinating less

[11] Ernest Gellner, *Legitimation of Belief*, Cambridge: Cambridge University Press, 1974, Ch. 1.

universally applicable interpretations, placing them at a 'lower' level. To put this slightly differently, it preserves, even enhances, the basis by allowing 'epicycles' in which the basis is interpreted for particular applications in order for it to become the basis for the unity of all. (By seeing theories in this way, we can recognize that we are not, in all this, very far from the views of Kant and Hegel – Kant if the theorizing is considered as human-mind-dependent, Hegel if the theorizing is considered as an expression of ontology.)

So we see the fashion in which a particular set of principles is maintained as sufficient for the interpretation of all that is, by elaborating the theoretical structure in which they appear. One 'scientific' theory may then manifest its position as basic by permitting another a subordinate position on the supposition that it is eventually reducible to the more basic principles. This multi-level 'opening' of the basic principles ends in a reduction.

PHYSICALIST EXPLANATION

Now, it is claimed that physical laws are universally applicable, and the case is defended on scientific and philosophical grounds. It is usually accepted that living organisms are open systems in constant exchange with their environment:

> It cannot stop absorbing food, ejecting waste matter, or being constantly traversed by a current of matter and energy from outside. Without a constant flow of order, the organism disintegrates. Isolated, it dies. Every living being remains in a sense permanently plugged into the general current which carries the universe towards disorder. It is a sort of local and transitory eddy which maintains organization and allows it to reproduce.[12]

Looking at any living organism in its environment overall, while it is an open system engaging in exchange with the environment and increasing in organization, it is suggested that its maintenance has to be paid for. It wears out and dies, and its maintenance carries the universe towards disorder, however slightly. And the negentropic character of each living thing is a subordinate, less universal interpretation within the universal entropy – an epicycle or 'eddy' within the general tendency towards disorder; this claim is an example of that 'protection' of certain principles

---

[12] F. Jacob, *The Logic of Living Organisms*, London: Allen Lane, 1974, p. 253.

as basic by allowing other principles a subordinate 'epicyclic' place within the overall explanation by the principles.

Perhaps the proper attitude to this is to accept our fate as pockets of life in a context of death, our own death and that of the universe, by God's grace making the best we can of our finitude in anticipation of our end and that of the universe. But questions need to be asked about the status of the physical laws which we have been discussing.

The suggestion of the universality of entropy is, of course, an instance of the phenomenon we mentioned at the outset, the attempt to specify the universal context from a particular vantage-point (or perhaps moving viewpoint) within it. And we claimed that such is impossible, that we cannot arrive at the total picture even from many extended vantage-points. This 'law' is in fact not a final theoretical formulation, because there can be no such thing without a known universal context by which to measure it, and we *have* – and can have – no full knowledge of that. 'No knowledge can be established, or even sought experimentally, about the *whole* of nature'.[13] But this is not to say that this 'law' should be disregarded. It is a useful relative differentiation within an open situation, differentiating or punctuating a known process from an unknown background; as such, it opens into other possible levels of explanation rather than incorporating them into itself as epicycles. In other words, this differentiation carries on an 'exchange' with others; 'entropy' and 'negentropy' interact rather than collide. And this suggests the need for a well-differentiated or multilevel approach to the natural world rather than a reduction to the laws of physics. When such a multi-level approach comes about, it should also take account of the relative differentiation of the 'code-reader' from the code which he interprets.

EVOLUTIONARY EXPLANATION

Evolutionary theory is related to the differentiation of human beings from other forms of animate nature, and many of the same points need to be made about it. The theory of evolution is a theory of high generality which unifies observations from widely varied sources, and unifies all sciences concerned with living beings, apparently functioning as a single account of the heterogeneity of the living world. Its basic claim is twofold: that all organisms at whatever time descend from at most a few living systems which arose spontaneously; and that species are derived from one another by natural selection of the best procreators. One need

[13] M. Grene, ed., *Interpretations of Life and Mind*, London: Routledge & Kegan Paul, 1971, p. 25.

hardly say that the theory, as one founded on history, cannot be directly verified or falsified; instead it must be interpreted and confirmed through interpretations made of it – a procedure which, if a particular interpretation is falsified, can preserve the theory inviolate by detaching the interpretation as a 'failed interpretation.' Nonetheless, the theory is taken to be confirmed *in certain aspects* by work during this century by physiologists and biochemists which suggests that all organisms appear to use 'the same materials for carrying out similar reactions ... the same ingredients and the same recipes'.[14]

The function of the theory of evolution should not be misunderstood. The point of the theory is not to focus on the human or even the 'survival of the fittest' but to concentrate on the whole 'ecosystem'; it is the conditions for the survival of the whole natural system which it attempts to describe, not those for the evolution of the human being. The theory shows that 'nature selects the survival of the ecosystem, at all levels, not the survival of the individual (subsystem)'.[15] Thus, to attempt to oppose it by discussing the human or by insisting on the uniqueness or finality of the human being is not to converse with the theory at all, but to talk about something quite different from the theory.

The confusion apparent in trying to shift the discussion away from the conditions for the survival of the whole natural system, and to the discussion of the human, is significant, however. It is a modern example of the ancient tendency to anthropocentrism, the same tendency apparent in turning all talk about creation into talk about the human being. It does to evolutionary theory what Bultmann does to the idea of creation. Bultmann suggests that the idea of creation and omnipotence

> is not an intelligible generally valid assertion which is discovered or perhaps believed and then held as proved ... and applied as a scientific idea. It always is true only as it arises. But that means that I cannot achieve the idea apart from my own existence; I cannot understand or 'interpret' something outside myself as creation of God or act of God ... I can speak of God's act of creation only if I know myself as 'a creature of God' in 'my concrete existence here and now'.[16]

Bultmann's view is that the ideas of creation and world are nothing other than speech about my existence and my world under the action of God.

But it is also important to see that the theory of evolution is itself partly responsible for its own misuse: like the claim that physical laws are

[14] Jacob, *op. cit.*, p. 13.
[15] A. Wilden, *System and Structure*, London: Tavistock Press, 1972, p. 218.
[16] R. Bultmann, *Faith and Understanding*, London: SCM Press, 1969, p. 251.

universally applicable, this theory also fails to establish its own meaning and function. There is a good deal of discussion about how the theory is to be interpreted, whether mechanistically or organismically, and there are significantly different versions available. Many appear to treat it as a one-level explanation, and others consider that concepts of more than one logical level are necessary. But that difference is less important than their agreement in supposing that the theory, however internally differentiated, is sufficient to explain the necessary conditions for life. Against this claim we would urge that: 'the sum total of necessary conditions for the coming into being of an individual, a species, a phylum or of life itself, are not logically or historically identical with the individual, or species, or phylum, or life itself'.[17] On the one hand, since we cannot be aware of these conditions, the theory cannot be taken as a sufficient explanation of life or of the conditions for the survival of the ecosystem. But, on the other hand, we cannot determine the limits of its usefulness either. Thus we cannot say that it is a comprehensively adequate explanation or a minimally adequate one: its place lies somewhere between the two.

Evolutionary theory does seem to describe the total system of nature as a closed system, in the sense that it provides a model of how things have to be, or 'universal' history viewed under the form of law, or 'plain' history derived from a model of how things must be. If the theory is correct, the system of nature is self-regulating to maintain its basic character; any divergence from the 'character' of the system is compensated for, as a drop in temperature in my house is compensated for by the boiler switching on and generating more heat. In that respect, evolutionary theory is like the physical laws universally applied. Either theory, or the two taken together, suggests that any freedom or real variation within nature is illusory, that they are mere appearances within a law-defined order.

To conclude that evolutionary theory reduces variation or freedom to an illusion is a mistake. The theory does do this but the theory is only a relative differentiation within an open situation, which distinguishes certain data from others, a foreground from the background, a known process from an unknown background. And as such, it opens into other levels of explanation, carrying on an exchange with them. As a theory it appears to be one level amongst others.

SPECIAL THEORIZING ABOUT HUMAN LIFE

The fact that explanation by physical laws and explanation by evolution-

---

[17] M. Grene, *The Understanding of Nature*, Dordrecht: D. Reidel, 1974, p. 149.

ary laws open into each other, and both may open into others, illuminates the much-discussed difference of inanimate matter from animate, and animate from human. There is nothing in each kind of explanation to suggest that others are necessary, just as nothing in inanimate matter would lead us to expect that there is also animate ('an event of zero probability' Monod says) and nothing in either that would lead us to expect human life: this is the 'closure' of the theories from each other. But the closure in each case is a relative one in an open, unknown situation – their background. And that fact would lead us to consider the theories as related to each other, opening into each other – however difficult this interrelation is to discuss.

There is nothing in either physicalist or evolutionary theories to suggest the necessity of theorizing about human being; and from physicalist and evolutionary viewpoints there is naturally resistance to 'special' theorizing about human life. But this resistance also points to a more radical disjunction of theorizing about the human from physicalist and evolutionary theories than simply that it is 'different 'or 'special', for theorizing about human life often quickly jumps from 'observation from outside' to 'introspection', analysis from the 'inside'; and this is taken to be unsatisfactory as science, committing the double sin of pluralism and subjectivism.

From the 'scientific' viewpoint, most behaviour studies comparing the human with animals have shown that the 'closure' of the human being, whereby he/she is distinguished from animals, is far less complete than was formerly thought. Many capabilities had been thought to be unique to the human, socially and as an individual: growth, learning, goal-setting and planning, discrimination, conceptualizing, stability, memory, simulation, tool-making, tool-using, language, counting, art, ethical sense, and reproduction. All are now seen as explainable, at least in part, as gradual evolutions from animal origins. On these grounds, there is no reason for supposing a complete discontinuity (closure) of the human being from animals. In other words, researches have served to extend the scope of evolutionary theory and to diminish the necessity for 'human' theory. And even though one should not take the intention for the deed and suppose that researches show these capabilities are simply extensions of animal ones, the question is posed whether there is any need for special theorizing about the human.

Neither is the evidence of the human being's consciousness, from the 'inside' of experiencing it, itself sufficient to show the need for special theorizing about the human, even though it may be exceedingly important in its own right (as existentialist and experientialist analyses have rightly shown). As we saw earlier, any giving of attention has as its correlative a relative closure by which I am constituted as distinct from that to which I attend. I may attend to something 'outside', to anticipations of some kind, or to myself, in each case either more concretely or more abstractly. In all these instances, my 'transcendence' (closure) from that to which I attend is a correlative of that attention by which something stands out from its environment for me. Any interpretation by which I select an object to stand out from its background is correlative with a relative closure by which I am identified as distinct and as a certain kind of person: to use one current language, my 'interpreting-as' interprets me also; or in Bultmann's language, truly understanding myself is understanding myself as from God.

I would not wish to gainsay the importance of these discussions of the personal 'identifying' which is the correlative of attending to what is 'outside' in the world, and in fact the explorations should be taken much further – as, for example, R. R. Niebuhr and Bernard Lonergan have recently done.[18] But to point at the activity of the experiencing subject to justify special theorizing about the human is to give only half the argument; it is to point to a correlative only, without accompanying it by pointing to a way by which, when seen from the 'outside', the human being stands out from other animals. Thus the activity of the experiencing subject is not sufficient as an argument for the necessity of 'special theorizing' about the human, even when the content of this experiencing is 'religious'. One might expect that, were the same vantage-point for non-human animals to be available to us as it is for ourselves, we might see considerable similarity between their self-identifying and ours, and that there is no absolute distinction between their 'transcendence' and ours.

All this points to continuity between the human being and animals, the relativity of any closure or distinction there might be. Three arguments point to the necessity of closure (in some degree) of human from other animal nature, however. *Firstly*, it is apparent that any discussion about behavior or self-identifying requires considerable extension when it refers to the human from its use in relation to non-human animal nature; this is evident in claims about the 'organized complexity' of the human being's behaviour and consciousness, in the individual and in social behaviour and consciousness. The complexity becomes of a very high order when we talk about human beings, nations, cultures and ideas, especially where they are growing, seeking goals and adapting to them, by comparison with what it need be for talking about animals.

Secondly, this argument for the relative distinguishing of the human from animals may be immensely strengthened by considerations drawn from the human being's self-identifying as distinct and as a certain kind of person, as we saw it occurring in any act of attending. The human's

[18] Cf. R. R. Niebuhr, *Experiential Religion*, New York: Harper & Row, 1972; B. Lonergan, *Insight*, London: Longmans, 1958.

self-identifying, which by itself is a correlative of his attention-giving, is a delicate, complex and accumulative process by which his character is built. While (like the first argument) it cannot stand by itself as an argument for the need for special theorising about the human being, when taken with the other argument it becomes strong.

Thirdly, it must be remembered that arguments about human behaviour and also those about human self-identifying or 'self-punctuation' in the activity of attending to or interpreting the environment, are various attempts to specify the universal from a combination of particular vantage-points, each suitably extended by talk about the complexity of the human being's behaviour and consciousness. And one might take any of the many others we have not considered, starting from social or individual growth, learning, goal-setting and planning, discrimination, conceptualizing, stability, memory, simulation, tool-making and tool-using, language, counting, art, ethics, reproduction, etc. In each case we would find the same thing, the attempt to specify the whole environment from a particular punctuation, the whole background from a particular foreground. And neither any one, nor all together, can yield knowledge about the whole of human nature; they are not capable, even all together, of specifying the totality of human nature. But when they are used, they are of course useful as relative closures, allowing relative differentiations within an open situation, and when they are taken as relative they do open into other possible explanations without attempting to subordinate them as what we earlier called 'epicycles'.

THE HUMAN BEING IN AN OPEN SITUATION

This argument that physicalist, evolutionary and 'special' human theories are relative closures within an open situation, opening into each other, is a necessary discussion if we are to take Christian understanding of creation and creature seriously, but it is not sufficient to justify a sudden jump into talk about God's creation of the world and human life. Nothing in these theories, severally or together, suggests that talk about a non-natural origin for the world and the human being is necessary. What does require such talk is the open situation in which they exist, in which we have seen theories producing relative closures, thereby differentiating various elements (physical, animal, human) from the open background. Even in making this claim, however, we must recognize that anyone who is convinced of the sufficiency of what we have called relative closures, severally or together, to explain reality, will have made the closures more than relative (except perhaps in relation to each other), and will have turned from what we earlier called critical to transcendental monism. To such people, wherever they locate this or these closures, our talk about the open situation will be fantasy.

Evidence is not altogether lacking that the situation is more open than they judge. For those who adhere to the notion that these physicalist, evolutionary, or human theories are sufficient still often suggest that the human being can and should stand out from what his/her physical nature and his natural and cultural evolution have made him and reflect on it in order to be responsible for it, all human beings complementing each other in the task by mutual adjustment or love.[19] Indeed, that suggestion seems implicit in current discussions about the human's responsibility for the ecosystem, or even in the claimants' own suggestion that they can understand the human being fully by their theorizing. One must not overestimate the power of this evidence, however, for it suggests only that the human being identifies himself/herself through this theorizing; interpreting the situation as something interprets the human being also. And he/she stands out from his/her theories, for example the evolutionary past, only in that way. It is mistaken, I think, to suggest that this is a response of faith, and the appropriate modern counterpart of the idea of creation,[20] unless it is accompanied by an identification from the 'outside' of the human as having such overwhelming responsibility.

We are in a strange position here. None of the attempts fully to determine the context can do so, because even when extended they are incapable of procuring knowledge about the whole of nature – they can only produce relative differentiations against an unknown background, and open into other possible levels of explanation. And yet they are seen as relative and open only by the supposition of a context so far undefined. The attempts which we have just seen, to suggest that the human being – as 'evolution reflecting on itself' – can stand out, punctuate or differentiate himself from the understanding provided by the theories which we have reviewed, and take responsibility for the direction of things, have the effect of making the human being a transcendental agent. There is more than a passing resemblance between this and the longstanding tendency in western thought to load the human with ever greater responsibility.

Theologians must guard against the urge to jump in at this point and suggest authoritative vantage-points from which the universal context may be ascertained, because the world has (they say) 'already been made', and made by an agent now revealed to us. From the incarnate Jesus, the electing God and the elected man, we can discover the basic composition and dynamic of the world. Sadly, the effect of making these claims is counter-productive. If through Jesus Christ it is claimed that we

[19] E. Samuel, *Order in Life*, Englewood Cliffs: Prentice-Hall, 1972, p. 396.
[20] Cf. J. Hick, *God and the Universe of Faiths*, London: Macmillan, 1973, pp. 97ff.

have access to the 'perfection' of the world from which it ought to be interpreted, Jesus is made the basis for a transcendental monism such as we have seen operating in the physicalist and evolutionary theories, and the use of an 'epicyclic' extension whereby we derive the doctrines of the Trinity and Creation from the event of Jesus Christ and then use these as anticipations of the coming of Jesus of Nazareth, only reinforces the appearance that this is another transcendental monism. Here, as we have seen in the cases of physicalism and evolution, the claim is made that we have within the world an authoritative vantage-point (provided, of course, that we are enabled by faith) wherewith to gain a view of the universal. Why counterproductive? Because the assertion of this monism as against the others has the effect of encouraging authoritarianism, and hence encourages other monisms.

PROTECTING OPENNESS

Quite the reverse strategy is needed, one which preserves the openness of the horizon in which such closures as physicalism, evolution, and humanism then become relative differentiations. And in preserving openness we seek to preserve not only tolerant open-mindedness, but a real openness. The most real threat to this possibility is a constant tendency to fix boundaries comprehending the world, either in the past by speaking of an 'origin', as a state of rest from which the dynamic of history began, or as a perfection from which the human being descended, or in the future by speaking of an 'end', a rest to which the dynamic will one day come, and in which the perfection will be restored. This fixing of boundaries, whereby the world in its existence and history becomes a totality, which is so deeply associated with the idea of God's creation (i.e. the eternal God created a temporal and spatial whole as distinct from himself), is what encourages attempts from within the world to ascertain the whole in its basic mature, whether they originate from within science, humanistic thinking, or Christian belief. Indeed, it is at the root of arrogance of most kinds and functions also as a solace for our own worry: 'This idea of an absolute purification of history, in an inertialess regime without chance or risk, is the inverse reflection of our own anxiety and solitude.'[21]

How then safeguard the openness of the horizon? Both Moltmann and Pannenberg attempt to meet this need, Moltmann by 'open questioning'

---

[21] M. Merleau-Ponty, *Adventures of the Dialectic*, Evanston: Northwestern, 1973, p. 5.

and Pannenberg by universal world history. Moltmann suggests that 'history as a whole' can be no postulate; the question of the unity and truth, the salvation and meaning of the whole becomes an open question which keeps time and the progress of human history in suspense, continually provokes new answers and makes all answers obsolete and temporary.

Pannenberg is as insistent on an open context for questioning as Moltmann, but he ensures it by suggesting universal world history as the necessary horizon within which questioning occurs. This is not to be understood as a knowable totality from which God's existence and nature can be inferred, a view which Pannenberg explicitly rejects: it is seen as a comprehensive horizon necessary for thought about God, which as a totality is not available but rather a matter of the eschatological future. While the historical reality of the world and the human being are not yet whole, and this wholeness is itself open to question, a conception of the actual course of history linking past with present with future, or of the whole of universal history, is necessary as a horizon to ensure openness. It is this horizon which allows a proper differentiation between ancient and modern (e.g. the horizon of a biblical text and that of the modern interpreter) and between contemporary and future. In other words, it avoids reducing the meaning of past events and texts to their meaning for today, protects the contingency of the future by preventing the collapse of the future into its meaning for the present, and might also safeguard against claiming that the past is normative for the present.[22] In our terms, it disallows any transcendental monism whose basis is the past, the present or the future, and for which other vantage-points are but epicycles – past and future where the present is the basis, present and future where the past is the norm, past and present where the future is the basic reference-point.

To disallow transcendental monisms (including theological ones), and focus attention instead upon the openness of the human being's context (universal world history) and the human's own searching (questioning about his destination) is an important *strategy*, but it does not get us far enough. It procures an openness for the human, and makes God into the author, authenticator or presupposition of the human being's openness to the world, the ultimate referent of the plurality of world religions, the ground of the human's desire to know, or the pathos correspondent to the *sympatheia* of human beings. But the effect of such re-statements has been to idealize openness, making a desirable predicate for the human into virtually the sole predicate of God. A number of consequences follow: (1) the idea of God is made as vague (or at least abstract) as

---

[22] W. Pannenberg, *Basic Questions in Theology*, London: SCM Press, 1970, Vol. I, pp. 129–136.

necessary to allow the vast diversity of claims made about him in world religions, with the result that little remains of God but his infinitude ('uncircumnavigability') and sheer deity as lord ('The deity of God is his rule'), and it is unclear in what way, if any, God is personal – personality and nonpersonality are taken as two aspects of the same infinite reality;[23] (2) the truth claims of particular religious traditions are relativized and particular elements of the traditions (or the traditions themselves) are taken as closed belief-systems which require to be opened through more or less radical questioning (which is frequently assumed to be only the *human's* questioning);[24] and (3) the place of historical *events* as the medium of God's presence or activity is neglected in favour of human *experience* as the locus of a responding to God (a 'reappropriation of events which establish faith'),[25] a responding which differs because of its interaction 'over the centuries with the different thought-forms of different cultures'.[26]

THE OPENNESS OF REALITY

To go beyond this strategic use of openness as a norm for the human to provoke the recognition of the cultural and historical diversity of human thought requires fuller exploration of the openness characteristic of reality and of God. On the one hand, it is mistaken when countering transcendental monisms to absolutize openness into an infinity which overflows every thought and differentiation. Such absolutizing converts openness into a closure, but one which is beyond understanding. Yet, it is claimed, the presence of this openness perpetually opens the human being cognitively and ethically. (Because of the resemblance of this position to new ideas of liberation, some enlist it in the cause of liberation while emphasizing our ignorance of ultimate reality and God.) But this idealizing of openness disregards basic questions about things as they are – about how there can be differentiated worlds and human beings in them, and also about how an unformed (unshaped) infinite *can* open the human being ethically and cognitively. A similar danger is implicit in the use of universal world history as a comprehensive horizon. The impression is

[23] W. Pannenberg, *Theology and the Kingdom of God*, Philadelphia: Westminster Press, 1969, p. 55.
[24] Cf. R. Hart, *Unfinished Man and the Imagination*, New York: Seabury, 1968, pp. 54f.
[25] Cf. W. Pannenberg, ed., *Revelation as History*, New York: Harper & Row, 1968, p. 138.
[26] Hick, *op. cit.*, p. 146.

frequently given that the horizon of the 'end' or universal history is as yet indeterminate, where actually if it is to be used to adjudicate rival claims to truth it must be determinate in some degree at least. The same holds true if 'God', in that version in which 'he' is presented as the ultimate referent of the world religions, is as abstract and unspecified as he is when thus presented. In both cases, 'universal world history' or 'God' is more a linguistic surrogate for 'universal convergence-point'. It is not clear if either can yield a notion of God (i.e. allow God to be God), as opposed to the hypostatization of a theoretical necessity for unifying the plurality of the human being's vantage-points.

On the other hand, though no one may be certain exactly what part of our knowledge of nature, history and human being is reliable, they are not themselves altogether 'open' and undifferentiated: all our theorizing belies this, by supposing that they are intelligible because in some way specific, even if very complex, and related within themselves in an intelligible fashion. But are the differentiations which are characteristic of them made intelligible for us now or in the future only by physicalist, evolutionary or human theorizing, severally or together? As we saw earlier in our discussion, such a conclusion is a mistaken attempt to specify the context by extending vantage-points taken from within the content; it is tantamount to saying that all that marks the world and the human off in the open context is discernible from vantage-points within the world and human life, where plainly they are differentiated otherwise also.

What is the reality which can thus be open and also differentiated? It is, of course, an environment for the world, animate nature and the human; it is the environment in which, through their mapped exchange with it, the world, animals and human beings are changingly and self-samely differentiated to be what they are. But this environment is itself differentiated in such a way that it impinges directly on them, engaging in a self-selected relationship with them in all of their aspects. Chronologically, it has impinged upon them in world-formation and human-formation (i.e. creation), in the establishment of particular destinies (covenant), and in the support and reestablishment of the possibilities of the world, human and particular destinies. In the process, as and when the human being has become developed enough, it has differentiated itself for the human *pari passu* with the world's differentiation for the human, and the human's differentiation for himself/herself. This is not, however, to say that the environment is closed and differentiated completely, and thereby equilibrial, stable and stagnant; indeed it could not be and also be an environment for the world and human beings. That is, it is dynamic, containing an element of contingency within it whereby it (and its exchanges) can have a future which is not wholly predetermined by what it has been; and this contingency affects not simply its relations with the world and the human but also its self-regulation and its goal-seeking.

THE SELF-REGULATION OF THE ENVIRONMENT

Any functional exchanges which the environment carries on with the world and the human being presuppose their own 'regulations' which express the selectivity (mapping) in the exchanges. The essential background of this, so far as the environment itself is concerned, is autoregulation, whereby the environment maintains itself (and indirectly the world and the human also, relative to their situation) within tolerable proximity to itself within a tolerable 'self-sameness'. This, we would expect, would correspond (as a self-regulative device) to the entropy described in physicalist theorizing, but it would be a self-regulative 'device' of a higher order appropriate to the self-maintenance of an environment which is a relative punctuation of openness, and also to its exchanges with the world and human beings, which occur in a fluid, unbounded area. Since for the environment itself this is self-regulation in an open range of possibilities, and since in its exchange with the world and human beings its 'self-sameness' is at the mercy of every disequilibrating factor, the key questions are: (1) what kind of autoregulation actually occurs (functionally) by which the environment maintains itself within a tolerable degree of self-sameness, (2) whether there is a 'centre' or 'organ' of autoregulation, and (3) what is the character of its internal mapping ('within itself').

For the first question, the answer can only be forthcoming through long-term consideration of (and intentional participation in) the exchange in which this environment engages with the world, animate nature and the human in their constitution and behaviour, and by supposing that this exchange is mapped for its part by the autoregulation of the environment, that is, that there is an identity (a non-duality) between the environment immanently in itself and its exchange with human beings. This is not, of course, to suppose that there is a regular identity between the two. The bond between the autoregulative centre and the world is much more problematic, being that between a self-regulation of a higher order in an open range of possibilities and one of a lower order in a range of possibilities much more constrained. The conditions whereby the one becomes 'known' (differentiated) for the other are those of an exchange which bears characteristics (mapping) of the autoregulative centre and also those of the other 'partner' in the exchange. Because of the difference of these characteristics, the exchange is much more surprising than regular. But this subject demands a special discussion which we cannot begin here.

From such considerations we can see that the autoregulation includes the possibility of radical origination and termination (whether that be fixed or ongoing) in world-formation and human-formation, and also, within the 'brackets' thus demarcated, a regulated (but not lawlike) exchange which includes those equilibrial regularities described in physicalist, evolutionary and special-human theorizing and also higher-order exchanges of a more open kind. The last-mentioned are those 'trajectorial' ones in which the exchange is between a purposive and adaptive environment and infra-worldly human and societal trajectories; the situation is what Waddington calls 'homeorhesis' or 'stabilised flow'.[27] In such exchanges, deviations from the trajectory or moral course are corrected by compensations which result from the autoregulation of the environmental trajectory.

THE AUTOREGULATIVE CENTRE

To speak in these terms is not far from talking of the economy of salvation within the 'brackets' of creation and eschaton. The question to which we then come is whether the autoregulation of the environment as thus described is simply functional or occurs through the activity of a centre of autoregulation. There are two answers between which we will not attempt to decide here; both suggest a 'centre', but of different kinds. As we saw earlier, a particular context cannot be fully specified without reference to another context beyond. In similar fashion, we can now see that the autoregulation of the environment may require reference to another 'level' which we can partly but not wholly know; the regulation would occur in the presence of that other 'level' (with the feedback which it brings) for the environment, and the presence may not be coercive (it may allow contingency). Alternatively, we may consider that, like the nervous system and cognitive functions of a human being, this 'level' is actually a differentiated regulative centre or organ controlling the functional exchanges of the environment. In either case, we should beware of separating the function (activity) and the structure (constitution) of the level or centre – the presence of the level, or centre for the environment, from what it is in itself.

What then is the character of the 'internal mapping' of this autoregulative centre or level? One point must be made at the outset. Functionally, in differentiating the environment in such a way that it engages in a selective relationship with the world and the human being in all of their aspects, originative and terminative, regular and trajectorial, what is required is a strongly informed and informative autoregulative centre or

[27] C. H. Waddington, *The Evolution of an Evolutionist*, Edinburgh: Edinburgh University Press, 1975, p. 221.

level. We must remember the openness, the scope of possibilities and possible disequilibrations in which this centre or level maintains its course as a relative punctuation in interaction with the world and the human. Secondly, whether we are talking in terms of functions or structures, it is necessary that the centre or level be as well differentiated internally as those with which/whom it interacts, and at the same time changingly so – so that it can stand as an originator, terminator, and as a trajectory of the kind discussed above. The first characteristic (strong informedness and informativeness) leads us to the notion of simplicity, while the second leads us to personality.

With these considerations we come into the arena of speaking about the one God who is also Trinity, and it should be apparent that we have, throughout this discussion of the autoregulative centre of exchanges with the world and the human being, been speaking of this God. Our discussion has been confined to very general terms and needs to be extended by considering the actual behaviour by which God has differentiated himself, the world and human being, as it has been known by the world and human beings living in intentional exchange with him. But the history of the surprising graces which have resulted in creation and redemption is another task.

7

Christ and Creation[1]

ALTHOUGH much might be achieved by such considerations, we shall not attempt here to provide a scriptural, or an historical-theological exposition of the topic 'Christ and Creation'; nor shall we be looking for the practical implications of the topic. Instead, we shall attempt to develop a means whereby we may grasp the topic from within a modern perspective; this should enable us to read the Scriptures and earlier theology anew, and also to maintain the truth of Christian claims about the contingency of the world and man upon the action of God in Christ. It will also readjust our accustomed perspective away from the idealist, personalist, and moralistic tendencies which nowadays affect it, not in such a way as to de-emphasize the importance of the personal and moral, but to raise them to new possibilities which – we suggest – are more true to their nature.

If we make a preliminary approximation of the subject matter which must be included in the topic 'Christ and Creation', we find that it involves the real world, Jesus Christ and God in a unified account in which the world and man stand as contingent to God and his inner being as formed and manifest in Christ. Thus it asserts that the occurrence and fulfilment of the world and mankind happen not arbitrarily or by human decision, and that the possibility of full development of human rational, observational, moral and personal capabilities does not arise from the capabilities themselves, but that these occur by God's action and that their fulfilment is bound to their intrinsic nature as contingent upon God's action. Secondly, it asserts that the action of God in the world and in human development and fulfilment is not arbitrary and unconnected with his own being, as though God were abstractly transcendent, but that the actions of God arise from his very nature. Thirdly, it asserts that the person of Jesus Christ, and the redemption of the world and man effected in him, are not latter-day after-actions or accidental occurrences unconnected with God's own being or with his previous and subsequent action in the world, but that these are integral to his being and his history with the world. And lastly, it asserts that the agency operative in Jesus Christ and his redemption is not secondary to that in God's creation and history with the world, but that the world and its history are formed by the same agency as seen at work in Jesus Christ and the redemption accomplished through him.

In order to proceed with our topic, we should attempt to 'stake out the

[1] This essay first appeared in T. F. Torrance, ed., *The Incarnation*, Edinburgh: The Handsel Press, 1981.

main traits of the real world as known through science'[2] in as clear and systematic a way as possible, carry out an equally thorough consideration of man and his history, and simultaneously discover their interrelatedness with, and contingency upon, God as formed and manifest in Jesus Christ. This task is so vast, however, that we must content ourselves here with clearing the way and establishing a programme for the task which will enable it to be completed elsewhere; we cannot hope within this small compass actually to supply a full statement of the account of Christ and Creation which is needed.

In order to clear the way, we must first consider a number of approaches often used for the topic which prevent a proper treatment of it. Then we will go on to suggest that another approach is required, which provides for the knower to be noetically qualified by the reality to be known, and in which the dynamic of thinking should follow from the nature of the object; such necessitates full study of the world and man, and understanding them not only as they are now understood by science but in their inner rationality. Beyond this, we shall consider a particular form of synthetic theorizing, information theory, which when noetically qualified will allow demarcation of classes of objects (e.g. physical, biological, human), showing the inner differentiation of the world, and also allow reconciliation of their differences without reductionism. The same synthetic theorizing can, when noetically qualified, allow differentiation of God from these intraworldly objects, and show his interrelatedness with them. Finally, we consider what this theorizing shows of the inner being of God, particularly as regards the contingency of the world and man upon the second person of the Trinity.

It will be evident from this statement of our purpose here that we set aside a number of alternative ways of approaching our topic: the collection and justification of beliefs, the study of human existence, the study of presuppositions, the study of being *qua* being, or of change, or of logic. These philosophical approaches may have considerable value in themselves, but they are of limited value in our present inquiry because they are distanced from the main traits of the world as known through science. If the world as thus understood is found to be related to the person of Christ, it would still be necessary to relate the connectedness to the real world – to find the same connectedness to be true of the real world. This would be especially problematic in the case of many of those approaches primarily occupied with beliefs, presuppositions, logic and human existence, for these deal with the world as it is for me, as it impinges upon me.

Since these approaches which deal with the world as it is for me provide such an important distraction from, and obstacle to, the

---

[2] M. Bunge, *Treatise on Basic Philosophy*, Dordrecht: D. Reidel, 1977, Vol. 3, p. 5.

approach which we will employ here, we should consider some of their main features before proceeding. In doing so, we can also consider the main tenets of similar philosophies of science.

Such views consider that the world as viewed scientifically, with physico-chemical or biological explanations, or mental or conscious processes as viewed physiologically or psychologically, or cultural or social processes as explained socio-economically or sociologically, are explored from the 'inside' as for-me and are made important by me. They are not accessible as they are in themselves, and so far as they can be known, knowing them requires a proper methodology and properly constructed theories. Knowing reality thus requires proper epistemology; epistemology is seen as antecedent to ontology, and science is a radically self-correcting constructive activity in aid of (instrumental to) our understanding, which provides an ascending structure of 'worlds' in terms of which the physico-chemical-biological and the mental-conscious and the sociocultural can respectively be understood.

Human understanding, according to this approach, relies on methodology or epistemology whereby theories are constructed, ordered and corrected by reference to the world as it is for-us. There is a methodologically-established demarcation of data available into 'worlds', and data may be excluded from 'knowledge' because they lie beyond these demarcated 'worlds'; unless religious beliefs were considered part of the sociocultural 'world', they would be excluded from the realm of methodologically-established knowledge.

Others, however, utilize the same approach in the service of religious belief, and in similar fashion consider that faith is a more-or-less free interpretative or constructive activity which should properly be a methodological exploration of the content of faith as for-mc. In that it sees faith as a constructive activity in aid of (instrumental to) theoretical understanding (or in some cases, in aid of practice only), with its own methodology, this approach to religious belief is directly comparable to the scientific approaches just mentioned. Much attention has been given to this comparability as a means of establishing the cognitive claim of religious belief.[3] But, despite the formal likeness to each other of these constructions (scientific, religious), they can be correlated only as formally similar. Since their content is delimited methodologically, and the methodologies remain distinct (only the fact of having methodologies remains the same), they can be correlated only by some factor outside of both – human experience or judgment, for example.

A similar problem occurs when history, not natural scientific knowl-

---

[3] B. Lonergan, *Insight*, London: Longmans, 1957; J. Hick, *God and the Universe of Faiths*, London: Macmillan, 1973; I. Barbour, *Myths, Models and Paradigms*, London: SCM Press, 1974.

edge, is at stake. When, as in recent historical approaches to the discovery of truth and of possibilities for practical reversal of the constraints depriving men of their proper freedom, history is explored from within historicality, it is supposed that doing so relies on the establishment of an historical methodology. This provides general rules for understanding past events, and the traditions within which they were understood, and for establishing their meaning-for-us either in reference to present unfreedom or in the context of universal world-history. An important debate focuses on the use of historical analogy in this methodology: are events and interpretations at variance with present understanding to be disallowed because they challenge the methodology, or allowed notwithstanding the methodology? Positivists would disallow them; others might or might not, depending on their historical-methodological norms.

Religious proponents of historical exploration utilize this same exploration of history-from-within in the service of religious belief. They suggest that religious belief is in general similar to ordinary historical understanding, in that both establish the factuality of data and their meaning by anticipating the totality of reality and human experience; religious and ordinary historical understanding are methodologically similar. But they differ in that the believer explicitly 'takes a stand' on his belief that God is the ground of the unity of history and therefore selectively interprets history from that theological interest.[4] Here again, however, this religious content is delimited methodologically, and as such is correlated with methodologically nonreligious history only by some factor outside of both – that human 'taking a stand' which causes non-religious history to be seen religiously.

The same primary features run through the positions, scientific and historical, non-religious and religious, which we have just summarized. In all cases, the nature of reality or of historical truth and meaning is to be explored from within the experience of the knower. To discover reality or historical meaning, however, depends on the use of a method which will enable correct construction, interpretation, or historical selectivity; knowledge or discernment of historical meaning follows from the use of method – ontology follows from correct epistemology. Some of the insights afforded by these positions are helpful, especially those which undertake a thorough elucidation of epistemology (e.g. Popper and Lonergan) or historical reasoning (e.g. Pannenberg), although this is not the case where the epistemological analysis simply establishes the comparability of religious with other interpretations of the world such as those employed in science (e.g. Hick and Barbour). Still less is it the case where epistemology is introjected into the inaccessible subjectivity of the

---

[4] W. Pannenberg, *Basic Questions in Theology*, London: SCM Press, 1970, Vol. I, pp. 77–78.

believer, as in most existentialism. We shall see later that a crucial issue is at stake here; thorough elucidations of epistemology (such as Popper's and Lonergan's) are valuable precisely because they suggest the necessity of hierarchically differentiated constructions or methodologies, and the others are lacking because they do not, suggesting instead a monoplanar 'flat earth' of different constructions, in a way which is at variance with the needs of modern scientific knowledge.

But the more problematic features of all these positions, so far as our present discussion is concerned, are those connected with the dependency of all understanding of reality and historical truth upon the experience of a knower and his method. As a result of this, events in nature and history are taken to cohere in systems, and to have meaning in relation to each other, only insofar as this coherence and meaning are discovered by or found by an experiencing subject (or conceivably by sharing subjects). Systematicity, as well as its goal of simplicity, either disappears because of this insistence or becomes a human construction. Nowhere is this more plain than in much present-day Anglo-American theology, where God's presence and activity are taken to be dependent on the believer ('God acts by being believed-in'), or communion with God is seen to be dependent upon the communicant. In such circles, systematic theology is a humanly-contrived matrix for events of this presence or communion, if indeed it ever is done at all. The loss of the possibility of an inner coherence between things, and of systematicity in science and theology, is important, and must be overcome if we are to be able to think of a primordial coherence in things, as our topic demands.

Another problematic feature of these positions arises from their use of methodology to demarcate data. One such demarcation is made between ordinary or natural events, such as those which can be discussed by reference to constructed worlds (physico-chemical-biological; mental-conscious; sociocultural) or to history understood analogically with the present constructed worlds *and* that which cannot be so understood, whether in nature or history. Thus ordinary events of nature or history – or for that matter, the facts of Jesus' nature, consciousness, or sociocultural situation – are methodologically demarcated from 'acts of God' or from God as transcendent ground for nature and history. Interestingly, this demarcation is frequently clothed in spatiotemporal conceptions such as 'within-context' and 'context', 'inner' and 'outer', and 'centre' and 'boundary' (or 'limit'), 'finite' and 'infinite', 'part' and 'whole'. But all the while the demarcation is *methodologically* established, and bears little relation to what is actually known of these spatiotemporal conceptions today.

When the transcendent ground is thus separated from the ordinarily-knowable, it lapses into the position of a 'brute fact' knowable only as the 'sheer transcendence' of an other. If it is to be known in any fuller sense of the term, it must be known indirectly through ordinary events of nature and history – as understood in terms of present constructed worlds. In other words, the transcendent other can only be connected with ordinary nature and history by an extrinsic relation made in human experience, never by an inner relation which presents itself to human knowing. Much argument may be offered – often very interesting argument, especially when used cumulatively – for this relation, but it always remains an extrinsic relation even when well justified, and cannot be an inner relation of the conditions of the world and man to their transcendent ground. The same is true even where a relation is established between the history of Jesus' life and mission and God, through the fact of the Resurrection and its interpretation. Even where carefully established by historical investigation, the Resurrection is an unusual relation in external history, and thus extrinsic to Jesus – not a confirmation of an inner relation between Jesus' nature and history and their ground. The limitation of the relation between the ordinary-knowable and its ground to one established in human experience – extrinsically – means that an inner relation between the conditions of the world and man and their ground in a logos of creation, cannot be established – or at least cannot be established without immediately being seen as a human construction; and such may always be nullified by reasserting in stronger form that methodologically-established demarcation between ordinary nature and history and the transcendent 'order'. So strong is this demarcation usually assumed to be that the claim for a relation between the ordinary-knowable and its ground, or between the conditions of the world and man and their ground in a logos of creation, is considered to be *arbitrary* and unjustifiable.

Lastly, we must consider an aspect of these positions which is particularly injurious to the topic with which we are concerned. If understanding of reality and historical truth is so much dependent upon the knower and his method or constructions, there is a serious danger that the programme for this understanding will be misconstrued – and will become the entrance-point for fundamental prejudices, perhaps quite unrecognized. This is the reason why Karl Popper attempts to eliminate from the programme for understanding all traces of the subjective act of thinking (knowledge 'consisting of a state of mind or of consciousness or a disposition to behave or to react');[5] the 'traditional' epistemology which concentrated on this is, he considers, irrelevant to the study of scientific knowledge, and must be supplanted by knowledge in the objective sense, which is totally independent of anybody's claim to know or believe or assent, assert or act. Thus, in order to remove the deficiencies of a knower and method-dependent knowledge, Popper studiously removes subjective factors such as intuition, concepts, definitions, etc., to a position ante-

[5] K. Popper, *Objective Knowledge*, London: Oxford University Press, 1972, p. 108.

cedent to the world of objective knowledge with which science is concerned.[6] He then places great stress on the growth of this knowledge.

But in a situation where there is no stringent method of establishing knowledge, and a greater willingness to equate it with belief and disposition, there can creep in the supposition that knowledge consists in a direct act, much like the act of perception, in which there seems to be a relation between the knower and the known. In the case of religious knowledge, this can lead to the attempt to know God directly – mediated, if at all, only by the activity of knowing and its methodological constraints, or by one's capacity to make that knowing of God cohere with a particular religious tradition. The danger introduced into religious knowledge by this attempt is twofold: (1) it prescinds too quickly from spatio-temporal, conscious, and social structures, thereby avoiding the mediateness of God's presence in them and treating them instead as circumstances or preconditions for the direct activity by which God is known; and (2) it prescinds too quickly from particular spatio-temporal, conscious, and social situations wherein God may be particularly presented, leaving them also in the position of preconditions to direct knowledge of God. The effect of this stress on direct knowledge is thereby to *reach through* creation and Christ without taking them fully seriously as mediations of God's presence. This is not to say that those who advocate this give no value to creation and Christ; their value, however, is that of preconditions or circumstances for the direct activity of knowing God – not even that of bringing that knowledge, for that capacity is taken to be natural to human beings.

By contrast with this position, it is necessary, in order to do justice to creation and Christ, to take both seriously as mediating the presence of God. In this respect, both Popper's and the direct-act view of knowledge just discussed are deficient. In the case of Popper's argument, the physical world (world 1) and mental states (world 2) interact with each other, and there is also a 'world 3' comprised of the contents of thought – a world of the products of the human mind which has a certain degree of autonomy and which influences the physical world; this world 3, which we learn culturally and socially, and grasp through a mental process (world 2), is the tool for (instrumental to) understanding world 1. The deficiency arises from the fact that world 3 objects, as Popper construes them, are instrumental only to the investigation of the (world 1) physical world, and thereby disallow the possibility that this (world 1) is a creation which mediates a creator – or that world 2 and world 3 may do so also. The problem with Popper's view, then, is that mediation of a 'higher' source in the physical, conscious, and theoretical worlds is disallowed.

On the other hand, the deficiency of the direct-act view of knowledge is

---

[6] *Ibid.*, p. 148.

that the physical, conscious and theoretical 'worlds' are together taken as instrumental to a 'knowing' which disallows the possibility that they may mediate a higher source in and of themselves, or that they may provide the parameters within which man's knowing must be constrained. In this direct-act view of knowledge, there lurks a residual idealism, that man's knowing (e.g.) of God is limited only by his relation to God; but is it not also the case that man's knowing occurs within parameters which are in some way established by virtue of his physical, mental and social (as well as historical) being – where God may be mediately present also?

We have dwelt at some length on the main features of certain approaches which deal with the world as it is for-me in order to show the problems which arise when such approaches are used in discussion of creation and Christ. The main problems, as we saw, were: the experience- and method-dependency of human understanding, the fact that coherence and systematicity in the world and between the world and God are extrinsic – achieved by human discovery – and never intrinsic, and finally the fact that the world and human knowing are disallowed their mediatorial function. It should be evident how seriously these problems affect the discussion of an inner relation between Christ and creation.

Clearly, another kind of approach is required, one which does not prescind from 'the main traits of the real world as known through science' and which yet allows their own interrelatedness with Jesus Christ to emerge without prejudging the case against it. What is such an approach?

Fundamentally, what is required is a noetic qualification whereby the 'knower' is capacitated by the reality to be known, and therein achieves a 'selectivity' whereby he can discern what are the basic conditions which define what is actually the case. Such a selectivity does not abstract from the physico-chemical, biological, mental, and sociocultural structures of the world, but finds the basic constraints which define what is actual and relevant – which are intrinsic to the real, not external to it.

This qualification is by no means simply a matter of knowing about these constraints, as though one were distanced from them. It is rather a qualification of all capacities available for understanding life in the constraints. It is thus more like a well-developed skill or ability comprised of knowing-of, aesthetic-recognition, and functioning skills, which cooperate together in a process with its own inner dynamic which matches the constraints and lives freely with them, all this together with others in personal interrelationships in a 'widely extended network of mutual trust'.[7] In these respects, it is more like the process of skiing downhill than the discovering of physical laws, principles of action or aesthetical regularities. As such it is very nearly indescribable and unprescribable.

[7] M. Polanyi, *Personal Knowledge*, London: Routledge & Kegan Paul, 1958, p. 241.

And it is also incapable of being separated into an antecedent methodology which can be considered in isolation from the actual process in which one is qualified by the reality to be known or lived-with; there is no forecourt to the temple, in which we can discover knowledge without knowing (as Hegel used to say).

What we have termed a noetic qualification is a qualification by an object or objects, but one which is a process with its own dynamic. It is, in the first place, a thinking of the object which brings that to a definiteness in accord with its own nature. In order for this to occur, there must be a constant correction by the object; the thinking of the object always requires correction by the object in order to be in accord with the nature of the object. In other words, the thinking never claims to achieve a final definiteness relative to its object, or to achieve a position where the correction is complete, although it should seek to approximate more closely to the particular determinateness of the object. Thus, a thinking of the object is a *complexity* of definiteness and openness: it combines *definiteness* – a definite thinking of the object which is a *positive knowledge* of the object, and *incompleteness* – an openness toward, or freedom for, the object to emerge more fully.

The combination of definiteness and incompleteness is not the static matter it is often claimed to be, whereby the two are alternatives between which the knower oscillates: either he knows (has correct definite knowledge qualified by the object) or does not. This digitalized either-or view of grasping or thinking the object is much less than human, even if it is very often used in discussions of knowledge in science and Christianity. Instead, the combination is dynamic: the noesis is a complex adaptive system reaching toward a higher simplicity. Each knowing, or definitive thinking of the object, is new information in a dynamic process which makes for new possibilities; this is a process of increasing complexity. But at the same time, this complexity – so far as it is a thinking of the object – operates within parameters which are not of its making; and what it seeks is maximal simplicity relative to the object.

Now, it is evident that the objects which qualify or capacitate man's understanding vary widely, but in all cases the dynamic of thinking of them should follow from the nature of the object. Thus physical objects differ from biological, and the conception of order or organization in the one differs from that in the other, even though superficially they can be made to appear the same. So also do human beings differ from lower biological organisms and their complexity and semiotic freedom make them open to more levels of their general environment than is the case for lower organisms which may be open to only a restricted environment.[8] So do all these differ from God, whose freedom and ordering are of

---

[8] A. Wilden, *System and Structure*, London: Tavistock, 1972, p. 360.

another level altogether. In the case of each object, there should be a noetic qualification of the knower in the dynamic process of his knowing.

The nature of the object in each case places an extreme demand on the knower to which no end can be set, for which no final success can be assured. In fact, this demand sets in motion that dynamic noesis to which we have already referred. It would be a great error to suppose that one can cut his way through this process by simple affirmations, whether favouring explanation in physicalist, biological, human or theological terms, for any such affirmation will appear authoritarian and the product of an unjustified monism.

The dynamic noesis should not operate at a naive level in which it is supposed that vague intuitive assertions are sufficient: the symbolic 'powers of operations' which primarily distinguish human beings from animals[9] – the application of that semiotic freedom mentioned a moment ago – must bring about coherent and consecutive reasoning of a theoretical kind. But this must be done, of course, in a manner qualified by the object, whether that be physical, biological, human or divine. One of the most difficult tasks, as we shall see, is the systematizing of such theorizings.

Two additional things must be said about this noetic qualification. *One* is that the theorizings to which we have just referred will necessarily be variegated, not because of their reference to physical, biological (etc.) structures, but because theories characteristically seek a greater economy and simplicity than reference to one domain alone allows. Thus we shall find that the dynamic noesis drives to theories of great generality which are not arbitrary but which contain generalizations of theories; these are corrigible but not refutable.[10] *The other* is that the noetic qualification is actually much wider than our recent discussion implies: since the object qualifies by its rational structure, beauty, and goodness, the qualification of the human being is noetic (in the narrower sense), aesthetic, and behavioural. At the same time, insofar as the object is itself integrated, it integrates the human capacities which it qualifies. Of course, if the qualification of the human being and his integrity depends on the object, it follows that the degree to which a human being can be qualified by (e.g.) physical structures is limited by those structures.

We have suggested that the aim with which one should approach creation and Christ is a noetic qualification by the object. Any demarcations within creation and Christ will arise from them rather than being introduced by the knower; such demarcations will occur in the spatio-temporal, human and social structures of the world, and not avoid them or take us beyond them, but at the same time will allow actual differen-

[9] Polanyi, *op. cit.*, p. 257.
[10] M. Bunge, *Method, Model and Matter*, Dordrecht: D. Reidel, 1978, p. 37.

tiations to appear – allow things which are extended in space and time to be differentiated from each other. In other words, demarcations and relationships will appear in creation, as inner to it.

We do not start in this from creation or Christ as though they were 'brute facts' or unknowable noumena: we are already under the influence of various inherited presuppositions about what they are and even how they take on this character (cf. our earlier discussion about knower-dependent views of reality). Even if they appear obviously to be the case, they require careful examination for several reasons: (1) they frequently block thorough understanding; (2) they make use of basic ideas – usually purely intuitive and prerational – which mislead because they have not fully been made exact; and (3) they confuse various levels of theory. For example, our inherited presuppositions cause us to read the Gospel in thoroughly mentalistic and moral terms, giving most attention to Jesus' self-consciousness and intentions, rather than in spatio-temporal, physico-chemical, biological and sociocultural terms. Where reference is made to time, life, consciousness, and sociality, they are left as intuitive – very much as they have been in science also. And no clear distinction is drawn between high-level theories (such as the Trinity) and models or parables applicable in interpreting portions of the Bible. Similar presuppositions operate in science, of course, and require careful examination there as well. The point is that the whole field of our understanding of creation and Christ is permeated by basic ideas which require careful attention.

Surely, attention to these tasks will lead one in the direction of a wide variety of special studies. But it must also be abundantly clear that if one seeks the inner rationality of the world, and the inner connection of that with Christ, they can only be found through such studies. Failing to do such work will inevitably lead to a rationality *imposed upon* the world through premodern ontology, or poetically, perhaps, and to a connection of that with Christ through an extrinsic relation. They will almost certainly appear to be speculative 'inserts' or anthropomorphic injections into the structure of the world. The task of allowing demarcations and relationships between creation and Christ to emerge from within the world will have been frustrated at the outset.

We can only hint very briefly at the consequences of these special studies. What they show is a world which is a 'totality of things, i.e. concrete individuals endowed with all their properties, some of which consist in their being able to change in definite (though possibly random) lawful ways'.[11] This world is comprised of changing things, and dynamic change is the natural state of things, in which they change through mutual influence; but things do not necessarily change in every respect,

---

[11] M. Bunge, *Treatise on Basic Philosophy*, Vol. 3, p. 268.

nor do they do so unceasingly. Some traits of the world remain invariant – the constants of the motion of a physical system, or the homeostasis of life processes. The world itself is also in flux, but is also in some sense an integrated system of processes which influence each other so that nothing is completely isolated: whatever exists is influenced by, or influences, some other things. This aggregation of things does not occur in a container of space and time, as though these were a 'fixed stage where things play out their comedy',[12] which would go on existing if all things were to cease to exist; this fixed framework view was shaken by the relativistic theory of gravitation. Nor does space-time constitute the prime or elementary substance of which every physical object is made. Rather are space and time a network of relations among things and their changes: 'space-time is the basic structure of the totality of possible facts.'[13] That is, the structure of space-time depends on its 'furniture', and a place in space-time is relative to a frame of reference and objective.

In an extremely summary statement, these are the results of special studies into basic ideas of science. They provide the general concepts of the world, individuals, changing and invariance, system and association, and space-time which allow us then to study things or individuals changing 'in' space-time and in the constraints which define what is actual or relevant. These general concepts, by the way, cannot be verified conclusively, but they are sustained because of their cogency, clarifying power, and closeness of fit with contemporary physics.

To study what occurs in space-time, one might review the attempts to provide an adequate explanatory framework by reference to physical principles, then by reference to evolutionary biology, then by reference to human life, showing that each is inadequate as a framework for explaining the whole of the natural world and, while differentiating its own domain (physical, biological, etc.) in a useful fashion, opens into other possible levels of explanation – right up to a differentiated environment in which they all exist.[14] But such an attempt probably places too much weight on the epistemological boundaries or limits of different kinds of explanation, and stresses too much the inability of any rational system to define its own boundaries (as described by Gödel, for example).

Recognizing that the noetic qualification by the objects studied brings about coherent and consecutive reasoning of an intensive kind, and thus involves dynamic theoretical work, it is preferable to employ adequately synthetic theorizings which will enable knowing of creation and Christ with such demarcations and relationships in and between them as may

---

[12] *Ibid.*, p. 278.
[13] *Ibid.*, p. 281.
[14] D. W. Hardy, 'Man the Creature', in *Scottish Journal of Theology*, 30:2 (1977), 111–136; Ch. 6 above.

appear. These will not be pictures or fictions which are instrumental to an intuitive or unspeakable, unthinkable apprehension of creation and Christ, but an actual theoretical grasping of creation and Christ – or, to put it more accurately, a qualification of certain theoretical work by its object.

There are several kinds of synthetic theories which are available, providing generic frameworks which help one to think of whole classes of entities in various domains, such as classical field theory, quantum field theory, game theory, information theory, network theory, and automata theory. They are all extremely general and empirically untestable, but they are (or should be) conceptually testable, and are properly classed as scientific. They have the particular advantage of being relatively neutral, not identified with one particular domain such as the human, and therefore escape the charge of being anthropomorphic. But the opposite danger is that they will be synthetic in the sense of being non-natural; they are sometimes said to be mechanistic, for example, and therefore incapable of synthesizing organic and human domains: instead of being qualified by such objects, they are disqualified. But this is a question which cannot be settled without seeing them used.

Taking one such synthetic theorizing, information theory, we can see that it allows demarcations within creation between the physical and biological domains. 'Whereas for the physicist the formation of a crystal amounts to a decrease in free energy and thus, by definition, to an increase in entropy ... for the biologist the passage from solution to crystal means an increase in patterning, and therefore an increase in negative entropy.'[15] Bound energy differs in the two cases, meaning a decrease in free energy for the physicist and an increase in energy for the biologist. So also does the use of information theory allow the demarcation of human being from the physical and biological domains, by virtue of the human being's generation of information through his openness to a relatively nonrestricted environment (where lower orders are either not open or restrictedly open) and his use of the input from the environment to modify the output to the environment.

The use of information theory also allows the reconciliation of the paradoxical disagreement between the physicist and the biologist. The *physicist* speaks of the fact that all natural processes generate disorder or entropy: an irreversible destruction of macroscopic order is going on. The *biologist*, appealing to our intuitive perception of the world as unfolding in time, suggests that everywhere order or information is being generated whereby a simpler state is being transformed into a more complex one. The two 'arrows' of time are in direct contradiction, thermodynamic with historical. But a theory generated from information

15 Wilden, *op. cit.*, p. 360.

theory reconciles *the two*, and also reconciles *both* with the time-symmetric character of physical laws at the microscopic level, suggesting that the universe is unfolding in time but not unravelling – instead it is becoming constantly more complex and richer in information.

Though there is much more to be said on these issues, what we see in the use of this high level synthetic theorizing is the possibility of a theoretical structure which is noetically qualified by its objects and which allows demarcations between domains of inquiry and yet reconciles their different results in an overall theoretical structure. It is, of course, under constant correction by its objects, but it also enables us to probe deeply into the character of creation in order to discover its inner patterns – and to do so clearly and with internal consistency, nonconstructively (i.e. without an antecedent epistemology), without definitions in terms of personal experience, and systematically. What exactly are the fruits? (1) By this procedure, we achieve systematicity but avoid various forms of reductionism, whether reducing 'downwards' – man in terms of his physico-chemical constitution, or reducing 'upwards' – the world in terms of its meaning and use for man. But at the same time, we achieve a greater degree of mutual translatability between apparently disparate explanations of the world. (2) The use of an overall theoretical structure enables us to grasp the inner differentiation of the world, and the fact that levels of organization (physical, biological, social) are necessary to each other as mediations, but also that the mediation does not exhaust what is mediated. The fact, for example, that two people are present to each other *in their bodies* and in the *physical sound waves* by which they hear each other, as well as in *symbol systems*, can be grasped and differentiated by the use of this theorizing; but *also* the fashion in which each is necessary to the others as a mediation, *and* the fact that we should look for something beyond the mediation, are *also* grasped by this theorizing. (3) Finally, the use of an overall theoretical structure can enable us to find the basic constraints which make our world, life and society what they are. This is not a search for abstract laws, but for the initial conditions, boundary conditions and symmetry conditions which provide the circumstance within which the world still operates and human life and society eventually came to be. They show the regularity and non-arbitrariness of the order within which we now live, but only in a general way: perturbations within and without, and the essential incompleteness of the information-store, create genuine novelty which disallows a deterministic view.[16]

Does the same synthetic theorizing allow a demarcation and interrelation to emerge between the sum of the domains of inquiry (physico-

[16] D. Layzer, 'The Arrow of Time' in *Scientific American*, 1977, p. 69, a view contrary to that expressed in E. Schoffeniels in *Anti-Chance*, Oxford: Pergamon Press, 1976.

chemical, biological, human, social) which we have been discussing, and God – and further, demarcations within God? Certainly, the theorizing does not construct the demarcations; its function is to be qualified and corrected by its objects, and to allow their own differentiation to emerge. But the pressure of God upon us, and upon this synthetic theorizing, does demand the differentiation of God from the sum of the domains of the world. The 'pressure' just mentioned is to be conceived of in terms of the synthetic theorizing, not simply intuitively or in terms which have their origin in some other synthetic theorizing. (Hence we may not simply speak here of the 'pressure', for example, of the history of salvation, although this might be appropriate in other circumstances.) Thus we should speak of the necessity of differentiating between the bound energy understood in different ways by the physicist and biologist and a bound energy of another and higher order, and of the necessity of differentiating between the human being's generation of information through his openness and use of a relatively nonrestricted environment and a higher order generation of information through openness and use of a completely unrestricted environment. Briefly, we should be differentiating a communication of a much higher order than that which we see characterizing the physical, biological and human world – precisely because we are under 'pressure' from this communication. And this would involve us in speaking also of the differentiation of a higher-order space-time which has its own unfolding and increasing richness – demarcated from the reconciliation of entropy and negentropy already discussed.

Notice, however, that, while the pressure of God upon us and our synthetic theorizing demands a demarcation or differentiation, the demarcation is not conceived within the synthetic theorizing as that had been developed by application to physical, chemical, biological and human domains – or in reconciling them. Of course, there is a constant tendency to drop back to these, so that, for example, we think of God's bound energy, information-generation and space-time richness in terms of the synthetic theorizing developed under the pressure of worldly thinking – the more so because even this worldly theorizing is so difficult. Thus, there is a tendency to employ 'monosemantic' secular thinking, instead of the 'disemantic' thinking which is required. But this reversion to a worldly synthetic theorizing must be resisted if we are to achieve a proper understanding of the transcendent identity of God. On the other hand, however, notice that the demarcation or differentiation of God is not a dichotomy: it is rather a demarcation which emerges according to the 'domain' of God when we grasp the inner differentiation of the world. That is to say, it is a demarcation which is *itself* of a higher order than the demarcations which emerged between the physical, chemical, biological and human domains. And as such, it is nonetheless to be grasped theoretically, however difficult this may be; we are not to abandon the theoretic task at this stage and lapse into an intuitive theology of 'openness', fashionable though that is, to a vaguely 'beyond' God.

There are very difficult issues at stake here. Probably the most important is the issue of whether and what this higher order domain is, as demarcated in the inner patterns of the world. There appear to be fundamental divisions of conviction here. *Without* a higher-order domain, or even *with* one conceived as a 'bare transcendence' (deistically) – which is very near to the same thing, the world collapses into an amoral pluralism. This is one fundamental position seen very widely today – especially in the ontological pluralism of much modern science, which can make so little of the intermediation and interconnectedness of physical, chemical, biological and human worlds. It is not easily compatible with Christian thought; indeed I doubt that it can be made compatible with it at all. On the other hand, with a *singular* higher-order domain with a *positive content* of a certain kind, not only does the nature of its demarcation from worldly domains become clear, so also does its mediateness in the worldly domains, as well as their proper relation to each other, become clear; and pluralism collapses into simplicity. The issue of simplicity is thus central to theorizing about the world and about God: it is the endpoint of synthetic theorizings, and can ultimately only be achieved in synthetic theorizing about God which is noetically qualified by God.

We should expect a positive theoretical grasping of God and his domain in, or relatedness to, the world to emerge in the noetic qualifying of the synthetic theorizing we have been discussing. So it does, identifying God through grasping the inner differentiation which occurs in God's being between the bound information characteristic of a higher organized system and the dispersed 'signal' information characteristic of free communication. The former has a higher 'information density', lacking the dilation of the latter; it is bound through self-regulation in a well-structured system with a high degree of 'stored' or 'condensed' information, whereas the latter has a lower information density and is dispersed and extended through time.[17]

With suitable development, this theoretical grasping can yield an understanding of God as Trinity who has, in the fashion of 'I am who I am', bound himself by self-choice in a high information density, condensing all the signal information by which his energy is directed. The specificity of God is seen in this 'density'; this is the information which is who he is, and which is who he may be *ad extra*. Thus we grasp God as specific in the second person of the Trinity, in an information density which arises from God's own self-determination and condenses all the

[17] Cf. J. Zeman, 'Information, Knowledge and Time' in L. Kubat and J. Zeman, eds., *Entropy and Information in Science and Philosophy*, Amsterdam: Elsevier, 1975, pp. 245–254.

directed energy of the third person. The interrelatedness of the persons is grasped also in this: the free energy of the third person, dispersed but directed (in the sense of channelled) is condensed or stored in the second person, in a fashion somewhat like memory, and hence always redirected in its free passage.

The self-determination of God, generating this information density, occurs in an unlimited field of possibilities, as we said earlier, and is also characterized by maximal generativity. Operating within a limited field and with limited generativity, the differentiated world and mankind are the product of the communication of this information and directed energy, and as such are contingent upon them for order and life/energy. Indeed, we find that the basic processes of the world and mankind – processes of decay, structure, development and learning – can be conceived of as successive dilation and condensation, and are contingent upon the dilation of direct energy (the Holy Spirit) through time and its condensation in the information density of the second person of the Trinity. Nowhere in the world itself, however, do we find the reconciliation of the world's decay and development that we find in the nature of God: the world is a growing complexity which lays waste to its own resources, and this cannot be resolved into ultimate simplicity outside of God, nor can one arrive at a maximally economic explanation of the characteristics of the world except by reference to God.

The information density of God is known to us only through contingent mediations; and considering the world and its increasingly complex life, even considering the entropy and negentropy of learning, does not enable more than fragmented glimpses (even if these can be very helpful) of the information density of God to occur. They certainly do not allow for the simplicity of the highly structured system of which this density is characteristic, to be grasped.

Where, then, is it grasped, and with it the basic information which is communicated in all the created order? Only in a particular time-encompassing event identified as such by its continual relevance to understanding the world and man, by the fact that the world and man may be understood and lived-in always 'from' this event, and the ultimate simplicity of God found in them. And this time-encompassing, lived-from event is Jesus Christ. He is the medium in which the information density of God occurs for mankind, and by which we may understand the domain of God in the inner logic of the world.

Like any human being, Jesus lived as dependent on basic levels of process, physical and biological and conscious, each level being dependent on the others, and all requiring a basic cosmic 'flow' of space-time and life and learning. Therein is Jesus' human nature, not only in his moral purpose or intentions or self-consciousness, as modern idealist-inspired Christology would lead us to believe. And only by recognizing his position in these levels and this flow, and the importance in them of his life, suffering and death, can we take full account of them and what may be mediated within them – and in the interrelatedness into which he brought them. For it is plain that his personal integration of the levels of worldly process and of the cosmic flow, the economy of his life and history, mediates the economy of the Trinity as differentiated in the created order. It is not only his consciousness of God his Father which achieved a time-encompassing memory and anticipation of all human relationships with God, but the entire economy of his life in the created order which did so. Thus we can say that his life mediates the information density which is the second person of the Trinity, upon which the entire created order is contingent, and that it mediates the focusing or channelling or condensing by which the Holy Spirit shines through the world.

8
Theology, Cosmology and Change[1]

THE NECESSITY OF COSMOLOGY FOR THEOLOGY

ALTHOUGH it is now frequently avoided, there is a necessary conjunction of theology with cosmology, history, meaning and practice, not to mention such issues as demography, sociality, humanity and culture. Where such connections are damaged or disappear, theology suffers – and so do all the others.

For the West, the universal acceptance of the Biblical account as a unified statement of the nature of the world and its history, with theological cosmology as its 'inner logic', provided the basis for a commonly accepted meaning for human life, whether social or personal, which in turn furnished an accepted order for practice.[2] The importance of the acceptance of a unified world-historical account for the meaning of life is seen amongst those imbued with 'classic' culture.

> Leopold Mozart – who had been educated for twelve years by Jesuits and after a year studying theology became a baccalaureate in philosophy – had brought up his young son as a Catholic, given him religious instruction, and in his letters to Paris had not hesitated to remind Wolfgang even as an adult to continue to practise his religion ... There is no doubt that Mozart's unquestioning faith, his holding fast to a meaning in life – on which he hardly reflected in theory – have their roots here. And this was expressed and responded to in a basic question in the catechism: 'Why is man created on earth?' Then as now, to some people this gives an answer to the whole of life: it may be sorely tried in the tribulations of that life, but is never seriously given up.[3]

Hence the doctrine of creation provided Mozart with the conviction of the givenness by God of 'an answer to the whole of life', and therefore of

---

[1] A paper delivered to the Society for the Study of Theology, 1993.
[2] Cf. Karl Barth's description of creation as the 'external basis' of the covenant.
[3] Hans Küng, *Mozart: Traces of Transcendence*, London: SCM Press, 1992, p. 23.

a meaning for life. His 'unquestioning faith' in this allowed his music to become an expression of the 'mystery of order'.[4] For him and for those of the 'classic' era, such faith provided consistent expectations for the order of life, and a coherent pattern for the enactment of this order through theory, human action and self-expression. It was that which enabled the craftsmanlike certainty – and its attendant freedom – which marked such music as Bach's or Mozart's.

But the accessibility of such a unified world-historical account, of the sort provided by universal acceptance of the Biblical account, has steadily diminished since then. The causes are complex, but the result has been the fragmentation of the elements formerly conjoined – into detached disciplines of inquiry – with corresponding consequences for human beings. On the surface, this might appear insignificant. But it has had the effect of confining each of the elements within a self-designated – while potentially also infinite – trajectory which is out of reach of the others: a 'private pinhole' through which to view everything. On the one hand, the conception of the object of inquiry and the means of attention and thought, as they operate within each of the elements, come to be isolated from other forms of objectivity and cognition. This isolation often produces impressive results: it allows the development of particular kinds of concentrated statement of the universal, in the form of scientific laws for example, but only by ignoring the data available from other forms of understanding.[5] The universal statement achieved is implicitly, if not explicitly, reductionist – the narrowness of its purview built into its premises. Hence the loss of a unified world-historical account is ultimately responsible for the various kinds of reductionism which characterize varieties of modern understanding. On the other hand, the conception of the human subject has suffered a corresponding fate: isolation (severance from its intrinsic relation to others), the need to concentrate universal meaning in the subject precisely when that subject is rendered indescribable, vain attempts by which human beings attempt to maintain and expand their meaningfulness through competition with others, etc. –

---

[4] 'There is one thing that one can find [in his music] – through all the dynamics, expressive power, colour and variation, right down to the extremely controlled and clear writing in the scores even until the month of his death – and that is a mysterious order ... the ordering of tones and sounds shows a "sense of form" which Ferruccio Busoni had already called "almost superhuman"' [*ibid.*, p. 18].

[5] Even then, as Stephen Hawking has said, 'It turns out to be very difficult to devise a theory to describe the universe all in one go. Instead, we break the problem up into bits and invent a number of partial theories ... Today scientists describe the universe in terms of two partial theories – the general theory of relativity and quantum mechanics.' [*A Brief History of Time*, London: Bantam Press, 1988, p. 11.] Nonetheless, science has moved from the hydra-headed phenomenon it was in the nineteenth century to a study increasingly unified by reference to a few powerful laws. The same cannot be said of social and cultural universalizing, from which most of the disturbances in the world today are generated.

all in effect an expansion of self-importance to compensate for the 'depletion' of the human subject.[6]

Those forms of world-historical account which persist in being synoptic – like religious understanding – suffer at the hands of such pinhole-universalizing. If they attempt to employ such 'universalizings', they find themselves compromised by doing so, swept into another kind of account which reduces them to its terms. If they do not, however, they are deprived of significant forms of understanding and lose the possibility of employing the 'fine-grained' theories and data which such forms of understanding bring. Most serious of all, they become detached from the world and human life when seen in such ways, and appear progressively remote from ordinary experience – which is probably the reason religious views have lost their adherents, especially amongst the young. In the face of such 'dysfunctionality', it is attractive to continue with their own trajectory, and use conceptions garnered only from that (which is why theology typically relies so heavily on the history of its tradition). Insofar as they do, they tend thereby to lose the 'raw material' available from other disciplines, and simply reinforce their own isolation. If instead they attempt within their own trajectory to advance to new understanding, their conceptual resources are limited – at least until the conceptions developed in other disciplines pass into common parlance and can be drawn upon without engaging with their source.

Granted the loss of the universal world-historical account provided by the Bible, we cannot rest content with the present fragmentation into 'pinhole universals'. The way forward is to attempt to reconstruct an account of the connection of theology with cosmology, history, meaning and practice while retaining the distinctiveness of theological and scientific convictions.[7] Before more adequate accounts can be undertaken, however, some attention must be given to the distinctive features which will need to be incorporated into them. That requires an attempt to grasp significant characteristics of current conceptions of cosmology – and also ways in which theological concepts can be redeveloped for effective interaction with cosmological discussions. It is to that attempt which the present paper is directed.

---

[6] See Donald E. Capps, *The Depleted Self*, Minneapolis: Fortress Press, 1993.

[7] This is frequently overlooked. The preoccupation of many participants in the discussion between science and theology is to develop a 'middle ground' or mediating philosophy by which each is interpreted to the other. Ian Barbour's *Religion in An Age of Science* [San Francisco: Harper & Row, 1990] is a sophisticated example of this, in which epistemological similarities between them are found, and both are interpreted through process philosophy.

THEOLOGICAL COSMOLOGY AS A COMMON AND EMERGENT TASK

In order to proceed with such a task, it needs to be recognized not only that we have the possibility of redeveloping a healthy relationship between theology, cosmology and the world-history upon whose basis human life can have meaning, but also that implicitly we are already actually engaged in achieving such a relationship. But are there any grounds for supposing that such a recovery is possible, never mind an actuality?

A major impediment in even posing such a possibility is that modern life and understanding are split into factions – whether in theology, cosmology, world-history or human life – and there is profound disagreement about whether and how there may be harmony between them. The main cause of friction has to do with a basic modern dilemma which cuts across ontology and epistemology, whether there is any way by which to establish what is present and knowable as having existence and value. Are we committed to a search which is so apprehensive about previous practices (as having authorized misuses of power) as to leave us in an endless analytic probing which leaves reality a 'fabric of traces'?[8] And is there any alternative apart from appealing to self-evidencing axioms?

The two extreme options can be stated as follows: On the one hand, there are some who claim that every claim to identity and value must be vanquished: they represent a profound opposition to any and all means of establishing centres of being and significance, and therefore to all attempts to ascertain metaphysical and axiological foundations.[9] They are opposed, on the other hand, by those who appeal to 'foundations' which provide metaphysical and axiological 'resting points'. Cognitive foundationalism – seen in religious fundamentalism in its many varieties and very widely elsewhere – is a good example of this, espousing secure (that is certain, self-evident, or self-evidencing) foundational truths –

---

[8] See Alexander J. Argyros, *A Blessed Rage for Order: Deconstruction, Evolution and Chaos*, Ann Arbor: University of Michigan Press, 1991, p. 4.

[9] 'Deconstruction makes common cause with much contemporary philosophical and critical thought in seeking to undermine both the identity of objects and the identity of the self.' Alexander J. Argyros, *op. cit.*, p. 157. 'From the perspective of deconstruction, there is nothing upon which we can ground an argument for evolutionary biology as opposed to fundamentalist creationism, since both are discourses, with their blindnesses and their insights, and neither one can be said to be more or less accurate than the other, there being no pathway open from the text to the world.' Robert Scholes, *Textual Power*, New Haven: Yale University Press, 1985, p. 99.

'master truths' with a content rich enough to enable a '*linear*, deductive exfoliation' of other truths dependent on them by which the world can be explained and its meaning or value ascertained.[10]

There is a further option available, that the two – underdefinition and overdefinition – are 'moments' in the process of achieving fuller understanding – aspects of a common search in which we are engaged: a common pursuit which itself exemplifies a dynamic, evolving, communicative order through which the theological and cosmological basis for world-history, and the direction of life, can be affirmed. It can even be said that we are already engaged in such an order, even where it has collapsed. And if this dynamic order can be acknowledged and understood, we may be able to participate in it more knowingly and responsibly.[11]

That is not to say that we should expect to find some standard recipe – a master formula – for all forms of understanding and life, since the character of the dynamic order will appear differently according to whether we are considering theology, cosmology, history or any of the many dimensions of life. Mozart's expectations for the order of life were found primarily *in* his music.[12] And we should expect that the dynamic order which we seek will be found *in* the theory, action and expression developed from it within *each* domain of understanding and life – however imperfectly it may be shown there. Except notionally, it will not be separable from theory, action or expression, as if it were somehow antecedent to them. Such dynamic order as is found in life is found *in* particular ways of theoretizing life, or patterns of consistent action or self-expression, and what can emerge from them. To the extent that we can find and participate in this dynamic order, we can find ways of reaching beyond both limiting positivities and endless, inconclusive analyses (relativism).

---

[10] Nicholas Rescher, *Cognitive Systematization*, Oxford: Basil Blackwell, 1979, pp. 39–55, 66–77.

[11] A partial counterpart is seen in Nicholas Rescher's suggestion that rationality is a 'dialectically cyclic' process. We repeatedly re-examine one selfsame issue from different, and mutually inconsistent, points of view ... We proceed in circles or cycles, returning repeatedly to a certain issue, viewing it now in this light and now in that ... yielding a sequential deepening of the case.' [*Rationality*, Oxford: The Clarendon Press, 1988, pp. 83f.] But the order which we are considering is more dynamic, social, historical and theological.

[12] A parallel point is made by Bernard Lonergan in relation to the study of Ante-Nicene cultures: 'Concretely, values are perceived only in the good of order itself, the good of order is perceived only in the particular goods that it ensures, and the only actual particular goods are those that men, by the operations that they have in fact carried out, have learnt how to produce or to acquire.' [*The Way to Nicea*, London: Darton, Longman & Todd, 1976, pp. 108f.]

THE PLACE OF COMPLEXITY IN MODERN COSMOLOGY

We are now at the edge of large considerations about cosmology as understood today, and these have to with such wide-ranging issues as the nature of being and change, elemental forms and their arrangement, diversity and relations, and life – not to mention their relation to, and their correlatives in, God. It is important to begin by noticing the fundamental shift which has occurred in modern cosmology:

> The age of absolutes, if it ever really existed, is now definitely and permanently passé. Einstein's work buried once and for all the concepts of absolute space and time, while Heisenberg shot down the belief in absolutely precise measurement. Gödel, of course, stamped paid to the quaint and curious ideas of absolute proof and truth. Even more recently, we find sociobiologists trying valiantly (and with some measure of success) to terminate with extreme prejudice the incomprehensible notion of absolute free will. Moreover, chaos theorists have been making a tidy living of late telling us that even if we did know the mechanism, we still wouldn't know the phenomena. Taken as a whole, modern science has redrawn the map of human knowledge so that it now shows potholes and detours not only along every side street and back alley, but on all the major highways and byways as well.[13]

If anything, this statement is too mild, for what it calls 'potholes' are – like some I have encountered on roads in southern Kenya – larger than the roads themselves, and so hazardous that they threaten to stop the inquirer in his tracks, if not to devour all possibility of further progress.

In addressing this redrawn map of human knowledge, two issues in particular must occupy our attention, the nature of complexity and the phasing of change. 'Complexity' in this case does not mean a multiplicity of individual entities, a 'many' of 'ones', and still less an abstractive unitive concept which might act as a surrogate for an unattainable 'one'. Nor is it to be equated with chaos or complete randomness, as if it were entirely lacking in order.[14] Complexity presumes structure and organization, though of widely varying kinds and degrees; it involves the relation of parts, and therefore the organization of multiplicity, and in this

[13] John L. Casti, *Searching for Certainty*, New York: William Morrow & Co., 1990, pp. 404f.
[14] In a universe such as ours, it is virtually inconceivable that there can be a complete randomness, even if there might be occasions of greatly reduced order.

respect it differs from randomness and chaos. But the sort of organization varies with what is organized – whether matter, life-forms, societies, evolution, ecosystems, or the economy of God's work in the world.[15]

The recognition of this variation in organization distinguishes current discussions of complexity from earlier ones which confined complexity to particular notions of the working of the universe. Examples of this strategy occur throughout the history of western thought: those which favoured the state of rest, the clockwork universe of mechanistic systems and even those which favoured evolutionary forms of organization. The preeminent concept which figured significantly in most of the others was that of linear relations, which sought to explain the order of nature in terms of a cause-and-effect scheme which could be applied throughout the cosmos; its most sophisticated form is the differential equation.[16] Classical physics operated with the supposition that the universe can fully be explained in linear terms, and that instances of complexity would eventually yield to that kind of explanation.

Even if such explanation is frequently appropriate,[17] it is now recognized that most of the natural world is more complex, nonlinear and not so readily predictable. More frequently, many components interact in diverse ways to produce unpredictable outcomes. The oft-cited example is the so-called butterfly effect: on one occasion, a butterfly flaps its wings in one part of the world and begins a sequence of events which culminates in a storm in another part of the world, while on another occasion nothing of the sort happens. Hence, alongside the continuing concern for linear explanation, there is new interest in nonlinear dynamic systems.

---

[15] That is the reason why the recovery of relational thinking in theology, which has been so much stressed in modern times, is only a first step in the development of adequate conceptualities for theology. What is required is more attention not only to the fact that relations are intrinsic (or internal) to their terms but also to their variety and dynamics – how they operate in differing situations. Without this, when used either for God and for God's relation to the universe, relational thinking will remain an abstract idea.

[16] 'An equation is linear if the sum of two solutions is again a solution. The motion of shallow waves on a liquid surface is very closely described by the wave equation, which – like most classical equations – is linear. The solution for a two-stone disturbance [when two stones are thrown into a pond] is just the sum of solutions for a one-stone disturbance, centred at appropriate points.' [Ian Stewart, *Does God Play Dice? The Mathematics of Chaos*, Oxford: Basil Blackwell, 1989, pp. 81f.] The clear implication is that the whole is exactly equal to the sum of the parts, each of which (or the sum of them) can be explained – and its behaviour predicted – by using a monodimensional explanation. Other factors, variations in both initial and subsequent conditions, are excluded.

[17] It is not to be forgotten that many of the most sophisticated of human activities, from the launching of spacecraft to surgery to common prayer, rest on repetition and predictability. And, as information theorists suggest, even musical satisfaction often rests on the incorporation of what is unusual in a repeating pattern. Cf. Monroe C. Beardsley, 'Order and Disorder in Art', in Paul G. Kuntz, ed., *The Concept of Order*, Seattle: University of Washington Press, 1968, pp. 191–218.

NONLINEAR DYNAMICS AND CHANGE

Two chief differences mark nonlinear dynamics. One is the attention given to small inputs which can alter what happens subsequently – factors omitted from linear dynamics because of the complications which they introduce. The other is sensitivity to 'initial conditions', which had to be clearly detailed if classic dynamics were to be applicable; in Newton's dynamics, they could be arbitrarily specified as if they were simply the beginning of a linear equation. For nonlinear dynamics, they are not so clearly specifiable: 'the initial conditions must be the outcome of the dynamic evolution itself.'[18] The implications are that neither in its initial conditions nor in the importance of subsequent inputs is dynamic process independent of antecedent and surrounding conditions, but is the result of, and alongside, many other factors. It also contributes to them: 'nonlinearity means that the act of playing the game has a way of changing the rules.'[19]

Bearing these things in mind, we must now turn to the question of how the dynamic evolution which features so prominently in these matters operates, the issue of what (somewhat crudely) we called phased change. With the advent of Einstein's principle of relativity (all motion in the universe is relative to the motion of something else), fixed frames of reference such as absolute space and time were no longer; the space and time of each individual depends on where he is and how he is moving relative to the position and motion of others. One's relationality becomes dynamic, and is seen as dynamically related to others whose relationality is similarly dynamic. As the consequences of this new understanding became clear, the 'old idea of an essentially unchanging universe that could have existed, and could continue to exist, forever was replaced by the notion of a dynamic, expanding universe that seemed to have begun a finite time ago, and that might end at a finite time in the future.'[20] With relativity theory, it was proved – from the way in which a star which collapses under its own gravity is trapped in a region whose surface eventually shrinks to zero size (volume, density and space-time curvature) – that correspondingly there must have been a starting singularity – a 'big bang'.

Not only Einstein's relativity but the cosmological results are important: they enable us to see the dynamic relationality of all that exists, and

---

[18] Ilya Prigogine and Isabelle Stengers, *Order Out of Chaos: Man's New Dialogue with Nature*, Boulder: Shambhala Publications, 1984, p. 61. Cf. Newton's dynamics which moved from dealing with problems *'with very special initial conditions* ... to being able to handle problems with arbitrary initial conditions'. [Julian Barbour, *Absolute or Relative Motion*, Cambridge: Cambridge University Press, 1989, p. 535.]

[19] James Gleick, *Chaos: Making a New Science*, New York: Viking Penguin, 1987, p. 24.

[20] Stephen Hawking, *A Brief History of Time*, London: Bantam Press, 1988, pp. 33f.

also to understand the general 'shape' of the movement of the universe, from the beginning of space-time to its end, from maximum density to continuing dispersion to density (although the outcome is a matter of question); and other theories – the second law of thermodynamics – tell us of the progressively increasing disorder (unusable energy) in the universe. While they tell us of the dynamic relationality which is intrinsic to all that is, these theories will not tell us how the universe has come to be shaped as it is, at the beginning or now. The secret of that, it seems, is a complex series of transformations, what can be called phasings and accumulations.

THE SHAPING OF THE UNIVERSE

From the compression of matter and energy found in the originating singularity, the whole universe has erupted in an expansion of that original reality. Recalling jazz in a 'sleazy backroom in New Orleans', Micheal O'Siadhail expresses it remarkably:[21]

> 'All right?' booms the saxophone man,
> 'everybody feeling chameleon?' The combo
> expands the tune of a well-battered song.
> An opulence of sound, clash and flow
> as a spotlight tunnels dust in its beam,
> glints the trumpet's bell and the hall
> turns hot and hybrid, beery listeners
> swaying and bobbing the mood of a theme.
>
> From rainbows of timbre a strand of colour
> floats into the air: the trumpet solo
> burping one phrase of a melody, ripe
> and brassy and buttoned down as though
> a song is breathing over its origins,
> those four hot-blooded notes weeping
> their pleasure again on an old civil war
> bugle. A sleazy backroom in New Orleans.
>
> Sax and rhythm. The brightness of a reed,
> winding tube and crook are working on
> another hue of the tune that moves

---

[21] Micheal O'Siadhail, 'Cosmos' in *Hail! Madam Jazz*, Newcastle: Bloodaxe Books, 1992.

into its own discourse: Bud Freeman,
Johnny Hodges, Charlie Parker. 'All right?'
he drawls, then scats a little as we clap
a tradition of subversions. But he's off again.
I watch as swarms of dust in the spotlight,

swirls of galaxies, and imagine he's blowing
a huge balloon of space that's opening
our world of order. In a waft of creation
his being becomes a music's happening.
A red-shirted pianist now leans to seize
a gene of the song which seems to veer
and improvise, somehow catching a moment's
shifts and humours. Hail! Madam Jazz.

Let the theme return, its mutants echoing
as a tune balances against its freedom.
One key – so open-toned and open-stitched.
A beat poised, a crossgrained rhythm,
interplays, imbrications of voice over voice,
mutinies of living are rocking the steady
state of a theme; these rifts and overlappings,
a love of deviance, our genesis in noise.

From 'an opulence of sound, clash and flow', 'a solo burping one
phrase of a melody', 'four hot-blooded notes weeping their pleasure
again' as 'a song breathes over its origins', 'winding tube and crook are
working on / another hue of the tune that moves into its own discourse',
'I watch ... and imagine he's blowing / a huge balloon of space that's
opening / our world of order. In a waft of creation / his being becomes a
music's happening.' 'Let the theme return, its mutants echoing / as a tune
balances against its own freedom ... mutinies of living are rocking the
steady / state of a theme.' That is an extraordinary portrayal of the
coming of the universe as we now understand it – a primordial billowing
of the universe into being whereby space and time themselves were constituted by movement, and mass and energy were together distributed
expandingly. The original 'billowing' formed a delicately balanced
matrix of conditions – not too fast or too slow, with elements neither
collapsed into each other nor too widely distributed to exert a significant
influence upon each other – by which the universe became what it is and

will be. The recognition of this 'self-shaping' by the universe – whereby it is internally coded to follow its own directions – is extremely important for modern understanding.

The 'coding' of the universe seems to have been achieved by dynamic means ('an opulence of sound, clash and flow'). Its self-shaping occurred through a series of transfigurations whereby energetic stabilities happen in such ways as to enable further expansion and stabilization. There was, for example, such a transformation when the original 'billowing', with its symmetrical and energetic interaction of elements, became more structured in the gravitational, electromagnetic and two nuclear interactions – 'those four hot-blooded notes', 'habits that the universe adopted for its primary actions'. And this structure of interactions, itself as delicately balanced as the original matrix of conditions, formed the constraints within which the integrity of the universe and all its future coherence has operated thereafter. In that sense, it is a *time-neutral* order of nature – the laws of physics – which defines what is possible.

In addition, there are varieties of *time-bound* order which – as initial conditions – define what is actual. They have arisen from further transformations of the universe, those which shaped the galaxies and their elements, and those by which were formed the sun, the earth, living forms and human beings, human societies and civilizations. Since these transformations occur differently, it is dangerous to suppose that they are themselves all of one kind, but in some respects there are continuities amongst them. One is their occurrence when the universe is in 'non-equilibrium conditions',[22] those where deterministic processes give way to stochastic (probabilistic) ones, an indication of their time-ladenness. Another is instability of motion which influences the structure and qualities of that which emerges.[23] Such characteristics can signal new forms of self-organization even within a universe which is self-shaped in the ways already mentioned.

What emerges from such a transformation is something with a 'determined intensity', rich enough in dynamic order and robust enough to concentrate the matter and energy of the universe in its own internal and external relations, and to sustain itself. In biology, 'the morphogenetic process of a particular species is intrinsically robust, [in] that it constitutes an attractor in the dynamical system whose alternative stable pathways or trajectories define different life-cycles.'[24] The perpetuation of the species cannot be satisfactorily explained by inventing a 'vital agency'

---

[22] Ilya Prigogine and Isabelle Stengers, *op. cit.*, p. 231.
[23] 'For instance, it is now realized that the transport phenomena going on in the host fluid phase during the growth of crystals and the solidification of alloys have a deep influence on the structure and the qualities of the solid phase.' Grégoire Nicolis and Ilya Prigogine, *Exploring Complexity*, New York: W. H. Freeman, 1989, p. 219.
[24] Brian Goodwin, 'A Science of Qualities', unpublished paper, p. 25.

– the action of a 'replicator' such as the 'selfish gene' which consolidates its position as a dominant species by eliminating others – because that naturally occurs in a context (the spherical cell) which is distributed through the whole structure of an organism in space and time.

Organisms are structures: self-regulating, transforming wholes generated by the distributed causal agency immanent in developmental fields that include genes and relevant aspects of the environment as part of its dynamic order. Each species is a distinct expression of this living order, a natural kind that reveals particular qualities of colour, morphology and behaviour as well as specific quantities of various substances. Organisms are intentional agents, engaged in expressing their natures, which are intrinsically holistic and dynamic.[25]

At the risk of generalizing again, we can say that such transformations continue in the history of human life in many ways. *Human beings* are themselves dynamic, self-regulating, transforming wholes which incorporate relevant elements of their environment (natural and human) but are also continuingly related to it as they form and transform themselves – a formation and transformation which is their history. As such, they are heavily dependent on the 'initial conditions' of nature and sociality: human beings cannot be (or become) what they are (or will be) without regularized interaction with their natural and social environment.[26] But they fulfill these 'conditions' by regular and ongoing change: they achieve their order and regularity through transformation. Recalling Einstein's insight into relativity, the relationalities by which their life is sustained are dynamic, with those of each human being and society dynamically related to those of others whose relationality is similarly dynamic. In that sense, human beings are deeply interdependent – far more profoundly so than is usually realized. The vibrancy of their lives derives from this form of dynamic spatio-temporality, in which they are distributed and diverse but deeply interactive and interdependent.

Nature and the *social* are also forms of dynamic spatio-temporality in their own right, and as such they are both distinct – the world as we live in it is shaped by their processes. The 'environment' and 'society' are always both antecedent to, but also shaped by those who participate in

[25] Brian Goodwin, *ibid.*, p. 25.
[26] Cf. D. W. Hardy, 'Created and Redeemed Sociality' in D. W. Hardy and C. E. Gunton, eds., *On Being the Church*, Edinburgh: T. & T. Clark, 1989.

them.[27] That is, they are self-regularized but also continuingly self-transformative according to their own processes.

But the natural and the social are also interactive and interdependent, and increasingly so. Society has steadily become more important as it has constituted itself by demographic, political, economic and cultural means.[28] Insofar as its dynamic self-constitution has become more effective, it has developed the power to organize its interactions with the material realm more securely, and this has brought with it an apparent lessening of the importance of materiality, and the world comes to be seen as manageable. (The results are by no means necessarily beneficial; and almost without exception, the consequences for the environment are dire.) But this is by no means universal, and those societies which lack an effective dynamic social organization continue to struggle for the material conditions of life.

As a result, there is now a profound uncertainty about what processes for the interaction of society and environment are rich and robust enough to serve as 'attractors' for the interaction of global society with the natural world in a dynamic interdependency, which will enable human beings to organize themselves into social wholes which have a dynamic of history which is suitable also for the natural world.[29] What are fruitful processes of transformation for societies interacting with the world in which they live? That is the major question facing humanity in the world today.

[27] 'A society is not a thing but a process. Any society – from the society of a family to the society of the whole human race – is a process of continuous self-creating ... Our interaction with a society is mutual in the sense that we form the society as it forms us.' But thus far, the shaping of society has been limited by the inability of society to know itself as a society: 'From the vantage-point of the end of the twentieth century, it is possible to perceive the activity of international society in the last five centuries, especially its activity in the twentieth century, as the pre-natal ordering of a society which has yet to be born into the world of its own consciousness, as the unselfconscious self-socializing of a society which did not yet know itself as a society. It is possible to say, with the benefit of hindsight and hypothesis, that international society has been ordering itself in spite of itself ... International society has been readying itself for a metamorphosis, for the sloughing of its self-unknowing. If so, it is also possible to suppose that international society, as it comes to conceive of itself as society, may at last find itself able to choose order as a social purpose.' [Philip Allott, *Eunomia: New Order for a New World*, Oxford: Oxford University Press, 1990, pp. 39, 263.]

[28] 'Cultural' here designates structures of meaning expressed in language and music, the sciences, the arts and their combinations.

[29] A democratic system of government, for example, confirms itself each time new representatives or leaders are elected. But under conditions where the equilibrium of the political process is seriously disturbed, a new form of government may be generated. Likewise, human beings both confirm the world in which they find themselves and also significantly reconstitute it, by transforming it into a technological-cultural product called 'the environment'. Where they seriously damage its equilibrium, its 'initial conditions' and subsequent dynamics are altered, and its self-transformation may proceed differently.

COSMOLOGY AS CONTEXT FOR THEOLOGY

Cosmology as thus seen must be the context for our understanding of theology today, not only surrounding it (the conventional meaning of context) but interwoven with it (the etymological meaning of context) – as much so as ancient Hebrew and Greek concepts have been. We should expect such cosmological understanding to open up possibilities for the understanding of God and his purposes which will enable them again to become transhistorical and transdisciplinary, and thereby allow them again to enrich the basis for life in the world now and in the future.[30] The *substance* of science should interact with the *substance* of theology.

How is it that theology can be made intelligible in the context of the cosmological process which we have been considering? And how can God be the agent of this process? Even if there are intrinsic limitations in the knowledge and awareness of those who are within the process, it is as likely to be possible to develop a theology for this cosmology as it is to develop the cosmology itself.[31]

It is important again to recall that the location for theology will be in cosmology itself, just as we saw that Mozart's expectations for the order of life were found in his music. One very important beginning is in the

---

[30] Interestingly enough, the genesis of the theological cosmology which has been most influential in theology, though decreasingly in science, was in the movement to transhistorical and transnational conceptions. It was clear enough to the writers of the New Testament that they had participated in the transfiguration of the history of human life in Jesus of Nazareth, but – as they were dispersed – they needed to find ways to affirm the continuing dynamic stability by which they were bonded together. If this was to be rich and robust enough for their new circumstances and audience, it required a more expansive statement of the transhistorical and transnational significance of the transfiguration which they had known. As it happened, however, the means available for doing so (the concepts and terminology of Greek thought) were centred on the logic of God's being in relation to the world, and on the relation of the unitive and stable resting-point of all to the diverse and changing world. The result was that the original terms of the discussion – a dynamic transfigurative event in which the economy of God's work in the world was reconstituted – were altered to the more static consideration of how the world arose from and returned to the perfection of divine rest. That alteration – with which to a very large extent Christianity has concurred ever since – is what has to be reconsidered if there is to be an interaction between the substance of Christian faith and modern cosmology.

[31] The limitations are those which spring from the nature of the reality with which we are dealing. As we have seen, reality as we live in it is complex and varied, dynamically relational, and emergent in its shape. If so, and if the 'nature' of reality is that it is spatio-temporally distributed and dynamic, it follows that it can only be known accordingly, that is distributively and through dynamic emergence – by many who agree it through time, and progress together toward its full realization. That is not to say that there may not be approximations available to those with vision, inasmuch as they can communicate it to others. In other words, the knowledge which should be expected is not 'simple' knowledge, but has – to borrow from the 'marks' of the Church – a unitive, sanctifying, universalizing and apostolic character.

event by which the universe was formed: 'all the energy that would ever exist in the entire course of time erupted as a single quantum – a singular gift – existence.'[32] It is astonishing to realize that there could have been such a burst of energy, but just as astounding to think that implicit in this outpouring were the conditions by which the resultant universe (a) was uniform and homogeneous in all directions, but with local irregularities, and (b) expanded at the critical rate which allowed it to maintain its inner relations without recollapsing.

Such features make it possible to conceive of an active abundance which surpasses such a singularity, so much so as to have been its origination and the source of its main features. Indeed, the logic of making such a claim drives one to assert that the basis of the singularity is in an unsurpassably active abundance:

The basis of Christian existence is not just a basis. It is also an environment of abundance created through this overflow of life, and giving reason for praise in all situations. If this is basic reality then all of existence can be thought through in the light of it … The beginning is with a basic reality which is good, attractive and generous.[33]

If so, however, this abundance has its own intrinsic character or energetic homogeneity by which it is self-maintaining – an implicit ordered dynamic by which it is itself. Of such a kind is the identity of God.

The identity of God as such, often called the 'immanent Trinity', can be theoretized in two ways: as a time-neutral theory, or as a time-bound one. (1) If Planck's equation $E = hv$ (where E is the energy of a light wave, v is the frequency, and h is a constant) says that 'energy and frequency are the same thing measured in different units'[34], one can say that the Spirit constitutes the energy of God, the Son the frequency (order) and the Father the constant rate of exchange between the two. As with Planck's equation, this only produces the 'right answers to certain questions'. (2) A time-bound theory, referring to God's own time, would run as follows: God's unity is complex and dynamic, and rests on his own energy to structure and restructure himself in self sustaining cohesion through what can be called 'energy events'. Hence, God is an energetic (Spirit-driven) unity which is yet true to its own initial conditions (Father) and ordered in its interactions (the Son). In their logical

[32] Brian Swimme and Thomas Berry, *The Universe Story*, San Francisco: Harper, 1992, p. 17.
[33] D. W. Hardy and D. F. Ford, *Jubilate: Theology in Praise*, London: Darton, Longman & Todd, 1984, p. 73.
[34] Freeman Dyson, *Infinite in All Directions*, New York: Harper & Row, 1988, p. 21f.

structure, both theories are more similar to traditional ones than they seem. While unlike traditional theories they give preeminent place to dynamic order in abundance, the one is logically similar to the Nicene formula and the other to a modern one.[35]

But such theories of the identity of God are not sufficient to account for the agency of God in bringing about the kind of universe in which we live. For that, we need to ask how this abundant dynamic order might generate a universe-originating singularity. A possible answer is found in 1 Corinthians 2.9–10:

> 'What no eye has seen, nor ear heard, nor the human heart conceived, what God has prepared for those who love him' – these things God revealed to us through the Spirit. For the Spirit searches everything, even the depths of God. For what person knows a man's thoughts except the spirit of the man which is in him? So also no one comprehends the thoughts of God except the Spirit of God. Now we have received not the spirit of the world, but the Spirit which is from God, that we might understand the gifts bestowed on us by God.

Beginning from the single quantum, the universe-originating singularity as gift, we can trace this to the basis of the gift in the 'searching' of God by the Spirit, one which draws out the implicit order – often called the Word – which is antecedently present in God. This is a 'stirring' which stirs God to be fully God by being *actively for* that which is beyond himself in a congruence which we identify as we speak of Christ. Both 'stirring' and 'congruence' become manifest in the giving of a singularity distinct from him, one marked by its own abundance, energy and order which are yet congruent with God's.

The relation between God and this singularity which is his gift is not ended with a once-for-all giving. Why? Neither the dynamic order of the singularity nor that of its dispersed 'parts' is fully self-evident, whether in the time-neutral laws of physics or in the time-bound forms of order which define the actual locally active regularities into which the singularity is dispersed. Even if it is not possible fully to establish their dynamic order, developing a fuller understanding of it rests on what has been called 'the help of extra information'; and this can be shown to require reference to the simplest hypothesis, which is the fullest possible source and range of extra information.[36] That is what is involved in continuing to refer both the universe-originating singularity and also its dispersion

---

[35] See Eberhard Jüngel's formulation of Trinitarian doctrine as 'repetition' in *The Doctrine of the Trinity: God's Being is Becoming*, Edinburgh: Scottish Academic Press, 1976.
[36] Elliott Sober in *Simplicity* [Oxford: Clarendon Press, 1975] suggests 'that the simplicity of a hypothesis can be measured by attending to how well it answers certain kinds of questions ... that the more informative a hypothesis is in answering these questions, the simpler it is' (p. vii).

into locally active regularities, to the 'congruent giving' which arises in the searching of God by the Spirit.[37]

The means by which such giving is actively manifest in them accords with the makeup of each. This is because the availability of God's dynamic order in the world is not through simple (one-to-one) conformation of one fixed state of affairs to another ('world' to 'God') but through a 'giving' – a dynamic interaction. Such dynamic order as marks them is, therefore, 'natural' to the world, but also 'natural' to God; it 'fits' both gift and giver.

The searching of God whereby this giving occurs, and the congruence which it finds implicit in the Father, continues in the dispersal of the originating singularity into locally active regularities through 'density fluctuations' (the distribution of matter in the universe as 'clumpy'). What we earlier called the transformations of the universe – those which shaped galaxies, sun, earth, life-forms, etc. – can be traced to this dynamic interaction of God with the universe, which triggers such changes and builds up the dynamic order appropriate to each. While they have one common feature – a 'determined intensity' which gives them a dynamic order which is robust enough to enable them to survive – they are not repetitions of some single order in God, but vary according to the self-structuring which occurs in local circumstances, giving it the characteristic pattern and dynamics by which it works. What occurs for each of these 'determined intensities' can be seen as a dynamic 'fidelity to its own being' which serves to structure its relations within and without.[38]

Apart from the dispersal of the abundant originating singularity into local dynamic regularities, is there a discernible pattern in this giving and congruence? Or – recalling the critic of Mozart who claimed that his music contained 'too many notes' – is it simply additive, resulting in greater and greater pluriformity? It clearly tends toward the richening of initial conditions, of the complexity of internal structure and of the range of possibilities open.[39] But each advance also incorporates previously

---

[37] 'Congruent giving' refers to what is called in the New Testament 'the Spirit of Christ'.

[38] Where it is normally thought that such self-structuring needs to be fixed in a 'closed organization' whose 'structure conditions the course of its interactions and restricts the structural changes that the interactions may trigger in it' [H. R. Maturana and F. J. Varela, *The Tree of Knowledge*, Boston: Shambhala, 1988, p. 95], it is more properly seen as a relative closure. Hence, rather than struggling to maintain closure, it may relax in being itself by relating fully to others. At the human level, it takes this form: 'It is part of the opening of one person to another that is the opposite of "hardening" one's heart, "stiffening" one's neck. It is the "letting go" of all one's objections and believing the word of another that one is really loved.' [Margaret A. Farley, *Personal Commitments*, San Francisco: Harper & Row, 1986, pp. 59f.]

[39] This is clear from the configuration of our galaxy. On some planets, chemical creativity never advanced beyond simple compounds, while on earth, its own internal dynamics and its position in the solar system permitted chemical creativity far longer, producing the first living cell.

established stabilities which require the maintenance of homogeneity in the universe and the sustaining of spatio-temporal relationships and structured interactions even as dispersion occurs. And in each case, these are developed in new and abundant possibilities for ordered and dynamic interchange.[40]

What kind of giving underlies this? It can be said that the basic character of the giving of God is seen in the shaping of the universe-originating singularity, and that this is presumed in all that follows it. But fuller understanding of the quality of the giving of God must be derived from the giving which is manifest in the history of the cosmos.[41] There we find expanded forms of giving, those more clearly aligned with historical views of God.[42] They are forms of giving which are implicit in the dynamic orderings of more advanced life-forms, those for example which are maximally informative for the 'determined intensities' which make up human life in all its varied aspects – demographic, social, personal, cultural. Such are the 'blessings' which expand and order the possibilities of life, those which further intensify ordered life in the world. These blessings expand the possibilities, implicit in all the universe, for spatio-temporal diversity and dynamic unity.

They are rooted, so far as God is concerned, in the continued 'searching' of the Spirit to further develop the congruence of the world and humanity with God's abundance, and thereby to fulfil God's bond in Christ with the unfolding of the cosmos. But, so far as the cosmos and humankind are concerned, while they are rendered possible by the constitution and dynamic ordering of the cosmos, their fulfilment rests in their direct participation in the activity of their giver, not only in an ever-greater appreciation of the abundance of the gifts which are given but in ever-greater responsibility for the development of the cosmos which is given. What is unique in the dynamic order of human beings and societies is that they are suited to this direct participation.

---

[40] As a new situation limits or confines itself to the characteristics of previous conditions, it loses its special character. This is the broader principle at stake where human beings confine themselves to 'the flesh', or human societies to 'nature red in tooth and claw'.

[41] In other words, the origin of the universe provides only a limited ontological basis for cognition of its divine source, while both ontological basis and possibilities for cognition expand as we follow the dispersion of the universe.

[42] 'It seems to me that if the word "God" is to be of any use, it should be taken to mean an interested God, a creator and lawgiver who has established not only the laws of nature and the universe but also standards of good and evil, some personality that is concerned with our actions, something in short that it is appropriate for us to worship. This is the God that has mattered to men and women throughout history. Scientists and others sometimes use the word "God" to mean something so abstract and unengaged that He is hardly to be distinguished from the laws of nature ... but it seems to me that it makes the concept of God not so much wrong as unimportant.' Stephen Weinberg, *Dreams of A Final Theory*, New York: Pantheon Books, 1992, pp. 244f.

By these means – by participating in the activity of the Trinitarian God in the unfolding 'economy' of the cosmos – human beings also share in the life of the giver of the cosmos. Doing so allows them to learn – and relearn – the meaning of life and to follow its direction.

9

Creation and Eschatology

INTRODUCTION

To address creation without considering eschatology risks serious distortion to both topics, and restricts the scope of fundamental theological discussion at a time when it badly needs to be opened up. One of the attractions of doing so, however, is to simplify the vast questions with which they deal. As we approach them, we need to remind ourselves how impossible it is to say even a fraction of what needs to be said about creation and eschatology today. I shall be limited to an attempt to sketch some major features about them.

What I propose to do is to explore ways in which to think about creation and eschatology *together*, and in doing so to question the interconnections between the two topics – to see how they intersect in important ways. We shall need to avoid conflating them, for that would lead eventually to a denial of the otherness of the two from each other and from God which conflicts with God's purpose for them. Along the way, we will employ very varied modes of access to the subjects – nature (where we must take the sciences seriously), history (where we must consider the nature of covenants very carefully), and relationship with God (where we must consider the dynamics of worship) – and some vigorous mental stretching! In all three cases, we will need to open up these modes of access somewhat, since as they stand they are more like intuitions of the reason, what Coleridge called the 'organ of the supersensuous', through which the understanding is to be ordered.

It is curious to mark how certainly – I may say instinctively – the reason has always pointed out to men the ultimate end of the various sciences, and how immediately afterwards they have set to work to realize that end.[1]

By way of preliminary comment, let me say that theology today does not bristle with confidence over the issues of creation and eschatology; and they are ripe for reconsideration. In that effort, it will be valuable to take them together – as different aspects of the same dynamic. When we do so, their full significance is more likely to be seen together than

[1] S. T. Coleridge, *Table Talk*, ed. Carl Woodring, Princeton: Princeton University Press, 1990, Vol. 1, p. 269.

separately. And their content is also best seen when they are interrelated. It is these issues, their mutual *significance* and *formation*, which we will have to explore.

It should be obvious that the *significance* of each is strongly related to that of the other, but somewhat asymmetrically. This is seen in the modern history of the issues: for the most part, at least among theologians, the consideration of creation has declined in modern times, and eschatology more so; and now there is better prospect of recovery from this decline for creation than for eschatology. (The same has been true for science, where there has been perennial concern for creation, but very little for eschatology.) And this asymmetrical decline and recovery is in no small part due to the *conceptualities* allowed in each. The onset of modern science – employing intensive methods more appropriate for uncovering special features of creation than contributing to broader issues – has frightened theologians into associating creation and eschatology too specifically with what seemed to be the inner core of theology, particularly the new covenant in Jesus Christ. While there have been interesting reconstructions of creation and eschatology within this perspective, without effective dialogical correlation with nature (as understood by the sciences) and the general history of the world and the human race, the method remains a narrow one.[2] In general, theologians have severely restricted their access to creation, and therefore to eschatology. We shall need to try to break through these difficulties.

WHAT ARE CREATION AND ESCHATOLOGY ABOUT?

First of all, what is *'creation'* about? Within the single term creation, two notions jostle each other. And in each of them there is some ambiguity.

On the one hand, creation may refer to the *universe* and that which begins and sustains it. Even here there is a difference of approach. The *universe may mean the totality of the universe* – in its total existence in space and time – of which the visible universe is just a tiny fraction. What we can *see* from the earth is 'relatively insignificant in comparison to the part which lies in our future'.[3] Or the universe can mean the *visible*

---

[2] The issue here is a very serious one: a 'monological' account of creation and eschatology, in which they are seen only from within the tradition of Christian faith, is inadequate without relating them dialogically to forms of understanding which arise without specific reference to the tradition.

[3] Frank Tipler, *The Physics of Immortality*, New York: Doubleday, 1994, p. x.

universe. The *visible universe* is that part which can be seen from earth, or known from its traces in the present composition of the planet and in each one of us. That is necessarily limited by what we can see – a sphere about 20 billion light-years across – and by what we can find of the forces which structure the universe, macroscopically and microscopically.

Depending upon the particular concerns and disciplines through which they are approached, one can focus on the *patterns or structure* of the world, those of its space-time, the plant and animal world, and those of humanity and human beings. In times past, these were seen in mutual correlation, as integrally related through the notion of creation; now, however, the most that is attempted is a unification of theories which is said to be capable of describing the universe in which we live, but only at a very fundamental level.

The visible universe is focused rather differently when we seek these patterns as the *field of relevant preconditions for life*, those which structure the life of a people – much as mythic accounts of creation did for early peoples. A feature common to these is that they provide an integrated account conducive to better understanding and well-being.

These are not simply descriptive in force. They are frequently also taken as *normative*, to designate *states or processes* which are constraints shaping or determining existence, its structure and dynamic, thereby manifesting *some normative authority*. What is the ontology of the universe, the world and human life? Is there purposiveness as such in them? Why is there something rather than nothing, or this state of affairs rather than that?

Here again there is difference of approach. Some – of a naturalistic bent – seek only for universal states or processes, what is ultimately the case with the universe – on the supposition that these are the only norms for the universe. Things are as they are, and it is sufficient – they say – to explain their order. But others find states or processes within the universe – its stability, motion and direction – which are normative in some other way than naturalistically. And these they consider to mediate a constitutive authority, which needs attention in its own terms.

Hence, summarizing these two, creation can refer to any factors taken as important to the determinative shape and purpose of the universe (total or visible), the world and human beings, and also to their mediation of an ultimate constitutive state or agency.

In some modern discussion, creation is not so much a matter of *straightforward* inquiry into a field (however extensive) and its constitutive reality, as one of *indirect* concern. It is seen as an issue co-present with others as their context or preconditions. Examples abound. The concern of ecology to sustain the proper balance of nature implies context and preconditions: what are the relations – whether static or dy-

namic – by which life in the world is rendered possible?[4] In phenomenological and theological accounts of humanity, creation is often treated
mainly, if not exclusively, as the precondition of freedom and redemption. In theology, if one is concerned directly with such primal features of
life as freedom or salvation, creation is found to be co-present with them
as the configuration of life in the world which makes freedom possible or
which provides the circumstance within which redemption can occur.
That is how Karl Barth, for example, can refer to creation as the 'external
basis of the covenant'.[5] We can also see another argument presented in
this way: if theology is primarily concerned with the Trinitarian God as
purposive, creation is the condition for the realization of the purposes of
this God, and receives its reality from the realization of these purposes.
Beginning from widely differing points, such examples show a common
strategy – *indirect inquiry* into creation, which limits consideration of
creation to those aspects which can be seen through some other primary
concern.

Now secondly, what is *eschatology* about? It is widely understood to
be the study of the last things, referring to the Greek term for 'last things'
(*eschata*). In that sense, the term is understood at two levels, cosmic and
personal, the end of the cosmos (invisible or visible), and the end of the
person, what to expect at the end (in the case of human beings death,
judgment, heaven and hell), and how God provides for these eventuali-
ties. In basic aspects, therefore, eschatology is similar to creation, the
discipline(s) concerned with the features of existence, since it attempts to
delineate the structure or order of the end, post-existence (if any) and the
normative authority by which these are constituted as what they will be.

Is such a topic, however broadly considered, capable of *straightforward* inquiry? It is at least notionally possible to consider eschatology as
the outcome of the preconditions for the universe, the world and humanity – separately or as combined in their ongoing history. Understood
in that way, eschatology is the outcome of the existence, structure and
dynamic of the universe and world as anticipated in their creation and
history. And just as the conditions of creation raise the question of why
they are as they are (something rather than nothing, this rather than
that), so the outcome of these conditions – in dynamic combination –
raises the question of what makes this outcome what it will be. This is the
question of what or who makes the eschaton what it will be – the
question of the constitutive agency of the end, whether nature, man or
God. Of course, we do not have messengers (at least, apart from the
resurrected Jesus) which have arrived from post-existence to tell us what

---

[4] Cf. John D. Barrow and Frank J. Tipler, *The Anthropic Cosmological Principle*, Oxford:
Clarendon Press, 1986.
[5] Karl Barth, *Church Dogmatics*, Edinburgh: T. & T. Clark, 1958, Vol. III, Part I.

occurs there. But our understanding – through the consideration of creation – of the conditions of existence at least gives us a format for conceiving what may or may not happen. That is a matter to which we shall need to devote more attention presently.

In earlier times, when the study of the world was more closely linked to its *moral* texture, and before the study of history alerted people so much to its complexities and contingencies, it was not only the physical conditions of the world and its life upon which eschatological understanding might be built. Fundamental moral patterns were seen as continuing also, and these too suggested the fundamental shape of the *eschata*. The characteristics of apocalyptic accounts are not as fanciful as it is now popular to suppose: they identify the moral issues taken into account in the final times, and show how they will be resolved.

But such views have largely been displaced in theology. In eschatology as in creation, theologians have leaned heavily instead on *indirect* inquiry. Like creation, eschatology can be taken as an issue co-present with most others as the horizon in which their ultimate outcome is specified. In that sense, it is seen as indirectly present in the very characteristics of life in the world, and in the very living of life: 'in life, we are in death'. As we saw, one way of understanding creation is as an issue co-present with most others, in which their preconditions are specified. Eschatology, understood in the same way, is co-present in the present configuration of the universe, the world or humanity, as the final outcome anticipated in their coming-to-be as they are, in their creation. Eschatology is that study in which their 'post-conditions' – their final outcome – are specified. And these are also indirectly present – co-present – at any point of their existence. Following a pattern of thinking typical of phenomenological thinking, Karl Rahner speaks of it:

Anamnesis and prognosis are among the necessary existentials of man ... If the presentness of man's being includes reference to the future, then the future, while remaining truly future, is not simply spoken of in advance. It is an inner moment of man and of his actual being as it is present to him now. And so knowledge of the future, just in so far as it is still to come, is an inner moment of the self-understanding of man in his present hour of existence – and indeed grows out of it.[6]

If we are not careful, however, such views make eschatology *adjectival* to the self-understanding of man in the present, to the understanding of redemption in Christ or to Trinitarian understanding. And in any case,

---

[6] Karl Rahner, 'The Hermeneutics of Eschatological Assertions', in *Theological Investigations*, Vol. 4, London: Darton, Longman & Todd, 1966, pp. 330–331.

too frequently such views take short-cuts, failing to consider the full set of pre-conditions and post-conditions for human existence.

ON THE RELEVANCE OF CURRENT SCIENCE

Where there are direct approaches to creation and eschatology (as distinct from indirect), modern science is relevant to the understanding of them. The widespread avoidance of direct engagement with creation and eschatology by theologians (as distinct from the indirect inquiries just mentioned) has created a vacuum which others – chiefly scientists – busily fill, whether through fragmented, specialized studies (whose significance can be somewhat overstated at times) or through comprehensive restatements of creation and eschatology. I shall mention one of these restatements as an illustration.

As mentioned previously, there are those who study the universe in its totality in time and space, and thereby draw very deep and general conclusions about the structure of space and time. One of these, Frank Tipler, has set out to study the future, because as he says it comprises almost all of space and time – the next 100 billion years or so – far more than the 20 billion years of its previous existence that we can see.[7] In doing so, he also seeks to rescue eschatology from the hands of theologians who 'with a few exceptions ... are quite ignorant of [it]'.[8] His procedure is openly reductionist, translating all other concepts (including biology) into the language of physics, regarding all forms of life as subject to the same laws as electrons and atoms, and incorporating theology into physics.

His reasoned conclusion is that the Omega Point (his correlate for God) created the physical universe (and Himself/Herself) in the sense that it emanated from God; that much, he says, is quite consistent with physics. Tipler supports the theological meanings of creation: (1) that the physical universe has a finite age, that time itself had a beginning; and (2) that the universe is not self-sustaining, and could collapse into nonexistence without the continuous act of God sustaining it. Furthermore, he says, the universe can and will eventually collapse as its temperature grows uniform; and yet we have the hope of resurrection – as all the information contained in our (and all historical) life is simulated in the mind of God. This is his integrated account of creation and eschatology.

Like this account or not, it is emblematic of what must be achieved in a direct approach to the task of providing a combined account of creation and eschatology, the successful integration of current understanding of

[7] Op. cit.
[8] Ibid., p. xiii.

cosmology (the structure and dynamics of the universe) with theology (normative conditions of the structure and dynamics of the universe grounded in a normative authority). If we wish to argue otherwise than does Tipler (or those whose arguments he uses), we must do so with the same comprehensiveness of argument.

Apart from those which arise both for God and creation from its emanationism, the chief fault of his argument is its poverty. Like many of the arguments which he uses, the synthesis which he weaves 'has something to say about everything, but does not tell us everything about anything' – or even enough about everything.[9] While, for example, it maintains many convictions which theologians would want to maintain, it does so only by avoiding their full meaning.

There is no way to overcome such poverty except by supplementing it by a more adequate account of creation and eschatology in relation to God. It is to the task of outlining the lines on which such an account might proceed that we must now direct our attention. We shall approach the task from several directions. For reasons of clarity, I shall keep these separate from each other, arranging them in linked sections.

THE NORMATIVE STRUCTURES OF CREATION AND ESCHATOLOGY

First of all, let us make a preliminary statement about what creation and eschatology involve when seen in relation to each other. *Creation constitutes foundational structures and dynamics which lead to, and delay, the end.*

The relation between creation and eschatology, put in the simplest terms, is this: in totality and in special aspects or regions, *creation as constitution makes reference to the conditions of continuance and ending possible; it both constitutes the universe in such a way as to delay its ending, and to lead to its end.* This is equally true for all aspects of the universe as known in the past and likely to be known in the future. This simple but general statement, if fully specified, would include those aspects of the universe which lend it *stability* and *direction,* and also those which make it sensitive to special conditions and therefore *turbulent* and *unpredictable* in outcome. (There is, in a sense, neither order which is not to a degree chaotic, nor chaos which is not to a degree orderly.)

That *creation is that constitution of the universe which keeps it from ending, and brings it to its end* is true differently for different elements of

[9] Martin Goldstein and Ilse F. Goldstein, *The Refrigerator and the Universe*, Cambridge, Mass.: Harvard University Press, 1994, p. 390.

the universe.[10] While the universe may last for 100 billion years, this earth will not; the earth will probably last longer than human beings; etc. For creation gives them different *'capacities for finitude'* according to their kinds and circumstances, and different possibilities for interacting with those other than itself. While all begin and end in some way, there is a different time-span for each, which will vary somewhat according to the local provision of needs and the use made of their 'capacity for finitude'. These are extremely varied and sensitive matters, and especially sensitive ones for all of the 'higher orders'.

Hence, in a general way, the two – creation and eschatology – are importantly connected: although not exhaustively, the one tells us the preconditions which are 'shaped' or 'completed' in the other; and the second tells us the range of possibilities – and then some – which have been allowed for in the first, and in the beginning, but appear through the complexities and contingencies of history. So, viewed ontologically, eschatology is the *unfolding* of what is *enfolded* in protology.

But that states it somewhat too mildly, for what occurs in creation is conditions without which there is no finite existence – without which there is nothing rather than something. Furthermore, what occurs is a certain order which allows for certain things to emerge – 'these' rather than 'those'. And when things of certain kinds come into existence, the structure and dynamics of creation keep them in being, and more or less self-same. Speaking of us human beings, these structures and dynamics constitute our existence and particularity, enlarge our possibilities and keep us from dying; yet they allow for us to die – and along with us, others in the animate kingdom, eventually the world as we know it, and later (possibly) the universe. Existence only continues insofar as the structures and dynamics of creation operate to maintain it; and then it ends. *Eschata* happen when these structures and dynamics *cease*.

From what source these derive, and how, we shall consider a little later. Rather than moving directly to those issues, we had better consider the *character* of the structure and dynamics of the universe and its members.

CREATION AND ESCHATOLOGY AS COVENANTAL

If creation constitutes the foundational structures and dynamics of the

[10] Whether the universe had a beginning as such, or will have an end as such, and if so what kind it was/will be, now much debated amongst scientists, should not halt the attempt to grasp the significance of the span from beginning (of whatever kind that might have been) to end (whatever that will be).

universe in such a way as to delay its ending, and yet bring it to its end, we need to know more about *how* – we need a theory of structure and dynamics for the created universe. It is clear that the universe is richly variegated in separate entities, species and individuals. It is also clear that these are normally associated with each other in different kinds of relationship. In other words, the universe is a relational field – determinate and contingent in the relationships of its members. How are we to think of the varied othernesses and relationships which we find there? We cannot simply name them – 'othernesses' and 'relationships' – without explaining how they operate.

The form of otherness-in-relationships which occurs in creation and eschatology is primarily covenantal. Why? Fundamentally, covenant designates the constitution of others *as others* combined with *continued relation* to them *as such*. In theological and human terms, covenant designates the recognition of others and the commitment to be with them, in such a way as to be binding, although not contractually, upon the parties involved.

There are clearly variations in the kinds of otherness and responsibilities – from inert to highly dynamic; such a constitution is clearly built into creation itself. And certainly in the history of Israel, and differently for the early Christians, there was growth in the awareness of and commitment to kinds and extents of otherness and responsibility as time went on; and the expectations about the importance of covenant as formative for the conception of others and the fulfilment of relations with them became much more profound. In this full sense the covenant – or in Paul's terms, being different but 'one in Christ', and in both ways both different from and related to God – became a primary avenue for the enrichment of otherness and relationship – between people and the natural world, between people, and between them and God. Freedom was assured in combination with relationships of well-being.

CONCEPTIONS OF COVENANT

There is also a variation and development – although not an irreversible one – in the *form* of covenants. The earliest conceptions of covenants were largely obligatory, focused on the power of the originating party (e.g., in the early days seen as 'backed' by the gods as guarantors), with the emphasis on determination, regulation and obedience. The 'grace' with which such covenants were established was a form of power, and the determinations and obligations were inflexible. By contrast, in both the Sinaitic covenant, and much more emphatically in the promissory one of Abraham and David, the 'grace' was a bestowal of freedom and benefits in return for loyal following and service; and continued following and service were expected, but the benefits did not cease if these were not as expected. A further development of the promissory covenant was, therefore, the inclusion of provision for alienation within the covenant designed to return the alienated to full standing, and thus construed as beneficial – a little like my daughter-in-law setting her child on the 'naughty step'. The covenant was not cut off, but included the possibility of disruption (e.g. of dynasty) and scattering (e.g. exile), and restoration upon repentance. These were profound developments in the understanding of otherness in relationship. They clearly anticipated the 'new covenant' established in Jesus, where God was at one with the people not only in their otherness but in their alienation, restoring relationships and justice.

The conception of otherness in relation could become very specific. One clear tendency was in the direction of ever more specific *obligations* expressed not as promises but as laws, laws governing the relations in the created order and between people which were seen as the 'law of God'. From this position, the history of covenant was retrospectively interpreted as the history of laws, which invited further legal refinement. This was a departure from the promissory conception of covenant, which had emphasized otherness itself and relation to others through promises, with a minimum of institutions and formalized expressions. It reflected the more complex social structures of latter-day Israel. And it brought a severe reaction from the early Christians, who emphasized a new freedom in Christ – beyond (but not against) laws. But the Christians themselves, retreating from promissory covenants, later resorted to legalized social structures in church and social life. Both the Roman hierarchical social structure used in much church order, and also the Reformed/Puritan 'covenant of grace', have left lasting legacies of obsession with governmental structure, law and legal protection.

Notwithstanding this overspecification of the structure and dynamics of creation, both as idea and as practice, covenant is the most helpful way of construing the dynamics of the establishment and maintenance of otherness in relationship. It remains basic to theology and its contribution to human affairs. At the same time, its significance is by no means as fully recognized as might be expected, and discussions – particularly constructive ones – of the topic are relatively rare, in theology or elsewhere.

COVENANT, CREATION AND ESCHATOLOGY

The importance of the conception of covenant for the present discussion is in the illumination it casts on the structure and dynamics of creation-eschatology. Within the constitution of otherness which is characteristic of all creation, we find two fundamental kinds of otherness, an *ordered* one built on determination and obedience and a *promissory* one which is built on trust and performance. The former is causal in structure, and lends creation the *stability* upon which all forms of existence depend. The latter confers *freedom*, not abstract freedom but one of remaining in relationship and acting in such a way as to confer benefit upon those who confer freedom. The former is *inexorable and without latitude*. The latter is *transformative*, comprised of the realization of freedom and the conferral of benefit; it includes the possibility of straying, redemption and return. The former is for *survival*. The latter is for *qualitative development* of all kinds, not least moral. But *both*, however, are expressions of divine gift, a gift carried *within* the span formed by beginning, continuance and end. In the last resort, the stability of the world and the developmental character of the world, as well as their ending, are formed within the opening constituted by divine gift and the response made by creation. They do not arise from by divine determination and obedience alone.

While the stability and dynamics of creation are *ordered* and *free*, human participation in creation deeply depends on the quality of the *free human response to the divine gift* by which there is both order and freedom – in all the ways through which humans affect the constitution of creation. The *quality* of this response rests on adequate appreciation of the mystery of the God whose *own life* is the gift of creation and humanity, order and freedom, who suffers to redeem it and us from the failure of our order, trust and community, and who imparts the energy for all otherness-in-relationships. This is the mystery of the character and life of the Trinitarian God.

CREATION AND ESCHATOLOGY AS RADICAL SELF-GIFT OF GOD

If creation is that constitution of the universe which keeps it from ending, and brings it to its end, we have now seen the general form of the structure and dynamics of the ways in which it does so – the differentiation of otherness in positive relationships. That leads us to ask how creation and eschatology as seen in these terms arise. How are they constituted as such? We suggest that – far from being self-constituted or a necessary act on the part of God – they are products of a certain kind of divine gift which constitutes the other as deserving fulfilment in its own right. The divine act constitutes the other (universe, world, humanity) for fulfilment within its time-span.

A major problem for understanding this is that the divine act which constitutes the other for fulfilment is frequently presented in such a way as to be much less conceptually rich and interesting than the infrastructure and history of the universe, the world and humanity; this is the origin of the practical atheism which undermines so much theology. Fundamental to the conception of the divine act of creation, therefore, is the existence of a creator from whose abundance the richness of creation as we know it originates and continues, and in which it ends – as distinct from (say) a bare causal principle which triggers, boosts or ends it.

Such a creator is *unbounded, incomparably ordered and radically alive*, not an empty infinite but one with a fullness of the perfections which constitute the otherness, structure and dynamics of creation – being, truth, goodness and beauty – and hence the complete source of all such things in creation's prevention and bringing of the end. As a mystery which lies 'beyond' the very relational field of creation constituted by it as 'giver' of it as other-to-be-fulfilled, the fullness of the Creator is known (so far as creation is concerned) only as that which actively constitutes this field. In other words, the character of the creator is known through its activation of the relational field called creation.

A second challenge is to discern the *manner of the creative act* of this Creator. It is the *fullness* of the creator's *gift of otherness* which constitutes it as source for the otherness-to-fulfilment of creation. How is this so in the creative act? It is as personal and free to be fully and radically self-giving through acting to originate that which is other than God. It is this which gives rise to our notions of 'universe', 'world' and 'humanity'; they are not self-generated. Each has its wholeness and freedom contingently, and all of them in mutual relations, from the radical self-gift of God. That is, the nature, structure and history of the world and humanity are found not in their self-standing but in the radical – but contingent – gift of being, truth, goodness and beauty by the Creator.

The nature of the *origination* which often dominates discussions of creation has to do with the *radicality of these gifts* by the Creator, not with conceptions of efficient causation no matter how powerful. Likewise, the notion of *creatio ex nihilo* (creation from nothing) derives from the denial of any source from which creation might have derived – other than the Creator's existence, and the fullness of truth, goodness and beauty implicit in it. Both are expressions of the contingency of the field comprised by creation (that is, the universe, world and humanity) on the radical self-gift of the Creator.

A further challenge is to understand the implications for the structure and dynamics of the world. While it is important to stress the contingency of the world and humanity on the radical self-gift of God, such contingency must not be misunderstood. Being, truth, goodness and beauty are fully realized in God, and are as *constant* in the self-giving of

God as they are in God; they are faithfully given to the world and humanity. It is this which confers upon both together (the relational field of world and humanity), as well as those which comprise each, an *inalienable structure and dynamics* proper to their existence together, beyond which they cannot go with impunity. Furthermore, the gift establishes the *quality* of this structure and dynamics, for elements of the world and human beings separately and together: they are to be related as those who realize the being, truth, goodness and beauty *in others* through care and compassion, not through self-serving which makes others instrumental to inflated needs.

The purpose of the world is therefore to *fulfil its finitude*. It is important to recognize that in the constitution of creation, the being, truth, goodness and beauty which are fully realized in God are not – and cannot be – completely given to finite beings, lest the finite be overcome by the infinite, 'become as gods'. The radical self-giving of God is for the world and humanity to *be themselves* – and fully such. It is this movement to fullness which forms the continuing course of the world and humanity, which forms the future whose arrival depends on the readiness of the recipient to move toward it. In other words, the fullness of God is present both in the gift of the condition of the world and humanity whereby they may move toward their fullness. Their future is, in this sense, hidden in the gift of God.

THE FEATURES OF CREATION

This awareness of creation provides it with some of its most remarkable features. The field of relations (in creation) which is the self-gift of God is a *plenum*, but *not one fully realized*. The first of these two features accounts for the seemingly *infinite depth of the stability* which we find in the universe, world and humanity, that which inflames the interest of those who wish to find and know their fundamental character through time-neutral observation. The second of the two accounts for the *indefinite dynamism of the universe, world and humanity*, in which they are seen as cosmically and historically open: because they are always moving toward an as-yet incomplete goal, they can be known only by anticipation through time-filled observation. The intersection between the two concerns and kinds of investigation – time-neutral and time-filled – is always a murky one, each always implying the other.

It was stressed earlier that God's self-gift is of the structure and dynamics comprised by the universe, the world and humanity. The same coupling of firmly given conditions with indefinite dynamism, is found in the field of relations within the universe, the world, humanity and God and between them. In that way, the radically loving self-gift of God not only *establishes* the boundaries of being, but *'shifts'* them[11]. This suggests that there is no fixed boundary either between God and creation, or within creation. *The very otherness between them may be a unity.* God's self-gift not only originates that which is separate but constitutes a unity between God and the other which does not compromise the other's being in filling it. And it both invests the other with fixed obligations which are expressed as laws, and also indefinitely enlarges the possibilities of the other in its self-giving, as seen (for example) in qualities of compassion and care for others and the world. This is the nature of the ethical dynamism of creation.

As seen earlier, the personal character and freedom of the Creator arise from the Creator's fullness of existence, truth, goodness and beauty. We now see that these characteristics arise within creation through the radical self-gift of the Creator, and are found throughout the field of relations in humanity and with the world. Precisely because this fullness of personhood and the freedom which flows from it are given to human beings, and to the world itself, however, there is the possibility of a radical misuse of the gift and its qualities (truth, goodness and beauty) by which they are alienated from their source (who is in turn treated as alienating) and taken as properties of the world and humanity. Even the constancy of the gift is taken over as these are considered intrinsic to those to whom God has given them. The result, evil in the case of the world and sin for humanity, radically dislocates all the relations proper to human beings in the world and fixes them within severely restricted conditions and purposes, structures and dynamics, thereby denying them both the true conditions of their being and the true future which they might otherwise anticipate. Such a dislocation can only be fully remedied by a decisive

---

[11] The term is taken from this poem by Micheal O'Siadhail:

> Nothing can explain this adventure – let's say a quirk
> of fortune steered us together – we made our covenants,
> began this odyssey of ours, by hunch and guesswork,
> a blind date where foolish love consented in advance.
> No my beloved, neither knew what lay beyond the frontiers.
> You told me once you hesitated: *A needle can waver,*
> *then fix on its pole*; I am still after many years
> baffled that the needle's gift dipped in my favour.
> Should I dare to be so lucky? Is this a dream?
> Suddenly in the commonplace the first amazement seizes
> me all over again – a freak twist to the theme,
> subtle jazz of the new familiar, trip of surprises.
> Gratuitous, beyond our fathom, both binding and freeing,
> this love re-invades us, shifts the boundaries of our being.

'Out of the Blue' in *Hail! Madam Jazz*, Newcastle: Bloodaxe Books, 1992, p. 118.

realignment of the 'boundaries' of and within creation, by a reestablishment of its structure and dynamics, of its stability and possibility. This is what occurs in the coming of the Redeemer, conferring new life in the presence of evil and sin.

CREATION AND ESCHATOLOGY AS COMPLETION

Beginning with the statement that creation is that constitution of the universe (or anything in it) which keeps its from ending, and then brings it (or anything in it) to its end, we went on to see the structure and dynamics of the created universe as those of a covenant with two aspects – ordered and promissory (including restorative alienation). We then saw that these dynamics of creation were the result of a radical self-gift/self-promise on the part of God, in which God gives to the other (universe, world, humanity) as other varying capacities for finitude, full possibilities of fulfilment within them, and redemption in the face of evil. These are sufficient for creation in its sustaining and ending.

It is as proper to creation to acknowledge and fulfill itself as the gift of otherness by God as it is proper to God to make the gift. The true character of its otherness from God, its structure and the dynamics of its fulfilment are realized through relating them to God. This means that the dynamic of this realization within creation-eschaton must be *identified* and recovered or *activated*. That occurs primarily in the activity of worship – which, of course, also activates the intelligent grasping of the structure and dynamics of creation-eschatology.

To appreciate the significance of worship for creation and eschatology, we must first understand its nature. In its *primary sense*, worship designates the response – acknowledgment in praise – evoked by the unfathomable depth of existence, truth, goodness and beauty ('glory') which is recognized as the source and end of all being, order and energy in existence. The response in worship is not self-generated but elicited by the quality of this glory whose plenitude elevates all that responds to it in the fullest acknowledgment of which they are capable. In its *secondary sense*, worship is the encompassing activity in which all that exists is brought into relation to that glory which is seen to have such abundance of being that it is wholly self-giving in constituting the universe, the world and humanity – and the dynamics by which they are, become and will end. In the one sense, worship is the *intensive* and *engrossing* manifestation of ultimate plenitude, in the other it is the *extensive* and *encompassing* direction of all the universe, the world and human life toward that which has brought them to be and move toward their fulfilment.[12]

Worship escapes the possibility of full or complete definition, for several reasons. Firstly, its concern with plenitude and the idea of God makes it *expansive* and *self-transforming*, reaching always for the yet fuller being which lies beyond present conceptions and practices, and lifting human faculties beyond confinement by such categories and forms. While it is not contentless or formless, this plenitude always exceeds grasp by human conceptions and practices no matter how far their reach is extended. In this way, it is fundamentally opposed to *idolatrous* substitutes for this fuller being and *magical* attempts to dominate and manipulate it.

Secondly, however, at its profoundest level worship is both a *synchronic* and a *diachronic* activity, and in that way traces the two aspects of creation (structures and dynamics) to the plenitude of the divine. On the one hand, it is stimulated by intimations of the possibility of the ultimate unity and meaning of all things, and also by convictions of the presence of this unity and meaning for and in all things, its engagement with them and with us. But, on the other hand, these are only developed and confirmed through the ongoing rediscovery of their presence in the order of things and in history; and history will be complete when all fully acknowledge the Lord (Rev. 15.4).

Thirdly, worship is *linked to all the features of life in the world* and *activates them in relation to their infinite and abundant source*. As such, it includes and activates all other forms of understanding and practice (such as the reason, understanding, ethical behaviour, etc.) through religious rituals, symbols, doctrines, moral practices, and also forms less directly associated with religion. It is by the placing of these others in the dynamic of worship that they achieve their proper standing and empowerment.

Through these three movements, worship both *identifies* and *activates* the transcendent source of order and energy in all of the cosmos. In it a primary and transformative impulse – the self-giving of holiness comprised in the being and activity of the Trinitarian God – is recognized as

[12] The first sense follows the strict designation of the English term worship (from the Old English *weorthscipe*, 'the condition [in a person] of deserving, or being held in, esteem or repute' [OED]). The term signifies the having of worth or positive value, or the honour or dignity which is *inherent* in the one in whom it is found, and is therefore recognized by others. The second sense becomes more widespread in the humanistic climate which has prevailed since the European Renaissance, and is further accentuated in twentieth-century developments, where worship is often (particularly in the USA) assimilated to the human task of constructing a full life. But more usually, worship incorporates the acknowledgement of a fullness of being, truth, goodness and beauty which is self-givingly constitutive for all else, and the responsibility of redirecting all else to the deepest possible relation to this plenitude.

creative of all the features of the cosmos in all its aspects, providing them with the fundamental orientation whereby they are freed for the fullest possibility which is theirs. It is within this recognition, concentrated in the dynamics of worship, that the development of human understanding of the 'nature' of the transcendent source occurs and continues.[13]

Secondly, appreciation of this abundant or all-sufficient source is appropriately achieved only in accordance with its nature and purpose. This gives rise to a particular dynamic of acknowledgment which – *synchronously* considered – has five aspects.

(a) Because this source is the infinite plenitude of being, truth, goodness and beauty, worship is offered primarily as *adoration* and *praise*, expressions of gladness for the very being and self-gift of this God, in attitude and language refined to exalt God. It looks beyond creatureliness and creaturely thought to the very source of this plenitude, both unknowable in splendour (the *apophatic* element) and also self-conferring (the *cataphatic* element) in such a way that human beings can – at least provisionally – adore and praise him.

(b) The adoring and praising of God brings to light the shortcomings of those who do so. A second aspect is therefore the *confession* of the faults by which they have distorted their relation to God and those around them. For Christians, this is not simply an expression of penitence, but opening themselves to the goodness by which God overcomes these sins in Jesus Christ.

(c) When the infinite plenitude of God is conferred upon human beings, and particularly in their salvation (cf. 'O come let us sing unto the Lord; let us heartily rejoice in the strength of our salvation.' Ps. 95), the appropriate response (the third aspect) is *thanksgiving*. This is a responsive movement of the hearts of those touched by the movements of God toward them, by which they show gratitude for God's acts.

---

[13] Such worship, and the understanding in which it results, embraces both mystery and illumination. In 'apophatic theology' such as that emphasized in Eastern Christian thought, for example, it is only within a divine darkness like that which Moses entered on Sinai in meeting God, and through the purification of the senses, intellect and words, that God is found in a union of 'pure prayer' [Evagrius Ponticus, sixth century AD]. 'Cataphatic theology', however, seeks to move toward God through the understanding of aspects of creation, while still recognizing that God is beyond the very things – 'Being', 'the Good' and 'Life' – by which he is called through the use of notions from the created world. 'With these analogies we are raised upward toward the truth of the mind's vision, a truth which is simple and one. [Then] we leave behind us all our own notions. We call a halt to the activities of our minds and, to the extent that is proper, we approach the ray which transcends being.' [Pseudo-Dionysius, sixth century AD] Both apophatic and cataphatic are ways of approaching God, in the one case through divine darkness and purification, and in the other through being raised upward through the mind's use of concepts from the created world. Contrasting emphases on mystery and illumination coexist in approaching the divine plenitude.

(d) It is equally important, however, that the world and these human beings be shaped through God's movements toward them. As regards 'the universe' in its various dimensions, God's actions are to be related to people and issues in the world through *intercessory prayer*, the fourth aspect. For Christians, this is a sharing in the work of Jesus Christ which holds together God and the world in his own suffering and dying, and a proclamation of God's infinite mercy as it is to be found everywhere. It is necessarily very specific, and requires involvement in the needs and pains of others. As regards those who worship, the movements of God's life are to be brought to bear on their lives – and all their details – in *petition*, the fifth aspect.

(e) This synchronic analysis of the dynamics of worship is intimately associated with the *diachronous*. Worship always draws from, and in turn sharpens, elevates and enriches the historical recognition of the nature of the plenitude whose movement toward human beings enables their adoration, praise, thanksgiving and petition. All of these involve the recalling (*anamnesis*) of the historical events by which divine plenitude has formed the basis of human well-being. The basis for worship is not (as Feuerbach thought) a metaphysical absolute which confines humankind in an alienated personification of himself ('God'), thereby dissipating his energies, but One whose history with humankind fulfils and energizes it.

Thirdly, as we have seen, worship naturally incorporates all the features of life in the world and activates them in relation to their infinite and abundant source. The way in which it typically does so is to focus on situations in which God's actions and purposes are intertwined with crucially important events, features and institutions of human life in the world. Hence, for example, Hebrew worship concentrated on divine presence and action in the crucial constitutive events of and in time (creation, exodus and passover), the immediacies of human life (flesh and blood in the practice of sacrifice), social institutions (law and government), personal behaviour (offerings and hospitality), particular spatial locations (the land and shrines), specially-endowed representative personages (prophets, priests and kings), etc.

The same features found in Hebrew worship are continued but radically transposed in Christianity, primarily through their comprehensive reshaping in relation to Jesus Christ. The very activity of God's blessing is seen to have occurred through God's relation with the world in Jesus Christ, through whom God chose his people even before creation – destining them to be holy and blameless, his sons in Christ, redeemed by his own blood from their trespasses to live in his grace and praise him. In effect, therefore, the fullness of worship occurs in Christ, and by being incorporated into Christ.

The implications of this transposition are extremely deep. The very

168

plenitude of God is seen in a new light, as decisively turned toward humanity in history in the promise of the fullest blessing, whose form is covenant and redemption (of mankind from the sin which blinds them to God and distorts all existence). It is through the very movement of God's holiness toward mankind in the life, suffering, death and resurrection of Jesus Christ that mankind is purified and redeemed. Hence the very synchronic and diachronic character of worship is changed into 'remembering the Lord's death until he comes'. And finally, God is fully knotted together with humankind – in the Holy Spirit reordering and reenergizing mankind for a new history with God, thereby conferring a new fullness of interactivity between human beings in their life together. All the ways in which the immediacies of life are incorporated in worship – institutions, rituals, personal behaviour, events of sacred history, etc. – are transformed through being refocused on the fullness of God's work in Christ and the Holy Spirit, and given new norms. All of life is so intimately united to the life of Jesus Christ in the Holy Spirit that it serves to honour, adore and glorify the Father.

CONCLUSION

Beginning with the statement that creation keeps the universe (or anything in it) from ending, and then ends it (or anything in it), we went on to view the dynamics of the created universe as a covenant with two aspects – obligatory and promissory (including restorative alienation). These very dynamics of creation were seen to result from a radical self-gift/self-promise on the part of God, in which God gives to the other as other (universe, world, humanity) varying capacities for finitude, full possibilities of development within them, and redemption in the face of evil.

But, as we have now seen, the self-giving movement of God towards the other requires recognition of the fullness from which this it arose. This does not violate the otherness which is established between them by the self-giving of God, but it does seek to maximize the relationship between them by all the means we have just considered. By doing so, all creation – that which keeps the universe from ending and that which ends it – is brought to glorify God. Creation and eschatology return glory to God – the very glory they are given through the *Trinitarian movement* of God toward and in them.

Then I saw a new heaven and a new earth; for the first heaven and the first earth had passed away, and the sea was no more. And I saw the holy city, new Jerusalem, coming down out of heaven from God, prepared as a bride for her husband; and I heard a great voice from the throne saying, 'Behold, the dwelling of God is with men. He will dwell with them, and they shall be his people, and God himself will be with them; he will wipe away every tear from their eyes, and death shall be no more, neither shall there be mourning nor crying nor pain any more, for the former things have passed away.' (Revelation 21.1–4)

Part Three: Society and Church

10

God and the Form of Society[1]

IN the General Synod Debate on 'The Church and the Bomb', Peter Baelz described the pacifist vocation, to which he stood very close, as 'a willingness to respond to the way of our Lord whatever the consequences and not to believe that it is the duty of the Christian Church to manage the affairs of the world'.[2] His own response was centred on the issue of being, and becoming, fully human; this was an issue which was as much one of social responsibility as of individual well-being. It could be described as a response made in 'open faithfulness', as – in the many important contributions he made to debates about ethical issues – he sought for ways of faithfulness which would soften the aggressive postures of those who claimed to possess the truth, and which would overcome conflicts of interest.

His concern in Christian faith was always with the transformative effect of faith on human beings. It was always, therefore, a social one, at least in part: the question was how people were to be brought together to a fully human life. But he also realized that the means to this end had to be societal, both governmental and ecclesial. On the one hand, the complexity of modern social life, so reliant on the interdependence of services and technology, had to be controlled by government: 'in the future there is likely to be much more control of our social life through Government action'. On the other hand, while it was not the business of the Christian Church 'to manage the affairs of the world', it might provide symbols of fully human existence; the question for Christians is

> whether there is any way in which we can understand the form of our society so as to give us a new orientation and a new impetus ...
> Are there any symbols of hope, symbols of community, symbols of individuality-in-community, which transcend both the system of a warring conflict of interests and the system of central planning of society by the state? Are there here any resources for hope? Since sooner or later we shall run short of that fundamental human emotion and outlook, are there any resources in the Christian tradition which, recognizing man's creativity as ambivalent, nevertheless help

[1] This essay first appeared in *The Weight of Glory: A Vision and Practice for Christian Faith*, edited by D. W. Hardy and P. H. Sedgwick, Edinburgh: T. & T. Clark, 1991, pp. 131–144.
[2] *The Church and the Bomb*: The General Synod Debate, February 1983, London 1983.

us to promote not only individual salvation but also the future well-being of mankind?[3]

It is to that question, of giving a new orientation and impetus to the form of our society, that this essay is directed. But the answer to be offered is not so much symbolic as social-structural. In the highly developed societies of present times, Christians cannot offer only transcendent symbols which illuminate and inspire; to do so is to remain in the realm of ideas which do not relate very well to the structures by which social life is organized. They must respond by developing social structures in which people may become fully human in interaction with God. In fact, they must learn to 'manage the affairs of the world' in their relationship with God, not in order to take over the affairs of government, but to give practical form to their life with God, and thus provide a more concrete manifestation of what this might mean for human affairs in general.

The argument which we shall present is that there is an inevitable interaction between conceptions of social structure and those of God. Indeed, social structures are, properly speaking, relative to the nature of God. But, as we shall see, modern conceptions of social structures have tended to make them more relativistic (as distinct from relative), probably in reaction to the absolutism which has continued to infect theology; and theology has tended to conspire in this by adopting a relativistic understanding of social institutions and of God. A more satisfactory reconception of social structures therefore requires a recovery of their relativity to a God who is seen himself to be relative to the world he has created and redeemed. This conception of the relation of social structures is far more consonant with traditional Christian understanding.

SOCIAL STRUCTURES AS RELATIVE TO GOD

The relativity of social structures to God is well expressed in an illuminating aphorism by the English poet-philosopher-theologian S. T. Coleridge:

He who begins by loving Christianity, better than truth, will proceed by loving his own sect or church better than Christianity, and end in loving himself better than all.[4]

[3] Peter Baelz, 'The Ethics of Strikes in the Caring Professions', *Crucible*, October–December 1975.
[4] S. T. Coleridge, *Aids to Reflection*, London: Taylor & Hessey, 1825, p. 101.

Where there is no recognition of the relativity of social structures to the truth of God, there will be a natural tendency to move in a negative spiral from greater to lesser preoccupations, from universal truth to self-regard. Preference for anything less than the truth (which is by definition universal and for all) leads through varieties of sectionalized identity and ultimately to self-isolation. And the only way of avoiding the spiral is to attend fully to the truth, and to find one's social or personal identity in that.

A like problem can be found amongst those who place love for a particular social order above that for truth. It is possible to parallel Coleridge's aphorism with another describing the state, social groups and the self. It would read:

> He who begins by loving the nation, better than truth, will proceed by loving his own group better than the nation, and end in loving himself better than all.

This would suggest that in the social sphere also, where there is not full attention to the truth, there is the same negative spiral from universal truth to self-regard; preference for that which is less than universal leads through preference for varieties of sectional identity (social groups or classes, for example), and eventually to a priority given to individuals.

When Christianity and the nation are viewed in this way, there is much to be learned from this parallel. It suggests a higher point to which both Christianity and the nation must be answerable, without which each will descend to lesser forms of coherence. But, particularly to the eyes of people in the 1990s, the form of the higher truth – the love of which would bring the highest form of social coherence – seems obscure. Is it – as some have claimed of the Kantian thinking which interested Coleridge – an imaginary ideal, 'an empty signifier of that total knowledge which the bourgeoisie never ceases to dream of . . . the phantasmal possibility of a knowledge beyond all categories, which then risks striking what it *can* know meagrely relative'?[5] It need not be, though it will always run the risk of becoming an ideology, a reified emptiness.

The higher point to which Christianity and particular nations are answerable may be a real goal, the goal of true social coherence which is anticipated in societies as they actually exist. And such a goal – genuinely but only partially realized in particular societies – would relativize both Christianity and particular civil societies to the position of instruments which may, or may not, support societies in the achievement of that true social being. In effect, reference to this goal of true social being would

---

[5] Terry Eagleton, *The Ideology of the Aesthetic*, Oxford: Blackwell, 1990, p. 77.

'put them in their place', making each instrumental to universal social coherence.

To relativize Christianity and nations to true social being is not to suggest that they have no value, but that their value is proportionate to their particular contribution to the achievement of true social being. And this, of course, will vary according to what they are. Both Christianity and nations contain within them different *kinds* of social unit. In each, we can identify 'formal units' with well-developed notions of membership and well-structured distributions of responsibilities, 'informal units' with less well-developed commonality and distribution of responsibilities, and 'fragmented units' made up of individuals with little notion of commonality where responsibility is assumed only by individuals.[6]

But if we follow the line of argument presented so far, each such unit has its value not in itself but through its contribution to true society; each in its own way should contribute to the achievement of true social coherence. 'Formal units' with their advanced organizational structure, 'informal units' with less well-developed polities, and 'fragmented units' with little commonality and mutual responsibility: all have true social coherence as their goal, and are to contribute to its achievement.

Interestingly, if this is so, there is a profound coordination of purpose between the different kinds of civil social units and the different kinds of religious ones. Each is in its own right to contribute to 'true society' in a way which is appropriate to the kind of social unit which it is. This suggests a fruitful relation between states (as the bodies with constituted responsibility for civil social units) and Christianity, or between informal units and sects, or between individuals as social and as Christian. If at each level both are obligated to find true social coherence, they meet in their common purpose. To take one implication of this, the state cannot conceive itself in quasi-religious terms, as if it alone knows or performs 'true society'; it must open itself to criticism. Nor can Christian bodies see themselves as quasi-states, with civil power derived from their knowledge of the truth; they must be reformed through their interaction with the truth.

If this position is right – that Christianity and the state, together with the variety of social units which they incorporate, are relativized by their obligation to contribute to true society – we have an important vantage-point from which to view current social structures, and from which to consider the contribution of theology to social structuring.

If we measure the modern social situation by the standards we have been considering, there are two features of modern societies which stand out. Both are kinds of relativism. The first is the movement toward simpler self-contained social structures and, underlying it, a movement

---

[6] See R. N. Adams, *Energy and Structure*, Austin: University of Texas Press, 1975, p. 57.

toward a simplification of human relationships. The second is the move-ment from the position in which social structures are relativized by the obligation to promote true social coherence to the more extreme rela-tivistic position in which certain kinds of social structure are taken to be exemplary forms of social coherence, and therefore important in their own right.

THE RELATIVIZING OF SOCIAL STRUCTURES

Despite the notable increase in the complexity of modern societies, it seems to be the case that modern societies in the western hemisphere – civil or religious – have not maintained the range of social units men-tioned before. In place of the formal, the informal and the fragmented units mentioned before, most social practice in the modern West has drifted towards a polarization of the formal (the civil state or the large-scale religious organization) and the fragmented (the individual, whether as citizen or as faithful), with a correlative de-emphasis of units more informal and local.

Hence there have typically been two conflicting tendencies, on the one hand that of states or churches which take it upon themselves to control their peoples, through the techniques of administration for example, and on the other hand that which attempts to safeguard citizens against the excesses of states or churches in doing so. Each has given rise to its own philosophy and practice.

In the one case, modern states have been concerned with the 'mass' of human beings and have various devices, including those for social admin-istration (e.g. statistics) and the management of wealth, as instruments to bring about social well-being. In the other case, there is an opposing movement to limit the excesses of states, and to do so through appealing to the notion of human beings as 'individuals' who by nature are endowed with rights to secure their own interests; in this case, the very existence of states is seen as the result of individuals freely contracting with each other to ensure the well-being of individuals, and they need to be restricted by constitutions and laws to prevent the arbitrary exercise of their power.[7] Similar tendencies are found amongst the churches, where there is a like polarization of large-scale 'institutions' which are regarded with great suspicion by those who emphasize the personal character of religious belief and life.

---

[7] A useful analysis of the major tenets of each position is found in Dag Österberg, *Meta-sociology: An Inquiry into the Origins and Validity of Social Thought*, Oslo and Oxford: Norwegian University Press, 1988.

The 'intermediate' – more informal – social units have tended to suffer. In practical terms, the supposition that society maintains itself in informal units, with strong customs and customary values, has been increasingly displaced. Referring to the like situation in the United States, one writer said:

> The influence of the democratic state has today become so pervasive, and our customary value sources so fragmented, that the process-oriented values of the Constitution that 'inform and limit' the governmental structure are thought by some scholars to be the 'values that determine the quality of our social existence.' As a result we live in something of a value vacuum. The 'megastructures' of society (which may include corporate conglomerates and large labor unions as well as large government bureaucracies) have overpowering influence – yet they do not typically seek to tell us what our lives really mean.[8]

What has largely displaced these more informal social units, however, is as much the notion of the individual as that of the state; the proponents of each of these have subsumed the notion of society into their own conception. It is either 'Societé, c'est nous!' or 'Societé, c'est moi!' Society *is* the state or individuals, not such informal units.

RELATIVISM IN RELATIONSHIPS

When we look more closely at the prevailing emphasis on the formal and on the individual, whether in civil or religious forms, we see that both incorporate a notion of human relationships which is in some ways very surprising, and also quite different from the relationships which often mark informal social units. This is best seen in the way by which those concerned with the state and with the individual define human beings. Neither of these defines human beings by reference to others; the relation of human beings to others is considered extrinsic to them. The chief difference between the two is in how these extrinsic relations take place.

In the case of the modern managerial notion of the *state*, the relations take place indirectly; the assumption is that human beings can be treated as 'externally related' by reference to some property or process which is common to them. The historical antecedent to this was the notion that

[8] Bruce C. Hafen, 'Law, Custom and Mediating Structures: The Family as a Community of Memory' in R. J. Neuhaus, ed., *Law and the Ordering of our Life Together*, Grand Rapids: Eerdmans, 1989, p. 103.

people were related by the 'property' of being governed. Insofar as governance was not only by a monarch but also through those appointed to governorship under him, people were related as 'classes' through the property of being governed by these appointees. Despite the required subservience to the governor, the positive feature of their situation was that people in each class were related to each other by the personal property of being governed; it was their common lot, which actually gave them their commonality. But now, where people are more likely to be seen as units (e.g. statistical units), they are 'related' only in a more 'factlike' way, their explainability (and manipulability) through some identifiable characteristic or process; hence, social improvement happens through controlling this characteristic or process. The most obvious example is wealth, where in the modern state people are explained in terms of their wealth, and social improvement is thought to happen through wealth creation and control. But much the same can be seen in the use which is made of education; people are explained in terms of their educability, and it is thought that the 'right' education 'socializes' human beings and ameliorates problems of social relations, such as those which arise from the class structure of society. Throughout, people are seen as related to each other through the characteristic or process by which they are 'managed'.

In the case of the notion of the individual, which is usually called the 'liberal' conception, the relations – also extrinsic to those involved – take place directly, in the sense that one individual is related directly to others. But directness of relation does not imply obligation, or relations which are necessary to the individual concerned. The view is based on several premises: (1) the human being is ontologically prior to society, and is defined ('externally') without reference to other human beings; (2) each human being is only contingently related to others (in the sense that this relation may or may not obtain), either through accidents of contact or through choice; and (3) each human being is only historically related to others (these relations arise only in, and last only so long as they are maintained in, finite existence). On this view, each individual is seen as a distinct being, and endowed with certain rights such as the liberty to seek his/her well-being through the enhancement and preservation of life, property or anything else seen as conducive to this well-being. As such, human beings are considered equal in their freedom to secure their own well-being. While this by no means excludes the possibility of a sense of responsibility for others, and the importance of conditions which would be conducive to universal happiness, the main thrust of the notion is the maximization of the freedom of the individual. Society then arises through the actual, contingent historical relations of such individuals. The civil state is constituted by individuals when they freely hand over certain natural rights, renouncing their right to punish intrusions upon their life, freedom and property; but it exists for the sake of individuals. From this vantage-point, the notion that human beings exist by their membership of a whole (such as a given society, state or church) is discarded as potentially, if not actually, totalitarian.

These are some of the main ways in which societies have been simplified in modern times, through preference given either to states or to individuals as the basis of society and thereby (even if not by design) de-emphasizing the informal ways in which societies maintain themselves. And what has accompanied them is favour shown for the notion that human beings are only related externally or extrinsically. Both these preferences deserve to be tested against other possibilities, that societies are as much maintained through informal units and through the intrinsic relatedness of human beings, whereby they are actually defined by relation to each other. Such possibilities do not imply that they may not also be related as states or as individuals, and through properties or processes or by their own choice, but may yield a stronger notion of how it is that human beings are related.

THE RELATIVIZATION OF THE GOAL OF SOCIETY

Accompanying the 'simplification' of societies and human relationships just described has been a movement away from the relativity of social structures to truly social coherence – from the position in which social structures are relativized by their obligation to contribute to true society. What appears to have taken its place is a more extreme relativistic position in which certain kinds of social structure are taken to be important in their own right, and present themselves as ideal. On the one hand, this has often brought states to present themselves in quasi-religious terms:

The wholesale aestheticization of society had found its grotesque apotheosis for a brief moment in fascism, with its panoply of myths, symbols and orgiastic spectacles, its repressive expressivity, its appeals to passion, radical intuition, instinctual judgement, the sublimity of self-sacrifice and the pulse of the blood. But in the post-war years a different form of aestheticization was also to saturate the entire culture of late capital, with its fetishism of style and surface, its cult of hedonism and technique . . .[9]

[9] Terry Eagleton, *The Ideology of the Aesthetic, op. cit.*, p. 373.

On the other hand, Christianity has tended to present itself as a divinely ordained, and therefore ideal, form of civil power.

The 'ideal societies' thus presented, whether by states or by Christianity, employ the notion of extrinsic relations discussed earlier. True society is not seen to arise from the essential relatedness or coherence of human beings; instead, it is to be achieved through the extrinsic relations in which human beings find themselves.

Where the focus is on states or large-scale societies, it is thought that the ideal will be achieved by appealing to human beings in general and securing their approval through an appropriate form of political process. If, for example, it is thought that states are best conducted on the principles of market philosophy, the implicit suggestion is that this is the most equitable way of securing the interests of most of their citizens and is therefore most likely to succeed in securing their approval. Where the focus is on individuals, true society is seen best to be achieved through securing a greater sense of responsibility on the part of individuals. Adherents of each often fault those who follow the other for their inadequate view of society.

It is interesting to watch proponents of the state or of individualism attempting to relativize each other, while supposing that their own position incorporates the possibility of a more ideal society. Hence David Jenkins, as an exponent of individualism, suggests,

It should be noted that there is a close connection between a growing awareness of the reality of exploitation and a developing understanding of human freedom and responsibility. To be able to point to exploitation as a feature of present human societies and of the world situation as a whole we must also hold that human social reality is a social construct and not just a reflection of some ordered reality which has its divisions and relationships built in by something like divine fiat or law. Justice then shifts from being a matter of attempting to see that everyone receives what is due according to their status and position in the ordered hierarchy, with the acceptance of vast differences between these 'dues', to a matter of concern for equality – in participation, in consumption and in enjoyment.[10]

In other words, the correct strategy for the development of true society is to undercut the features of traditional notions of the state, that is a simple causal relationship which is supposed to hold between the 'divine' act or law, the structure of human societies and the social exploitation which results from such structures. We are to relativize existing social orders as 'social constructs' and instead – as the individualist position requires –

[10] David Jenkins, *The Contradiction of Christianity*, London: SCM Press, 1976, p. 71.

develop understanding of human freedom and responsibility. As people become more concerned for equality, a truer society arises:[11]

> Thus the pressure of God and his kingdom upon us at the present time is particularly to be seen in the rapid spread of the discovery that everybody is human and even more particularly in the rapid growth of the awareness of everybody that they too are human.[12]

It seems, however, that neither the modern view of the state nor that of the individual has a strongly developed notion of true society. A fairly common view of justice is that it has to do with 'the distribution of rights and privileges, powers and opportunities, and the command over material resources'.[13] But the definition of what is fair distribution and command is made by those who maintain control over the processes and characteristics by which people are related to each other. Their position is protected. It is therefore rather sanguine to claim that justice is actually being achieved.

It seems that states and individuals have reduced the notion of true society to what they can manage without threatening too much the interests of those in a position to control the processes by which human beings are related.

THE MARGINALIZATION OF 'GOD'

We have now seen the two kinds of relativism to which modern understandings of societies seem to be subject. We first considered the movement toward simpler social structures, based respectively on the primacy of the state and that of the individual. Accompanying this we found the supposition that human beings are related only extrinsically. Secondly

---

[11] This individualist view frequently sets itself up against a view which it calls traditional, while failing to realize that such a position is by no means normal now. To be sure, examples of the 'traditional' view are still found in places where absolutist states still survive; the view which prevails in the western nations, however, is not such a 'traditional' one, but rather one which suggests that states have an obligation to develop for the betterment of their citizens. The main problem arises from those who sustain the 'givenness' of their relatively privileged position, by their ability to maintain control over the processes or characteristics by which they are related to others. They may do this either by maintaining such control in a 'betterment-orientated' state or through an individualist position. Both have proved relatively defenceless against the manoeuvres of those who are bent on protecting their position.

[12] *Ibid.*, p. 117.

[13] Brian Barry, *A Treatise on Social Justice*, London: University of California Press, 1989, Vol. I, p. 292.

we saw the movement from the position in which social structures are relativized by their obligation to contribute to true society to the more extreme relativistic position in which certain kinds of social structure are, in their own right, the proper form of social structure.

Though they are often presented and accepted as such, these movements are not theologically neutral. *Historically*, they have emerged alongside a marginalization of the Christian understanding of God; it is no longer considered necessary, whether in state or church, to consider the form of society theologically. But *conceptually* also, they require the marginalization of God as Christians understand him; to suppose the normalcy of these kinds of relativism undercuts the presence in human social structures of the social coherence which is embedded in God's very being and work, together with the deeper and more varied form of human relationality which that presence implies.

How is that ostensibly Christian societies and churches have marginalized God in such ways? Strangely enough, they seem to do so by revising – or domesticating – the conception of God so that he is seen to be marginal, one who is by nature disinvolved from social structures and human relationships. That is, they do so by relativizing God, allowing him only extrinsic and occasional relations with social structures and human beings.

Historically, the disengagement of states and churches from their obligation to promote true society, replacing that by their own ideality, reflects the supposition that God *is* disengaged from the world. That is the premise of the 'natural religion' which has been widespread in the West since the eighteenth century. There God is thought only to be extrinsically related to the natural world, not defined by his relation to it any more than it is defined by its relation to him. Instead, there are processes or characteristics through which he is related to human beings, such as the natural 'infusions' of energy by which God is seen to operate in the Newtonian universe or amongst human beings. Hence his relation to them may be mediated through an historical process in which he and they are engaged, for example; this is a fairly common position for late twentieth-century theologians. Or he may be thought to be related to them, and they to him, by direct choice; this is an alternative common in theology also. But there is no intrinsic relation between God and the natural or social orders.

In this view, it is possible to satisfy religious people by maintaining the sovereignty of God, through what can be called a magical view of his operation, in which he is occasionally related to the world when it pleases him. For example, he can be seen as providing a justice which modern states cannot.

It often seems that God is pictured as doing more perfectly what the state is failing to achieve. In an age of civil disobedience he was 'the author of peace and lover of concord' who is able to give 'that peace which the world cannot give' ... Today God is thought of by many people in the North Atlantic nations as the celestial grandmother, indulgently handing out benefits and performing more satisfactorily the role which an under-financed welfare state tries vainly to fulfil.[14]

Conceptually also, modern relativistic views of society and the individual require the domestication of the Christian understanding of God. But, strikingly, this distorted form is then *transferred* to modern views of society and the individual.

First of all, the movement toward simpler social structures reflects an inability to comprehend the complexity of God's own life and relation with the world. This is often characteristic of the strongly monarchial view of God which prevails in the West. There, God is seen above all as absolute and simple, related in the selfsame way to all his creation as its ultimate explanation. Because such a view disallows all diversity or particularity as fundamentally unreal, the complexity of nature and humanity is unintelligible. When this view is extended to social structures, what results is that simpler ones are considered preferable, and this authorizes the preference for *either* monolithic states *or* those based on solitary individuals. In effect, the *monarche* of God is transferred to states and individuals.

A further result of the wish to explain everything by reference to the simplicity of God's being is the supposition that human beings are essentially alike, repetitions of God (or his will) in finitude whose destiny is to be reincorporated in an absolute unity with each other and with him. Since likeness is so strongly the norm, the manifest difference of people is puzzling, and both the complexity of their relations and the unity which might occur in this complexity are unthinkable. Human beings are too different to be intrinsically related; they can be related only extrinsically to each other and to God.

When the *monarche* of God is transferred to states and individuals, it follows, secondly, that social structures are themselves the arbiters of social coherence; they are no longer relativized by their obligation to promote an ideal true society which is beyond them. Those agencies (governmental or individual) and processes by which a society achieves or retains its unity are preferred. By contrast the complexity, pluralism and changeability of the society are regarded as alien, as aberrations. Furthermore, justice is seen as conformity, as requiring a return to the

---

[14] David Nicholls, *Deity and Domination: Images of God and the State in the Nineteenth and Twentieth Centuries*, London: Routledge, 1989, p. 30.

norms of the society, its identity and its enduring character. Whether in large societies or small, the transference of such a notion of God to states or individuals promotes something approximating to a totalitarian view of society or the individual.

If current understandings of social structures are as deeply interwoven with the domestication and transference of 'God' as we have suggested, a more satisfactory reconception of social structures will require a recovery of their relativity to a God who is seen himself to be relative to the world he has created and redeemed. This conception of the relation of social structures is far more consonant with Christian understanding.

THE FORM OF SOCIAL STRUCTURES AND GOD

The development of more adequate social structures is correlative with uncovering the presence and activity of God in them. That will mean turning away from the 'simple' social structures in which the conception of God's activity was domesticated and transferred, and acknowledging the diversity and change which are found in modern society as the location of the presence and activity of God. It is clear that the processes by which society structures itself are inherently non-linear and randomly variable (stochastic), that they are relatively unstable and unpredictable, and that they are too complex to make it possible to construct models adequate for dealing with all their characteristics.[15] On the other hand, they can be dealt with as self-organizing fields of relations, through which 'operating units' of society arise, and in terms of the energy which they require as they do so. In similar fashion, God's presence and activity in society can be discussed in terms of the fashion in which order arises through energy.

Human social life in the world appears to be a complexity of inter-related human beings, whose identity and relations change through their regular interaction. Each individual life is to some extent a self-producing and self-maintaining structure which is capable – given the energy and power – of constituting and maintaining its unity and distinctness, chiefly through structuring its components and their relations and conditioning its interactions with other lives. In so doing it orders itself by restricting changes in its structures and relations. But such lives, singularly and together, are also defined by their relations – they are internally related to others. And such relations are structured by existing forms of societal

[15] Cf. R. N. Adams, *The Eighth Day*, Austin: University of Texas Press, 1988, p. 4.

structure (formal, informal and individual). Each of these forms of social structure is in turn – given the energy with which to do so – self-constituting and maintaining through change, and for better or worse. Each is benevolent, in the sense that it promotes the possibility of moral formation for those involved, or harmful where it does not. No social structure is neutral.

If we consider God in these terms, we see him as self-structured (in accordance with his own self-determined conditions) and self-identified in a complex and dynamic unity which rests on his energy to structure and restructure himself in self-sustaining cohesion. He is in a structured dynamic relation with his world, and capable of restructuring himself and his relations with the world insofar as constructive or destructive perturbations arise in the world. Hence he is seen as an energetic unity (the Holy Spirit) which is true to its initial conditions (the Father) through ordering its interactions (the Son). But this is to be regarded not so much as a 'state of affairs' in God as an energetic faithfulness maintained in his dynamic relation to the world.

Seen in these terms, both the *nature* of society and of God may be uncovered without supposing that diversity/complexity and dynamics/change are alien. On the one hand, society is seen as its structured interrelations which are developed through the dynamics of its life. On the other hand, God is seen as a dynamic structured relationality in whom there is an infinite possibility of life.

If this is traced out more fully, the Trinitarian life of God may be seen to inform the structuring of social life, through it bringing about that 'unity in holiness' which marks God's own life. It also helps us to see how the self-structuring of God is to be seen as a self-structuring which occurs in an ongoing 'relation' with human life in the world. In this relation all the characteristics of the divine interact ongoingly with those of human life in the world. This 'interaction' suffuses human participation in the interaction, both as individuals and in the dynamic relationality which occurs in their social structuring. It can and does occur without their awareness, preconsciously so to speak, but it occurs to best effect when, in various ways appropriate to them, human beings interact with the Spirit through their own social structuring.

It is in the energizing of his relationality that God reaches his fullness, and in this ordered relationality interacts energetically with human beings to enable them to structure their life together. In their turn they exist in a relationality whose form is derived from God: their self-relationality is also their sociality, both together being structured by the presence and activity of God ('love the Lord thy God ... love thy neighbour as thyself'). But their relationality (self-relationality and sociality) is also given its dynamic energy from God; their moving toward themselves and towards others are energized by God. They need not attempt to 'possess' their relationships, by relativizing particular forms of social structure and by domesticating the notion of God and transferring it to themselves. They need instead to rediscover their own relativity to God in their relativity to each other, and thereby find new social life from God.

11

Created and Redeemed Sociality[1]

INTRODUCTION

IF we compare societies in the modern world with those in the ancient, we find modern societies much less cohesive. Furthermore, they do not expect to be cohesive. It seems that a reduction in expectation for society has taken place. And correspondingly, there is no sense of loss when societies do not in fact function well, as at present.

It does seem that the social institutions of the western world are now in a state of disarray, despite the valiant efforts of many good people to make them otherwise. And, since many religious institutions have followed the patterns of secular society, directly mirroring them or depending on their stability in order to carry on an independent existence, the problems of society have affected religious groups very deeply as well. Even if one is much more optimistic, it still seems that society and its institutions lack a rationale by which to proceed on firm pathways; and lacking this they are prey to shifting policies or to the manoeuvres of the powerful.

The possibility of human society needs to be intelligently grasped and acted upon to achieve its highest potential, the more so with the growth in complexity which characterizes human society through history. What we seem to see in our day is the effects of such a growth in complexity outstripping the intelligent grasp and action by which society may fulfil itself, with a corresponding instability – if not decay – in society and its institutions.

There is another dimension which must be added to such an explanation, for natural human society, as well as the means by which it is grasped and acted upon, manifests a pathological tendency whereby society becomes self-destructive, turning against itself and undermining the conditions which are necessary for its fulfilment. Society is not simply the unwilling victim of its own complexification; it is also active in its own self-destruction.

It is of great importance therefore that *the foundations of the possibility of society be intelligently grasped, and the possibility thus revealed*

[1] This paper was delivered to the Society for the Study of Theology as a Presidential Address at its Annual Conference in April 1986, and appeared in *On Being the Church: Essays on the Christian Community*, ed. Colin E. Gunton and Daniel W. Hardy, Edinburgh: T. & T. Clark, 1989, pp. 21–47.

acted upon. Only thus may the direction of society be identified, and pathological deviations discovered and remedied. To address this task is to ask about the position of society in the doctrines of creation and redemption, from which the issue of society has come to be disconnected. To ask about the basis of society in creation and redemption is also to ask about the nature and life of the Church, whose witness is to the possibility of a true society in the wider society around it.

FOUNDATIONS AND THE PROBLEMS OF INDIVIDUALISM AND IDEALISM

What are the foundations of the possibility of society? One way of approaching the question is to recall one of Coleridge's most well-known, but not well-understood, aphorisms:

> He who begins by loving Christianity, better than truth, will proceed by loving his own sect or church better than Christianity, and end in loving himself better than all.'[2]

At first sight, this looks simply like practical advice about priorities. But closer examination shows that it is intimately tied to Coleridge's view of reason as the transcendent capability of the human being for truth. The view was dangerously similar to Kant's, as Coleridge knew, and might carry him along the trajectory which Kant had begun; the book *Aids to Reflection* was intended as a corrective to Kant's moral philosophy. The problem was that, though Kant had allowed a vestigial place for God, the implication of his view was that the human subject should replace the divine subject as the locus of the plenitude of being and truth. And, for those who followed, this meant that the creator God must die and be resurrected as the creative human subject; he must die for the human subject to achieve his true place. As God created the world through his Word, so man creates – constructs – a world through his conscious activities and unconscious projections. *In the last analysis, therefore, the 'other' was always found to be a dimension of the subject's relationship to himself.* Since it is the solitary human subject which stands at the centre, this 'turn to the subject' always left the individual subject 'constructing' other subjects, or conceivably being deconstructed by them, finally perhaps achieving absolute knowledge when the other is fully reflected in the subject (Hegel). But, for Kant as well as Hegel and

---

[2] S. T. Coleridge, *Aids to Reflection* in the Formation of A Manly Character, London: Taylor & Hessey, 1825, p. 101.

those who came after, the end was limited by the beginning, and since the beginning was individuality, the end was no true society, only intersubjectivity; and the way commended from the one to the other was no true way, but ultimately the exercise of power.

But Coleridge avoided the trap of displacing God by the human subject. He saw reason as the organ of the supersensuous in man, as the organ there of a truth beyond man. And this was not simply a philosophical view; it was also a religious one, for human reason and will – when properly used – were seen to correspond to the divine reason and will which were themselves trinitarian in form. For man, therefore, loving truth was primary, as a coordination of will and reason, and this brought a correspondence of man's will and reason with those of God, the Trinity. It was unacceptable, therefore, to begin otherwise.

> He who begins by loving Christianity, better than truth, will proceed by loving his own sect or church better than Christianity, and end in loving himself better than all.

Since loving the truth brought participation in the Trinity, for man to love something else (in this case, Christianity) before truth was to undercut the proper use of will and reason, and in doing so to undercut their correspondence with God the Trinity, and replace them with something less. And once the rot had started, it would naturally lead to further debasements; when man no longer loved the truth, loving a lesser substitute would bring him to love still lesser substitutes. He would enter a downward spiral, whose end was in the least of all, self-love.

What is particularly interesting for our present purposes is that Coleridge's dynamic transcendentalism has a direct social implication. Loving the truth provides a universal sociality which is lost when preference is given to a particularized form of society; and preference for one particular society breeds more limited particularisms: love of Christianity stimulates sectarianism, and eventually the social disappears altogether; the only thing left is the individual self loving himself. Adhering to anything less than the universal sociality which arises in loving the truth is the entrance to a downward spiral to the least social.

What lies under the surface of Coleridge's remark is a concern with transcendentals – what have been called 'necessary notes of being', such as unity, truth, goodness, beauty. As traditionally conceived, these are the forms through which being displays itself, through which being is determinate; they constitute an answer to the search for the fundamental features of the cosmos. In the 'secularized' discussion of transcendentals which marked the 'turn to the subject' in Kant's philosophy, they were not 'necessary notes of being' but embedded in 'consciousness as such' in such a way as to provide the presuppositions for the possibility of science and morality; they needed to be uncovered by a process by which their use was analyzed. In its endeavour to provide a proper basis for science and morality, Kant's philosophy concentrated on the 'consciousness as such', and was therefore universal in intent, but this was the universal in the individual consciousness; this philosophy began and ended with the individual consciousness. Not surprisingly, most of those who came after Kant concentrated on the transcendental ego, even where they developed notions of intersubjectivity, thereby confirming Kant's individualism.

But does Coleridge reach full sociality? It is true that in Coleridge's discussion, Kant's concern with 'consciousness as such' disappears, and is replaced by the dynamics of reason in relation to truth whose operation needed to be uncovered by reflection upon practice (try it! was the motto of *Aids to Reflection*). But if his view of the dynamics of reason is not focused on the consciousness, it is still the individual who is operative in the dynamics of reason in relation to the truth, and it is the mode of his individuality which changes from universal to solitary: 'He who begins ... will end by loving himself better than all.' In the beginning, that is, the 'he' is a universal individual and at the end a solitary one. Ultimately, this remains a theory of universal individuality, rather than one of universal sociality.

It is this view, whether in the extreme form found in Kant (and those, like Kierkegaard, who follow him in this respect) or in the modified form found in Coleridge, which leads to Bonhoeffer's suspicions about transcendentalism as the foundation for a view of society. He found the conceptualities provided by the 'metaphysical scheme' of transcendental idealism unsuitable for application to the church as an empirically real community of believers:

> We must reject the derivation of the social from the epistemological category as a *metabasis eis allo genos*. From the purely transcendental category of the universal we can never reach the real existence of alien subjects. How then do we reach the alien subjects? By knowledge there is no way at all, just as there is no way by pure knowledge to God. All idealist ways of knowledge are contained within the sphere of the personal mind, and the way to the Transcendent is the way to the object of knowledge, to grasp which I bear within me the forms of the mind: thus the object remains an object, and never becomes a subject, an 'alien I'.[3]

These objections are well-founded if the transcendental category of the universal is individualist and idealist. For in such a case, the individual could reach neither the alien subject, nor his real existence. It is under-

[3] D. Bonhoeffer, *Sanctorum Communio*, London: Collins, 1963, p. 28.

standable why Bonhoeffer should therefore turn to the ethical sphere as a means of recovering responsibility to the alien subject in his empirical reality. As he saw it, it is only in the ethical sphere, where one acknowledges the thou of another person and God, that the other is truly acknowledged and genuine sociality is established.

But it is not necessarily the case that the transcendental universal is individualist and idealist. And we suggest that it is neither. In the first place, both Kant and Coleridge, and also Bonhoeffer in his reaction to them, mistake the alienation of individuals in empirical reality for transcendental reality. *The transcendental universal is sociality; and this, rather than individuality, must be the basis for understanding.* In the second place, there is no necessary cleavage between the transcendental and the empirically real, of the sort often attributed to Kant and assumed by Bonhoeffer; rather, *the transcendental should be understood as the basis of the real.* By either of the two major traditional accounts of transcendentals, for example, they were understood as general features of the empirically real, not distanced from the real. On one account, as suggested earlier, transcendentals are 'necessary notes of being', the forms through which being displays itself, and through which being is determinate; as such they constitute fundamental features of the cosmos. On the other account, transcendentals comprise the presupposed basis for the establishment of knowledge through argument and agreement. They are:

> what is *ultimate and irreducible* for all who argue – no matter what their position. For by arguing – and this means even in the light of any doubt however radical, which, as doubt, should have a meaning – they have established for themselves and implicitly recognized both the transcendental presuppositions of epistemology and the theory of science in terms of the language game of an unlimited communication community.[4]

By either account of transcendentals, therefore, *the transcendental universal should manifest itself in the empirically real.*

TRANSCENDENTAL SOCIALITY AS PRACTICAL

Given the ideologies and events of modern times, one might readily

---

[4] K.-O. Apel, *Towards a Transformation of Philosophy*, London: Routledge & Kegan Paul, 1980, p. 138.

doubt whether there could be a transcendental sociality manifest in the real which was either Godly or fully human. That is why, in their turn, Coleridge's concern for the consequences of a displaced love, the turn by Bonhoeffer to the ethical sphere and the concern for the pragmatics of human communication which has marked twentieth-century philosophy, are significant. With the exception of Coleridge, all alike abandon the discussion of transcendental sociality and instead concentrate on what is necessary for the practice of human community. They do so in many ways: Bonhoeffer's consideration of ethical responsibility in relation to one's fellow man and God, and Habermas's more rational attempt to achieve mutual understanding in communication that is free from co-ercion, might serve as two examples.

There is now strong pressure to concern oneself only with the practical or pragmatic, and to develop intermediate notions with which to do so, and to concentrate attention only on those. Hence the prominence given to the pragmatics of human communication or the ethics of human relationships. But this strategy is inadequate for several reasons. The conventions of pragmatics and ethics rest on the supposition of a tran-scendental sociality which is not only possible, but actually present in the practical or pragmatic. Secondly, pragmatics and ethics cannot neces-sarily provide insights into overall behaviour or the structure of sociality. Thirdly, what is found in pragmatics and ethics cannot readily be trans-ferred to uncharted fields, where knowledge is scarce.

Rather than abandon the attempt to find a transcendental sociality manifest in the real, one which is Godly and fully human, we should treat the two as equally necessary aspects of sociality, and as importantly different levels which are not necessarily in conflict. Coleridge's concern with the transcendental basis of 'being-with' must, so to speak, meet the concern with that which occurs in practice as one is with another (or, in Bonhoeffer's words, answers the call of another).

How are we to conceive of the relation of the transcendental basis of sociality to practical sociality? The most fruitful way is to regard them as interconnected levels, the one testable only through the other. Thus, the social transcendental is like what is sometimes called a 'generic semi-interpreted theory' in science, such as general classical field theory, quan-tum field theory, game theory, information theory, network theory, etc. Like such a theory, it is comprised of notions which are assigned no factual interpretation, has a reference class consisting of a whole family of genera; and it is only conceptually testable unless it is given further specification (which makes it another kind of theory). In contrast to such a theory, what we have called practical sociality is like a 'generic inter-preted theory' such as classical mechanics, general relativity, or the syn-thetic theory of evolution, etc. Like such a theory, it is comprised of notions which are assigned a factual interpretation, has a reference class with an indeterminate number of species; and it is only conceptually testable until there is added to it a concrete situation through which it can be empirically testable.[5] (Practical sociality is actually only practical when it is dealing with a concrete situation.)

Such a clear distinction between transcendental and pragmatic levels is important for the issue of sociality. This can be seen by considering one notorious example of the way in which the social transcendental (though not identified as such) has been 'fleshed out'. At various times, the accounts of creation and the formation of society in Genesis have been used to support the notion of 'orders of creation', which in turn was used to establish a hierarchy of races or preferred groups, thus justifying claims to superior races and providing support for the policies of Aryanization in the Nazi era and Apartheid in South Africa, not to mention a myriad of other subjugations. In such cases, as one often finds in an improperly developed theology of creation, one finds a dualism selectively breached, a wrong view of human self-sufficiency and a confounding of God with aspects of the world and its history: God's presence in the world is recognized only through the medium of the history of a particular people (the 'superior race'), the people elevated by that history are allowed a wrong self-sufficiency (national autonomy) and God's will is wrongly confounded with a particular state of affairs (the existing racial divisions).

There are two strategies noticeable in the response to this use of the 'orders of creation' argument. (1) One mistakes an *interpretation* of a 'generic semi-interpreted theory' for the theory itself, and because that interpretation is falsified, abandons the theory itself. Thus Barth and others mistook a false use of the 'orders of creation' argument for the argument itself, and abandoned the very possibility of such an argument. (Barth abandoned it after his *Ethics*, and others did likewise; there has been confusion about the argument ever since.) In effect, that strategy involves the abandonment of the possibility of a social transcendental. (2) The other recognizes that the particular interpretation of the theory (that which established a hierarchy of races) was falsified by its consequences, and then restates the argument in another form. (Bonhoeffer attempted to transform the argument into 'orders of preservation' which prepared for the coming of Christ, thereby nullifying the supposition that some were to be subjugated.) What is important here is to recognize that a failure at the pragmatic level does not falsify at the transcendental level; it only shows that the particular interpretation of the transcendental level has failed.

As can be seen from such a case, arguing that there is a social transcendental does not guarantee the quality of a particular content for it. That

[5] M. Bunge, *Method, Model and Matter*, Dordrecht: D. Reidel, 1973, pp. 38–43.

requires a further movement identifying the basis of the unity, truth, goodness and beauty of society. Such a movement, like the doctrine of creation itself, is a fundamental operation of human thought and life, and perfect results should not be expected.

CREATION AND THE SOCIAL TRANSCENDENTAL

One way of pursuing this has been the doctrine of creation, and we may use that as an illustration of what is involved.

(i) In classical Christian theology, 'creation' is a summary indicative word for two things: (1) for all the formed or ordered cosmos, as distinct from that which is unformed or lacking in order on the one hand, and from God on the other hand; and (2) for the primary relation which this bears to God. In the first sense the word 'creation' designates that which has its own proper 'nature', through its inner constitution for example, whether by reason of its distinction from that which lacks such a nature or by reason of its constitution by God. In the second sense, the word designates the fundamental relation of this 'nature' to God: since, by reason of the primacy of God, there can be no other source for the ordered cosmos, the fundamental relation is seen as causative, e.g. derivation from God's action.

Theology of creation raises questions which are pertinent to these two senses of the word 'creation'. In their classical form, questions pertaining to the first sense have to do with the constitution of this cosmos as distinct from that which is not itself, and from God, and how this is to be explained. Those pertaining to the second sense have to do with the constitution of the cosmos by God, and how this is to be explained; hence they are concerned with the theology of nature, whether as understood from God's action or presence in nature ('natural theology'), or purely by reference to God's self-communication (as in 'revealed theology').

(ii) While 'classical' forms of thinking about creation take the cosmos in its relation to its source as their starting-point and emphasize the importance of explanation, the advent of modern understanding, which is traceable to humanistic, philosophical and theological influences, has brought a concentration on fields of inquiry within the cosmos. This concentration has in effect removed reference to God as the necessary source of the cosmos, and replaced it by reference to factors within the cosmos considered in their own right, each of which has become the province of specialists. The main areas of modern investigation – cosmology (including anthropology), history, epistemology, semiotics – have been steadily developed by reference to themselves, largely in contradistinction from each other, and it has been taken that each should be understood in terms of rational patterns which can be found within the area being investigated. Correspondingly, since interest has been transferred to factors operative in each area, pursued by the appropriate specialists, the possibility of a unified view of the cosmos has receded, and interest in God as the source has diminished sharply, almost to the vanishing point. Where interest in creation as a whole has remained, it has been transferred to specialists in a particular area, usually the physicists. Where interest in the Creator has remained outside the field of specialists (the theologians), attention has been concentrated on maintaining the 'fact' of the createdness of the world as such, and showing the 'necessity' of God as presupposition, whether for the cosmos, human life, history, truth, or authentic communication. These have proved so difficult, in the presence of powerful explanations developed within each area, that development of particular issues in the createdness of the world (such as sociality), and of their relation to the Creator, has been left to one side.

We see, then, that the notion of creation was used in two senses: (1) for all the formed or ordered cosmos, as distinct from that which is unformed or lacking in order on the one hand, and from God on the other hand; and (2) for the primary relation which this bears to God.

These senses of 'creation' designate the *results* of a fundamental operation of human thought, that of thinking the formed or ordered cosmos to its limits, to the frontier which distinguishes it from what is not itself, beyond which this ordering is lost. The process requires ascertaining the fundamental features of the formed cosmos, the division of the formed from the unformed, how this forming occurs, and by what agency it occurs. These are the typical movements involved in thinking of creation. It is not, of course, that such thinking does (or should) take place in a vacuum, or move according to its own trajectory. It begins from the formed cosmos, penetrates to its most basic conditions, ascertains the limits beyond which these conditions are not present, meets the elemental forces by which these conditions are constituted, and finds how they come to be present, determining by what means they come to be. Of course, such movements are not limited to rational operations such as those mentioned. They are also found in life itself, where one becomes aware of the elements which constitute life, and also the point at which they are absent, beyond which these elements of life are lost, in the process meeting fundamental life-giving forces by which the elements of life are constituted, discovering how this happens, and by what agency this occurs. Questions about the 'meaning of life' very often take this form.

Intimately associated with such operations are all kinds of 'sins' of omission and commission. Fundamental features of the ordered cosmos may be omitted or falsely placed; limits may go unrecognized or false limits may be established, wrongly placing the division of formed from unformed; the forming of the cosmos may be falsely identified; and the operative agency may be falsely understood.

As a fundamental operation of human thought and life, and with such difficult tasks, we should not expect the consideration of creation to produce perfect results; it must instead be a project of thought and life which should be capable of self-correction. This is not to suggest that it is simply a human construct; that would be to prejudge the issue of its correspondence with truth. The process is a dynamic order, and therefore always contingent, but in its contingency should correspond with truth.

In just such a fashion, the movement to a social transcendental is a project, which in its contingency should correspond with truth, but which should be capable of self-correction. The same is true for the social transcendental. The aim is to establish an element which will justify a true society, and thus inform the pragmatics of human society. But the danger of establishing an ideological substitute is very great; to paraphrase Lukacs, 'to say "we" is the beginning of ideology'. On the one hand, the supposition of universal human solidarity provides a fundamental consolation for human social life; on the other hand, the threat of a restricted or wrong basis for human solidarity is a constant accompaniment – the highest always seems to contain the lowest. As the discussion of the 'orders of creation' argument showed, universal human solidarity is too often based on the notion of assimilation to a particular social group, whether that is based on suppositions about national identity, economic and political practice, culture or religious belief.

THE DYNAMIC OF SOCIAL TRUTH

What kind of dynamic should therefore be employed in the project of establishing the social transcendental? Above all, it will need to be of such a kind as to allow the emergence of a social transcendental which corresponds with the truth of sociality. At the same time, it will have to take account of the manifest failure, through irrationality and wickedness, of human thought and life to appropriate a social transcendental which corresponds with this truth. This suggests a dynamic which is both affirmative and critical. As affirmative, it will be a projective realization of society, and thus a raising of the most basic conditions for this by affirming them in thought and life. Furthermore, it will be capable of generating 'richer and more open-structured forms of order' in a social universe of constantly expanding complexity. As critical, it will identify and negate inadequate conditions based on unsatisfactory categories or particular societies, whether sub-human (e.g. mechanical, organic or animal) or human (e.g. particular human groups, practices, cultures, beliefs). In different terms, the dynamic is a dialectic of hope and 'reality'. But it must be remembered that both affirmation and criticism are directed to the emergence of a social transcendental which corresponds with the truth of sociality.

Two further consequences follow from this brief statement of the dynamic which is necessary for the establishment of the social transcendental. On the one hand, the affirming, projective realization of society will bring an aversion (a) to the confinements of what has been deemed to be 'natural' law or social order, and (b) to the moralistic following of patterns found in nature or history, of the sort advocated by Stoicism or such neo-Stoic movements as Capra's *Tao of Physics*.[6] Instead, it will respond to higher possibilities for society which are found through affirmation. On the other hand, the critical negation of inadequate categories for society will mean that society will not be 'natured' (understood through subhuman categories) nor will nature be 'socialized' (as providing 'a mute and purpose-less basis and pre-history for human society'), with the concomitant possibilities for the exploitation of the natural world for the 'good' of society.

Nonetheless, the dynamic by which the social transcendental is established, whether relatively true or ideological, testifies to the search for a common meaning which is necessary for the formation of society. In formal terms, what is achieved *a posteriori* testifies to the presence of a social transcendental *a priori*. Another way of expressing this would be to speak of meaning as constituted through a determinate/indeterminate relation, in which anything meaningful is 'constituted only in relation to the general host of other possible determinations that are excluded in this particular case and are therefore indeterminate'.[7] If so, the establishment of societies testifies to a common determination involved in the meaningfulness of society as such, and this is the social transcendental. Such a common determination or meaning would include the 'necessity' of society and social order, whether as a universal feature (or 'fact') of the human condition, or as a feature of the evolution of humanity, or as that which justifies attempts to establish the pragmatics of human social behaviour.

It remains the case that this social transcendental or common meaning, though universal to the human condition, is contingent; it could conceiv-

---

[6] F. Capra, *The Tao of Physics*, New York: Bantam Books, 1977.
[7] G. Lukacs, *Hegel's False and His Genuine Ontology* (The Ontology of Social Being, Vol. I), London: Merlin Press, 1978, p. 9.

ably be otherwise; and those who claim for it a particular content – the primacy of individuals or of the state, for example – suggest that is otherwise. And the dynamic of establishing it, which has its own proper operations (the affirmation and critical negation mentioned above), is also contingent. How then are such operations formed and preserved?

One important answer is that they simply are. That is to say, though contingent, they are also necessary to the human condition. Human beings, to be such, are social and form societies; and they do so in the diverse ways which are appropriate to a world increasing in complexity. This is not to suggest that human beings are subject to some kind of mechanical or organic necessity; the necessity is a social freedom which arises from the presence of the social transcendental. Looking for another with whom to share life, for example, is not in the first instance a cultural or sexual necessity; it is founded in the social character of human being as such.

THE FORMATION OF THE SOCIAL TRANSCENDENTAL AND ITS DYNAMIC

It is more difficult to say how the social character of the human being, the social transcendental, as the element which justifies all society and thus informs social pragmatics, is formed and preserved, and the dynamic of bringing it to its true form perpetuated.

Let us look briefly at two answers from modern Christians. One is provided by Bonhoeffer in a programmatic (though largely unexplicated) statement:

> Social community is in essence given with community with God. The latter is not what leads to the former. Community with God is not without social community, nor is social community without community with God.[8]

Bonhoeffer derives sociality directly from relationship to God; human sociality arises in (is given with) relationship with God – as a necessary part of it, not as a *post facto* addition to it. Therefore human sociality is

[8] Quoted in E. Feil, *The Theology of Dietrich Bonhoeffer*, Philadelphia: Fortress Press, 1985, p. 8.

inseparable from community with God; human and human-divine community are mutually necessary.

P. T. Forsyth supplied one of the few, and admirable, parallels to Bonhoeffer's view:

> I desire to write of a holy Church as the moral guide of society. By a holy Church I mean a Church holy in its calling rather than in its attainment either in work or truth. I do not allude to the Church as an authority, but as the apostle and agent of the authority ... The great problem before civilization is the moral problem ... the whole social problem. It is the issue on which civilization depends for its permanence; and yet it is the problem which civilization alone is least able to solve. But it is the problem on whose solution Christianity stands or falls ... (1) The main work of the Church is determined by the nature of the Saviour's work in the cross, and not by human demands. (2) This work was the condensed action of His whole personality – His whole holy personality. (3) The Saviour's work being personal was therefore ethical, and not official. But by ethical I mean that its keynote was holiness. The great need of the Church therefore is not work, but sanctity in the ethical evangelical sense. (4) The *essence* of Christ's work was the securing once for all of the Kingdom of God in the real world unseen, by an ethical and spiritual victory ... The historic *scope* of this work of the Saviour was the whole of society.[9]

As few others have done, Forsyth recognized the social problem as primary for civilization and for Christianity; there is an inseparable connection between the two. And the Church is called as an apostle and witness to society as a whole on behalf of One whose work was for the whole of society, its witness being determined by Christ's achievement in securing the Kingdom of God through an ethical and spiritual victory.

Bonhoeffer and Forsyth alike recognize the centrality of the 'social problem', and that there is an inseparable connection between society and God. Furthermore, both recognize that the Church shows by what it does (as apostle and witness, not by the authority of its being) that God in Christ and the Cross has brought about ethical holiness, not for individual human beings so much as for all society. But there are two problems with their views. One is that they suppose the necessity of God's specific work in Christ as the solution of the social problem; the

---

[9] P. T. Forsyth, *The Church, the Gospel and Society*, London: Independent Press, 1962, pp. 5–6, 10.

other is that they suppose that witness to the work of God is specific to the Church. In the first case, Bonhoeffer, for example, states the mutual necessity of social community with community with God as a matter of definition, without explication or defence. And both Bonhoeffer and Forsyth base the solution offered by God to the social problem on what can be called the ontology of 'gift': social community is the response to the gift of God, fulfilled in his achievement in Christ. In the second case, both Bonhoeffer and Forsyth suppose that the Church is the place where this response is made, not as cause for pride in the Church or for claims to its authority independent of Christ, but as apostle to society as a whole.

One effect of these views, therefore, is to eliminate what one could call 'general sociality' or created sociality present in the human condition; there can be no such thing as the social transcendental present in human society as an element of nature, because its place is always taken by the specific gift of God in Christ. The other effect is to eliminate the general dynamic whereby the social transcendent should be brought to correspondence with truth; its place is always taken by the specific apostleship and witness of the Church to something which occurred in Christ. Confronted with the need for sociality, both leap immediately to the specific gift of God and to the apostolicity of the Church on behalf of this gift.

There are two wider effects which result from their claims. First, in moving immediately to the specific gift of God in Christ proclaimed by the Church, they lose their commonality as created social beings with the society to which they speak. They put themselves outside the society to which they speak, and put Christian faith in the position of pronouncing God's work to society. Second, in proclaiming the specific gift of God in Christ as one of the grace which comes through God's victory, without relating this to God's work in creation, they narrow God's work unduly.

The consequences of these views are damaging. In the first place, despite the fact that Bonhoeffer and Forsyth identify the importance of Christian faith for sociality, and do so with such power and earnestness, they set Christian faith apart from common sociality, in effect privatizing the Christian contribution to sociality. In the second place, because they unduly restrict God's work to that of redemption, they lend substance to the views of those who underrate the importance of religious faith. In the presence of sharply increased contingencies in modern life, not only those which have to do with the disappearance of external natural resouces but also those related to crises in institution and personal freedom and meaning, it is widely claimed by social theorists that religions are obsolete because they are incapable of dealing with these contingencies. And where religion does deal with the contingencies which are common to modern life through 'contingency management praxis' (Luhmann), it is a 'bourgeois stabilization of capitalistic action systems', and obsolete as a medium of identity formation.[10] The challenge thus presented to religion is powerful. It undercuts any unduly simple view of God's work in sociality, of the sort to be seen in one restricted to redemption and the Church.

But there is another danger to be seen amongst those who oppose the contribution of religion, that of what could be called social sollipsism, or confinement within self-established parameters. In such a case, the theorist (or practitioner) overcomes social complexity by a constructed (or supposed) social theory which is basically incapable of being affected by anything that is other or different from itself. This is a self-closure within a particular social theory which ultimately disallows anything else, and is ultimately more sterile than the religions which are excluded. Ironically, this is the kind of crisis-management which was decried in religion. Unquestionably, if religion requires richness in meeting contingencies, social theory and practice do also.

Rather than trace the social transcendental, as the element which underlies all society and thus informs social pragmatics, to God's specific act of redemption in Christ, it should be traced to the *Logos* of God operative in creation. This divine ordering is what ultimately implants in the human condition the 'being-with' which is natural to it. And rather than trace the social dynamic (of bringing the use of the social transcendent to its true form) to the apostolicity of the Church, it should be traced to the truth of God present in creation. Hence it is to this dynamic that we trace the capacity of human beings to generate 'richer and more open-structured forms of order' in a social universe of constantly expanding complexity.[11] As stated earlier, the social transcendent – by virtue of its presence in finite human beings – is, though a necessary feature of human beings, contingent in form. But this contingency manifests the sociality of God present for humanity in created society. And the social transcendent is 'raised' to its true form in a social dynamic. We can now understand that for it to be raised to its true form is for this dynamic to generate richer possibilities of social order to meet the contingencies to which human beings are subject, particularly in the modern world, rather than simply to maintain the same range of possibilities for social order which were available in simpler situations.

This identifies the existence of social being in humanity (the social transcendental), and the movement of social being through the social dynamic, as due to the presence of divine sociality and hence the Trinitarian presence of God. To carry the argument further, as we should prop-

---

[10] R. J. Siebert, *The Critical Theory of Religion: The Frankfurt School*, Berlin: Mouton, 1985, pp. 372–373.
[11] Cf. T. F. Torrance, *Divine and Contingent Order*, Oxford: Oxford University Press, 1982.

erly do, would require an extensive discussion of the contingency of God as social; but this is more than can be undertaken here.

THE SOCIAL TRANSCENDENTAL AND THE PRACTICE OF SOCIETY

In conclusion, we must remark briefly on the ways in which the concept of the social transcendental requires further development. Strictly speaking, the social transcendent is what might be called a 'nest' of categories, and requires refraction through them all. Another way of speaking would suggest that the social transcendent, as a project of thought and life, requires specification through appropriate themata. A more technical designation of such categories or themata would be 'generic interpreted theories', those patterns of thought and life which are assigned a factual interpretation and have a reference class with an indeterminate number of species, as distinct from the higher level 'generic semi-interpreted theories' such as the social transcendental itself, which are not assigned such factual interpretations and have a reference class consisting of a whole family of genera, in this case societies. They are not therefore to be regarded as empirical descriptions, but as intermediates between the social transcendental itself and practical or empirical sociality. In a sense, they serve as a two-way street between the transcendental and the practical, enabling the social transcendental to guide the practical and also serving as a testing ground for a particular understanding of the social transcendental. They might be called 'intermediate' categories or schemata.

In order to arrive at a conception of the social transcendental in its fullness and simplicity, it would be important to pursue the number and interrelation of such categories; but we shall not attempt to do this now. Instead we shall give a first sketch of the *areas* in which they fall, and of the *dynamics* to be found in these areas.

In identifying the categories or schemata, it is important to recognize those which are conditions *for* human society and those which are conditions *in* human society, and to recognize that such conditions are ramified through history – as, for example, conditions through which the social transcendental is realized are historical (though perhaps in different degrees) rather than timeless. The conditions *for* human society are, loosely speaking, situational: sociality is formed and constrained by ecological conditions, such as location on a delimited land area and the natural resources which are available there. The conditions *in* human society are: (1) those of social institutions, the presence of laws, customs and political organization, with the constitution of leaders such as rulers, governors or a 'superior' class; (2) those of economic arrangement, including those of production and distribution; (3) those of personal relationship, including natural bonds (whether of blood affinity or loyalty) and those constructed bonds of a more 'spiritual' kind such as friendship or compassion; and (4) those of communication, such as language, symbols and culture.

All of these are also, in a sense, both the product and the producers of a history in which their effects have become, and become, more distributed and complex. And there is a sense in which the history which they produce is also the history of the world, and thus in turn provides the conditions for human society itself. For there can be little question that human society provides the organizing activity by which the world itself emerges, a world which then provides the 'materials' for human society. More simply, that which causes finds itself caused by what it has caused. But that is too simple. The historical dimension is not so simple as many would have us believe: sharp distinctions are not only created but blurred through constant mobility and merging; there is great difficulty in maintaining clearly defined social differentiation except through blind adherence to the 'simple fact that they are different'.

Human social activity, occurring in these ways, is therefore capable of reconstituting its own ways. While, for example, laws, customs and political organization appear to be an immutable 'social cosmology' by which people and things are assigned positions and powers, such a 'cosmology' can be transformed, even reinvented, to meet new demands. Hence the institutionality of society has its own historical dynamic. Indeed, it must have if it is to escape the premature stability of which modern social theorists complain, or the injustice of repressive societies to which those concerned with social liberation are opposed. For these are complaints about the fixation of society in inadequate forms which can be answered only by recovering the dynamics of institutionality.

The social transcendental of which we have been speaking, in its manifestation of the Divine Trinity, is found in such primary schemata, as the witness of the Old Testament and the New makes clear – despite the tendencies of modern interpreters to personalize their message in individualist terms or to treat it as cultural history. In fact, one of the most important aspects of recognizing the social transcendental is that it provides a corrective to widespread misinterpretations of the Bible, enabling us to grasp its meaning through a fuller set of themata than are normally in use.

In order to achieve a full picture of the social transcendental, it would be necessary to look at these themata one by one; but to do so would require a book. We must content ourselves with a sample, considering the issue of territoriality.

It is quite clear that the community of the Jews in ancient times was formed in part by their occupation of distinct territories, and the gradual coalescence of territorially-identified groups through organizations serving some special purpose (e.g. the amphictyony). The availability of the conditions for a viable economic life was also important. Early Christianity presents an interesting transformation of this means of social formation. Places remain important, but the astonishing missionary journeys of St Paul seem to be motivated, not simply as the result of a personal call, sustained by the companionship of Christ. They had more to do with his discovery of the presence of the risen Christ in the world itself. He found that the world itself was not empty but filled with the presence of Christ – a Christlike place, so much so that traveling the world was for him a constant finding of Christ. And he found that the peoples of the world were themselves Christlike; speaking to them was a constant rediscovering of Christ. If the social transcendental is found in the formation of societies by place, the determining element of places is here found to be Christ: they are Christomorphic. This is the basis for Paul's conviction that Christ is the head of all creation and salvation, without confinement to place. This has the effect of annulling social identities constructed by excluding others from an identifying place.

In order to understand the existence and quality of the social transcendental in such circumstances, we would need to consider all those conditions *in* human society which we mentioned before: (1) those of social institutions, the presence of laws, customs and political organization, with the constitution of leaders such as rulers or governors; (2) those of economic arrangement, including those of production and distribution; (3) those of personal relationship, including natural bonds and those constructed bonds of a more 'spiritual' kind such as friendship or compassion; and (4) those of communication, such as language, symbols and culture. Each and all not only come into existence but also achieve a qualitative difference in the history of the Jews and the redemptive work of Christ. That is what forms from *created sociality* a truly *redeemed sociality*. And the one is necessary to understand the other.

12

The Public Nature of Theology[1]

INTRODUCTION

OVER my many years in England, it seemed to me that people almost always felt that social life was stable, in such a way as to allow everyone to know where he or she stood. And because it was reasonably stable, individuals could proceed with their lives in a reasonably confident manner. Since the very character of society was substantial, people felt they could proceed confidently within it. But progressively in western social life, not least in England, the awareness of stability in social life has tended to diminish. There is much to be said about why this should be so, but the scope of human action is one main factor. In the western hemisphere, there are possibilities for human life and action which have progressively expanded in various ways, though of course not equally throughout society. These enable people to find new ways of organizing their life and furthering their own purposes and benefits, possibly to the disadvantage of many others. The result has been a destabilizing of hitherto-accepted social institutions.

The major issue confronting us is whether it is possible to have a new vision of what public life really is all about – a new vision of the common good and the purpose of society. Is it actually possible, with the increasing diversity of interests one finds amongst peoples in the western hemisphere, to derive or develop a new society, or a new vision of society, where some kinds of universal values will still inform a highly diverse social life? Another question is whether it is possible to develop a new notion of those institutions – universities and churches, for example – which may contribute to a new vision of society. Is it possible for universities and churches actually to respond to the shock of a destabilized society and to the uncertainties of vision which are shown by society today? So far as the churches are concerned, is it possible for the churches to promote a new idea of what is good in social life and do so from the deepest awareness of the truth of God's work in human life?

These are the issues which I shall discuss today: the shock which has occurred for society and its institutions; the question of how it is possible to have a new vision of social life; and the contributions of institutions of higher education and churches.

[1] An Address to Chaplains in Institutions of Higher Education in the UK, 1991.

THE DESTABILIZING OF SOCIETY

I think it is unquestionably the case in the western hemisphere that there is much of what could be called social disintegration, or in extreme cases social collapse. We see the collapse of societies in Eastern Europe, or the collapse of society in riots in Los Angeles. These are not unusual or peripheral phenomena. They are, in fact, extreme expressions of a phenomenon that is well known throughout the societies of the western hemisphere.

We should not idealize the past, but in years gone by there were ways in which people identified themselves and their societies, ways which were fairly stable and fairly clear. These have now become diversified, so that what people thought of as 'society' or 'the nation' has become increasingly diverse and diffuse. I do not myself use the language of pluralism for this, a language that many like to use: 'how pluralistic everything has become', they say. Such language masks the very difficulty of discussing what it is that has happened. It is widely said, for example in America, that everything has become pluralistic to such an extent that there are no principles by which people can agree to live. And there is some evidence for this, that everyone proceeds according to his or her self-interest, or the interest of a particular group. It is therefore said by Americans that there are no fundamental principles by which they can agree to proceed in social life.

I do not think that the increasing diversity of life in the western hemisphere necessarily requires a loss of national unity and the conception of a stable society. It does, however, make the formation of society into a *task*. Societies must recognize for themselves that their society, or their sociality – the very means of being a society, is not something on which they can presume that they all agree. Agreeing it is a task that they have to undertake. One of the implications that can be drawn out of the diversification of society in England, as well as in the other countries of the western hemisphere, is that England faces the task of building its society anew, and repeatedly. Thus far, England has succeeded in presuming that it is a society, that it has a national unity. But does it? I suspect that the proper response to the question is: it may, if it will *build* a national unity. The correct response to the confusion about social unity and society is not to pretend that there is already have some kind of national unity, but instead to recognize that we have a task before us, the task of *building* a society.

That is a serious task for all the leaders and institutions of society. What leaders have the vision to proceed with the task of building a society? I don't know your feelings about your Prime Minister, but there is rank despair in America about the two alternatives for US President, because it is felt by almost everyone that neither candidate – and no political leader in sight – has the capacity to provide a vision for the national future, for a future that is worth striving for. Instead America is driven into confusion by the play of market forces amongst self-interested groups. Every person and group, in fact, appeals for something which is in their own interest, with few paying attention to the common good.

SOCIAL UNITY AND THE CHARACTER OF THE CHURCHES

Who, therefore, will provide a vision of the unity of a society, a vision of a society that is worth striving for? As regards higher education, I hope you will see that the task of building social unity has implications for what chaplains do in institutions of higher education. It seems to me that the Church becomes very important at that point, because the basic character of the Church – in this country, I might add, not in America – is such that it can make a strong contribution to the task of forming social unity. I don't mean that by itself it can provide a vision of the future, but it can certainly assist a society in providing a vision for the future.

Now let me explain what I think is the specific character of English Church life, which is more important than the usual historical analyses reveal. Church life is in this country has a specific and unusual character. This does not apply only to the Church of England, but is shared in different ways by all the Churches. I am hesitant, furthermore, to give Anglicans anything with which to puff themselves up – they do that too much anyway, which is another topic we could address.

It seems to me that the specific character of Church life in England is its immersion in social life. By that I mean that amongst all the ways by which life is carried on amongst a people, the very interesting peculiarity of English Church life is how deeply it is involved in each of them.

There are basic ways by which a society, or any group of people, proceeds with living. (1) It tries to know about the world in which it lives. A conventional word for that now, pursued in highly specialized forms, is Science. (2) It tries to know how to operate well as a society; it has a variety of means of conceiving of itself as a society and a variety of ways in which it practises society. These come under headings like politics, economics, community life, family life, and so on. A society has well-recognized practices for being a society. (3) A society also has a language which it develops to enable its members to speak amongst themselves and discover their unity, and to speak of itself. (4) It has a culture which is very important for its self-identity as a society; and the culture employs means by which to sustain itself through the printed word, through radio and television and all sorts of other instruments for the sharing of meaning. These, therefore, are some of the typical ways by which a society operates: knowing about the world, knowing and practising itself, and having language and culture. All these serve as instruments by which a society is itself and develops itself.

The special character of English Church life is that it operates through the means by which this society is a society. In other words, the preeminent character of English Church life is its immersion in the ways by which the society is a society. That can easily be tested. Suppose, for example, that someone starts changing forms of worship, or the language of worship that is used. A public controversy starts, not limited to 'church people'. All hell breaks loose. Why? Because the language of worship is a way by which the society has identified itself, and for someone to start to fiddle with it is actually to damage the means of social unity. There are all sorts of other examples that could be used. The point is that Church life in this country is deeply immersed in the means by which English sociality occurs, and that is its peculiar character.

In a very important sense, therefore, theological matters are in the public domain. They are actually immersed in the means by which the public is a public, and do not stand outside public life. Let me draw the obvious contrast. In America, although it was never intended to be this way at the genesis of American life, religion has been privatized. It has been turned into something which is a matter for 'consenting adults'. And the result of that, after years of withdrawal, is that the churches are actually finding themselves less and less capable of operating in the public domain. They operate within a special corner of life which is reserved for Sundays. American religious life is unbelievably Sunday-located. They may be, as one critic said recently, 'the most religion-mad people in the world', but it is religion of a very peculiar type. It is religion that is confined to a special locale on Sunday, if it is there at all. That is the obvious contrast, an example of privatized religion. English religion is by its nature public religion. I do not mean 'folk religion' – that's an artifact constructed by the sociologists. English religion is by the nature of the case public in the sense that it is immersed in the devices and means by which the public sustains itself. The great tragedy is that by and large the Churches do not realize this. They don't realize what is the special role that they have in English life. That worries me deeply.

Actually this is so little realized that the English Churches tend to be confused about what they are trying to do. As a result, they always tend to react in a sectarian fashion. They become preoccupied with understanding who they are and what is their special role. As they do so, they tend to withdraw from their immersion in society, withdrawing from their strength into weakness. They withdraw into a 'place' where they can feel themselves and from which they think that they can contribute something very specific. But in doing so, they withdraw from the very place where they are strongest. (And by the way, this is not any the less true of the Welsh or the Scots.) The proper place for religion in England is right within the places by which English society continues. This is not a place where any kind of sectarian, self-interested, self-conscious Church can function effectively. It is a mistake for English Church life to retreat from its immersion in the very sociality of England.

THE TASK OF HIGHER EDUCATION

Now, let us begin to explore these issues under a slightly different disguise. Let's switch the scene to higher education and try to consider what higher education is, and what might be the place of the Churches in it.

I have a strong notion of the place of higher education. Traditionally, societies always managed to set up for themselves special groups of people who were responsible for guiding what was best in society. That can be done in a number of ways, but one way is to entrust to people in higher education the task of finding the best for society. In other words, universities in the past have been charged with the task of finding what is best for society and imparting that to society itself. A rather elegant way of putting this is to say that the university is a means by which society transcends itself, by which a society reaches to something which is beyond its present grasp and tries to make it possible for itself. That could be accomplished as a university provides the kind of knowledge which the society needs, the kind of skills and devices needed to enable it to function as a society, or through the elevation of culture. There are many different ways in which the task could be accomplished.

That is a very, very high view of the task of higher education. I do not suggest, however, that higher education as it exists in England now is seen that way. Instead, that is the traditional role of higher education in this country. To use graphic images, it was a wonderful 'balloon' which society threw up to enable it to lift itself. But people have been firing arrows at the 'balloon' for some time, and it may be down on the ground by now. Perhaps this is for good reasons, some of which may be things never questioned by those involved, including the Churches. Is it really right for society that people in universities should be so elitist as a group, so abstractive in their forms of learning and so esoteric in some of their knowledge?

Are those things really necessary to the contribution of universities to society? Maybe they come under the category of the old epithet, 'as good as gold and fit for heaven, but of no earthly use'. Even if they are assumed to be necessary characteristics of higher education – that of course it has to be for the elite, of course it has to be abstract, of course it has to be esoteric – there are real questions about these things. And people have therefore been firing arrows at the balloon for some time. When they now talk of making education useful, of bringing education within the reach of a larger number of people and of making education concrete, perhaps those things are legitimate.

Hence, I am by no means supposing that the old ideal of higher education as 'society transcending itself' is unassailable. There are some ways in which it ought to be 'shot at'. My questions have to do more with what is happening as a consequence. It seems to me that English education is pursuing headlong a policy of Americanization. If you are interested in the bad (and good) consequences for a society which can result from practices in higher education, America is an instructive example. From familiarity with the results of American education, I really do question whether the policy which education is following in this country is actually in the best interests of society. It may be in the short-term interest of society, but is it in the best interest of society? That's a matter for careful consideration.

THE CHURCHES AND HIGHER EDUCATION

Just what is the responsibility of the Churches in higher education? Suppose you take the view, as I do, that the strength of the English Churches is their immersion in the means by which a society tries to be its best, tries to be itself. Suppose that you do not go the sectarian route, and withdraw into the task of establishing individual or group identity as Christian, attracting a group of consenting adults to share in this. What then is the role of the Churches in institutions which are actually trying to undertake the basic tasks of higher education while also trying as best they can to cope with all the changes that have come about recently? What is the task of the Churches in higher education?

Of course that raises the question of what the Churches are all about. I have given you some indications of what I think is the chief strength of the Churches in England. One response that the Churches can make is to consider the social purpose of higher education, and think about what ought to be done in it. That would mean that the Churches should be engaging in exactly the kind of conference you are engaging in, addressing the tasks of higher education and seeing what is the Churches' responsibility in that. But instead of doing that occasionally – once every few years – they would need to do it often, and not by delegating it to chaplains. If the task of the Churches is precisely to think about what higher education should do for society, they would be in a position to help the universities identify themselves and their future, given their present circumstances.

If we suppose that the task of the universities, the institutions of higher education, is to help society transcend itself, perhaps the task of the Churches is to help the universities, the institutions of higher education, engage in that task in the fundamental ways which they have at their disposal. Perhaps the task of the Churches, in other words, is to become the means by which – the mediation by which – universities can perform their function for society. That would be consistent with the view of Church life which has been at its strongest in this country. As I have been trying to make clear, the Churches are at their strongest in this country precisely where they are immersed in social life.

How does that actually occur? How might the Churches actually assist the universities in this connection? Avoiding the view that Churches should just stand on the fringes of higher education and preach at higher education, they will employ the special values which arise in Christian faith. Do not mistake me. It is necessary to be deeply Christian and theological in what is said to universities, but not by preaching at them from a distance. So the task of the Churches might well be to assist universities to rediscover their own identity and vocation, and then assist them to develop this vocation, doing so from a Christian faith which is immersed in social life.

CHAPLAINS IN HIGHER EDUCATION

How can that actually happen? There is a very practical problem. I recognize well enough that most of you are reasonably isolated; as chaplains, you are in ones or twos, or maybe threes, in universities which predominantly do not give you much of any role. I suppose there are some places which are not necessarily well represented in gatherings like this, the Oxfords and Cambridges and Durhams and places like that, where the Church has a very well institutionalized role which is well within the social framework accepted in such universities. They ought to be here because they, above all, ought to be thinking about what they should be doing. But most of you are not from such places. Most of you exist in your ones or twos or threes, faced with an indefinitely large task, of how to minister somehow to university populations from a few thousand to many thousands, which are constantly in motion, constantly in transition.

It is a fearsome task, so part of the question about what the Churches should be in higher education comes down to what the role of an ordained (or specially appointed) person is in university chaplaincy. Is it possible to do the kind of thing that I have been suggesting, for one person to be the representative of a Church which is attempting to help the university achieve for society what universities are set in being to achieve? Is it possible for one, or two, or three people in a university situation, to do that sort of thing, to do the mediatorial task, mediating within the university the goals of its own life, so that the university can direct itself accordingly, while at the same time doing so from a position – relatively speaking – of voicelessness?

Actually I think it is very difficult, for one reason. Most of you probably have a notion of what an ordained person is which makes it very difficult to engage in a task of that sort. If we speak specifically about Anglicans for a moment, the conventional view of ordained ministry amongst Anglicans is that it confers power; ordination sets a person in being, and establishes this person in place 'from on high', in order to mould the situation and people around him/her. But this understanding of ministry is incompatible with the situation in which you find yourselves as chaplains.

I can never speak in these terms without remembering a story that was told to me once by a vicar in Birmingham who had had quite a notorious career with motor cyclists. So he was thought to be a good person for the Diocese of Birmingham to put into a new housing estate. They found him a council house in a housing estate in northern Birmingham where the Church was not within eye-shot, or within the comprehension, of the people who lived there. He was moving into his house and was trying to get rid of all the packing material left by the movers. So there he was one day, jumping up and down on the packing materials in the dustbin outside of his house, to try and fit more packing materials into the dustbin. Just then a little girl and her mother wandered by, and the little girl said to her mother, 'Oh, mummy look at that, there's a vicar in the dustbin!' 'Jolly well where he ought to be, too!' came the mother's response. Your situation as chaplains is not so very different. You are in a position of marginality in the university. Yet you have inherited the notion that ordination brings some sort of power to fashion everyone in accordance with your vision of Church life.

I have been suggesting the Church is at its strongest when it operates in the very mediations of social life which are handled in higher education; and higher education is under some threat as a result of what has been happening in social life. And despite the fact that as chaplains you are fairly marginalized and with a notion of your role which suggests that you should be powerful, I have been suggesting that you should be able somehow to help the Church speak effectively within the universities' attempt to raise social life to its true stature. I think you can do that, but probably only by altering your notion of ordained ministry and adopting another one.

The fundamental task of the ordained person is not to be a person of power who can 'collect the troops' and marshall them into a 'great army' for Christ. The fundamental task of the ordained person is, in an important sense, to build those characteristics which have marked the Church (as One, Holy, Catholic and Apostolic), but within the university as such. I do not mean that chaplains should build a self-enclosed sectarian society, but that they should work to hold up for the university the vision of the society which it exists to serve. And if the university's task is to promote society – through knowing about the world, through knowing how to achieve social order, and through developing language and culture – the task of the ordained person is to enable the university, by doing these things, to promote a society which is marked by unity, wholeness and world-engagement. Insofar as this is done, the chaplain will be engaged in building society through the university through the Church.

The task of the chaplain therefore is to mediate to an institution of higher education its own task in society. Within this task, he/she will help other people to identify their vocation within the university's purpose for society and persist with that. That is to say, the task of the chaplain will be to enable people in the university, whether they be staff or students, to rediscover their vocation within their ordinary sphere of learning as a contribution to the well-being of society, and then to enable them to unite in helping the university to achieve its purpose for society.

A SPECIFICALLY CHRISTIAN TASK

There is a specifically Christian aspect of this which becomes visible where the contribution of the university and its members perpetuates God's work. For those who can, even in very limited ways, perceive this, the end-product will be gathering in worship, in what is above all the particular characteristic of Christian Church life. The task of the chaplain in higher education is not to be a powerful person, but to help other people within existing academic life to identify their vocation in the university as it builds society, and eventually to find their work, and their place in the university, as God's work.

As academics they will continue to be concerned with those things I mentioned before, with understanding what is this world in which we live, how we operate as a society, and how we develop the common culture and language with which to be a society. These are jobs that are the work and concerns of everyone in universities, in one way or another. What the chaplain has to do is to enable people to identify this vocation, within their fields of study, as a contribution to society – and help them develop that as Christians. Thereby he/she builds the Church amongst them, gathers the Church and builds it for worship. In other words, the chaplain's task is to help people identify their own responsibility as those who contribute to the well-being of society through their particular field of academic study, and then enable them to find that this makes them part of the One, Holy, Catholic and Apostolic Church.

The task of the ordained person, therefore, is assist in the re-creation of universities and their role in society, and to help academics find their role in that. To do so is to carry out the work of a Church which is immersed in the development of society. And if they do so, they will be recreating the Church and bringing it to worship. There are many different ways in which that has to happen, which you can identify better than I can. The end-product of the whole thing, however, is not in fact for the chaplain to be the great person but for the university to serve society.

The reason for this is not that Christianity is merely functional in the development of a better society. It is, of course, an embodiment of the long-standing Christian commitment to what is sometimes called 'the life of the mind'. But there is a much more strongly theological impetus underlying it. The fundamental commitment of Christians is to the supposition that by higher education, or by the things of the mind, people are brought into contact with the world which God has created, the society which God has fashioned, and the culture which has been developed to promote human fulfilment.

Christians need to understand their commitment to these things as the basis for their work in higher education. It is this which will enable them to foster the universities in their purpose, and assist academics to identify their vocation, as something specifically Christian. The real concern of Christians is with how knowledge of the world, the working of society and the working of human culture actually exemplify God's activity in the world, but they can also assist those without such a commitment to fulfil the role of higher education in building society.

Their more ultimate task is to find how institutions of higher education – being concerned with the world, society and human culture – also exemplify what is the highest basis for such things, the work of God. And gathering them in worship will show that they ultimately come from God and are to be returned to God. So the ultimate task of chaplains in higher education is to help people see how the world in which they live – and the world of learning, science, society and culture – actually comes from God and is to be returned to God. But their proximate task is to promote the university as a place where society may transcend its present limitations, and this is a task in which all university people may join.

CONCLUSION

These are difficult tasks. And chaplains require much more assistance than they presently receive. They need help in understanding how God works through the ways in which society fashions itself and the ways in which institutions of higher education help society refashion itself. How to help people identify their vocation in academic life as something which comes from God and returns to God is an equally serious question. These are issues which need serious attention amongst theologians, and amongst chaplains.

Facing them will bring you, and through you university personnel, to an understanding of how God is God by working in human society in the world – how God is Father, Son and Holy Spirit by engaging with human beings in the formation of a good and just society in the world. Hence higher education, and your place in it, are – at least potentially – operating from the deepest truths of God's actions in history.

I have been trying to say that society is in a kind of shock at the moment, and that the shock is being felt in most social institutions. English universities have always existed to enable society to flourish through understanding the world, developing the means of sociality and the culture which is necessary for full humanity. The formation of social institutions and the immersion of Church life in this, are where English Christianity is at its strongest. If society is to be renewed in England, both universities and Churches will have to address these responsibilities. As chaplains, you have the opportunity to focus these responsibilities for university and Church. All I have been trying to do is, in fact, to re-direct you to this fundamental task.

This is a deeply Christian task because fundamentally the well-being of society, as well as these institutions which serve society like universities, come from and are to be returned to God. Social life manifests the Trinitarian activity of God, and fundamentally those of you who are concerned with helping universities to serve society in improving itself, are actually operating within the Trinitarian activity of God. It goes without saying that all of these things need to be discussed much more fully than is possible now. Heaven knows there's a lot more to be said on all of them than I have had time to say.

13

The Future of the Church: An Exploration[1]

INTRODUCTION: THE NEED FOR A THEORY OF THE CHURCH

ONE of the things I have particularly noticed about life in the Church, whether here or in England, is how little time people spend thinking about the nature of the Church – surely a key issue for them. They will be found arguing about what the Church should do in order to keep up the numbers of those attending, how the Church might be a more effective witness in today's world, what people should believe – or what quality of life they should show – if they are to be members of the Church, or who is suitable to lead the Church. These are difficult questions which can claim the energies of all the members of the Church, and they should not be underrated.

But there is another question which is presumed in all of these others. What is the Church, the nature of the society which is called the Church, and how does it exemplify faith in God? And within that, more specifically, what are the Churches – those which in the USA are called denominations? They are frequently made to seem like historical accidents, compromises which arose in Britain when neither traditional (Roman) Catholicism nor continental Reformation Calvinism or Lutheranism prevailed, and which happened to be transferred to North America *via* the British – and were perpetuated by people of a certain 'cultured' class.

I want to suggest to you that the social life of people is actually a direct manifestation of God's work amongst them, and their response to it. Likewise, the form of their social life is an intrinsic part of God's work amongst human beings. This is true in general; as an article in a London magazine said in 1830: 'A state without religion is like a human body without a soul, or rather like a human body of the species of the Frankenstein monster, without a pure and vivifying principle.'[2] But there are also societies which attempt particularly to manifest a Godly form of social life; and these are called 'churches'. For them, the specific content of Christian faith is actually to be mirrored in the form of their society, in

[1] An Address to Trinity Church, Princeton, N.J. Summer 1994.
[2] Fraser's Magazine, quoted in *The Times Literary Supplement*, 9 April 1993, p. 14.

all the dimensions which make up this form – the ways their people associate together, the ways they organize themselves and distribute responsibilities and benefits, their institutional form and their leadership, even the means by which they communicate amongst themselves.

And their mission in wider society is to show communities, nations and international life their own true life. By this reckoning, the churches in the USA, as well as those elsewhere, have significantly failed the nation, because they have not mirrored for the nation what a Godly society would be.

This is one way in which Anglican Churches are quite distinctive. Other churches give priority to statements of belief, confessional or otherwise, and treat the Church as a witness (or sacrament) of those – as if the two could be separated. But for Anglican Churches, belief is manifest as the Church itself exemplifying the truth of social life: the form of faith is the Church as the form of social life, and one is not fully in faith apart from participation in the social life of the Church.

This gives a special urgency to our question today: 'the future of the Church' is for Anglicans also the future of faith itself. That which builds up (or undermines) the Church builds up (or undermines) the work of God in the world which is evidenced in the Church.

THE CIRCLE OF GOD'S LIFE IN THE WORLD

But what is the form of the social life of the Church which exemplifies its faith? Is it just 'togetherness' of some sort? No, it is a particular quality of social life maintained through a complex structure of social life which is itself dynamic and changing, but is also constantly in need of reformation. We need to try to appreciate the many dimensions which make up this dynamic structure, and also how they can be renewed for the future. There are two main points I shall be making throughout what I say: (1) that without a full recognition of this dynamic structure, and constant attention to its transformation, the Church will – if it has not already – become ossified, a dinosaur surviving from the past; (2) but it is also of critical importance that this transformation be an expression of profound, dynamic Christian faith, and not simply an assimilation to the currents of the surrounding society. I think there is ample evidence that the Anglican Churches are profoundly problematic on both scores, that they oscillate between two kinds of self-loss: ossification (the dinosaur syndrome) and assimilation (the look-alike syndrome). If we are to have a full future, we must get a grip on ourselves, learning the art of transformation in accordance with the economy of God's life and work in the world.

Let me try to describe the issues involved in this. In Anglicanism, the Church is best seen as a number of linked issues. Perhaps it is easiest to see them as linked in a circle:

– the people of the Church in localities
– united in specific ways:
     by common worship according to a set pattern
     by the ministry of the baptized exercising the gifts
          conferred on them by God
     with a clear organization by which tasks are assigned to them
     for the common good (pastoral, teaching, service, evangelism,
     etc.)
– for certain specific purposes:
     to be one (as God is one)
     to be holy (lifted through the life of God)
     to be catholic (joined to other churches)
     to be the mission of God in the world
– these purposes sustained in three particular ways:
     by education in faith (theology)
     by an ordained ministry
     by deepening theological research.

In other words, there is a primary circle – people united through worship, ministry and order – whose purpose is to be united in holiness, catholicity and apostolicity. This circle is aided by certain kinds of stimuli: education, ordained ministry, prayerful thought (inquiring ever more profoundly into the life and work of God in the world). But it is the main task of the people themselves – all who stand in this circle – to make it into a *deepening spiral* of ever-greater participation in the work of God in today's world, which is our vocation as Christians.

LOSING THE CIRCLE

There are two things which worry me particularly: where we break this circle apart, making each part self-important; and where we lose our capacity for an ever-deepening participation in the work of God in today's world, turning the Church either into a museum of ancient life and understanding or into a look-alike of the surrounding world. Let me give you some examples.

One is the danger of one part substituting for the whole. For a long time, there has been a tendency, both here and abroad, to suppose that the Church is somehow centred in the priest. In the recent struggle of the Church of England over whether to ordain women to the priesthood – which led to a decision in favour of ordination – the supposition shared by all sides in the debate was that the priest was in some sense the direct presence of Christ in each church; and that led some to believe that the (male) Son of God had to be represented by a male priest, while others took the view that Christ was the Saviour of all and could be represented by male or female priest. But no one asked what was the office of priest, and both sides were wrong to suppose that the Church is centred in the priest.

The origins of that idea were probably in the view that the clergy were a kind of religious aristocracy whose very presence was the Church. And later they came to be understood as experts – the modern counterpart of the aristocracy. Today we live in a world where we are accustomed to defer to experts, on the supposition that we need them to do for us what we cannot do for ourselves – doctors to doctor us, entertainers to entertain us, lawyers to resolve our disputes, professionals of all kinds whom we can admire – and praise if they do well – or blame if they do not do well enough for us. And that notion lingers on for priests when they are expected to be the experts in teaching, pastoral care and so on. They soon become the substitutes for others who are as capable of teaching and pastoral care as they are. That is one example of how the circle of which I was speaking is undermined: the characteristics of the circle of people which are the Church – worship, ministry, organization – are seen to be the job only of the ordained.

For another example, take the question of education. Education in holiness is a prime need for the Church: to be able to discern the ways of God in the world, and to follow them, is a deep and basic requirement for Church life; it is life-building/-sustaining for the circle of people who are the Church. This is a matter for careful prayer and thought. But that has become a low priority in most churches, which are usually content with (in effect) kindergarten-level information in a world which is increasingly ignorant about the substance of Christian faith. [This is largely the result of the centring of Christianity on human experience from the 1950s onward.]

It is not enough to transfer the responsibility to bishops and clergy. They ought not to be held up as the 'educated' Christians, because education is the need and responsibility of the whole circle of Christians in each place. In any case, they are rarely in a position to fulfil the role of the 'educated'. The institutions in which they were trained are usually a compromise between modern academic habits and professional training. On the one hand, every branch of theological learning has become a highly specialized discipline to which students are only introduced. On the other hand, clergy are supposed to be capable in all the tasks associated with parish life – administration, teaching, preaching and pastoral care, and every one of the parish tasks has become a form of professionalism. It is simply impossible to combine all of these things – academic specialism and professional training – in one human being. But the more basic problem is that neither of these has much to do with learning that ever-greater participation in the work of God in today's world which is the chief purpose of education in the Church.

What is presented as education in most churches closely mirrors the educational practices which I have just been describing. On the one hand, there is often study of the ancient heritage of Christian faith, as if that in itself will help us understand God's work in today's world. But, even if that has its place, it will not help us *enough* in discovering the patterns of God's work in today's world. On the other hand, education is often used to familiarize people with programmes of church activity, and to deepen their skills. But, even if that also has its place, it is easily detached from participation in the work of God in the life of the Church. In both cases, education usually fails to *deepen awareness of how* God's life and work are evident in the world today, and how we may *follow* that. Don't mistake me: these things we commonly do are not wrong, but they are not enough.

Those two examples should give you some indication how the dynamic life of the Church is less than it should be, because we tend to displace our responsibility for worship, ministry and church order onto those who are supposed only to assist us, and because we lack an educated capacity to discern and follow the life and work of God in the world. To return to the quotation I cited earlier, the Church itself is 'like a human body without a soul ... without a pure and vivifying principle' – the life and work of God which its vocation is to follow.

What are the results? Because our awareness of how God's life and work go on in the world is not sufficient, things can go badly wrong in our worship, our ministry and our common life – in the very form of our social life. And because they go wrong, the mission of the Church – to show communities, nations and international life their own true life – will fail. 'Unity? A universal community? True holiness?' people will ask, 'What do the churches have to show us but disunity, discord, harm done to people, impurity and lack of faith?'

By now, perhaps, you can see the dangers besetting life in the Church today. But I do not want to say that there is no good in the life of the Church. After all, even if haltingly, we still sense what is our task – to be responsible together for living God's life and work amongst us and showing it in the world, through our worship, ministry and common life to be one and holy and to extend this into the world. But we must go much further: if we are the circle of God's life in the world, how do we restore that circle and make it a deepening spiral of participation in the life of God in the world? It is not too much to ask that we get our act together, and do the job properly!

MAKING THE CIRCLE A DEEPENING SPIRAL

All the elements in that circle have a *certain role to play*; and yet they are deeply reliant on each other. More than that, they must learn how to animate each other: each to lift the others: the life of God lifting the world by means of the Church, the life of God lifting the Church by means of all who are baptized, who are themselves stimulated by a faith-full education and leadership to appreciate ever more fully the life of God in the world.

I wonder if you know the story which is told in England about heaven and hell. Heaven, the story goes, is when the English are the police, the French are the cooks, the Germans are the engineers, the Italians are the lovers, and the Swiss are the bankers – that way each aids the others by means of their special gifts. Hell, however, is when the English are the cooks, the French are the engineers, the Germans are the police, the Italians are the bankers, and the Swiss are the lovers – all undermining the others because they are not following their special gifts. Without taking that joke too seriously, it does show that a proper distribution of responsibilities is crucial for the common good. So it is also in matters of the ordering of common life in the Church: let each do what it is his/her gift to do, while also being sustained (animated) by others with their gifts.

Just as important is the task of *raising each person to holiness*, holiness not in some abstract sense but holiness in the task of (baptized) ministry. How? It seems to me that this happens primarily through worship. Let me explain.

As Christian people, we are concerned to participate in God's work in the world. The way by which we show that is to *perform* our participation each Sunday (and perhaps on other days as well) through common worship in the Eucharist. There we give thanks for God's continuing work in the world through Jesus Christ and the Holy Spirit, and are joined to it. But we do more: our giving of thanks *involves* us in what God has done, and we are joined to God's ongoing work through our participation.

But this is only fully related to our own ministry when we take our own life and work into our common worship, incorporating our ordinary life into God's continuing work. Every one of us at worship is the same person who lives somewhere, amongst other people in a neighbour-hood, in a community with a government which provides services, does some form of work or service in public or private, in a natural environ-ment – in a much wider and often more troubled world. As witnesses to life in these places, we could draw these concerns into our prayers if we wished. Changing the image, we are like the outstretched fingers on a hand at worship; the same fingers which draw everything into the hand can also be those which distribute what the hand contains. We ourselves at worship are the means by which the life of others – and our ministry among them – are drawn into God's work and redistributed. In that sense, our ministry can be set within worship, and we can be made holy for our ministry.

The third element from which the Church is made is its *ordered common life*. How is that developed? It is important to recognize that we already are the Church in these ways – even if not as much as we should be. Some would say that our common life is simply the result of our likeness to each other, or because a clever team of clergy and vestry plan a good programme of organized activity. But those are not the primary issues. There is a deeper kind of commonness already amongst us. As the Church, we are all already bonded together (made one) in Christ by the Spirit of God. And, to the extent that – in all sorts of church activities – we recognize our responsibility toward others, we are already part of the apostolic mission of God in the world. But there is a lot more for us to do if we are to share more fully in God's life amongst us. Our task is to be one, holy, catholic and apostolic more than 'in a measure'.

The way by which we can reach higher is to align our common life with God's life in the world. By discerning and following in God's life in the world, we can order our common life so that it achieves the funda-mental tasks of the Church – to manifest God's life in itself, and show the world at large what it is really like to live from and in God's life. By being one in Christ, we can show the world what the compassionate love of God is like. By being made holy by the Spirit of God in Christ, we can show the world the liveliness which God confers on the world. By being made catholic by God's life in us, we can show the world what it is to live across the divisions by which nations, peoples, cultures and interests are divided. It's a tall order, already begun in us but needing to be carried much further.

WHAT KIND OF STIMULI?

When I say that God has already begun to do it in us, it is not because of our reliance on an *ordained ministry*. It has happened because of our common commitment to the life of God amongst us. By Baptism, every person is committed to this task, 'promised to God' for participation in his life. And we have varied ways of participating in his life, the particular vocation to which we are called – 'apostle, prophet, evangelist, pastor, teacher, to equip the saints for the work of ministry, for the building up the body of Christ'. (Eph. 4.11–12) But these are callings for all of us, and not specific to any one person, whether the priest or anyone else.

And what is the role of the priest? The task of the priest is rather different. Against the constant temptation to localize the Church in the priest ('wait until the Rector comes'), the priest is to lift up and enrich other people who are called to a variety of ministries themselves. Priests are not to 'substitute' for their people; they are not to *displace* the ministries to which laity are called by Baptism. Instead, they are to *support* them. Drawing upon the same active Spirit of Christ which enriches others in their ministries, priests are to recall other ministries to unity, holiness, catholicity and apostolicity, above all in the worship of the Church, at which the priest presides.

What kind of education is needed to deepen Church life? Education is a crucial part of all of this, for all those who participate in God's work. Above all, it helps people discern their task, and know how to activate their participation in God's work in the world.

That places an extraordinarily high expectation on theological education. It cannot consist simply in the learning of what could be called arcane knowledge and practice. It must provide the means for discerning the work of God in today's world, by all the possibilities which faith and modern critical scholarship afford. That is exactly contrary to the tendency of most of what we call theological scholarship today, which is more often caught either in a heartfelt piety detached from critical scholarship or in a neutralized scholarship which is detached from genuine faith.

All of us, and certainly theological education, need to be awakened to the task of discerning the work of God in today's world. [That is the assignment the Center of Theological Inquiry has set itself. It seeks to reunite faith and critical scholarship, and to revive the capacity of intelligent faith to speak in the crucial areas of modern life – of the truth and meaning of faith in a scientific-technological universe, of the social implications of faith in a world whose social structures are under threat, of the proper nature of human life where no one is any longer sure of what are the norms for human life, of the possibility of speech and culture as vehicles of Godly and human understanding, of how to achieve mutual respect and understanding amongst the world's religions, etc. These are nothing less than the attempt, faithfully and intelligently, to identify the life and work of God in the world's life.]

CONCLUSION

You will recall that we began with the view that the form of faith for Anglicans is the Church, a Church which does not exist for its own benefit but for the sake of showing a Godly form of social life to the world – a Church committed to healing the social life of the world. We have been trying to discover the dynamics which will enable the Church to fulfil this mission.

The picture which I have been presenting for you is that of a circle, a Church comprised of people bonded together in common life by their ministry to each other, ordered and made holy in worship. The 'pure and vivifying principle' which prevents this from being a dinosaur or a look-alike for other forms of society is its participation in God's life and work. Its future is in participating in that, and thereby becoming a form of society which can show healing to a world faced with the collapse of all lesser forms of society. The future of the Church is in its being true to itself – one, holy, catholic and apostolic – in its vocation in the work of God in the world.

Part Four: The Configuration of Theology

14

Rationality, the Sciences and Theology[1]

INTRODUCTION: THE INTERFACE OF CHRISTIAN FAITH AND THE SCIENCES

THERE is a *prima facie* reason for the concern of Christian faith with knowledge and rationality, and therefore with the sciences and the pursuit of rationality. For, at the least, Christian faith is concerned with mankind's attempt to understand its position in the world, and its theology with attempts to do so in a fully disciplined manner, wherever and however this is done. Because of the importance which they have assumed for the understanding of human life in the world, and because of the importance of their method in doing so, the sciences must be considered by Christian faith and theology. This is no longer an optional 'extra' to faith and theology, if ever it were. The sciences and theology meet in the understanding of mankind in the universe, and in the discipline of that.

It should not be a unilateral interest on the part of Christian faith. Insofar as faith and its theology actively manifest their concern, the sciences in turn are bound to be concerned with theology. It is a sad feature of our day that this reciprocity is most frequently seen only where there is conflict, for example in those episodes – remembered or present – where theology is seen to be restricting the freedom of science and scientists are defending science.[2] There are much more sophisticated accounts of the intersection of the concerns of the two, in which theology and the sciences are seen to be of assistance to each other; but these are largely ignored by those (from either side) who see the two necessarily interfering with each other.

In fact, there are two dimensions at which theology and the sciences intersect, *human existence in the world* and the *understanding and development of its basic conditions*. (1) The existence of mankind in the

---

[1] This essay first appeared in *Keeping the Faith: Essays to Mark the Centenary of Lux Mundi*, edited by Geoffrey Wainwright, Philadelphia: Fortress Press, 1988 and London: SPCK, 1989.

[2] The most obvious example is the opposition offered by Christians to the teaching of evolution in schools in the USA, accompanied by a claim for 'equal time' for the teaching of 'creation science'. See Michael Ruse, *Darwinism Defended*, Reading: Addison-Wesley, 1982.

universe is the 'natural' location, not only for mankind and the universe, but for Christian faith. Whatever this existence is, it is necessarily the condition for both mankind and its faith and theology. Therefore, insofar as *either* the results of the sciences and technology *or* those of faith affect the situation of man in the universe, they will affect each other. And each, the sciences and technology, and Christian faith, must take account of the effects of the other.

It is surprising to look back to the time when *Lux Mundi* was written, and find that the effects of the sciences and technology upon mankind could largely be ignored in restating Christian faith. Likewise, the consequences of faith upon mankind in the world could be seen to be of such a kind as not to impinge upon scientific understanding of mankind. But that can surely no longer be the case for either; the situation of mankind in the universe is deeply affected, even mediated, by the sciences and technology on the one hand and by religious faith on the other. Globally, but particularly in the prosperous places of the world, human understanding and life are infused by the sciences to a remarkable degree. Most of the benefits and necessities of life as we know it are provided with the assistance of the sciences, and the advances with which people are most concerned – as well as the problems which accompany them – are those in which the sciences play a very large part. Furthermore, it is evident that the sciences are important for all levels of society, and for all of their activities, even those which at first sight seem most remote from the world of the sciences. And few would wish it otherwise. On the other side, the importance of religious faith for the situation of mankind is now no longer ignored either; the effects of religious world-views – or the lack of them, as in what is (somewhat dubiously) called secularization – is seen as increasingly important.[3]

(2) It is also evident, however, that in important respects, the position and content of the sciences and of theology occupy a mediating role in relation to each other in their understanding and development of the basic conditions of mankind in the world. As T. F. Torrance has suggested, 'our understanding of the on-going universe itself cannot but enter into the coefficients of our theological statements'.[4] The sciences and technology, but also faith and theology, have had a deep effect on the disciplined search for (and development of) the basic conditions of mankind. The means by which the understanding and development of these conditions are pursued are now mediated through the practices of the

---

[3] The legitimacy of the notion of secularization, as employed for example by Karl Lowith in *From Hegel to Nietzsche: The Revolution in Nineteenth Century Thought*, London: Constable, 1964, is persuasively contradicted in Hans Blumenberg, *The Legitimacy of the Modern Age*, Cambridge: MIT Press, 1985.

[4] Thomas F. Torrance, *Divine and Contingent Order*, Oxford: Oxford University Press, 1981.

sciences and technology, frequently with the assistance of those (for example, philosophers) who assume the role of reflecting on these practices in order to purify them. On the other hand, the position and content of theology is of no small importance in the understanding and development of the basic conditions of mankind in the world.[5] The mediation by both the sciences and theology of the basic conditions of mankind in the world deserves recognition by both.

That is not to say that their mediation is invariable. On the contrary, in recent years, it is possible to see that notions of the position and content of each has varied considerably, with consequent variations in the view of their relations. (1) When science was seen in positivist and antitheoretical terms, Christian faith was seen to depend on direct experience, whether in Christ-formed knowledge of God (Barth) or in the experience of salvation rooted in the justifying act of God (Bultmann) – each a positivist and antitheoretical account. The claim about their interaction was therefore that faith and the sciences were positive and antitheoretical but offered sharply different possibilities, each useless in the view of the other, of knowing man in the world before God. (2) When science was seen to allow a larger place for theory, as falsifiable conjecture, theology assumed the position of falsifiable conjecture which required justification by appeal to experience, usually cumulative rather than instantaneous.[6] Correspondingly, the view was taken that the relation between the sciences and theology had to be settled by 'empirical' means, by 'looking at developments in the sciences ... and then thinking about any possible implications they might have for Christian theology.'[7] (3) When the sciences came to be seen as interpretations making use of world-views or paradigms, faith was also seen as interpretation of the world through models and paradigms. And the effects of the sciences upon faith were seen as those of one form of interpretation of the world on another, because the means of reflecting upon them were mediated by a view of the sciences as theory-dependent interpretations.[8] In all these cases, reflection on the nature of science and religion and their mutual interaction has been conditioned by the possibilities which it was thought the sciences and theology afford for understanding: positivist, empiricist, and idealist (a modern form).

---

[5] From two different directions, historical and epistemological, the work of Wolfhart Pannenberg in *Theology and the Philosophy of Science*, London: Darton Longman & Todd, 1976, and T. F. Torrance in *Theological Science*, Oxford: Oxford University Press, 1969, has been of considerable importance in this respect.

[6] Cf. Basil Mitchell, *The Justification of Religious Belief*, London: Macmillan, 1973.

[7] Arthur R. Peacocke, *Creation and the World of Science*, Oxford: Oxford University Press, 1979, p. 47.

[8] John H. Hick, *God and the Universe of Faiths*, London: Macmillan, 1973, Ch. 3; cf. Ian Barbour, *Myths, Models and Paradigms*, London, SCM Press, 1974.

Given the importance of science and technology on the one hand, and of faith and theology on the other, for the conditions of mankind in the universe, it is easy to lose sight of their limitations. Both as they affect the condition of mankind in the world and in the requirements of their theories, their demands sometimes prove excessive.

In practice, both can be seen as incurring expenses which are disproportionate to their benefits. This is most obvious, perhaps, in the case of the sciences. The expense of scientific research has frequently risen to levels which are unbearable within limited resources. As scientific research advances, its requirements – in terms of equipment, energy and talent – increase geometrically as the results available at one level of inquiry are exhausted and the researchers proceed to the next level. The infinite possibilities of research are necessarily limited by what is economically possible in one locality.[9] The technological counterpart of this problem is in the transference of the benefits of scientific research to large numbers of people, which requires an exponential increase in the use of resources. To achieve this transference is frequently impossible within the limited resources available in one locality. The exploitation of natural resources there or elsewhere is often required, an exploitation which is unacceptable for the future of mankind as a whole or for the future of the natural environment. But much the same is true in the case of religion, where the advance of religious institutions places heavier burdens on those who bear them, often without being able to call upon wider resources.

In theory also, their demands frequently prove excessive. Within both the sciences and religion, there has been a strong tendency to idealize the means and goal of inquiry, and to impose these idealizations as normative. In the sciences, 'knowledge' has been taken to be that which is supported by – or at least not falsified by – good evidence from observation and experiment. Of course, the by-product of this set of notions is the establishment of an elite of those who are most practiced and effective in observation and experiment; they are thought to be the guardians and practitioners of knowledge. With that goes the credit for historical achievements: it is thought that the knowledge produced by the sciences and their practitioners was responsible for most major human achievements through the past few centuries. Since the Renaissance, as human beings have concentrated on the task of improving their situation, it is seen that the sciences developed the most efficacious means of pursuing this task – sometimes through on-going corrections in the direction of their work, sometimes through more sustained considerations of the nature and derivation of the skills by which they worked, for example sensibility, understanding, and judgment. In Christianity, 'faith' was

---

[9] Cf. Nicholas Rescher, *Scientific Progress*, Oxford: Blackwell, 1978, pp. 194 ff.

idealized in similar fashion, as that which exercised a total claim on the believer, while also providing the grace by which it should be exercised. Hence, much as knowledge was supported by observation for the sciences, faith was supported by the presence and power of its 'object'.

Each has produced what could be called a 'confinement in factuality'. For with such knowledge (in the case of the sciences), or such faith (for theology), the result takes on the character of a self-evident state of affairs – a 'fact' or a 'belief' – which is to be assumed, and which requires no further examination. That is very like the view of scientific statements which was accepted by the scientific positivists of the Vienna Circle: 'In science there are no "depths"; there is surface everywhere ... Everything is accessible to man ... '.[10] Whether in the sciences or in theology, such 'facts' could then be used as an unexamined axiom, from which conclusions could simply be drawn. In theology, such an axiom might be: 'it is the case that God (who is of such and such a sort) is ... , that he created the world (simply originated it) and all that is in it (with their established characteristics) ... , that he redeemed mankind (transforming it into the likeness of himself).' Resting in such notions, whether scientific or theological, as if they were 'facts', involves treating the particular meaning ascribed to them as equivalent to that to which they refer, as if the referents themselves were as accessible as the meanings ascribed to them. In effect, this confines the referents to the limitations of the referring expressions.

The attractions of the old notion of a unified and unchanging basis for epistemology and ontology for science as well as for religious people continue very strong, for obvious reasons. The medieval description of God, which so closely approximated to that notion, continues – largely unmodified – amongst Christians; and they are strongly inclined to the supposition that God himself is the one, unchanging basis for all knowledge and reality. But while they may be able to sustain it in its own terms, they hold this view without being able to sustain it by reference to present-day notions of epistemology and ontology. And many questions have arisen within theology, producing a tension between 'foundationalism' and 'constructivism'. Like one form of objectivism in science, a foundationalist position in theology finds in revelation (for example) a content-rich source from which statements can be derived, while constructivism, like relativism in science, suggests that all concepts are culture-derived though perhaps employing 'thick descriptions' to maintain their content-rich material.[11]

The high cost of such attractive and usable idealizations in the sciences

---

[10] As quoted in John Watkins, *Science and Scepticism*, London: Hutchinson, 1984, p. 137.
[11] See Ronald F. Thiemann, *Revelation in Theology*, London: Notre Dame Press, 1985, and George F. Lindbeck, *The Nature of Doctrine*, London: SPCK, 1985, respectively.

and theology should be recognized nonetheless. There are two difficulties with treating them as normative. One has to do with their adequacy as indications of what occurs in the sciences and theology; in so simplifying that which is achieved in knowledge and faith, they may be untrue to the complexity of the process by which they are achieved and maintained. Indeed, it may be untrue to the relation of the sciences and theology: their simplicities may blind them to their commonality and thereby keep them apart. The other has to do with making them normative: if their derivation is too narrow, they cannot be used as universally normative. If, for example, the 'facts' of the sciences are derived from the sensible and repeatable, observation and experiment, they cannot be treated as normative in other matters. Or, if the 'facts' of Christian belief are derived from faith through grace from God, in such a way as to exclude matters of scientific 'fact', they cannot be treated as normative in wider areas. While – insofar as they are adequate to the practice of science or faith – they can be treated respectively as normative for the sciences or faith, their use must be limited to that domain. Of course, this will not be the case if their derivation is not so restricted, as when one derives from the world *and* God. This is what lies behind the refusal of many scientists today to employ an axiomatic-deductive method, and that of theologians to begin from God's presence to the world.[12]

It could also be claimed that the use of such restrictive approaches has other and wider consequences. On the one hand, it so limits the interaction of the human being with that which is to be known as to promote a nearly mechanistic interrelation of the two, excluding from science and faith those who seek a relation with the conditions of mankind in the world which is more free. This is the source of the mysticism, pluralism and aestheticism, and even the anarchic tendencies, found within and outside science today.[13] 'If it feels good, do it!' or 'believe what you will' are the sort of slogans which have a very wide appeal; and they form the basis of life and understanding for very many people, subject only to the constraints within which they live. Such views undercut the contribution of the sciences and theology, leaving it unclear how the stability and developments which they have afforded to mankind can have come about.

On the other hand, the application of such restrictive methods in the sciences and theology is frequently enervating. Using such methods in the sciences will sap the energy of reason from other areas of sense-related life and understanding, expropriating their achievement in these connections and requiring them to admit that their work is esoteric and unscien-

---

[12] See Nicholas Rescher, *Cognitive Systematization*, Oxford: Basil Blackwell, 1979, and Ronald F. Thiemann, *Revelation and Theology*, Notre Dame: Notre Dame Press, 1985.
[13] Cf. Paul Feyerabend, *Beyond Method: Outline of an Anarchistic Theory of Knowledge*, London: New Left Books, 1975.

tific or untheological. Likewise, in theology, using a restrictive notion of faith will sap the energy from other aspects of life and understanding, detaching the 'real God' from the 'real world'. Recent scientific discoveries of order emerging from spontaneity, and theological emphases on 'nonorder' testify to the search for more dynamic methods.[14]

Of course, the recognition of the limits of the methods of the sciences and of Christian faith opens a space for those attempts to speak of knowledge and faith beyond these norms. But it does not in itself restore the credibility of knowledge, faith and their relatedness. It is to that task that we must address ourselves in this essay.

How does one reappropriate the possibility of knowledge and faith in their proper relationship? One important way is to begin from their commonality in mankind. This suggests that both are intrinsic features of fully human life and understanding in the universe. In other words, the concentration or integrity of life as lived, and the most concentrated acts of the human mind, are intrinsically human activities. And as such they can be the subject of endless human activity, whether in the sciences or in the humanities. But it can also be said that they are intrinsic features of mankind's life before God, and as such directed to their source. 'Knowledge of God is the basic act of the human mind and ... faith in its intellectual aspect is the adaptation of the reason in its response to the compelling claims of God as he makes himself known to us in his Word.'[15] If these things are so, natural life and the sciences, while having their own norms which disallow specific reference beyond the domain of the natural world, are also manifestations of the direction of human life and understanding to its source and end. The sciences and theology are separate but interdependent. But it does not suffice simply to point to this intersection, or to claim it. That only states schematically what needs to be reappropriated.

Why should this be so? Why will it not suffice to repeat the intrinsic connection of that which is fully human to that which is of God? It is primarily because both the sciences and theology, in the forms in which we know them, are increasingly dislocated and disempowered by a new context, a new basis for understanding, which is overtaking both of them. As we will see later, it is hardly appropriate to refer to a dislocation of such magnitude by such neutral words as 'context' and 'basis', for they will require a vastly different understanding of the sciences and theology and their relation.

---

[14] See Ilya Prigogine, *From Being to Becoming: Time and Complexity in the Physical Sciences*, San Francisco: W. H. Freeman, 1980; Daniel W. Hardy and David F. Ford, *Jubilate: Theology in Praise*, London: Darton Longman & Todd, 1984 (in the USA, *Praising and Knowing God*, Philadelphia: Westminster Press, 1985), pp. 96–99.
[15] Thomas F. Torrance, *Reality and Scientific Theology*, Edinburgh: Scottish Academic Press, 1985, p. xi.

Our reappropriation of the relation between the human and God must allow for this, and the conclusion of this essay will suggest how it may do so. But before we attempt to do so, we must face questions about the nature of knowledge and rationality and how they are made possible by God, and how such knowledge and rationality are mediated through materiality and history. In other words, we must attempt to reappropriate the intrinsic connection of knowledge and rationality, as mediated in materiality and history, to the nature and presence of God. That is a task which requires a wide discussion of the issue, as that has appeared through the centuries. Within this discussion, we will need to face the kinds of distortion which afflict the understanding of God, knowledge and rationality, materiality and history, and which have severed the proper connections between them. Doing so is unavoidable, and really requires much more space than we have available. We shall, therefore, have to be quite selective, focusing particularly on features which are often overlooked.

KNOWLEDGE, RATIONALITY AND THEIR POSITIVE CONTENT

Knowledge, what is that? Rationality, what is that? Perhaps, above all, they are refinements of what human beings have acquired through wisdom, their own or received from some source, problematic as the notion of wisdom may be. As such, it would seem that, though they may be refinements of the achievement of wisdom – and may seem very different – they are ultimately inseparable from it. They are also implicated in whatever may be the character of wisdom. One consequence of this might be that, because wisdom is concerned with more than rationality and knowledge, they are not to be dissociated from whatever else is involved in wisdom. If wisdom is also concerned with certain goals for rationality and knowledge which lie beyond what they are, preeminently with the achievement of goodness and beauty, or with their achievement in human life in the world, then rationality and knowledge are not to be dissociated from these goals or 'values'. Whatever it is in which the respective refinements of rationality and knowledge consist, these refinements should not omit the consideration of their use in bringing about goodness and beauty. If rationality and knowledge are connected with wisdom, they are indissolubly connected with goodness and beauty, through their derivation from wisdom if not directly.

Through the centuries, most views of rationality and knowledge have followed the basic features of this picture. They have done so selectively, to be sure, but they have in the main done so. Look, for example, at the strategies which are commended for the development of knowledge. At first glance, it seems a particularly modern strategy to suppose that knowledge and its movement are to be assimilated to the 'positive content' of knowledge, that to which knowledge refers in order to be knowledge, or the 'object' by relation to which knowledge is considered to be knowledge. If this supposition is made, knowledge is that which incorporates this positive content, and knowing – the movement to knowledge – is then seen to be the pathway to the incorporation of this positive content, whereby knowledge is derived from this content. But further thought shows that this is essentially the strategy followed by all theories of knowledge through the ages. We will look at examples of this in a moment, but not before considering several other issues.

On the one hand, the positive content of wisdom to which knowledge is to be assimilated in order to be knowledge seems simple; on the other hand, it seems exceedingly dense. As the goal of all knowledge it seems to have the possibility of being maximally informative for knowledge, while also being appropriately conducive to other aspects of the well-being of mankind in the world. These qualities lead to the supposition of its simplicity.[16] On the other hand, as manifested in knowledge it seems to be so mysteriously deep as to require it to be seen as a complexity in which various aspects or levels are present. This depth leads to the supposition of an inner complexity which is incapable of being known without comparable complexities in the structure of knowledge (for example, using basic categories or establishing an inner proportioning or dynamic), and in the relation between knowledge and other aspects of the well-being of mankind such as goodness and beauty.

Another issue has to do with the question of rationality. We have spoken so far of the assimilation of knowledge to the positive content of wisdom. Seen in such a way, knowledge has its source in, and is authenticated by, the positive content of wisdom; and rationality does not as such appear, except perhaps adjectivally to show when knowledge has become 'rational' knowledge by virtue of its 'proportioning' to the positive content of wisdom. But insofar as the content of wisdom is seen otherwise, as an agency or in terms of a consciousness, the way is open for knowledge to be considered also in terms of agency or consciousness, a knowing. Seen in such a way, the activity of knowing becomes important. In other words, attention can shift from knowledge as such to the instrument of knowledge, from the state of knowledge to the activity of the agent who knows – his rationality. And if this is to be assimilated to its proper content, it is an assimilation of knowing-activity or rationality to the agency of wisdom or rationality. This assimilation may be marked by the simplicity and the complexity of the agency of wisdom; the assimilation

---

[16] See Elliott Sober, *Simplicity*, Oxford: Clarendon Press, 1975.

is not necessarily a simple correspondence, but may also be seen as the inner proportioning of the agency of knowledge.[17]

A further issue arises over the position of the material (sensual) and historical. If knowledge is to be assimilated to timeless and immaterial wisdom, or rationality to a perfect (because changeless) agency of wisdom, the consequences of materiality and change must – so far as possible – be avoided.

But if, as later became the case, materiality and change are seen to be the medium of wisdom and rationality, it is an important task to employ the material, sensory observation and historical understanding in assimilating knowledge and rationality to wisdom and its agency. Here again, the issue is often identifying the simplicity and complexity of wisdom in the simplicity and complexity of the material and the historical.

VARIETIES OF ASSIMILATION TO WISDOM

Such considerations permit us to identify in a few major examples a fundamental pattern of knowledge, and of rationality, through the ages. We see that Platonism assimilates knowledge to the 'positive content' of an absolute whose inner complexity is the eternal forms. In such a case, there is a clear direction of knowledge to a transcendent content, even though that content is simply abstract. But much later, attention is directed more explicitly to the positive content of the rational mind, with the transcendent assuming the position of a guarantor or informant. With attention switched to rationality, for example, Cartesianism assimilates rationality to the rational content of the mind, as guaranteed by the perfection of God. Locke's view gives much more importance to materiality and history, and finds rationality in the right judgment of sensory and historical content. With consciousness of the world taken as the mediation of wisdom, Kant (like Descartes) assimilates rationality to the rational mind as it is exercised upon the material and historical world. With a still more active view of consciousness of the world as the mediation of wisdom, Hegelian idealism assimilates knowledge to the movement of Spirit as it moves from abstractness through concreteness to the self-possession of wisdom. But in all these cases, 'positive content' for knowledge or rationality is found in it, either by itself or in its relation to the world, and only guaranteed (or attracted to itself) by an unconditioned or absolute. The absolute, already abstract in Plato, is seen only in its operation on the mind.

[17] Interesting examples of this 'inner proportioning' are found in Augustine, Calvin and Schleiermacher, for all of whom the agency of knowing is to be proportioned to that which is known, while the notion of a simple correspondence is to be found, for example, in Descartes and Kant.

In each case, actual knowledge or rationality – knowledge on the way to being knowledge, so to speak – is considered the mediation of this positive content; insofar as it is knowledge, it has become so through assimilation to that positive content; and the dynamic of knowledge or rationality is seen as a growth to a mediation more adequate to that content. For Platonism, it is the dialectical ascent to the eternal forms, so far as that is accessible to human beings, which combines an exemplary searching for truth with the happiness which is the concomitant of such a search;[18] for Cartesianism, it is a rational *ascesis* by which human knowing is purified in accordance with the perfection of God; for Locke, it is education in analysis and judgment; for Kant, it is the rational redevelopment (through the agency of transcendental reason) of the activity of human understanding; for Hegelian idealism, it is the self-transcending rationality of Spirit culminating in Spirit's self-appropriation in its object; and so on. All alike presuppose that knowledge or rationality (as the case may be) occurs when its 'positive content' is achieved, and that knowing is rightly ordered in accordance with this content.[19]

This is, perhaps, the notion that underlies the claim that 'we have, in the West, no ways of knowing, rational or irrational, that we can describe without Greek models of description.'[20] For, underlying every one of these views of knowledge is the supposition that the basic pattern characteristic of Platonism – assimilation to 'positive content' – should be followed, even if the kind of content which is supposed is altered very radically (from a transcendent content to one found in the human mind or spirit).

Associated with this strategy has been another, that of dualism. It has been typical of the pattern we have described, and also of its variants, that the 'positive content' to which knowledge has been assimilated has been, shall we say, protected from interference or contamination by what is seen to be inconsistent with its character. At the most fundamental level, this has meant that knowledge or rationality itself is distanced from

---

[18] Cf. Augustine, 'For if he is happy, as indeed he is, who lives in accordance with that part of the soul which appropriately governs the rest, and this part is called reason, does he not, I ask, live in accordance with reason who seeks after truth in an exemplary way.' *Confessions*, 1.7; G. O'Daly, *Augustine's Philosophy of Mind*, London: Duckworth, 1987, Ch. 7.

[19] W. Pannenberg suggests that 'modern philosophy is totally dominated by the Augustinian idea that man cannot understand himself in his relation to the world without presupposing God as both his own origin and the origin of his world ... The starting-point is Augustine's idea of *veritas* as presupposed in all human consciousness.' *Theology and the Philosophy of Science*, London: Darton Longman & Todd, 1976, p. 306. It is, however, the reference of knowledge to what is supposed as its own positive content that is central to the history of philosophy, not the presupposition of God; that would be to mistake the history of philosophy's ultimate reference for the history of religion.

[20] Harold Bloom, *Agon: Towards a Theory of Revisionism*, New York: Oxford University Press, 1982, p. 5.

the very positive content to which it should be assimilated. That is to say, in the knowledge of this content, there is also an unknowledge, because in some basic sense human understanding as such interferes with – or in extreme cases contaminates – the positive content of knowledge.

What it is that is problematic for knowledge is differently conceived. Often, as in the more intellectualist views of knowledge, the senses are held responsible, as though every ascent of knowledge to wisdom were weighted down by the impulses of the body. Hence, in the Platonist-Augustinian view, the purity of 'truth' cannot be expected to arise from the senses,[21] any more than in the Cartesian view, rational certainty can arise from the senses. At the very least, there is a dichotomizing of truth and bodiliness.[22] But sometimes it is the movement of the world which is blamed: 'what constantly changes cannot be grasped'.[23] If so, knowledge cannot arise from the contingent except by grasping the (timeless) truth of contingent events, whether for a Plato or an Augustine or a Descartes.

New views of the senses and of history slowly arise with the Renaissance, however, and thereafter it is not the senses or the changeable as such which are regarded as contaminating knowledge, but their improper use. Knowledge requires to be derived from the senses and history, and – as in the empiricist view – rational judgment cannot arise from innate ideas given in the mind or from the accepted truths of the past; they are the contaminants and must be set aside in favour of a fresh derivation of knowledge from the senses and history contextually understood.[24]

A further stage occurs with Kant and Hegel. There too, the assimilation of knowledge to its positive content requires stringent safeguards: it must arise from the senses and history; yet it must be of such a kind as to guarantee itself as knowledge. Kant provides these safeguards by excluding potential contaminants: (a) knowledge is sharply distinguished from what has not been touched by the rationality of the forms and categories which are operative in all knowing, from the sensual/historical as it is merely 'in-itself' – the phenomenal from the noumenal; (b) knowledge is sharply distinguished from that which is less than rational – knowledge from deficient knowledge (which includes that of the self, the world and God); and (c) knowledge is sharply distinguished from those activities which are not knowledge in that basic sense at all, those which

---

[21] See G. O'Daly, *Augustine's Philosophy of Mind*, op. cit., p. 92.
[22] Modern examples of such a thing occur in the writings of D. H. Lawrence, who finds a false dichotomy in the sexual act, where the bodily act of intercourse is not itself pure love where the mind 'observes from above'.
[23] Augustine, *De Diversis Quaestionibus Octoginta Tribus*, 9, quoted in G. O'Daly, *Augustine's Philosophy of Mind*, op. cit., p. 92.
[24] On this view of history and the importance of context, see Amos Funkenstein, *Theology and the Scientific Imagination*, Princeton: Princeton University Press, 1987, Ch. IV.

have to do with goodness and beauty. In Hegel's idealism, the assimilation of knowledge to its positive content requires consideration of the achievement of this positive content through historical change: knowledge is achieved through its passage into the sensory and historical, and the repossession of knowledge from this passage. The sensory and the historical are necessary to the movement of rational Spirit itself, but are contaminants insofar as they are not raised to the true (that is, the rational) quality of the Spirit. Hence, Hegel's view of the achievement of the positive content wherein knowledge consists requires not simply those contingent dualisms (of infinite and finite, for example) which Spirit 'creates' and transcends, but also the subordination of those movements which are less than absolutely rational, whether they be aesthetic, religious or even historical. In all cases, the very attempt to proceed to knowledge involves the elimination of what is considered to be incompatible with the positive content which is the heart of knowledge.

It is a significant aspect of these dualistic strategies that they procure full knowledge and rationality by concentrating on 'purity' of knowledge itself, what we have termed its 'positive content', and excluding the impure. The exclusion of the impure serves the pursuit of purity. The consequences, of course, are very serious, for everything which is inconsistent with this 'positive content' must be eliminated, whether arising from the senses and materiality, from the less-than-rational self or from a rich transcendence. Viewed from the standpoint of the Judaeo-Christian tradition, they are barren rationalisms.

Such strategies lie at the heart of traditional views of knowledge and knowing rationally, and form the core of traditional views of the sciences and epistemology. The differences introduced by different suppositions about what is the 'positive content' of knowledge (or rationality), and about what are its appropriate mediations, make the strategies seem more different than they are; their basic pattern is very much the same, directing knowledge or rationality to their positive content or 'wisdom', correcting them accordingly, and eliminating 'contaminants' through exclusion by dualisms.

This fundamental pattern has provided a vehicle of astonishing power for western thought, even where the pattern is adapted very extensively. What remains of it, and what now to do, are the chief questions facing us in this essay. But that it does remain can hardly be questioned, even in those who today claim fundamental shifts in 'paradigms' of thought.[25]

---

[25] It is noticeable that the notion of 'paradigm-shifts', as seen in the writings of Thomas S. Kuhn for example, is constructed on the supposition that all knowledge in a given time is formed through the assimilation of theory and practice to a particular 'positive content', which may collapse when new theory and practice can no longer be assimilated to it. In our terms, it is overcome by the contaminants it would formerly have been able to exclude. See *The Structure of Scientific Revolutions*, Chicago: University of Chicago Press, 1970.

THE COMMONNESS OF PATTERN IN KNOWLEDGE AND CHRISTIAN FAITH

The pattern which we have been tracing suggests that knowledge and rationality, in their fullest senses, occur when they are assimilated to their positive content. Knowledge and rationality are, in a sense, mediations of their own positive content. Whether this positive content is strictly within the possibilities of human knowledge and rationality, or requires reference to a higher 'wisdom', is a matter of disagreement. And the kind of a 'higher wisdom' which is present is also a matter of disagreement, whether it is an absolute or something richer in content, and whether the presence is attracting or informing. These issues are often resolved by sleight-of-hand, where a particular thinker simply adopts a consistent position without argument.

Nonetheless, the pattern has been a constant accompaniment to Christian thought in the West, and there are striking affinities between the two at many points. Indeed, there are those who advance the much stronger claim that there is a necessary connection between the two, and that modern science not only *did not* but *could not* have arisen apart from Christianity. For example, it is said that

> the scientific quest found fertile soil only when this faith in a personal, rational Creator had truly permeated a whole culture, beginning with the centuries of the High Middle Ages. It was that faith which provided, in sufficient measure, confidence in the rationality of the universe, trust in progress, and appreciation of the quantitative method, all indispensable ingredients of the scientific quest.[26]

The contribution which Christianity made is impressive, even if only because the richness of its understanding of God, of materiality, of particularity and of history, provided a constant attraction to the sciences, bringing them out of the barrenness of Platonism to search for richer understanding of the mind and its operation in materiality, particularity and history.

But how much of the pattern which we have traced was attributable specifically to Christian faith? The possibility of knowledge through assimilation to the positive content of wisdom? No. The supposition of simplicity and depth in this wisdom? No. The possibility of rational agency through assimilation to the agency of wisdom? No. The me-

---

[26] Stanley L. Jaki, *Science and Creation*, Edinburgh: Scottish Academic Press, 1974, p. viii. See also *The Road of Science and the Ways of God*, Chicago: Regnery, 1978.

diation of wisdom in the natural order of matter and history? No. All of these have other sources as well. But the possibility remains that Christianity, concentrating these emphases in its own powerful presentations, co-authored the pattern, emphasizing certain features, and thereby added immensely to the power of this pattern in the West. That is not, however, to say that the connection of Christianity and modern science was, or is, necessary – only that there is a massively important contingent connection between the two, whereby each is significantly affected by the other. It is another question, which we must face later, whether the connection of Christian faith is necessary for the well-being and acceptability of the sciences – and perhaps of both Christianity and the sciences – today.

The issue of the relation between Christianity and this pattern for knowledge is not so easily dismissed. The argument which we have just put is based on what is discernible through the history of culture, on the fact that 'things have happened this way'. From that point of view, there is an intimate link between Christianity and the pattern of knowledge which is in general use in the West, but the link is a contingent one because the two have happened to develop together. The argument traces the pattern of knowledge used in the West and its affinities with Christianity; the form of the argument is *a posteriori*. But to Christian faith, many of the characteristics of the pattern of knowledge appear as contingent in a different sense: knowledge has happened according to this pattern because it is of the nature of knowledge that it be assimilated to the positive content of wisdom and be so through history. To put it slightly differently, Christian faith sees it to be of the nature of wisdom that it generates knowledge in and through history. And it sees that this generation of knowledge has occurred broadly within human life, as well as specifically in Judaeo-Christian experience, the one as a broader correspondent of the other more specific one. So the affinity between the broader generation of knowledge and the more specific one arises because of their common source in the generative power of wisdom, because they are both contingent upon the generative power of wisdom.

Nor is this view limited to Christian faith. Insofar as one who knows recognizes that this knowledge is generated by the positive content of wisdom, and acknowledges that the same generativity also occurs in the more specific ways of the Judaeo-Christian tradition, he may recognize the affinity between the two, not simply as an accident of history but as contingent upon the nature of wisdom.

It is particularly interesting to recognize that by this account, the affinity between the two – knowledge and Christian knowledge, both deriving from the nature of wisdom – may be recognized in both static and dynamic forms. Hence knowledge occurs, and occurs in and through history, and in both cases occurs through its assimilation to the positive content of wisdom. This may be recognized both by anyone who knows and by the Christian who knows, who should therefore be able to see the affinity between them occurring both in the static occurrence of knowledge and in the dynamic achievement of knowledge in and through history.

The argument can be put more readily without such circumlocutions. The wisdom to whose positive content knowledge is assimilated through history, and which is thus known *a posteriori*, is found in Christian faith to have as its positive content the God who presents himself for human beings to know in history, known also *a posteriori*. The affinity between the two, which may be seen as an accident of cultural history, is shown in Christian faith as arising from the nature of wisdom itself. Nor is this confined to Christian faith: insofar as, for one who employs this pattern of knowledge, wisdom is recognized as that which gives itself to be known in history, he has some degree of affinity with the Christian. And that recognition is widespread amongst those who employ the pattern. But the claim that the one who employs the pattern of knowledge is therefore dependent upon theological ideas must be treated with some caution.[27]

ASSIMILATION TO WISDOM IN THE JUDAIC TRADITION

From the beginning, there is an intermingling of the pattern of knowledge which we have discussed with the subject-matter of theology. We must now look much more carefully at the positive content which is provided for the pattern of knowledge in the Judaeo-Christian tradition.

The supposition of the presence of wisdom in the natural world in such a way that its positive content might be the determinant of knowledge is to be found in Greek attempts to identify the 'powers' of nature through mythology, and in Judaic summaries of wisdom manifest in the practice of wisdom. But despite such similarities, there are many qualitative differences between the presentations. There is, for example, far greater passion about the importance of wisdom and its implications for the practice of life amongst the Jews, whereas amongst the Greeks there is far more patience with the development of exact statements of the conditions through which knowledge can be gained and society can be rightly ordered. There is a difference, therefore, in the form of their concerns, even in their similar concern for assimilation to wisdom.

Not disconnected from this is the more vivid awareness of time and

---

[27] Cf. Harold Nebelsick, *Circles of God: Theology and Science from the Greeks to Copernicus*, Edinburgh: Scottish Academic Press, 1985, p. xiii.

movement which is to be found in Hebrew understanding, and the determination which is exercised upon knowledge by one who will be there (in the future) as he himself desires and wills to be there:

(And he said:)
Thus shall you say to the sons of Israel,
I AM THERE sends me to you.
(And God said further to Mosheh:)
HE,
the God of your fathers,
the God of Abraham, the God of Yitzhak, the God of Yaacob,
sends me to you.
This is my name in world-time,
my remembrance for generation after generation.[28]

In both cases, the Greek and the Hebrew, wisdom is seen to be itself and yet present in knowledge and practice as their determinant despite the inadequacy of human beings to receive it. As we saw before, its positive content is 'maximally informative' and therefore simple, but also exceedingly dense; its presence in knowledge requires extensive elucidation in law and practice – as witness the extensive presentation of laws and practical wisdom to be found in the Old Testament. There is a great deal of hesitancy about elucidating the implications of this density for wisdom itself; and where this is done, it is never done in such a way as to confine the positive content of wisdom to a law-like pattern.

There is a greater willingness amongst the Jews to speak of the agency of wisdom, however. The self-sameness of wisdom (in its simplicity and density), arises not from its regularity but from its self-determination – which may at times seem changeable. Correspondingly, the agency of wisdom is seen to be the positive content of responsible action on the part of 'his' people. So there are the foundations of a notion of human rationality which is proportioned to the positive content of the agency of wisdom, in addition to the notion of human knowledge assimilated to the positive content of wisdom.

A further distinction arises over the issue of the importance of materiality and sensuality. For Platonic understanding, anything – even beauty – which is associated with materiality and sensuality is too far distanced from the ideal, the positive content of wisdom, to act as a medium of wisdom; the dialectical ascent to wisdom must begin outside materiality. And even Aristotle does not altogether overcome the distancing of materiality from wisdom.[29] But materiality is not so distanced from

---

[28] Exodus 3.14–15, translation of Martin Buber and Franz Rosenzweig, quoted in Pamela Vermes, *Buber on God and the Perfect Man*, Chico: Scholars Press, 1980, pp. 85–86.
[29] See Richard Sorabji, *Time, Creation and the Continuum*, London: Duckworth, 1983, pp. 230–231, who claims that the same is true of St Thomas Aquinas.

wisdom in Hebrew understanding. It is not simply the 'place' through which there is an epiphany of the wisdom, but itself the mediation of wisdom. Hence, human territory and behaviour are themselves mediations of wisdom and its agency. Why else should one worry about being in a strange land?

Likewise, history is of greater importance for the Hebrew than the Greek. Here one should note the character of the Old Testament text, which – apart from law and wisdom – is predominantly concerned with the interweaving of historical narratives through which the identity of God and his people is established. They are not therefore to be treated as time-neutral transparent screens through which the timeless purposes of God are to be discerned, but as historical mediations of the wisdom and purposes of God. To be sure, this poses a most difficult question for the 'nature' of wisdom. Is it 'substance-like', so that 'all events, ideas and movements in history have at bottom something in common, which manifests itself in them all and makes it possible to understand them' in terms of that 'common' thing?[30] It is only with difficulty that wisdom is seen otherwise than as a 'common thing' with a singular positive content which is the point of reference for all knowledge. But this is undoubtedly the implication of the Hebrew understanding of history. By that standard, a 'substance-like' notion of wisdom appears a simplistic abstraction.[31] To understand wisdom in its mediation in history, and to assimilate knowledge or rationality to the positive content of wisdom or its agency, therefore, demands a *hermeneutic* of wisdom.

There is another dynamic present in the Old Testament than the historical one, though the one is not readily extricated from the other. This is the dynamic of praise, whose elements are readily discernible, particularly in the Psalms. There is reference to an addressee, the Lord, whose identity and position are established, not only by who he is but by what he has done and will do. Those who address themselves to the addressee are identified, self-involvingly and imperatively, and when and where the address of praise should be offered (that is now and always, here and everywhere). And the movements and modes of activity by which praise is offered are designated; economic activity (offerings), political and

---

[30] See Jürgen Moltmann, *Theology of Hope*, London: SCM Press, 1967, pp. 254–255.

[31] 'And in nothing is Scriptural history more strongly contrasted with the histories of note in the present age than in its freedom from the hollowness of abstractions ... The histories and political economy of the present and preceding century partake in the general contagion of its mechanic philosophy, and are the *product* of an unenlivened generalizing understanding. In the Scriptures they are the living educts of the Imagination ... These are the Wheels which Ezekiel beheld, when the hand of the Lord was upon him, and he saw visions as he sate among the captives by the river of Chebar. *Whithersoever the Spirit was to go, the wheels went, and thither was their spirit to go: for the spirit of the living creature was in the wheels also.*' S. T. Coleridge, *The Stateman's Manual*, in *Lay Sermons*, ed. R. J. White, London: Routledge & Kegan Paul, 1972, pp. 28–29.

social activity, personal activity and symbolic means of praise are the most usual.[32] Hence praise is seen as a comprehensive activity representing all that humanity is and does, always and everywhere; nothing stands outside of it, 'framing' it as it were. And, even more important, it is drawn out of mankind by the positive content of God (his position and his activity, for example), and it is directed to 'raising' God through celebrating his presence throughout the world – or, alternatively, mourning his 'absence' from where he 'is'.[33]

This movement of praise is significant for knowledge and rationality. It establishes the relation between the positive content of wisdom (or its agency) and knowledge (or the knower) or the mediums of wisdom (materiality and history) differently, thereby avoiding the supposition that wisdom is fixed and substance-like or that there is – or should be – a fixed correspondence between them. Instead, wisdom (or its agency) and knowledge (or the knower) and the mediums of wisdom are drawn to their proper excellence in God and his truth. Hence in praise – openness to that excellence – the very notion of God and what is truth are opened through a simple yet dense affirmation. Simultaneously, the direction and mode of assimilation to that truth are expanded according to the truth of what is attended-to. Still again, the movements and modes of human activity are reproportioned through their assimilation to this truth. The effect of this is to avoid hypostatizations or 'substance-like' thinking at every point. Truth, wisdom, rationality, cognition, practice, economics, politics, society, persons and symbols are all 'desubstantialized' in this movement of praise. Only insofar as they are 'raised' by their assimilation to God do they become what they are.[34] This has important implications for the expansion of wisdom, knowledge and history, as we shall see later.

The movement which is to be seen in praise significantly affects knowledge and rationality in another way. It is a noticeable feature of Greek understanding that it prescinds from the particular, moving immediately

---

[32] Daniel W. Hardy and David F. Ford, *Jubilate: Theology in Praise*, London: Darton Longman & Todd, 1984, published in the USA as *Praising and Knowing God*, Philadelphia: Westminster Press, 1985, pp. 173–175.
[33] See Kornelis H. Miskotte, *When the Gods are Silent*, London: Collins, 1967, p. 141.
[34] See George Herbert's hymn:

Seven whole days, not one in seven, I will praise thee;
In my heart, though not in heaven, I can raise thee.
Small it is, in this poor sort to enrol thee:
E'en eternity's too short to extol thee.

But Herbert's piety has caused him to interiorize the raising ('In my heart, though not in heaven ... ') rather than to treat it as a matter of raising *wisdom* through *knowledge* of the *world*.

beyond this to the universal; every particular is seen as an instance of its universal form or of universal categories – the universal imposed on the particular, one is tempted to say. And the consequences of this are found eventually in Descartes and Kant, for example, who develop theories of universal rationality through which particulars are to be seen if they are to be known (or acted upon) rationally. Hebrew understanding, by contrast, always finds the universal in the particular. To be more accurate, it begins from the particular in its spatio-temporal location, those factors which 'place' it and manifest its particularity, pre-eminently its economy or self-ness in its history, and – where human 'beings are concerned – society, polity, persons and communication. And this 'location' or particularity is then expanded in praise to be 'everywhere', without displacing other particularities. The universal is therefore a world of particulars, each contingent upon its place yet joined by an expanding truth found in the praise of God.[35] The consequences of this way of thinking are found much later in medieval nominalism, the Reformers, the inductive thinking of Francis Bacon and modern observational science.

With these considerations in mind, we can also see that the western notion of progress is only attributed to the Jewish understanding of history by a considerable oversimplification. It is true that for the Hebrews history is important as the medium of wisdom in the world, but 'progress' is an example of a 'substance-like notion' which is a simplistic abstraction of wisdom as present in world-history. Whatever is the presence of wisdom in world-history, it does not permit the 'every day in every way I grow better and better' philosophy of progress. There is, therefore, no clear line or 'key' to the development of knowledge or rationality, of the kinds suggested by Descartes or Locke or Kant. It is unlikely that there is even a dialectical line of development of the sort found by Hegel; even the line of abstraction, concreteness and self-possession appears too simple and 'substance-like' a notion of the presence of wisdom in the mediation of history. The course of history itself needs to be 'raised' to become a fit vehicle of the positive content of wisdom.

ASSIMILATION TO WISDOM IN JESUS CHRIST

It is precisely this set of emphases which are taken up and given a fresh

---

[35] This accounts for the striking concern for particular places and histories which one finds in the Old Testament, which are interwoven in a master narrative of the history of the Jewish people.

concentration in Christian understanding; and it is through the recognition of these emphases that the arrival of Christianity is to be seen – they form the pre-understanding with which one must approach the task of understanding Christianity. Thereafter, through the centuries of the Christian era in the West, it is primarily through the fresh concentration of these emphases in Christian understanding that the influence of these factors upon subsequent views of knowledge and rationality is exercised.

It is in no small part due to a preparedness for the particular that one man, Jesus Christ, could be seen as the concentration of wisdom in its presence in the world. This man, furthermore, is seen as imparting, not a theory of wisdom which has a general form, but the presence of wisdom in the practice of life for those who are assimilated to it in practice.[36] The imparting is seen, furthermore, to carry the 'maximal information' in which the simplicity of wisdom or God consists, while also being so mysteriously deep as to require extensive elucidation:

There were many other things that Jesus did; if all were written down, the world itself, I suppose, would not hold all the books that would have to be written.[37]

Such assertions recognize the intrinsic similarity of Jesus to the wisdom which he presents.

The same characteristically Jewish willingness to speak of the agency of wisdom – as the positive content of responsible action – is also found in relation to Jesus. It is seen in Jesus' preparedness to accept his position as one who by his agency imparts wisdom, which is recognized by those who hear him doing so: 'He taught them as one who had authority.'[38] There are two things noticeable in this. On the one hand, the activity of Jesus in knowing seems to be assimilated to the agency of wisdom (God), though in a fashion appropriate to his humanity: he constitutes goodness himself, but also retorts, 'Why do you ask me about what is good? One there is who is good.'[39] On the other hand, there is – in Jesus' agency or activity in knowing – the mysterious simplicity and depth associated with the agency of wisdom in God. In both respects, we find within his

---

[36] Despite some limitations, Dietrich Bonhoeffer's *Cost of Discipleship*, London: SCM Press, 1948, and *Ethics*, London: SCM Press, 1955, are valuable expositions of the person and work of Christ as the presence of God for those who respond to the call of Christ which constitutes their relation to their neighbour. The limitations arise from the dualisms implicit in the exposition, with individuals set apart and related only through response to being called and the Church called out of the world to respond to the world.

[37] John 21.25 (Jerusalem Bible).

[38] Matthew 8.29.

[39] Matthew 19.17.

imparting of wisdom, an active agency which appears to be the imparting of the agency of God in the imparting of wisdom. Hence, there is in Jesus a, if not the, concentration of the agency of wisdom, of rationality.

It is obviously expected by Jesus that those who respond to his agency will be assimilated to his (and hence God's) agency of wisdom – having in them 'the mind of Christ'[40] – as they deal with the world around them. In other words, they are to perpetuate his agency in wisdom, though obviously within their limitations. It is for that reason that the attempts of Jesus' followers to grasp the truth of him, his life and death and his teachings, are not – so long as responsibly done – at odds with his own agency, even if the form in which they do so – typically interpretations and teachings – are not the same as that of his life and teachings. Interpretation is exactly what Jesus' followers should do, and rational interpretation, in the form of statements of teaching and practice, is a perpetuation of the agency of Jesus in the impartation of wisdom. These are not, therefore, to be dismissed as the result of the interference of human beings or of a 'rationalizing' of his life and teachings.[41]

This issue appears again in later, particularly post-Medieval, Christian theology, where the issue of consciousness looms large. In late Medieval nominalism, as well as in John Calvin and in Francis Bacon, human awareness assumes a pivotal position. In such discussions, the issue is how human awareness makes a freely rational response to the pattern of God's agency in wisdom as found (in concentrated form) in the 'book of nature' and the 'book of God's Word', according to the pattern of God's agency as found in Jesus Christ. But, helped by the didacticism left from certain kinds of Medieval and Ramist scholasticism, this was met by various kinds of attempt to confine the agency of human consciousness in predesignated patterns. At that point, the right attempt to assimilate the agency of rational consciousness to Christ's agency (of the agency of God's) wisdom was deflected into an abstractive view of logic which was quite at odds with it, evidently drawn from an abstractive view of the Logos as found in Greek philosophy. As a result, the freely rational response to the pattern of God's agency in wisdom was overwhelmed by rationalism. That was a radical distortion, a caricature, but it was readily

---

[40] 1 Corinthians 2.16.
[41] These have become common accusations. See Maurice Wiles, *The Making of Christian Doctrine*, Cambridge: Cambridge University Press, 1967, pp. 157–158, who sees early doctrine as the imposition of interpretations, particularly of a Platonic kind, on the figure of Jesus. In different vein, Bernard Lonergan, in *The Way of Nicea*, London: Darton Longman & Todd, 1976, sees doctrine as the product of 'differentiated consciousness', as distinct from the 'undifferentiated consciousness' which prevails in the New Testament. He does not suppose that it is an alien intrusion, but the result of the characteristically human tendency to reflect rationally. He fails to recognize that it is required by response to Jesus as agent of wisdom.

enough mistaken for Christianity. And subsequent attempts to provide for free scientific inquiry were set up in conscious opposition to this caricature of Christianity.

But the story of the concentration of wisdom in Jesus Christ is not fully told by considering his agency of wisdom. There is also the question of materiality to be faced. We recall the Jewish preparedness to find materiality as the mediation of wisdom. This was not some abstract 'quiddity' with which they were concerned, but the materiality of being bodily, living and dying in a place with others, related to them through the mediums of exchange (economics), social organization (polity), interpersonal relationships and communication. And so, it is necessary also to see the wisdom presented in Jesus Christ in these terms, not as preeminently a person independent of these factors and occasionally addressing them, but as one whose being and behaviour is the presence of wisdom in those mediums. Nor is his reality to be seen 'shining through' these mediums, epiphany-like. He is to be seen as the coincidence of wisdom with them, and not accidentally so.

Separate though they are often made to seem in modern discussions, such dimensions (even the word makes them seem separate!) as bodiliness and life, community, exchange, social organization, interpersonal relationships and communication, always meet in the reality of life in the world. While the Jews fully realized their practical importance, and the importance of wisdom for them, what we find in Jesus was one in whom wisdom reconstituted such dimensions of materiality. To consider how he did so would require a wide-ranging discussion of his reconstitution of the ways in which things and people in the world are 'placed' in space and time (through their being, life and death), their sociality, economy, polity, interpersonhood and communication – far more than can be attempted here. But throughout, we find him changing them from *within what they are*, and thus assimilating them to wisdom. For him, like the Jews, what they are is highly particularized as *this* place, sociality, economy, etc. But within these, he manifests freedom from the close restrictions of the particularities to which the Jews had tended to confine them, and correspondingly a finding of wisdom in and for other particularities, a fact which can readily be seen in his comings and goings between Jerusalem and alien territories like Galilee, or in his freedom from accepted practices of sociality, economy, etc.

There is good evidence that Jesus' representation of wisdom in these factors of materiality was passed to those who responded to them – insofar as they were assimilated to the wisdom manifest in him in their materiality. This can be seen in Paul's freedom to find (and also enhance) the reconstitutive presence of Jesus everywhere. He manifests a freedom to travel and to be with others in compassion, as in the case of those with whom one was not normally free to relate, the aliens and outcasts, the 'lost sheep'. Places remain important, but the astonishing missionary journeys of St Paul seem to be motivated, not simply by a personal call, or sustained by the companionship of Christ. They had more to do with his discovery of the presence of Christ, and hence the transformative wisdom of God, in the materiality of the world itself. He found that the world itself was not empty but filled with the presence of Christ, and in him the wisdom of God. The materiality of the world was Christlike, and in that was present the wisdom of God, so much so that travelling the world was for him a constant finding of Christ and the purposes of God. With that came a transformation of the 'ordinary' materiality of the world, its societies, its economics, etc. For example, he found that the peoples of the world were themselves Christlike; speaking to them was a constant rediscovering of Christ. If wisdom was found in the particularities of places, societies, economics, etc., for Paul the determining element of particularities was found to be Christ: they were Christomorphic. This is the basis for Paul's conviction that Christ is the head of all creation and salvation, without confinement to place.

But how was the materiality of the world filled with the transformative wisdom of God in Christ? To put it briefly, it was reproportioned in accordance with the wisdom of God as present in Christ. And this reproportioning called forth an acknowledgment of praise in which materiality recognized its own positive content as arising from the action of God. The reconstitution of materiality by Jesus, as well as the sharing of others in that reconstitution, was therefore intimately linked to the return of materiality to its source in the wisdom of God.

As we saw earlier, the dynamic of praise in the Old Testament consists in the direction to God of movements and modes of activity (bodily, living, economic, social, political, etc.) which are themselves based in the factors of materiality which we have since discussed. But with the presence of the wisdom of God in materiality in and through Jesus, these movements and modes of activity in materiality are reproportioned. In order for this reproportioning to have its full effect, however, it must be acknowledged – the appropriate form for which is praise. When they acknowledge this reproportioning, they acknowledge the one through whom they are reproportioned.

It was evident to the early Christians that there is a richness in the movement by which the wisdom of God was present in Jesus and that this richness reconstituted things. This was in striking contrast to other wisdom:

> Where is the wise man? Where is the scholar? Where is the philosopher of this age? Has not God made foolish the wisdom of the world? For since in the wisdom of God the world through its

wisdom did not know him, God was pleased through the foolishness of what was preached to save those who believe.[42]

In effect, God in Christ reconstituted not simply wisdom but the material factors in which wisdom was present, and this was known in so far as those material factors acknowledged it. Participating in this dynamic is what is important. It cannot be 'possessed' by worldly wisdom, only received and returned in praise. So those who do not take possession of wisdom may be drawn in praise to the excellence of God's wisdom through its presence in Christ, if they allow the mode by which they apprehend to be expanded or developed in accordance with that to which they attend.

This has vast implications for the activity and results of knowledge. The actual source of wisdom – the wisdom of God – cannot be hypostatized by human beings as 'their' wisdom. Instead, the excellence of it draws human wisdom beyond itself, expanding and developing it according to the wisdom of God insofar as it will allow its mode of apprehension to be expanded in such a way as to be suitable to the excellence of the wisdom of God. But this wisdom of God is also present in materiality, in Jesus and those who are formed by the presence of Jesus. As such, it reproportions all materiality, to such a degree that nothing can be hypostatized or substantialized; all the factors of materiality are reproportioned to the excellence of the wisdom of God which through Christ is present in them. So there is no longer the constancy of order – everything in its place, knowing its place – which was the case with the older views of wisdom, whether Jewish or Greek, but order itself is reproportioned by this 'new' wisdom of God in the material world through Christ. Praise is the human being's participation in this reproportioning.

But it must also be seen that this reconstitution is not complete. It might be more accurate to say that it is varyingly completed, in some ways more so than in others, and for some not so at all. To put it somewhat differently, there is an 'unhealed wound' in praise, which is healed in varying degrees, both in the human participation in movement toward wisdom and in the reproportioning of all things in their relations.

Most basically, there is the partly-unhealed wound of life itself. For life itself, which is the basis for praise, is lived only by healing over the threat of death. 'I will sing to the Lord as long as I live; I will sing praise to my God while I have being.'[43] This is the wound which is again and again opened by the threat of death, whether for nations (as for the Jews in the

---

[42] I Corinthians 1.20–21.
[43] Psalm 104.33.

Holocaust) or for individuals, and which appears to end the possibility of praise.[44] Apart from that, there are situations in which all relationships, including that with God, whether for societies or individuals, are blocked, as a result partly of damage inflicted and partly of a strong sense of integrity; and self-defensiveness (to preserve the self) is often combined with self-negation (self-destruction). More frequently, capacity for relationships of all kinds oscillates. And beyond the question of capacity for relationships, there is the still more difficult issue of the proportioning of relationships in a manner suitable to the partners. 'Pay all of them their dues ... Owe no one anything, except to love one another.'[45]

The problem is whether such wounds can be healed, and if so how. Is praise possible any longer, or is it only singing on the tomb of God? Is even lamentation, praise in the darkness, possible? 'What does your greatness mean, Lord of the universe, in the face of this weakness, this decomposition, and this decay?'[46] What does praise mean in such a threat to the life of a whole people, in which all proportionalities are lost, or indeed for any person for whom relationships and proportions are lost? It may appear simply a goad: 'Why do You still trouble their sick minds, their crippled bodies?'[47]

The intractably strange answer given by Christianity is that the wisdom of God which is present in Christ and which – through our praise – reproportions all things, is in those alienations of life and its material circumstances which Christ suffered, and there begins its reconstitutive work – only to be continued by those who share in this alienation and find the proportions of new life in praise.[48] Only in such a fashion does participation in the wisdom of God through Jesus Christ heal, restore and reproportion.

To what view of history does this lead? It was clear enough that the Jewish understanding of history was based on no supposition of a 'common thing' with a singular positive content which is the point of reference for all understanding in and of history, and that what was necessary is a thoroughly historical interpretation of the appearance of wisdom in history, a hermeneutic of wisdom. That view remains in Christianity, but it is allied with a new positive content. Wisdom is now found in materiality and history through the presence of Jesus as the concentration of wisdom. And this concentration of wisdom is present in the extreme alienations of life and its material circumstances, there to reconstitute and reproportion them. Wisdom in history is therefore

---

[44] Psalm 119.19.
[45] Romans 13.7–8.
[46] Ellie Wiesel, *Night*, New York: Bantam Books, 1982, pp. 63–65.
[47] *Ibid.*
[48] See Rowan Williams, *The Wound of Knowledge*, London: Darton Longman & Todd, 1979.

known as alienation and reconstitution, and by those who share the life of the one in whom it is alienated and reconstituted.

History itself is also seen as wounded and reconstituted. There is no constant presence of a triumphant wisdom of history, nor is there the possibility of possessing the healing power of wisdom, its source or its effects. Instead, God's own excellence appears through the rediscovery, not only of the meaning of history but of its manifestation in materiality, in what is called the kingdom of God. Therein is the reproportioning of mankind and the world.

All this is the positive content of wisdom so far as Christianity is concerned. And it is assimilation to this positive content – in praise particularly – which for Christian faith constitutes (and heals) knowledge and rationality. It is, of course, possible to summarize the content in either of two forms, as knowledge or as the direction of rationality. But for either it can be said that the positive content is only knowable (or rational) through assimilation to it in the factors of materiality and history; and this requires assimilation from the position of one estranged from it.[49] As knowledge, the content can be summarized in the doctrine of the Trinity; as the direction of rationality, the content can be summarized as personal faith seen as an active and involved knowing achieved through what is sometimes called 'in-dwelling' which is at the same time 'outer-directed' to the agency of wisdom in God.[50] While neither ontology nor revelation are irrelevant to these summaries, the positive content to which knowledge and rationality are to be assimilated calls into question the use of traditional notions of ontology and revelation.

THE RATIONALIZATION OF CHRISTIAN TRADITION

In various ways, the wisdom of God thus represented by and through Jesus in the factors of materiality was reinterpreted by means of philosophical ontology, just as the representation of the agency of wisdom was reinterpreted in terms of philosophical epistemology. So, likewise, the dynamic of praise, in which things reproportioned acknowledge the

---

[49] Compare the more limited statement, largely based on a communicational view of the relationship of God and mankind: 'The Trinity of the economy of salvation is the immanent Trinity.' Karl Rahner, *Theological Investigations*, London: Darton Longman & Todd, 1966, Vol. IV, p. 87.

[50] See Daniel W. Hardy, 'Christian Affirmation and the Structure of Personal Life' in T. F. Torrance, ed., *Belief in Science and in Christian Life: The Relevance of Michael Polanyi's Thought for Christian Faith and Life*, Edinburgh: The Handsel Press, 1980, Ch. 4.

source of their reproportioning, was reinterpreted by such philosophical hierarchies as 'the great chain of being'.

It began very early. Sometimes, as in the Book of Revelation or Augustine's *City of God*, concern for the purity of wisdom itself led to the kind of dualistic view in which the purest form of this materiality was to be found in an other-worldly place supervening upon this world, but more often the concern for this wisdom in material existence took its shape more from Greek sources. And this translated the concern for wisdom present in the factors of materiality into quite a different form, in which they were largely divorced from materiality itself in a search for supramaterial 'quiddities' like 'substantiality' (instead of spatio-temporal and historical place), 'persons' (instead of living beings), and so on. And the ubiquitous transformative presence of Christlike wisdom in materiality was restated in such abstract notions, through the use of which it was actually detached from the very materiality in which it had been present.

The same retranslation appeared much later in a different way. Concern for the same factors of materiality is found in the division of the sciences found in Francis Bacon's *Advancement of Learning*; there it was placed in the dynamics of history and mediated in the dynamics of consciousness, in which was to be traced the activity of wisdom imparted by God. After Bacon, however, the freedom of consciousness to discover wisdom from God in the 'book of nature' and the 'book of God's word' was swallowed up in the disciplines and conclusions of the separate sciences. As each of the sciences developed, the freedom of consciousness was confined by the norms of the separate sciences. These separate sciences were themselves rationalized forms of the ancient Christian concern with the factors of materiality. (The ancient concern with place became the sphere of physics, with animate beings that of biology, all the while searching for the 'economy' or 'politics' of nature in natural law. The ancient concern for societies became the sphere of sociology, for economy that of economics, for social organization that of politics, with the media of human contact that of semiotics.) In effect, consciousness and the world which it studied lost contact with the presence of wisdom in consciousness and materiality. Reference to the wisdom of God present in materiality was forgotten. It was replaced by reference to man's own consciousness of the world, rationalized either through particular pursuits (in the separate sciences) or by a general theory of rational consciousness (as in Descartes, Locke, Kant and Hegel).

Why did the sciences turn in this direction? One possible explanation is a fundamental error about the 'positive content' of knowledge and rationality, which led to a certain kind of search for simplicity and depth within knowledge of the world (i.e., with the factors of materiality) or within the rationality of the knower himself, with the result that this positive content was itself emasculated.

The search for knowledge of the world was developed through the separation of the sciences, there being a science for each one of the factors of materiality. Indeed, there was an analytical severance of their connections with each other, in effect relocating the positive content of knowledge within each one – a fact which explains the monopolistic tendencies discernible in the sciences. Furthermore, the preferred method within each field was to proceed to this positive content in its simplicity through the use of an analytic method reaching level by level back to what was the heretofore hidden inner 'reality'. If in physics, for example, the deepest 'substantiality' of things or laws of nature was sought, the search proceeded by the discernment – usually through measurement – of more and more exact quantities and regularities. As thus used, the analytic method itself was a particular avenue to simplicity, to that which was deemed to be the maximally informative – regarding matter and motion in these cases – in the mysteriously complex depths of a particular factor of materiality.

And, having begun within a separate 'science', the search for this maximally informative content went on, attracted by a kind of absolute positive content. Yet such a narrowly conceived positive content proved shadowlike and vacuous. In other words, an abstractive method produced an abstractive result. That which was found to be maximally informative was also abstract from normal material existence and from the source from which material existence derived. As we found to be the case in Greek philosophy, there was a loss 'at both ends' – in the richness of materiality and in the richness of wisdom. Thereafter, one could only reconstruct the relations of such abstractions by means of artificial connections.[51] Though neither the development of the separate sciences nor the search for maximal informative content was in itself problematic, they became so when they were used to produce an abstraction from materiality in place of the simple materiality which they sought, and when they lost the richness of the positive content of wisdom.

Much the same happens where there is a search for simplicity and depth within the knower himself. If an ideal of pure rationality is set up, in effect this establishes a pure positive content to which the practices of rational thought are to be conformed. The way by which thought can be assimilated to this pure positive content, is to search for the simplicity of rationality (pure reason in its use) in its complexity (forms and categories), and then to employ these in thought. But this actually divorces

---

[51] A particularly interesting example of such a reconstruction is to be found in P. W. Atkins' *The Creation*, London: W. H. Freeman, 1981, in which the first stages of spatio-temporal existence are explained through a series of abstractions artificially connected. But scientific literature abounds with examples; the search for ways to 'unify' science provides many examples.

thought from the richness of that which is thought (the 'world' in Kant's terminology), from the richness of the thinker (the 'soul') and from the richness of the wisdom of God present in and for both. Again, there is a loss 'at the ends' which is only matched by a loss in the dynamics of knowledge.

It is worth adding at this point that the subject-matter of Christian faith itself may suffer the same loss if, like a science or a notion of pure rationality, it wrongly conceives its positive content and searches for 'pure faith'. This is only avoided when there is a full reproportioning of faith to the wisdom of God in Christ.

ARE KNOWLEDGE AND RATIONALITY NOW TO DISAPPEAR?

Perhaps it can now be seen that notions of knowledge and rationality as they operate in the sciences and in Christian faith are related at important points. Both operate with a common pattern, concerning themselves with the assimilation of knowledge to its positive content. But their use of the pattern is so different that they are frequently at cross purposes in the area with which we are primarily concerned, that is the possibility of knowledge and rationality.

There are many ways in which they draw deeply on each other, their differences notwithstanding. From Christian tradition comes the emphasis of wisdom (or agency of wisdom) present, a wisdom which is rich and nonabstract, simple and deep, in knowledge (or its agency), where for the sciences the emphasis is on abstractive positive content (whether in knowledge or rationality). From Christian tradition comes the emphasis of wisdom present in particularities (or the particularity of awareness) for those fully assimilated to its effect on particularities, while from the sciences come emphases on generality. From Christian tradition comes the emphasis of wisdom (or its agency) present in materiality and its factors, proportioning and reproportioning them, known through being proportioned or reproportioned by it, while from the sciences come emphases of substantiality and regularity ascertainable through a detached knowledge. From Christian tradition comes the emphasis on the rich dynamism by which wisdom is present for mankind in the world, in which mankind may participate through praise; and from this rich dynamism comes the 'attractive' character of wisdom for the Christian, where for the sciences the tendency is to hypostatize the object sought for, and the means of seeking for it. For Christian tradition, too, history is a time of incompletion and contingency in which wisdom is present in the dark places as well as the light, where for the sciences, history is a regularity and in that sense fixed in its meaning. Each, as we have said, draws on the other.

As we said much earlier, however, both are now being judged for their adequacy by reference to a new situation. While presented as utterly new, in many respects the new situation combines many of the features of the scene which has been emerging for the past two hundred years. What is this new 'post-modern' situation? It defies generalization, and in actuality resists any synthetic picture. But even at the risk of generalizing, it is above all a picture of plenitude, consisting of an endless complexity and dynamism of meaning at every level. Imagine any connection which appears in the history of knowledge, and then imagine that connection being seen as a complexity of interrelations; the picture thus obtained would not be inappropriate. Hence, so-called 'correspondence' notions of knowledge and rational agency, in which a simple one-to-one relation is drawn between words or concepts and realities, is vastly oversimple; all such relations are multiple and complex. The same argument affects all supposed affinities, emphasizing their 'difference', 'deconstructing' the simplicities on which they are founded. The consequence is that all that gives a solid foundation for knowledge and rationality, particularly the 'onto-theology' of the western tradition, and its 'logo-centrism', are dissolved. And with them go conventional notions of knowledge and rationality.[52]

A further indication of the immensity of the changes implicit in these suggestions can be given by referring to a problem in topology. If one cuts a hole in the inner tube of a bicycle tyre where the valve is, and begins to pull the rest of the tube through the hole, what happens? The issue with modern understanding – though hardly fully appreciated yet – is that one can repeat the exercise at an infinite number of points on the tube, drawing the tube through *after* it has been drawn through at an infinite number of other points. That is a fascinating prospect, not only a testimony to the amazing creativity of human understanding but an indication of the possibility of an endlessly multiplying complexity in knowledge. If such major endeavours as those which have to do with the factors of materiality we discussed earlier provide more and more holes through which other endeavours – and even their own – can be drawn, then knowledge becomes fuller and fuller, with no limit in sight. It is, as we said, an indefinite plenitude.

Perhaps it is because Nietzsche is so influential in this post-modernism that it has been taken both as a 'reduction of meaning to mere nothingness' and as anti-Christian, suggesting that all Christianity is a sacrifice of

[52] See Joseph O'Leary, *Questioning Back: The Overcoming of Metaphysics in Christian Tradition*, Minneapolis: The Winston Press, 1985.

the intellect to maintain a 'theological construct' called the Word of God. But what should be clear by now is that those characteristics of 'Christian tradition' which are thus accused are in fact not Christian tradition at all, but the product of various kinds of rationalism imposed on Christian faith.

It would be far too much to claim that Christian faith has refounded the possibility of knowledge and rationality in this new situation. But precisely because by its faith in Jesus Christ it is prepared for the presence of the Wisdom of God in particularity, in the factors of materiality and in the reproportioning of all 'things' and relations as their maker and redeeemer is praised in them, Christian faith at least has the means by which to rediscover the possibility of knowledge and rationality in the new situation.

15

Faith Embedded in the Particularities of History[1]

INTRODUCTION

As historical beings contemplating history, we do so with sensibilities formed in certain ways – themselves the results of certain trajectories of historical formation. So the notions of historiography with which we approach nineteenth-century theology are likely to be the results of the influence of the nineteenth century or perhaps a refinement of it. With some reflection, those notions can be traced, and perhaps redefined – or redirected where they are problematic.

But these notions of historiography may be more questionable than such a strategy recognizes. Is the historiography which seems to have resulted from the nineteenth century still allowable? The answer to that query will depend on what history is now seen to be. Indeed, 'how history is now seen to be' may bring us to ask again what it was that nineteenth-century notions of history were. Perhaps they made hitherto unrecognized contributions to a different understanding of history.

In order to fix in our minds the possibility that there are other notions of historiography than those habitually drawn from the nineteenth century, let us begin by mentioning two others before identifying the one derived from nineteenth-century thought and analyzing some of its hidden features. Afterward, we will need to suggest an alternative.

HISTORY AS A FIELD OF POTENCIES

This is history conceived as the 'discourse ... of intimate identification, indeed kinship, in a mythically literal sense, with the rest of the earth's society – a speech and technology of power, though not so much a power *over* other things as the power *of* these other sentient beings.' History is therefore 'the learning of their human powers and abilities from these other-than-human beings.'[2]

---

[1] A Paper for the Annual Meeting of the Nineteenth Century Theology Group, American Academy of Religion, November 1992.
[2] Calvin Luther Martin, *In the Spirit of the Earth: Rethinking History and Time*, Baltimore: Johns Hopkins University Press, 1992, p. 18.

As such, history is akin to the 'dream-time' practices of the Australian Aboriginals described in Bruce Chatwin's book *The Songlines*:

The Aboriginals had an earthbound philosophy. The earth gave life to a man; gave him his food, language and intelligence; and the earth took him back when he died ... [They] were a people who trod lightly over the earth; and the less they took from, the earth, the less they had to give in return ...

My reason for coming to Australia [Chatwin says] was to learn for myself ... what a Songline was – and how it worked ... Every Wallaby Man believed he was descended from a universal Wallaby Father, who was the ancestor of all other Wallaby Men and all living wallabies ... Each totemic ancestor, while traveling through the country, was thought to have scattered a trail of words and musical notes along the line of his footprints ... these Dreaming-tracks lay over the land as 'ways' of communication between the most far-flung tribes. A song ... was both map and direction-finder. Providing you knew the song, you could always find your way across country ... as long as [a man] stuck to the track, he'd always find people who shared his Dreaming, who were, in fact, his brothers ... from whom he could expect hospitality. So song is a kind of pass-port and meal-ticket ... In theory, at least, the whole of Australia could be read as a musical score ... And [the Aboriginals] could sing [all the white man's gear, even] the railway back into the created world of God.[3]

Though not based on a Christian understanding of God, this shows deep similarities to biblical faith of the sort found in the Wisdom Literature, and its capacity to find in the right practice of human relationships the presence of the divine. It is not unlike the statement from the Book of Proverbs: 'The fear of the Lord' is in 'turning your ear to wisdom and applying your heart to understanding ... For the Lord gives wisdom, and from his mouth come knowledge and understanding ... Then you will understand what is right and just and fair – every good path.'[4]

THE RELATIVITIES OF HISTORY

The two theories associated with the name of Albert Einstein – special

[3] Bruce Chatwin, *The Songlines*, London: Pan Books 1988, pp. 14–17.
[4] Proverbs 1.7; 2.2, 9.

and general relativity – suggest another view of history, applied so far only in cosmology. According to these views, mass and energy and spatio-temporal position are deeply interrelated, so that one should not think of substance and movement as distinct from each other or from time. Nor is space-time uniform; its curvature in the vicinity of matter makes gravity a property of space and time. Despite the fact that we try to think in the 'straight lines' of historical spatio-temporal existence, and indeed to 'flatten' everything in unidimensional terms, space-time

> seems to possess a 'curvature', analogous to that of ... [curved] surfaces, but more complicated because of the higher dimensionality, and mixtures of both positive and negative curvatures are involved for different displacements.[5]

Hence the things of the world have a certain mass, which is conserved, but which is also partly composed of (and therefore changeable into) energy. The things of the world are therefore dependent upon their energy, and vary with their capacity to draw energy into them and use it effectively. Their mass depends on their relations, and vice-versa.

History therefore resembles an elastic sheet or trampoline, with the curvatures of the sheet dependent on the mass and energy of things as they relate to each other.

> If you placed a cannonball on it, a large indentation was the result. An orange would make a smaller dent in the trampoline, and have an inclination to roll toward the deeper hole. Stars and planets have the same effect on space that balls have on a trampoline; heavenly bodies actually put a dent in the space around them, altering the geometry of space itself. Larger objects in this dented, curved space tend, like a cannonball on a trampoline, to pull less massive objects toward them.[6]

This elastic sheet is, in a sense, the story – though not a linear sequence – of the relativities of position and relations of things in the universe. And it requires varieties of explanation, only some of which are directly testable empirically.[7]

---

[5] Roger Penrose, *The Emperor's New Mind*, Oxford: Oxford University Press, 1989, p. 207.
[6] John Boslough, *Stephen Hawking's Universe*, New York: Avon Books, 1985, p. 32.
[7] See Mario Bunge, *Method, Model and Matter*, Dordrecht: D. Reidel Publishing Company, 1973, pp. 38–43.

THE NINETEENTH CENTURY AND THE TRIUMPH OF HUMANISTIC HISTORY

Elements of the two views we have just sketched were clearly present in the nineteenth century, particularly amongst those who were attempting to reconstrue history in response to rationalism. Coleridge, for example, used Faery as a vehicle for the restoration of the human imagination in history, whereby the human is restored to full participation in nature, to integrity of spirit, and to encounter with Absolute Truth and God.

> The Mariner surveys his world, but there is no place to rest his eyes. Decay and death surround him. Sight brings no life-giving sense of connection. 'A wicked whisper' – coming from his own unloving heart – dries up any possible prayer. The Mariner's entire being assumes the weight of separation. Reconciliation comes as a result of seeing differently, a curing of the distemper of the 'inner spirit'.[8]

> That religion is designed to improve the nature and faculties of Man, in order to the right governing of our actions, to the securing the peace and progress, external and internal, of Individuals and of Communities, and lastly, to the rendering us capable of a more perfect state, entitled the kingdom of God, to which the present life is *probationary* – this is a Truth, which all who have truth only in view, will receive on its evidence. If such then be the main end of Religion altogether (the improvement namely of our nature and faculties), it is plain, that every Part of Religion, is to be judged by its relation to this main end. And since the Christian Scheme is Religion in its most perfect and effective Form, a revealed Religion, and therefore, in a *special* sense proceeding from that Being who made us and knows what we are, of course therefore adapted to the needs and capabilities of Human Nature; nothing can be a part of this holy faith that is not duly proportioned to this end.[9]

And in different ways, Kant, Schleiermacher and Hegel were committed to the exploration of the assumption that nature, man and history are a purposive unity from God.

In their attempts, however, a pivotal place is accorded to the human being – always in their views authenticated by right relation to the Absolute, but always also human in being so. When, however, that was coupled with what has been called 'historicism' and also with new atten-

---

[8] Jeanie Watson, *Risking Enchantment: Coleridge's Symbolic World of Faery*, Lincoln: University of Nebraska Press, 1990, p. 102.
[9] S. T. Coleridge, *Aids to Reflection*, Aphorisms on Spiritual Religion, Aphorism III, London: Taylor & Hessey, 1825, p. 180.

tion to the relation between the nature of human beings and the conditions of their natural and social existence, the result was 'history turned outside in'. By this we mean that increasing prominence was given to history conceived as the history of human thought and action when seen by human beings. It was not that the importance of proportioning human nature in relation to nature and God was denied, so much as ignored. Instead, interest was transferred to human thought or action 'in' history and 'about' history. History therefore became the history of human thought or action as determined by the humanity of human beings, and as occurring 'in' a spatio-temporal container or context, from which God might be distinct. The symptoms of the later view are clearly seen in the work of Ernst Troeltsch:

> The history of mankind merges in the evolutionary history of the earth's surface; it takes its rise in the prehistoric life of primitive peoples; it is determined throughout by the general laws of geographical conditions, and by the various phases of social life, and forms an unspeakably complex, yet altogether coherent, whole of unmeasurable duration both in the past and in the future. It is as a part of this array and system that we must survey and estimate our own existence, and find its rationale and origin.

And, having established the seamless web of history which is the explanation of man, and employed analogical and critical thought to reconstruct the past and correct extant traditions,

> we gain at length the idea of an integral continuity, balanced in its changes, never at rest, and ever moving towards incalculable issues. The causal explanation of all that happens, the setting of the individual life in its true relations, the interpretation of events in their most intricate interaction, the placing of mankind in a rounded system of ceaseless change – these constitute the essential function and result of modern historical reflexion. The latter, viewed as a whole, forms a new scientific mode of representing man and his development, and, as such, shows at all points an absolute contrast to the Biblico-theological views of later antiquity.[10]

But despite its claims to be 'purely scientific', such history was confined to a certain place.

The humanities celebrate representation – not representation of

[10] Ernst Troeltsch, 'Historiography' in James Hastings, ed. *Encyclopaedia of Religion and Ethics*, p. 718.

things in the external world, but representation of things in the human mind ... Whether Plato or Aristotle accurately described the way things worked in Greece has always been less important than that they described them in a way that later human minds could comprehend ... The purpose of the literature and art that constitute the humanities is to affect and inform human mentalities, to impress them with novel information.[11]

It is this tradition of humanistic history which has largely been continued in the twentieth century and its interpretations of the nineteenth century. We must now consider some of the ways in which it is perpetuated, often through unquestioned assumptions.

'NINETEENTH-CENTURY THEOLOGY' AS HISTORIOGRAPHY

On the assumption that history is 'without inherent unity', it is said that history offers 'an irreducible number of histories according to presupposition, topic, and scale.'[12] If so, periodizations provide for historians both scale and the order which belongs to scale. As such, they are used in a way similar to the axiomatizations used by the formal scientist.

They bring into order a mass of happenings which of themselves have none. By distinguishing sequences of events and cutting them into shapes, the historian is able to give coherence to what otherwise remain formless. His divisions enable the events of the past, undifferentiated in themselves, to be differentiated into intelligible groupings ...

A period is 'the outcome of the need to relate generic continuity to temporal discontinuity' and identifies 'a sequence of events as a new epoch ... to type it by certain characteristics which are considered not to hold in the same way at other times.'[13]

A periodization forms a new frame of reference (a context) within which to order evidence anew, while not necessarily isolating it from others (context as interwovenness[14]). In that way, the 'axiom' provides a proximate field of connections – a 'what' facilitating a 'how'. And the development of each reinforces the other, the frame of reference devel-

[11] Richard Newbold Adams, *The Eighth Day*, Austin: University of Texas Press, 1988, p. 173.
[12] Gordon Leff, 'Models Inherent in History' in Theodor Shanin, ed. *The Rules of the Game*, London: Tavistock 1972, p. 151.
[13] *Ibid.*, pp. 150f.
[14] The original meaning of context, from the Latin *contexere*, is 'to braid' or 'interweave'.

oping, and being developed by, the connections found in the evidence. If 'nineteenth century theology' is a periodization, it will therefore be supported by connections found in the data provided by the period.

The periodization of the 'nineteenth century' does not necessarily imply that it is sharply distinct from all others. Insofar as the historian who has periodized it also identifies its connections with persistent features of the course of mankind and history, for example, it will also be seen as continuous with previous (or subsequent) eras, though to some extent a modification. Maurice Wiles' comment about Jaroslav Pelikan's five-volume *History of Christian Tradition* provides an illustration of a disagreement about continuities and changes:

> Pelikan insists from the outset that what he is concerned with is the history of *doctrine* (what the church believes, teaches and confesses), a concept wider than dogma but narrower than theology. The line of demarcation between doctrine and theology is almost impossible to draw ... And when we reach the nineteenth century, that line becomes increasingly hard to draw.[15]

Pelikan sustains his sharply-delineated view of doctrine – the 'high doctrine' of previous ages – throughout his *History*, thereby deemphasizing the distinct periodization of the nineteenth century, and any modification it brought. Wiles, however, emphasizes the periodization much more, together with the modification brought by the period.

A periodization does not determine the particular emphasis of the history of the period to be written. That is decided by the category or categories through which the historical period is seen. In themselves, these are as variable as are events, movements and people and the ways by which they can be studied. But in practice, they are not. And the study of nineteenth-century theology is decisively marked by preference for certain categories of explanation, particularly those which provide the possibility of tightly-knit continuities – those of linear causality, for example. Hence, history is confined within causalities which disallow reference to nature or God.

> Here one can say that the 'social factors' (although this is a misnomer) really only tell us about features of the Church that are relatively unsurprising, whereas its surprising, unique features are precisely the reason why it made a historical difference, why we are still interested in it at all. There is something, then, almost contradictory about trying to level it down to a 'social' level. In reality, one is not measuring 'social' as against 'religious' influences, but rather the

[15] Maurice Wiles, Review Essay on Jaroslav Pelikan, *The History of Doctrine* in *Religious Studies Review*, Vol. 18, No. 1, January 1992, p. 2.

influences of surrounding pre-constituted and themselves contingently historical modes of social organization as against the new socio-religious element, in a new social grouping, the Church. So the most *significant* social element in the new situation escapes 'sociology' altogether, and can only be referred to its own textual self-genesis.[16]

With the wish for tightly-knit continuities which can be established through particular forms of explanation, and a developing toleration for coexistence amongst explanations, study of the nineteenth century can be marked by a chaos of viewpoints. It is easy enough, and fascinating in a certain way, to range through the period, picking up this text, person or movement or that, with this emphasis or that, with little effort to achieve coherence in results. For this reason, the nineteenth century can at times seem more like a workable focus for the specialisms of a significant number of people – those who have learned their academic trade through study of Schleiermacher, Hegel, et al. – one which provides enough of a common conceptual world for them to be able to work together, advance their specialisms and learn from each other.

As should now be clear, periodization and categorization are devices of humanistic history which manifest the nominalism which pervades the modern practice of historical theology, a nominalism which finds no 'inherent unity' in history but instead construes history by 'presupposition, topic and scale', and do so in a fashion which places the human interpreter above the history which is his/hers to interpreter. If so, we should be able to see the results in views of the historian *vis-à-vis* the past.

ANTIQUARIANISM AND ANACHRONISM

If there is no 'inherent unity in history', there is also none amongst historians, as we can see by considering four genres of historical study which have been identified by Richard Rorty: (1) historical reconstruction of 'unreeducated primitives', (2) rational reconstruction of past figures by those who know better, (3) forming the canon of those who count as significant by reference to some standard and (4) doxography, the telling of the history of thought within a fixed format – history and format unaffected by each other.[17]

[16] John Milbank, *Theology and Social Theory*, Oxford: Blackwell, 1990, p. 117.
[17] Richard Rorty, 'The Historiography of Philosophy: Four Genres' in *Philosophy in History*, Cambridge: Cambridge University Press, 1984, pp. 49–75.

The first two can be labelled 'antiquarianism' and 'anachronism' respectively. In many ways, they are two sides of the same coin: the second treats the dead as contemporaries with whom to exchange views (the dead as counterparts), thereby displacing them from the past to the present, while the first distances them by virtue of their thought and context (the dead as different). Rorty's view is that both genres are important as long as they are clearly differentiated:

> We should do both of these things, but do them separately. We should treat the history of philosophy as we treat the history of science. In the latter field, we have no reluctance in saying that we know better than our ancestors what they were talking about ... There is nothing wrong with self-consciously letting our own philosophical views dictate terms in which to describe the dead. But there are reasons for also describing them in other terms, their own terms.[18]

The reasons in each case, however, have to do with the interests of the historian involved. In the one case, we find partners – 'pen-pals' – in the truth we believe we have found. In the other, it is because 'it helps us to recognize that there have been different forms of intellectual life than ours' and thereby makes us aware of 'the contingency of our self-awareness'.[19] Both are undertaken, therefore, for their value to the historian, whose position becomes pivotal.

> There is, in our view, nothing general to be said in answer to the question 'How should the history of philosophy be written?' except 'As self-consciously as one can – in as full awareness as possible of the *variety* of contemporary concerns to which a past figure may be relevant.'[20]

Rorty's view concentrates responsibility on the historian and his/her awareness, making the intuition of this person pivotal in the play of 'contemporary concerns' upon history, without informing it by a fuller (and more disciplined) appreciation of the possibilities of history implicit in these concerns.

[18] *Ibid.*, p. 50.
[19] *Ibid.*, p. 51.
[20] *Ibid.*, p. 11.

HISTORY AS THE CANON OF THE SIGNIFICANT

As we have already seen in the earlier discussion of periodization and categorization, humanistic history takes on itself the responsibility of forming the canon of those who count as significant, and establishing the terms in which their significance is seen. In that way, the writing of history confers dignity on those chosen for attention, much as the writings of a 'nineteenth-century theology working group' bestow significance on those studied.

In doing so, it also establishes the relative value of the periods being considered. But as regards what is their relative value, there are considerable differences. At one extreme are those for whom the value of historical antecedents is only in the successes of the present, and can thereby be forgotten.[21] These are people who 'historicize the present' and thereby 'disremember the past',[22] whether rationally or irrationally.[23] At the other extreme are those who identity themselves very closely with historical antecedents whom they see as forming or informing current understanding. For the first group, the present has become so powerful, for one reason or another, as to displace reference to the past – except perhaps as the beginning of the present. For the second, the power of the present is seen as an extension of the past.

There is a major issue between them. To what extent does the present stand – like the Colossus of Rhodes – astride the port of what is permitted to pass as knowledge? Humanistic history which aspires to the status of science is more likely to place itself in this position, where that which takes a more gradualist view of its work is less likely to. Rorty himself is an example of the former.

---

[21] 'Historians of science feel no need to justify our physicists' concern with elementary particles or our biologists' with DNA. If you can synthesize steroids, you do not require historical legitimation.' *ibid.*, p. 57.

[22] Michael Kammen, *Mystic Chords of Memory: The Transformation of Tradition in American Culture*, New York: Alfred A. Knopf, 1991, p. 655.

[23] The following is an example of the irrational means of doing so: 'The second early warning sign of thinking is memory, which is when you suddenly think of something that happened in the past ... Memory isn't necessarily fatal. As long as it only happens every once in a while. But if you should get in the habit of remembering things ... it could mess you up. Especially if you start to wonder what it all means. And whether you should take it into account in deciding what to do next. You shouldn't. The thing is, memories don't mean anything. The past is history. And it isn't important. Or worth worrying about. If you start to have attacks of memory, And you feel like you might start to wonder about it or take it into account for some reason, Do some drugs instead, Like maybe something hallucinogenic, Because hallucinations are safer than memories, If you're trying to prevent an outbreak of thinking.' [R. F. Laird, *The Boomer Bible*, New York: Workman Publishing, 1991, p. 615.]

Philosophy should be expected to display a relationship to history that closely resembles the relationship of the sciences to history. As long as the sciences aimed at discovering the timeless and eternal order of things, philosophy was led to conceive its task in much the same terms, and conversely ... Philosophy investigated the time-transcendent structure of human reason or human nature. When the sciences transgressed preconceived ontological schemes, yet appeared gradually to approach the Truth, philosophy too might hope to find the law of its development in assumptions or antici-pations of a final and perfect stage. The pattern can be observed from Hegel until today; names as different as Charles Sanders Peirce, Karl Popper and Juurgen Habermas come to mind in this context.[24]

Charles Taylor is an example of the latter.

Philosophy is an activity which essentially involves, among other things, the redescription of what we are doing, thinking, believing, assuming, in such a way that we bring our reasons to light more perspicuously, or else make the alternatives more apparent, or in some way or other are better enabled to take a justified stand to our action, thought, belief assumption. Philosophy involves a great deal of articulation of what is initially inarticulated. Now, one way of making the historical thesis about philosophy is to argue that suc-cessful articulation frequently requires – though it never simply reduces to – recovering previous articulations which have been lost. In other words, the kind of redescription we need in order to take a justified stand frequently requires that we recover previous formu-lations, precisely the ones we need to give an account of the origins of our present thoughts, beliefs, assumptions, actions.[25]

The two stand uneasily alongside each other within the humanistic history which was generated by the nineteenth century.

The same difference of view is found in the kind of value which is accorded to past and present. There are those who find the past formative for the ordering of present thought. This does not require reference to 'big sweeping *geistesgeschichtlich* stories – the genre of which Hegel is paradigmatic'. Any tradition which is reappropriated as in any degree formative for later thought serves that purpose. The reliance may simply be on previous *thinkers* as providing a *pattern of thought* which is necessary for the continuance of what is considered significant. Can

---

[24] Rorty et al., *Philosophy in History, op. cit.*, p. 95.
[25] Charles Taylor, 'Philosophy and its History', *ibid.*, p. 18.

Christian theology be sustained if those responsible for it cannot recall the major disputes of Athanasius or Augustine? or if they cannot identify the major emphasis of Calvin, Luther, Schleiermacher or Barth? So, at least in Christian thought, there is an implicit reliance on past thinkers, as providing suitable patterns of understanding: who should figure in the pantheon of thinkers is more debatable. By and large, those of the nineteenth century would figure only for those convinced of the importance of modernity.

Or concern can be transferred from establishing a canon of the thinkers who embody patterns of thought to discerning the patterns themselves, for which previous thinkers are exemplars. This is the genesis of idealist, phenomenological and realist views of history, in which historical variety and contingency are deemphasized in favour of a preoccupation with the recurrence of pattern – whether viewed as 'interesting' or as normative. The historical question is whether given figures are near or far relative to a recognized pattern.

Just as there were questions about the relative value of present and past, so there are questions about the status of the pattern: is the pattern a human product of history-making, or is it somehow inherent in history – so that history as such has a meaning which is drawn out by recognizing it? Rorty himself, and an increasing number of 'new historicists', take the position that patterns are simply a matter of 'historians making history' – as if there were no choice between accepting patterns ineluctably imposed and creating them.[26] Those who see truth as already incorporated in history, however, will concentrate on questions of proximity to truth rather than on 'making history'. For them, the issue is whether a given historical thinker meets the standard for access to truth. And where people do so, even if separated by a millennium, the historical distance between them evaporates, and they are seen as contemporaries. Present and past are as one in proximity to truth, and historical time disappears.[27]

Though it can as easily be found in modern forms of idealism and phenomenalism, we will illustrate this from modern 'theological realism'. Here, the purification of knowledge is considered to occur through conforming oneself to the inner structure of knowledge which is given through God's self-impartation. The results are clear:

> One is the privileged position which it accords to those who live in the 'occurrence', the metascience by which they understand their position and the knowledge which they achieve ... [This] is the

---

[26] See William Dean, *History Making History: The New Historicism in American Religious Thought*, Albany: State University Press of New York, 1988.
[27] For those more concerned with historical process, this was the difficulty with Bultmann's view of history.

product of the deep relation in which they participate; they and the statements by which they express the fruits of this relation are 'transparencies' ...

Remaining within the factuality of knowledge provided by reality also makes for an exclusivist and 'occasionalist' [view of history], ... a very sharp distinction between those who respond properly to truth and those who do not, between when they do and when they do not. On the one hand, in the 'fact' of proper response to truth, human beings achieve knowledge. On the other hand, outside the 'fact' of proper response to truth are those who impose 'self-willed', 'distorting idealization[s]'[28] on reality.

[Even where] there is more recognition of the contingency of knowledge, though still within the 'fact' of proper response to truth, ... [and a] welcome emphasis on the richness of reality and conceptualities opens the way for a more positive notion of ideas and practices, ... it is not less exclusivist; what is permissible is wider, but it must – and must always – be authorized by reality. This leaves the question of whether the many mundane devices which human beings use in their life and work, from sacraments to technology, are not still too much discounted; contingent structures though they are, they may constitute proper response to an ineffable reality. The truth of history is more than the achievement of correct accounts of truth.[29]

Despite the variations we have now seen in the means for establishing the 'canon of the significant', however, the tradition of humanistic history which has been derived from the nineteenth century encompasses them all, allowing each variation as legitimate within history found and told by human beings. All make the position of the historian pivotal in uncovering the truth in history.

DOXOGRAPHIC HISTORY AND THE PROBLEM OF HISTORIES OF DOCTRINE

What is considered unacceptable are the ways by which previous historians have foreclosed the issue of how history should be interpreted. For example, it has been a common practice in the past to write histories of thought by using a canon of accepted persons matched with a set of standard questions, with some variations in how rigidly these are inter-

---

[28] T. F. Torrance, 'Divine and Contingent Order' in A. R. Peacocke, ed., *The Sciences and Theology in the Twentieth Century*, Stocksfield: Oriel Press, 1981, p. 93.
[29] Daniel W. Hardy, 'Thomas F. Torrance' in David F. Ford, ed., *The Modern Theologians*, Oxford: Blackwell, 1989, Vol. I, pp. 88f.

preted. The genre appears to have begun through mixing the question-centred approach characteristic of the medieval disputational method with the person-centred approach more characteristic of post-Renaissance and post-Reformation discussions. More recently, under the impact of a growing historical awareness, the tendency has been in the direction of studies of persons or movements carefully contextualized, with standard questions treated more discursively. Nonetheless, the continued use of this method suggests the viability of a self-same canon of matched persons and questions. And this prejudges the issue of the interpretation of history by 'master' historians 'with as full awareness as possible of the variety of contemporary concerns to which a past figure may be relevant'.[30]

Rorty's term for this kind of history is 'doxographic' – for example 'the story of philosophy from the pre-Socratics to the present day' told in such a way as to suggest that all were talking about the same field of issues. He regards it as always a half-way house, a *'half-hearted* attempt to tell a new story of intellectual progress by describing all texts in the light of recent discoveries. It is half-hearted because it lacks the courage to readjust the canon to new discoveries.'[31] This is why it is treated with contempt by those, for example *geistesgeschichtlich* intellectual historians, who are prepared to be more prescriptive about who and what count as significant. Theirs is the kind of history – checked by their peers – which should be encouraged, and contrived connections of people and questions given up.

The fact remains that this kind of history has been a conventional resort for those who wish to maintain an inherent meaning for history as understood by certain classical thinkers, and to trace its evolution through human questioning and life, a genre as old as Augustine's *City of God*. Given the preoccupations which we have found to be characteristic of the humanistic history begotten by the nineteenth century, however, the problems likely to be found with such histories are monumental: not only any thematization of the meaning of history ('development'), but the parameters ('church belief'), periodization and localization of thought – not to mention the task of historical explanation – are all likely to provoke comment, since all have been rendered much more complex in modern discussion.[32] Inevitably, it seems, the 'sieve' is considered problematic in all sorts of ways. But is it even conceivable for history – and history of theology – to sweep away the past and have an entirely fresh construal of history?

The humanistic history which is the legacy of the nineteenth century

[30] Rorty et al., *op. cit.*, p. 11.
[31] *Ibid.*, p. 63.
[32] Cf. James O. Duke, Review Article on Jaroslav Pelikan, *The Christian Tradition, Religious Studies Review*, Vol. 18, No. 1, January 1992, pp. 4–6.

judges such 'doxographic history' as if it were the product of a master historian whose techniques are to be tested by reference to the full range of present-day discussions. In doing so, humanistic history mistakes another kind of history for that which its own tradition sponsors, and misunderstands the *genre* of the history being attempted, one which subordinates the historian to the communities in whose service he/she intends to be.

Nonetheless, writers of history of doctrine – as well as the communities which they serve – are now more aware of their historical transience and the necessity for creative redescription of the conditions of understanding, belief and action by those who have recourse to earlier redescriptions. This is more than simply accepting the beliefs of earlier ages as given principles; it is understanding their genesis and also redescribing them in terms which will support present activity. In other words, they understand that the genre is not necessarily well-served by histories comprised only of standard sets of questions and persons in the history of theology. Fixed configurations of issues and people may be less than helpful in the task of creative redescription, except possibly as 'regulative principles'. Worse still, they may displace attention from the central task which faces the modern-day believer, creative redescription in the circumstances of today, and may thereby subvert the historical dynamic of theology itself. It is for these reasons that the place of the old 'doxographic history' – with its time-neutral lists of people and questions – has been taken by a deep immersion in the historical character of all thought, precisely in order to rediscover its movement in the present. That is of great practical importance at many levels. At the most personal level, it is one of discovering how *we* should move on, and move history with us. More widely, it is the question of how rationality, society and culture – as the most fundamental features of humanity – are called onward.

While it is understandable that the tradition of nineteenth-century humanistic history, with its emphasis on the master historian charting and correcting history, should wish to subvert 'doxographic history' in its own favour, it remains a question whether the alternative it provides is sufficient to the task of rediscovering the movement of history and how human beings are called forward. Does it not, rather fashionably under present circumstances, overemphasize the capacity of human beings to 'transcend' their limitations, and to be free in a unrestricted 'market' in which every individual or social group competes for position by maximizing their position?

A NEW HISTORY OF PARTICULARITIES

We have been considering some of the implications of the view of history which has been developed from the nineteenth century, and whether they are sufficient for the present. And, as we said earlier, we may be driven thereby to consider the possibility that the nineteenth century may need to be freshly assessed for unrecognized contributions to a different understanding of history.

Amidst a collapsing ideal of history as seen through the eyes of self-transcending heroes, is it possible to identify an alternative? Unquestionably, history needs to be reconceived in terms of the emergence of significance within and from particularities. The notion is well-suggested by this poem:

> Remember how at school we folded and unfolded
> sheets from a jotter, scissored chunky *m*s and *n*s,
> a saw-edge,
> a clump of paper squared, melodeoned.
> Then delight as it reopens
> a fulness of design, transfigured wounds
> unfolding in a page
> berries, acorns.
>
> The moment's contours scatter in the light.
> A crossbeam gathers in pattern and fringe,
> traces of passion,
> hologram of thought, memory's freight
> until a beam rethrows the image,
> an intensity unpacking stripe and whorl;
> each fraction
> an implicit all.
>
> Acorns of memories, berries of dreams.
> Does every pilgrim's tale sleep in one moment?
> Some inbred
> whole uncodes in a tree's limbs,
> spreads in slow workings of environment.
> Soil, air, water, sun quicken
> a word in the seed.
> Time thickens.[33]

In such a view, historical significance ('time thickens') arises within the contingent, dynamic interconnections of nature, culture and society.

Aleksandr Solzhenitsyn has employed a similar understanding in his

---

[33] Micheal O'Siadhail, 'Disclosure' in *The Chosen Garden*, Dublin: The Dedalus Press, 1990, p. 79.

historical novels of the events of 1914–17 in Russia, treating them as 'knots' (critical historical moments) for which to develop 'concentrated and minutely detailed accounts of events within strictly limited periods of time, with complete breaks between them'.[34] What is distinctive about this mode of writing is that it takes its point of departure from the energies which arise contingently within complex relations between people, their society, their culture and their natural situation. But within these appear the deeper issues which are ages-old, particularly those of religion. A good example is this conversation between students and a young woman professor who they think has avoided the difficulties of the present situation by studying medieval papal documents:

[A student speaks:] 'But for practical purposes the history of the West, or all that we need of it, begins with the great French Revolution . . .'
[Another student:] 'No, with the Enlightenment . . . Why do we need to know about pilgrimages to Jerusalem? Or paleography?'
[The professor replies:] 'You mustn't jump to conclusions – don't mistake the branch for the tree. The Western Enlightenment is only one branch of Western culture, and by no means the most fruitful. It starts from the trunk, not from the root.'
[A student:] 'What would you say is more important?'
[Professor:] 'If you like, the spiritual life of the Middle Ages. Mankind has never experienced such intense spiritual life, with the spiritual so far outweighing the material, either before or since.'[35]

So, despite apparent confinement within one 'knot' of history, other 'knots' can appear there, unlinked by linear causality or an historian's generalizations.

Full appreciation of such 'knots' within 'knots' – the appearance of heritages within the particularities of events – demands multifold sensibilities and analyses capable of identifying the complex means by which they are carried forward in the later situation. Furthermore, they must be capable of identifying the historical dynamic which is operative as they are carried forward. For these heritages constrain events and behaviour while at the same time being refashioned by them to serve as constraints for future refashioning.[36] Thus, for example, the historical heritage of

---

[34] Aleksandr I. Solzhenitsyn, *August 1914* (The Red Wheel, Knot I), New York: Farrar, Straus and Giroux, 1989, Publisher's Note.
[35] *Ibid.*, pp. 788f.
[36] Anthony Giddens, *The Constitution of Society*, Berkeley: University of California Press, 1984, p. 374.

Christian faith is embedded in – intrinsic to – the particular ways by which it is creatively refashioned.

While these 'knots' (and the knots within them) can be indicated through narrative – the subtitle of Solzhenitsyn's *Red Wheel* is 'A Narrative in Discrete Periods of Time' – the larger task for historical theology is that of identifying the dynamic by which the most concentrated forms of human life in the world – rationality, society, and culture interacting with nature – exemplify the work of God in the world. For this, existing views of these forms of human life and of the work of God in the world are unlikely to suffice, since they are both static and self-contained. What will be required is understandings of rationality, society and culture – and God's work in them – which are both conditional and contingent upon their future. That is a task for which much can be learned from the archetypal figures of early, pre-humanistic nineteenth-century theology, even if not even they dreamt of the conditionality of human life in the world upon its future. Not even they fully realized that the history of the world and humanity is, above all, a promise of what they may become – achievable only if they respond together in freedom.

If the world has not approached its end, it has reached a major watershed in history, equal in importance to the turn from the Middle Ages to the Renaissance. It will demand from us a spiritual effort; we shall have to rise to a new height of vision, to a new level of life, where our physical nature will not be cursed, as in the Middle Ages, but even more importantly, our spiritual being will not be trampled upon, as in the Modern Era.[37]

---

[37] Aleksandr I. Solzhenitsyn, 'A World Split Apart' in *East and West*, New York: Harper & Row, 1980, p. 71.

16

English Crypto-Atheism and its Causes[1]

INTRODUCTION: RECOGNIZING A HISTORY

IT could be claimed that, for a race with such a long and distinguished history, the English are peculiarly unaware of the historical genesis and formation of their distinctive characteristics. They identify certain ways of doing things, whether in thought or practice, as 'natural' to human understanding and behaviour, rather than as products of their own particular history. Nor do they see that this singular history continues, with its own dynamic, to shape present convictions and practices.

This is as much true in religious matters as elsewhere, where there is a certain tenacity to ways deeply rooted in habits and institutions, as if things could not be otherwise. Theologians from elsewhere are greeted warmly enough, but their insights – so far as they are understood at all – are distilled and reshaped in the ongoing dynamic of an English tradition which is far stronger than is generally realized. But there seems to be little awareness of the fact that this is occurring, and still less of the direction which the tradition is taking. There is some value, therefore, in inquiring into the nature and characteristics of this tradition, and how they may be related to the present tendencies of English theology.

I propose therefore to engage in an exercise in intellectual history, and to concentrate on certain central strands which particularly affect theological concerns. This should make it possible to identify the main features of a particular movement in modern English theology, one which might be called 'crypto-atheist' in character, at least if it is measured by a more widespread 'consensus' view. The aim is to understand the inner dynamic of the English theological tradition as it operates in certain modern theologians, and to check its correspondence with a view less prominent in modern English academic theology but which is, nonetheless, the consensus view of modern theology. It should thus be possible both to find the historical origins and provenance of theological views which are taken to be 'natural' in Britain today, and to establish whether they are indeed 'natural' to the wider Christian tradition – or as inevitable as many in England seem to find them.

We shall look briefly at how a tradition may operate in a particular

[1] Birmingham, June 1984.

national culture, and then at the long-standing traditions of English theology, and finally at three particular modern English theologians. Throughout, we will refer also to a consensus view of Christian theology which can be found in as diverse figures as F. D. E. Schleiermacher, Karl Barth and Karl Rahner, although of course they develop this view in markedly different ways. To avoid becoming mired in the details of their differences, we shall concentrate on one particular issue, that of the understanding of the bond between God and man.

THE OPERATION OF TRADITIONS

I do not suggest that the traditions of English theology are easy to get at. Their position is somewhat akin to the 'fiduciary frameworks' which Michael Polanyi discusses, which operate as an unarticulated position underlying all our knowing and doing. As such central concerns, they are often the most difficult to identify and appreciate. They seem to operate as the reference-point around which important issues rotate, or (to change the metaphor) the *cantus firmus* of the music which is made, themselves not fully exposed, while at the same time being used as the medium of relationships with others and the standard by which judgment of the others is made. How these concerns are appropriated, perpetuated and used is a fascinating matter: the one who 'has' them does not fully 'know' them or how they originated, even if he uses them constantly. They must emerge for him over the period of his use of them, partly from himself and partly from his training, and do so slowly, and perhaps never fully; they are also the slowest to change.

These concerns come into operation, of course, in the work of any theologian, and also in the interpretation of him made by another. They are the stuff of which theological – indeed any rational – work is made, whether the direct work of a theologian or the indirect work of an interpreter, and they lie at the heart of what is done. One might see Schleiermacher's piety and Barth's ontology as examples of such frameworks or concerns; each is central to the theologian's position and interpretation, and is rendered consistent and elucidated by him only with difficulty, over a period of time and perhaps never fully satisfactorily. This is not to suggest that they are 'simply human', 'culturally conditioned', or whatever: that would prejudge the issue of what in fact these concerns are, and in individual cases they may actually be 'located' very differently. In a broader sense, one can call these frameworks or concerns the bearers of traditions in which people participate, as Schleiermacher's and Barth's (despite their differences) were bearers of a

Calvinist tradition. Here again, this is not to say that they were merely culture-bearers.

THE COMMON TRADITION OF ENGLISH THEOLOGY

Is there a common tradition of which the fiduciary frameworks of contemporary English theologians are the bearers? It seems to me that there is, a tradition which touches on knowledge, morality and aesthetics. Let me give a brief indication of the main features of the tradition in these areas.

(a) A long-standing tradition, dating at least from Francis Bacon and loosely following Calvin, places human knowledge at the intersection of the influences of nature and revelation, of 'the waters flowing from below and above', and gives chief attention to the development of this human knowledge as the organ of the two. In this, primacy was given to humility, weighting the 'wings' of knowledge to prevent it from soaring and thereby depriving the 'book of nature' and the 'book of the Word' of their determinative importance. But, very early and increasingly, the emphasis changed: the analysis of human knowledge and its machinery became important in their own right, and the results became determinative for the content of legitimate piety. In this way, the implicit tendencies of English practice coincided well with Kant's strategy for knowledge, although not with his transcendental derivation of the possibility of knowledge; and his strategy also put piety 'in its place'. As we shall see, this combination thrives in English theology today, placing human standards of knowability in a determinative position.

(b) Closely allied with this is the question of morality. When Calvinism arrived in England, it was spread in a scholasticized form in which the will of God for man (the decrees of election) was treated as a foundational principle from which human life and virtues (or their converse) were to be deduced as a logical system. That had the effect of logicizing the action of God in creation and salvation, and encouraging Christians to check their salvific status 'against the chart'. One's relative position as more or less moral became important in its own right: and the longstanding tradition of moralism in English religion began. This was further enhanced by the 'Anglican' attempt to use religion as an instrument of national unity: proper morality was as important for civil reasons as for religious. Unlike American moralism, however, this was not associated with a work-ethic (and still is not!); it was associated with an hierarchical class system – morality was measured by moral codes proper to classes, not by a single chart of salvation. In a sense, this also prepared the English for Kant's strategy of morals, which made the necessity of moral behaviour (the moral imperative) important in its own right and allowed for the use of particular moral symbols as possible extras. The English agreed with the moralistic tendency inherent in this view, while associating with it code-systems as operative symbols particular to each class.

(c) A third element in English understanding which is as important as the views of knowledge and morality is the aesthetic. The ancient ideal of a pure 'interaction' with God, a beatific vision whereby God in his glory is found to be near – present for – one who is pure in heart, and through being near, perfectly actualizing man's being by the light of his Spirit, underwent a complete transformation in eighteenth-century England. It was now associated with the sensuous vastness of Newton's cosmology, the infinite and eternal of extended space and time. This spatio-temporal vastness, taken up in the romantic idea of the sublime, was to be participated in through an expansive sensuous imagination. But this imagination was also seen to have its own dynamic, and to serve as an 'interior vastness'. Both 'object' and means of 'participation' were thereby changed from those of the supernatural beatific vision to those of natural sensuous imagination. As a result, there arose a confusion between God's transcendence and natural vastness, and ontological differentiation in this transcendent vastness (such as had occurred in the doctrine of the Trinity) became unintelligible; and there opened up an interior vastness which also cannot readily be thought. These could not be appreciated properly through scientific thought; and the only appropriate expressions were artistic or literary.

The Operation of the Tradition in Modern English Theology

This brief sketch of the long-standing tradition which is found in English understanding – knowability as a determinant, moralism through moral codes and naturalistic aesthetics – enables us to appreciate certain underlying concerns which operate in English theology and form its views on most subjects. The tradition is found in different mixtures in the work of different theologians, not necessarily very clearly, but functioning importantly to form their views. Let us look at the most general features of the responses of the theologians, and afterward at particular cases.

First, it is necessary to focus on a central feature of Christian theology, by reference to which we may evaluate the views of characteristic English theologians. It seems to me that there is a consensus amongst modern theologians that corporate piety (in a broad sense and not necessarily confined to the Church) is the location or resting-place of a real relationship of God and man. To take several examples, Schleiermacher, Barth and Rahner would agree with this position, however differently they might develop it. The question which we must now answer is whether current English theology can fully allow such a position, or whether the use of the tradition which we have described changes the position out of all recognition.

How, in general, does English theology respond to this concern with corporate piety? While Schleiermacher and Barth go to great lengths to stay within the possibilities which they find this piety affords, even enjoying the fulfilment of man which is implicit in it, the whole issue of whether there is such a piety, and the possibility of freedom and joy in it, has become far too agonistic in current English theology to allow such a position. This is evident in the consistent problematizing of all notions which serve to indicate such a piety. As a result, faith – the having and resting in such a piety – is more and more treated as a heroic path demanding personal commitment, development and self-transcendence. If we take Don Cupitt and Maurice Wiles and John Hick as characteristic examples of current English theology, we will find that they construe this corporate piety, and the relationship between God and man to be found in it, almost exclusively in anthropological and personal terms, while varying in the means which they employ. Hence, Cupitt focuses on heroic moral freedom which constitutes the meaning of life, Wiles on personal aesthetic experience as constituting the meaning of life, and Hick on personal cognition in experience; and each is more or less confined by his starting-point.

THE BOND BETWEEN GOD AND THE HUMAN BEING

This response, though varying in form, raises a fundamental question about the acceptability of the consensus view. Is there a bond between God and man of the sort suggested by the consensus? And if so, what is the medium through which it occurs? The importance of these questions cannot be overstated. But the thrust of the English tradition leaves this bond, however conceived, highly problematic, by rendering aesthetics, knowledge and morality unsuitable mediums for such a bond. As a consequence, the relationship between God and man becomes unimaginable and unimportant, if not corrupted, very much as it was in the situations which Schleiermacher, Barth and Rahner faced in their different times. What is more, those who attempt to reassert such a bond between God and man are forced by this situation from dogmatics to apologetics; they must defend the basis of their theology in doing their theology, lest the whole thing be seen simply as assertion. Strategies for doing so are in short supply, because most fall into the traps laid by the aesthetic, moral and cognitive techniques which operate in the received tradition. And where one finds that the bond of God with man involves all of these areas, there is particular difficulty in defending or elucidating the bond.

Well, 'an empty pocketbook concentrates the mind wonderfully', as the saying goes, and forces one to make choices. A further consequence of the presence of the tradition (aesthetic, cognitive and moral) outlined is to force choices about strategies. The outcome varies widely, and different strategies bring different evaluations of the consensus view and its most powerful exponents. Let us review some of the most basic strategies chosen, together with their implications for evaluation and interpretation of the consensus view.

The most fundamental response to such an alien situation, one which is made by many major English theologians, is to be pressed back into the domain of what is most personal. This, I think, is a peculiarly significant move for a race as reserved as the English, and accounts for the strangely opaque character of much English theological writing. This 'resort to the personal' is found in theologians as diverse as T. F. Torrance and D. M. Mackinnon, Don Cupitt and Maurice Wiles, as well as many others. And what usually accompanies it is the suggestion that this is the way in which all human contact with natural, human or transcendent realities operates. On the face of it, this would seem to bring a preference for a piety seen in the terms of personal idealism, existentialism or experience, with a corresponding impatience for anything 'externally' given, like revelation, unless it is translated into terms of a 'personal vision'. But Torrance's use of Polanyi's *Personal Knowledge* to explore the way in which a personally-held fiduciary framework is used as tacit knowledge in our approach to the world shows that the consensus view can be considered personal without being the less a God-centred theology.

The issue here turns on the question of what a 'personal' theology is, and what can be admitted as personal. It would, I think, be admitted by all that a personal theology is one in which all that comes to us is, in a measure at least, subject to our determination as free and as participants in the 'shared reality of the public world'. As such, we are at least codeterminants of the content of theology. That may allow the possibility of referring to another codeterminant or cogent, or may not. Some, for example Don Cupitt, are altogether unwilling to allow any other codeterminant at all, because such a thing compromises our autonomous spiritual freedom by heteronomy. There is even doubt, on Cupitt's part, whether the shared reality of the natural and social worlds should be allowed to affect the content of our determination, so alien are they in the modern technological situation. The religious must for him be an *a priori* practical principle freely adopted and self-imposed; 'God' is thus only a reification or codification in symbolic terms of the best direction for inward self-realization – a somewhat different position from that of Kant. And any suggestion that 'God' is other than a symbol lending coherence to the free finding of meaning, that 'God' is a descriptive term for an agent rather than an expressive term, is alienating, the more so as it is accorded a content which in some way surpasses that of man.

It seems to me that Cupitt's view is more significant, although not necessarily more satisfactory, than its present treatment in English theology allows. It suggests that Christianity is a self-consistent meaning-system constituted by free moral self-realization, and eliminates reference to any agency which is in any degree inconsistent (and is therefore 'external') as alienating. Hence he is proposing a radical theology focused on human action, closed to reference to any other factor, a closed picture which excludes reference to any other agency – a self-enclosed and largely philosophically-tested piety of meaning through action. Very much the sort of thing for the untroubled world of a Cambridge don! Such a view is very narrowly 'personal', and has drawn the circle of what is legitimate as personal very restrictively. There can be nothing which is not internalized, and language must therefore cease to be used denotatively. Its function is expressive and generative when 'I bind the religious requirement unconditionally upon myself'.[2] We meet here what could be called an 'interior aesthetic' of the person, which takes up the moralism intrinsic to the English tradition in an aesthetic drama in which mythical representations like God become progressively less valuable as spiritual life advances.

IMPLICATIONS FOR THE RELATIONSHIP BETWEEN GOD AND HUMAN BEINGS

The view has interesting implications for the interpretation of the consensus view. Firstly, it would suggest that the appearance of God as a necessary correlative of human identity is transitional, becoming otiose as spiritual development occurs. This is radically at odds with the God-man relationship in the consensus view, which requires reference to a

---

[2] Don Cupitt, *Taking Leave of God*, London: SCM Press, 1980, p. 93.

codeterminant, upon whom one is dependent, as a necessary and permanent part of human knowledge and moral action. Secondly, it misinterprets those more sophisticated versions of the consensus view (for example, Schleiermacher's) which state this God-man relationship in less than baldly objective terms, in order to provide precedents for itself. Cupitt sees Schleiermacher as initiating the trend to subjectivism seen in modern theology by basing his theology on religious experience in such a way as to play down the old supernaturalism and the 'great dogmatic affirmations', thereby beginning the more recent reduction of Christianity to 'values and attitudes with hardly any doctrinal underpinning at all'.[3] In other words, Schleiermacher began the trend of which Cupitt's view is the culmination. But what Schleiermacher was doing was not at all what Cupitt suggests: he was relocating the relationship between God and man in human consciousness as such, and finding the proper content of that in Christian piety (after the example of Calvin). He was finding a new medium for the bond between God and man, not beginning the move to 'Christian Buddhism', and was drawing from that bond certain conclusions about God, man and the world, as expressions of piety, certainly not as direct implications of science or morality. His theology does not posit the same location or kind of bond as does Barth's (for example), but is not therefore to be seen as undermining the 'great dogmatic assertions' so much as reconstituting them in another medium.

The more usual view in 'personal' theology, however, is not so extreme. In a version such as appears in Maurice Wiles, the discussion remains as one about man, and thus it does not seem able to ask directly whether there is a codeterminant alongside man's self-determining. Because it is self-confined in human experience, it seeks a proof of God from experience. Thus it asks about the reasons for being a person who can make an absolute commitment, who is the God who is believed in, and whether such commitment is well-founded. In any case, man's commitment is highly contingent: man's natural situation is seen as one of contingency in geography and time, and this religious belief is tied to particular circumstances; it has therefore to be recognized as subject to intrinsic limitations – his freedom is always contingent and relative to those circumstances. Yet he responds in an absolute commitment 'as a whole person' to his environment and tradition. As a total personal act, however, that may be founded on delusion; we cannot suppose that its absoluteness corresponds to the absolute and universal One to which it refers, or indeed is justifiable at all. So critical reflection on its legitimacy is demanded, in general and for the particular content associated with it. But believing or 'trusting in reality' as such is found to be legitimate, on the grounds of its anthropological universality. The more particular con-

[3] *Ibid.*, p. 35.

tent associated with this is seen as imaginative expression, metaphoric in the unity and novelty which it provides. Jesus, for example, is seen stereoscopically, as the subject of history and as a man with a costly sense of God's all-encompassing reality, the same quality of life that marks out some outstanding Christians.

The form of Wiles's argument is, as we see, thoroughgoingly personal, eschewing all direct discussions of codeterminants in man's experience in favour of the critical reflection on what it is personally to be a Christian – and locating that in absolute commitment to God, a concept which is so personal as to transform us. Correspondingly, the conception of God must, according to Wiles, be a 'profoundly personal concept, yet one that bursts the restrictive bounds of what it is to be an individual person as we know that in our finite human experience'. And the conception must be of 'God in relation to us, for any knowledge of God that we have is so inextricably bound up with our particular experience of him that what we can say about him can never be wholly separated out from the limiting and distorting prism of that contingent experience.'[4] In the end, this leads Wiles to affirm, with Gabriel Marcel, a Spirit or 'presence from which all other presences draw their life and worth'.[5]

It is an interesting personal theology which Wiles presents. No moralism which employs 'God' as a transient concept, this is a Spirit theology, in which the presence of Spirit requires recognition, openness and transformation in order for the presence to be full.[6] And there is no possibility of demarcating presence from recognition, or full recognition from the contingencies of existence. Like the consensus view, Wiles is claiming the appearance of a codeterminant as necessary to fuller identity as an individual person. In place of the immediate self-consciousness as the locus of this codetermination, however, Wiles considers the individual in the dynamic of his relationships, and places God (Spiritual Presence) in the position of transformative agent – very much the same location as Bonhoeffer and the later Barth use.

What is more significant, perhaps, is the way in which this Presence (God) is understood. He is not to be described, but intuited; and the means which Wiles prefers are aesthetic. Likewise, the deposit of previous faith with which Wiles wants to find continuity is an aesthetic, mythopoetic or literary one. An essentially aesthetic and subrational awareness is thus checked by artifacts which are treated as being of the same kind. So we have, in place of the presentations of the codeterminant which are common in the consensus view – which are rational, existential or idealistic (in the sense that they are mediated in the consciousness) –

---

[4] Maurice Wiles, *Faith and the Mystery of God*, London: SCM Press, 1982, p. 120.
[5] *Ibid.*, p. 123.
[6] *Ibid.*, p. 124.

an aesthetic (but not sensuous) perception. And that does not allow straightforward discussion of determination by God; instead God is seen as 'personally acting' in and through our recognition of his acting.

Furthermore, where the consensus view normally makes Christian content intrinsic to developed awareness of this Presence, Wiles has stepped back from this, and made it extrinsic, something which is found to be consistent with awareness of the Presence but not intrinsic to it. In other words, normal Christian claims about Christ and the Trinity of God are not necessary to the recognition of the Presence, but historically-conditioned mythopoetic utterances about the Presence which are no longer intelligible or suitable to the recognition of it.

Again, what is most interesting is the way by which Wiles has developed his view. By remaining at an aesthetic level, he has declined to *think* the Presence, and has thereby displaced doctrine to a second-order activity. Nor, it seems, can the Presence be thought or differentiated for itself; it can only be recognized through its activity inextricably interwoven with ours. Interestingly enough, this obeys the strictures placed by the consensus view on speculative knowledge (knowledge derived by means inappropriate to relationship with God), and also – like the consensus view – emphasizes total commitment. But interesting differences appear which suggest that the pattern of Wiles's theology may be as much influenced by the English tradition. This is not the extended moralism of Don Cupitt, but other facets of the English tradition have seriously affected Wiles's view. Suppositions about how things happen in human experience have become normative for what is theological. The theoretical problem of discerning or knowing God's action has been abandoned, and in its place we are asked to consider the legitimacy of aesthetic expressions of meaning in events. God, in the form of an active sublime with its own moral content (cf. romanticism), is recognized in the moral transformation which recognition of him brings. And the truth of this can only be expressed imaginatively in aesthetic symbols or literary forms. Man's legitimacy in believing rests on finding the truth by such means. True to the spirit of the English tradition and its modern personal form, God's codeterminacy has been displaced to the aesthetic sphere.

CONCENTRATING ON THE HUMANLY KNOWABLE

A still different form of this 'personal theology' is found in John Hick's theology, and this – unlike the other two – concentrates explicitly on knowledge, its possibility and its nature. So this will usefully complete our study of the impact of English tradition on contemporary English theology.

Hick has followed the English tradition in its determination of knowledge by what is taken to be humanly knowable, largely by following some tendencies in post-Wittgensteinian philosophy. In order to allow some possibility for the development of knowledge in religion, he has then proceeded to change the form of religious knowledge as well as its content. The way by which he does this is to differentiate between experience, myth and theology in religion.

(1) Religious experience is 'the whole experience of religious persons constituting an awareness of God acting towards them in and through the events of their lives and of world-history, the interpretative element within which awareness is the cognitive aspect of faith'.[7] Christian experience is a special form of this, for in interpretation (the cognitive aspect) experience is experienced according to a particular tradition (Christianity in this case). (2) Myth, on the other hand, is comprised of the great persisting imaginative pictures by which a religious community expresses in universal terms the special meaning and importance of certain items of mundane experience (e.g. redemption by Jesus). Again, Christian mythology is a special form of this. (3) Theology uses the data of experience to speak in a systematic and explanatory fashion.

In the past, Hick says, theology and mythology have been closely intertwined; and because men knew too little to be able to identify myth as myth, theology was misled. Now that myths can be identified because of the advances of science, theology can go back to the data of Christian experience. Those data are already knowledge, because interpretations are the cognitive element in faith, and theology seeks to systematize them. The data are interpreted according to particular traditions of experience (preserved by myths), and there is no way before 'eschatological verification' to decide upon the truth of these traditions. Indeed, all traditions, particular though they are, participate in the universal and are therefore of equal value: 'all your ways are my ways', says God. A parallel situation occurs in goal-setting: life is an open process of goal-setting in which man must find his way through obstacles in a vale of soul-making.

What is interesting about this is to see what strategy is being employed. It is a development of the option presented by Schleiermacher, with the assistance of the philosophy of the later Wittgenstein. The language has changed somewhat, and a supposedly neutral term – 'experience' – has become central. In place of the supposition that human experience is necessarily religious in some respect, Hick uses the term vacuously, suggesting that all the specificity of experience arises from interpretations

---

[7] John Hick, *Evil and the Love of God*, London: Macmillan, 1966, p. 281.

which are particular to some culture and tradition, or to individuals. In other words, whether one has religious experience is accidental, rather than a necessary aspect of being human. What is more important, the content which is intrinsic to the consensus view of the relation between God and man has been displaced in Hick's understanding of communion with God. Where the consensus view develops content considered to be intrinsic to the God-man relation, and does so in such a way as to yield definite understanding of the codeterminative relationship of God and man, Hick considers all such content to be 'experiencing-as' in terms of a particular cultural tradition, and thereby to have the structure of metaphor. So the emphasis is on presence of God in particular interpretation, rather than presence in the consciousness of man as such. In other words, the view of the God-man relationship which characterizes the consensus view has become a completely human experience known in a completely human fashion.

The English tradition of moralism has also entered into Hick's extensive use of Schleiermacher as an archetypal example of what he calls the 'Irenean' type of theodicy. We saw earlier that one's relative position as more or less moral was important in the kind of Calvinism disseminated in England, promoting self-conscious morality. This is developed by Hick into a theology which sees our present human existence as a phase in God's gradual creation of finite beings who are to live in conscious filial relationship with him – whereby, after the evolution of man, God is now, through our free responses, fashioning 'children of God' out of human animals.[8] In doing so, Hick alters Schleiermacher's structural and phenomenological analysis of sin as the presupposition of redemption, into an 'historical' one in which sin is virtually inevitable as man is created at a distance from God 'precisely in order that he may come freely to God, drawn by redemptive grace'.[9] So man must in freedom strive for morality, exactly as the moralist tradition suggested. And Christ, rather than being the redeemer as for the consensus view, becomes 'one of the points at which God has been and still is creatively at work within human life'.[10] Moral striving, in the good English fashion, is self-sustaining, and goes on until transformation is finally achieved.

A TRADITION OF CONFINEMENT

Throughout this review of three kinds of 'personal theology' which have

---

[8] John Hick, 'Evil and Incarnation' in Michael Goulder, ed. *Incarnation and Myth: The Debate Continued*, London: SCM Press, 1979, p. 80.
[9] Hick, *Evil and the God of Love*, p. 238.
[10] Hick, *Incarnation and Myth*, p. 80.

been produced in Britain, we have seen attempts to find a place in the English tradition of aesthetics, knowledge and morality for the bond in which God and man are related. The very confinement which characterizes these three aspects of the tradition – knowledge to what is considered knowable by man, morality to man's moral personal experience of (or transformation by) the sublime – has forced these theologians in the directions which they have taken. One has been seen to elevate man's moral autonomy to a heroic moralism; another has been seen to reconstitute the God-man relationship as a presence aesthetically realized; the third has reconstituted human life as human experience which may (accidentally) be religious in a particular way. In each case, they have been forced by their own cultural tradition, which is largely areligious, to compromise the essential features of the consensus view of Christianity.

Their intention, of course, has been otherwise, to carry out the reinterpretation which is needed to make Christian faith intelligible in the modern situation. But the 'modernity' to which they seem to think themselves answerable is itself the product of the English tradition whose features we have traced, and by no means unquestionable. There seems little doubt that Christian faith must be made intelligible in the modern situation. Perhaps a more serious, and more probing, critique of their own cultural tradition – the tradition which produces both their understanding of Christian faith and their view of what it is to be modern – would have prevented such a compromising of Christianity, and of modernity. But, as we saw at the start, the English are largely unaware of the genesis of their own distinctiveness, and have never really engaged in such a thing as the analysis of their own cultural history.

17

The Cultural Reduction of Religion and the Agenda of Theology[1]

INTRODUCTION

ALTHOUGH in some limited respects religious life and institutions remain strong, society as a whole in the western hemisphere has moved steadily in the direction of residualizing them. The movement is not confined to social forces external to religion. It seems that those responsible for the study of religion and religious education, and frequently also theologians and religious institutions, collude in practices likely to place religious commitments and practices in a residual position. It is to the understanding and correction of this situation that this paper is directed.

THE RELIGIOUS SITUATION TODAY

It is unlikely that the diminished place of religious belief and commitment is due to a single cause. But the multiple causes may have certain common features. Preeminent amongst these is the assimilation of religious beliefs and practices to the very tools which have been used to analyse them. There is an offsetting of what is understood by the means by which it is understood through which the former becomes subject to the latter, and ends by being confined to it. Interestingly, therefore, the substantial content of religious beliefs and practices is methodically diminished.

To point to this dilemma is not to decry the use of these methods in itself. Their use is often the product of attempts to take religious beliefs and practices seriously. And whatever the practices in the past – and it was often assumed that religious authorities should be interpreted and criticized only from within – there is little question that other tools are needed now. But problems arise when these are used to *recast* religious beliefs and practices, a procedure which is strikingly similar to 'assuming what is to be proved'. Amongst many possible illustrations, we will begin with the equation of religion with culture.

[1] A Paper for the Symposium on Christian Theology and Religious Education, North of England Institute of Christian Education, Durham, July 1994.

RELIGION SEEN AS CULTURE

Religious beliefs and practices have – at least in some sense – a transcendent *content* but an innerworldly *location*. It is a marked feature of much current study of religion that both of these are regarded as *cultural* in origin, and as such only *human*. They are therefore best understood in any and all the terms applicable to culture: texts, language, stories, rhetoric, societies, politics, social action and the self-understanding which produces and is formed by such.[2] Culture is a category of no small importance, and is often used – in the triangulation of economics, the individual and the field of social action – to designate the fashion 'in which social groups create common values, objectify them in the institutions of everyday life, and hand them down in the form of social utterances'.[3]

But, well-intentioned and fruitful in some respects though this may be, the supposition that *religion* is *primarily* cultural – that is, that it should be entirely recast in ways appropriate to cultural analysis – is much more problematic. It has the character of a self-fulfilling prophecy – if not a confidence-trick: 'look at religion, and you will see how like a culture it is'; and, so capacious are the categories of cultural analysis made to be, and so indefinite is the understanding of religion, that the fit between the two is made so close as to dissolve religion into culture without remainder.

This is not to suggest, as would those who oppose religion to culture, that religion is not in any degree cultural. *How* they are related is the question. As one way of relating them, consider the view of religion of which S. T. Coleridge spoke in his most widely influential book, *Aids to Reflection* [1825]:

---

[2] Apart from a very generalized definition – 'a certain kind of environment as changed and shaped by man, and also the human activity that leads to the cultural pattern' (*Sacramentum Mundi*, ed. Karl Rahner, London: Burns & Oates, 1968, I, 45) – 'culture' is more likely to be described as the product of the consistent practice of one of these modes. Rhetoric, for example, yields a definition like this:

> Human cultures have multitudes of ways to persuade, as they have many ways to build houses and raise children. The totality of these choices is what we mean by *culture*: it defines people as a cohesive group and gives meaning to their lives. With diligence and goodwill, members of one culture can gain some understanding of the ways of another, may even come to admire them, but can never hope to have the same visceral, empathetic response to the structures of other cultures that they have to their own. (Robin Tolmach Lakoff, *Talking Power: The Politics of Language*, New York: Basic Books, 1990, p. 238.)

[3] Alex Honneth, *The Critique of Power: Reflective Stages in a Critical Social Theory*, Cambridge: MIT Press, 1991, p. 25.

The great fundamental Truths and Doctrines of Religion, the existence and attributes of God, and the Life after Death, are in Christian Countries taught so early, under such circumstances, and in such close and vital association with whatever makes or marks *reality* for our infant minds, that the words ever after represent sensations, feelings, vital assurances, sense of reality – rather than thoughts, or any distinct conceptions. Associated, *I had almost said identified*, with the parental Voice, Look, Touch, with the living warmth and pressure of the Mother, on whose lap the child is first made to kneel, within whose palms its little hands are folded, and the motion of whose eyes *it's* [*sic*] eyes follow and imitate ... from within and without, these great First Truths, these good and gracious Tidings, these holy and humanizing Spells, in the preconformity to which our very humanity may be said to consist, are so infused, that it were but a tame and inadequate expression to say, we all take them for granted.[4]

Here 'the great fundamental Truths and Doctrines of Religion' are directly connected with 'whatever makes or marks reality' through what might be called 'cultural formation' by the mother, which is instrumental to the connection. It was this 'association' which allows the formation of the Reason of the growing human being to be suffused with Divine Light:

In Wonder all Philosophy began: in wonder it ends: and Admiration fills up the interspace. But the first Wonder is the Offspring of Ignorance: the last is the Parent of Adoration. The First is the birth-throe of our knowledge; the Last is its euthanasy and apotheosis.[5]

In this view, therefore, we see cultural influences instrumental in the connecting of the 'Truths and Doctrines of Religion' with reality, a combination within which Reason develops as the 'organ of the super-sensuous' into which pours 'the Light that lighteth every man's individual understanding'. Cultural influence is therefore instrumental in the primary education of the child from which the development of reason and divine illumination proceed. It is a means to connect reason and reality, and not constitutive of reason in its most fundamental sense, still less of religion. That is one way by which to relate culture, reason and religion without dissolving religion (or reason, for that matter) into culture. For Coleridge, to disperse them into culture would be to make 'the

[4] S. T. Coleridge, *Aids to Reflection*, Spiritual Aphorism B IX, Collected Works, Princeton: Princeton University Press, 1993, pp. 237f.
[5] *Ibid.*, p. 236.

Understanding, "the mind of the flesh", into the measure of all spiritual things'.[6]

But the fact that cultural influences play an important role in the formation of reason and religion is easily expanded into the supposition that both reason and religion *as such* are constituted by cultural forces, and are relative to particular cultures.[7] This extension is not so easily sustained, however, and in any case the position leaves primary questions – for example, those of the nature of reason and reality and of continuities in the rational grasp of reality and those of God's own truth – untouched.

THE IMPLICATIONS OF RECASTING RELIGION AS CULTURE

It is important to grasp the effects of the recasting of religion as culture. Considering religion as culture may lead to the supposition that it is primarily a human construct which can be understood exclusively by the study of human practices.

Hence, on the one hand, primacy is given to the human person as proponent and student of religious commitment and practice. Both believing and study are placed within the realm of human capability, which invites humility and circumspection in both – believing as human beings only (insofar as one is capable of it), and studying belief as human beings only (insofar as human beings can do this). This involves the scaling back of the transcendent content of faith, and also of the education which is appropriate to such a faith. Empathetic but neutral (i.e. non-evaluative) faith and observation are normalized.

In effect, these separate the believer and the student from the transcendent illumination of *reason* and *religion*. The result is what might be called a 'deficient subjectivity' for the religious believer and the student, and an education which – judged in these terms – is deficient.

There is a further issue. It has become usual to suppose that the 'objectivity' of religious commitments and practices is culturally established, and best appreciated where they are studied

empirically, and as displaying power, rather than studying them as

---

[6] *Ibid.*, p. 239.
[7] 'According to Thomas Kuhn, for example, scientists who work within different scientific traditions – and thus operate with different descriptive and explanatory "paradigms" – actually "live in different worlds."' Nicholas Rescher, *A System of Pragmatic Idealism*, Vol. III, Princeton: Princeton University Press, 1994, p. 61.

topics for evaluation ... [with] the primary emphasis ... on the descriptive and historical mode of approaching the phenomena, without importing into the study normative associations (we hope) from any one tradition.[8]

Such an approach need not, but when combined with other preconceptions often does, result in a conception of religions with minimal reference to their fundamental determinants – to those elements by which they are configured.[9] In the case of Christianity, it is often considered unnecessary to refer to the determining role of the Trinitarian God and the fundamental structure of Christian religious theory and practices which such understanding of God implies. The result is what can be called a 'deficient objectivity'.

Incidentally, these problems are so severe that the argument about the place accorded to religion or religious education in public institutions is relatively unimportant. No matter how much time is given to them, the results will be poor, because with these deficiencies religious commitments and practices can never be given the seriousness which they deserve.

THE BACKGROUND AND FOREGROUND OF THE PROBLEMS

Yet these problems pass largely without notice, primarily because the suppositions on which they rest are so thoroughly built into current practices as to pass without notice. These suppositions derive from views which originate in the European Enlightenment and pass into current educational practice in Britain not only from those sources but also from the forms in which they have been embraced in the United States. The primacy of the believer and the student as independent of illumination (in worship, for example) is, of course, commonplace in Kantian and post-Kantian thought, with a few notable exceptions such as Coleridge and Schleiermacher. The practice of viewing religion descriptively as an historical-cultural product, and attempting to grasp its power as 'a coherent

[8] Ninian Smart and Steven Konstantine, *Christian Systematic Theology in a World Context*, Minneapolis: Fortress Press, 1991, p. 29.

[9] If it is thought that the primary power of religions rests in the religious experience which they incorporate, for which reference to the divine source of such experiences is the product of human reflection, the position of what are here called 'fundamental determinants' is shifted from 'close and vital association with whatever makes or marks *reality*' (Coleridge) to the culture-bound possibilities of human thought.

account of the major types of religious experience',[10] has spread through the influence of the social sciences and cultural studies.

The combination of the two has been strong in the United States at least since the 1950s, given powerful impetus by the adoption of what has been called an 'experiential-expressive' approach, which equates religion with 'inner feelings, attitudes, or existential orientations'.[11] This served to focus anti-intellectual religious tendencies there which treated any theoretical element as the product of human reflection upon experience. It embodied the anti-theological tendencies which have severely undermined church-based religious education in America since then.

The same approach appeared in the United Kingdom a little later. In part it is traceable to the impact of historical and social-anthropological approaches to religion, in part to the influence of Rudolf Bultmann and Paul Tillich, and in part to the promotion of religious studies here by those heavily influenced by practices in American university education.[12]

The result in the USA, and also in some quarters in the UK, has been the normalizing of religion presented without normative assumptions. The version in which this is commonly accepted includes the supposition that worship and doctrine are two amongst a number of elements in 'religion'. The effect is twofold. It severely limits the determining role of active relation to God in worship, and the reconfiguration of human life in the world which that requires, and in its place elevates religious experience. And it reverses the role of fundamental beliefs and practices in religion. From conclusions derived – often through centuries-long painful struggle – from the intelligent worship of God which transcended the possibilities afforded by current intellectual endeavor, they are transferred to the position of reflections on human experience which are subject to the categories of thought available in particular cultural circumstances. The effects are very drastic for the configuration of religious theory and life, removing its two most fundamental determinants from their central position.

[10] Smart and Konstantine, op. cit., p. 173.
[11] George Lindbeck, The Nature of Doctrine: Religion and Theology in a Post-Liberal Age, London: SPCK, 1985, p. 16.
[12] The immediate background of the view they imported into the UK was the struggle for the acceptance of the teaching of religion in American publicly-funded universities from which it had been excluded. The basis on which it won acceptance was that it was to be studied without reference to its value.

It must be recalled that religious beliefs, practices and education – as well as any reference to God – are completely disallowed in state-funded education or public space in the United States, a possibility never envisioned by those originally responsible for the measures which separated church and state in a nation under God. This not only denies education in religion to the wider public, but also affects religious education in the churches, both by requiring it to concentrate on imparting of fundamental information and by making the neutralized presentation of such information normal in them.

The problematic character of the strategy we have now considered is easily overlooked, because the primary characteristics of religion have been so thoroughly displaced by now that they are forgotten. And, as we have already noted, the strategy is not attributable to a wish by its advocates to disparage religion. On the contrary, it was one form of attempt to take it seriously amidst increasing uncertainties about the truth and relevance of religious beliefs.[13] Although sometimes concentrated in modern philosophy, these uncertainties are probably not so much primarily philosophical in origin as they are the result of the progressive complexification of scientific, intellectual, social, cultural and religious life. Complexity and diversity in such matters seem to undermine universal rational, social and religious concepts and principles – and the capacity of institutions to respond constructively.

But the 'strategy' is problematic because it compounds the difficulty. If religion is recast as culture, it loses its primary impulse and determinants. And the terms on which it is allowed in religious education – as one form of cultural study – are poor, because on these terms it must struggle to find a place amongst an ever-increasing range of – ostensibly more relevant – alternatives. And it is judged not on its intrinsic value but by its functional value in today's world. It thereby finds itself competing within a variety of cultural discourses in a wider market-place of interests governed by the politics of functional interests. The place which it occupies is a very fragile one.

THE RELIGIOUS RESPONSE: A NEW PRAGMATISM

Such a placing for religion is not unconnected with a second phenomenon of our time, a 'practical reduction' of religion in the religious institutions and amongst those directly committed to them. The reduction is not so much in quality, although that may occur too, as it is in the ability to mediate between increasingly wide divergences of view

---

[13] It is relevant, however, to note that those now engaged in religious studies in the United States are united, not by any agreement about subject-matter and methods, but only by common consent that they are not concerned with theology. (See Ray L. Hart, 'Religious and Theological Studies in American Higher Education: A Pilot Study' in the *Journal of the American Academy of Religion*, Volume LIX, No. 4, Winter 1991.) Those who insisted that religious studies should become normal in British universities frequently imported a comparable polarization – that the only alternative to religious studies was 'confessional theology'.

about what religion is. This leads to a predisposition in favour of religious variety.

When new syllabuses for religious education were being constructed, and there was powerful advocacy for the assimilation of religion to culture, the churches' contribution to new syllabuses for religious education in schools was often naive and uncertain. Why? They themselves already half-believed in the need to present the variety of religious views, and that such religious differences were cultural in origin.

What accompanies this 'practical reduction' is an inability to develop intelligent criteria for adjudicating between the varieties. This is partly due to the fact that the place accorded to theologically-informed judgment has declined markedly in religious institutions. Instead, theology is most often seen simply as the process of reflecting on experience, although constrained by the traditions accepted in these institutions.[14] The possibility that theological judgment derives (at least in part) from illumination by God is no longer unquestioned. What has taken its place (for good or ill) is a newly politicized situation in which there is competition within and between several options, a competition which can only be resolved through consensus.

The options found most widely today are these: (1) new attempts to recover the relevance of faith, (2) a variety of authoritarian claims (as they are now perceived to be) and (3) habitual practices of living with the cultural residue of a once-strong Christian faith. The competition within each of these and with each other has produced a situation in which it is usual for their value to be established by pragmatic means.

Amongst these competitors. the first is seen where, in their struggle for survival, religious institutions have sought ways to become more relevant and useful. Employing the *lingua franca* of the day, they have presented themselves as forms of understanding and practice with only the most general connection with the tradition in which they stand. There is little motivation – or often ability – to trace the connection of the one with the other; hence there are frequent disagreements about what faith implies for understanding and behaviour today. While this can easily be illustrated from the life of the churches in the United Kingdom, a cartoon which appeared not long ago in the United States sums up the dilemma, as well as the impact of cultural factors. A pastor is shown with a friend, telling him: 'Mike, the church has to *deliver* for its members – we have to offer it all!' Mike replies, 'Where's God fit into all this?' 'God?' the pastor responds, 'Well, God's still the draw for sure. He's got the big name.' Mike responds, 'Do you ever evoke it anymore?' And the reply comes:

[14] This, for example, was the arena within which the controversy about the ordination of women to the priesthood took place, as a debate about whether reflection on experience should extend – or be constrained by – traditional practice.

'Um, frankly, Mike, God comes with a lot of baggage, the whole male, Eurocentric guilt thing ... '[15]

The second competitor is seen amongst those individuals and groups who speak authoritatively, whose proclamation provides powerful challenges and promises stability and better prospects for those buffeted by uncertainties and perceived injustices. Their impact is great because what is offered seems attractive, particularly to those who are anxious; and they are confidently presented and base themselves in frequently simplified versions of the great traditions of Christian faith. But their appeal is strongly connected with the powerful rhetoric and personality of those who proclaim them, and the simplicity with which they offset the confusions of the time. These features are strongly connected with the 'deficient' subjectivity and objectivity to which we referred before (pp. 295f.), to which they provide an authoritative response. They bear no small resemblance to the well-known story of the lecturer whose text happened to be seen by a student. Marked at one place in the margins were the words, 'Argument weak here: shout!'

The third competitor is seen in the members of an increasingly wide group who respect the contribution which Christianity has in the past made to the possibility of a good society, and to the 'values' which are necessary for life. These are people who generally admire the place which Christian faith and institutions have occupied, and who are willing to grant them a hearing for the sake of the good which they may continue to do. But they are not committed to their value as such. For them Christianity is an historically-based culture which may benefit society, not a matter for religious commitment.[16] Correspondingly, it does not include the expectation either that Christianity is capable of answering their spiritual yearnings or that it can stand up to the pressures of modern life. Although it might conceivably make a positive contribution in special circumstances, on the whole it is taken as powerless to obstruct the tragedies and difficulties of modern life. For example, it would not convince a suicidal young person that life is good.[17]

In practice, those concerned for matters of religion today are likely to be drawn from one of these three competing groups. And most religious people today seem to be a varying mixture of the three, with one or

---

[15] Garry Trudeau, 'Doonesbury', 21 May 1993.
[16] This is the most likely basis for the present agreement that religious education is needed in schools in England.
[17] Two vivid examples come to mind. One was a brilliant 30-year-old anaesthetist educated in the nihilism of her father who committed suicide recently. The other a 21-year-old American from a gun-loving rural area who one winter evening fired his handgun in the air. When at the same moment his friend slipped on the ice, and he thought that he had killed him, he dashed into the woods and killed himself. The issue in both cases was the absence of a well-grounded and effective conviction that life is good.

another element prevailing at any time – living embodiments of a complex of positions. If we were to imagine the conversation between them, it would go something like this: 'We need a relevant faith!' 'No, we need to return to the faith of our forebears!' 'Both of you calm down! All we need is to explore the possibilities which the religious traditions afford for a good life.' Religion – in the United States and the United Kingdom – is more likely to be a pragmatic mixture of these three tendencies, with the loudest voices prevailing.

And it is exactly this admixture which constitutes and limits the effect of religious institutions. These cries are seductive, because the situation has declined to such a point that the majority of those who serve the field of religion, as well as members of the wider public, find it difficult to imagine anything beyond these three positions.

Furthermore, the very fact that all of these positions coexist in public, as well as in private, lends support to the view that religion is a cultural matter after all. For it to be otherwise would require a theological resolution between them – as distinct from coexistence and mutual confrontation – which is informed by the worship of God and the fundamental determinants of Christian understanding and practice. And that in turn would require well-grounded criteria for judging between them. The theology of the churches at present is insufficient for the task.

The Locus of Theological Responsibility

We have been considering the prevailing characteristics of the current religious situation as seen both in those responsible for the study of *religion and religious education* and in *religious people and institutions*. While amongst the first group we found tendencies to recast religion as culture, amongst the second we have found such disagreement that the value of religious claims is decided only through mutual confrontation – which in turn lends support to those who wish to recast religion as culture. In effect, therefore, religious people and institutions comply in the recasting of religion as culture. Now we must look at a third group: it might be hoped that those who accept responsibility for the formation of theology would be in a position to contribute to a theologically-informed understanding and practice of religion.

Who does accept responsibility for theology? In the first place, it is striking that such theology as is done outside the universities, in the churches for example, is almost entirely occasional and for special purposes. This is a state of affairs which more befits the relatively stable situation of the churches hundreds of years ago than it does the highly turbulent climate of today. The churches still suppose that the needs of theology are met in the universities.[18]

The position of university theology in the wider context is itself a question. Amongst those concerned for theology, religion, religious education or religious institutions, it is a matter of debate whose influence is more important – who is/are the villains and who the victims. Each tends to complain about the misguided ideologies of the others. All, however, together with others in wider circles, are linked in a complex feedback loop. Where the loop begins is not so important as how it continues, and who can alter and improve it.[19] Here, university departments are often considered to have a decisive influence. But such as they have is severely limited, not only because of the confined position which universities now occupy but also because their work is often regarded as irrelevant by those responsible for religious education and religious institutions.[20] In any case, such contribution as they might make to what we have termed the 'feedback loop' is affected by their practices. It is to these that we now turn.

[18] In this discussion, for 'universities' in the United States read 'theological seminaries'. Few universities and colleges in the USA, indeed a progressively diminishing number, accept any responsibility either for sustaining religious belief or for theology as such. Where it survives, the institutions are often polarized by conflicting demands – denominational authorities seeking greater control in the name of 'orthodoxy' and academic staff resisting in the name of 'academic responsibility'.

[19] One way of interpreting the purpose of the present conference is to explore the possibilities latent in this feedback loop. One important lead, however, is to question the suppositions mutually reinforced within the loop. That is what is attempted in the present paper.

[20] In this connection, it is important to recognize the place of universities today, and the role of theology within them. The ancient view was that academies, and later universities, were necessary to the well-being of society itself. And in the times before societies were 'advanced' by social, military and economic forces, they fulfilled this purpose. Religious factors, and theology also, were a necessary part of the way in which they did this. But later on, universities were confined to a primarily educational role. And later still, issues of faith ceased to play an explicit role in universities as such, and were consigned to faculties of theology or departments within other faculties. Churches were also allowed only a more limited position; and their leadership had to be provided by special institutions, theological colleges – in the USA seminaries – whose primary function was vocational and educational. In England, at least until recently, religious educators were educated separately in institutions which were primarily vocational and educational. These shifts have serious implications for what can be achieved by university departments of theology; those who work in them are divided from the churches and from religious education, except insofar as they – with the assistance of conferences such as the present one – are reunited with them. In time, particularly where the nature of the work undertaken in university departments of theology is not agreed, such shifts result in *ideological* justifications, for example that university departments are for 'pure scholarship' while church or educational establishments are for 'practical training'.

AGREEING THE TASKS OF THEOLOGY

The characteristic most often found in university departments of theology throughout the western hemisphere is their difficulty in arriving at agreement about coherent programmes and priorities for theological study – which seems to reflect a deeper uncertainty about what is their subject and their goal. Typically, their programmes represent an uneasy compromise between the normalcy of an historical approach to religion and sets of conventions about periods and disciplines which survive from the hey-day of Christian theology.

In practice, their programmes often presuppose the normalcy of forms of study detached from active relation to God in worship and from the determining role of believing. Within – or apart from – the conventions just mentioned, it is often assumed that adequate theology will result from the free play of choices about content and method which marks many aspects of university theology today.[21] And the onset of 'new' methods and approaches – new hermeneutical approaches, for example – only exacerbates the situation.[22] The very freedom allowed in religious 'subjectivity' and 'objectivity' – whether for those who teach or for those who learn – raises important questions, particularly about how far religion is open to 'reimagining'.[23]

A different version of the same dilemma appears where many fields of specialist study, and within them many kinds of interdisciplinary study,

[21] This is more extreme in the United States than in England, but is apparently rising here through the insistence that courses be 'modularized' to allow maximum flexibility and choice. In the USA, it is often called the 'cafeteria system', whose extremes were reached following the student uprisings in the late 1960s and still continue. It can also be seen as the result of the growing ascendancy of individualism and market forces.

[22] There is probably a link between the supposition that religions and their theologies are cultural systems and the value placed on creativity in methods and interpretation. Both are strongly reminiscent of Romantic organismic views.

[23] This is an issue which has stirred enormous controversy recently in the United States. A conference was held in 1993 in Minneapolis – and funded in part by contributions from the Presbyterian Church (USA). It was designed to 'challenge and expand our horizons in undreamed of ways' and thereby reduce 'the pain of exclusion or marginalization experienced within the church'. Appealing to the 'catholic and evangelical truth' that 'the Church in every culture has used and adapted biblical symbols, images, stories, and words in worship,' a variety of 'extravagant language' was used which in some cases went to extremes, for example: 'I don't think we need folks hanging on crosses and blood dripping and weird stuff.' ('Re-Imagining: A Theological Appraisal', by Joseph D. Small and John P. Burgess, *Presbyterian Outlook*, 7 May 1994, pp. 11–13.) The conference has widely been taken as a betrayal of Christian faith: 'If they found in cultural developments a disclosure of God equal to that of Scripture, why should they have been surprised when that culture dismissed their Bible? ... We have no *right* to be surprised, because we, too, have placed modern culture side by side with scripture as the source of our understanding of the will and nature of God.' ('Minneapolis: The Real Issue', by A. J. McKelway, *Presbyterian Outlook*, 4 April 1994, pp. 6f.)

are in use. It readily happens that the nature of 'theology' goes by default. Theology is what *results* from the interplay of the specialist fields of study, or the use of different kinds of interdisciplinary study, for example those based in historical-critical scholarship, in cultural studies or in the history of ideas. In other words, 'theology' is constituted by the outcome of interspecialist or interdisciplinary discussions. Frequently, where departments of theology agree to allot a certain amount of time to each of these fields and disciplines, *de facto* they agree that theology is constituted by the sum total of these allotments – the aggregate of the separate gardens, as it were. The preconfiguration of study by theology and its object are lost in an ongoing redefinition.

Such practices could be rationalized if there were to be agreement that theology or theological inquiry should be the *motive* in study and teaching. If it were accepted that theological inquiry should be the stimulant for study, at least there would be attention to the dynamics of the subject, even if not to the configurations required by its objectivity. This would bring both scrutiny and selectivity to the selection of subject-matter and method. If so, it might then determine and incorporate what is significant for study, and thereby avoid both the chaos of an indefinite range of demands and a 'theology' which is only pragmatically defined.

The danger, however, is that such a strategy would be based on a *notional* 'theology' or 'theological method'. In other words, it would only transfer the difficulties of lack of definition and direction to another level, one at which they intersect with other anxieties about the peer groups to which their practitioners are responsible.

> Can a theologian speak faithfully for a religious tradition, articulating its ethical and political implications, without withdrawing to the margins of public discourse, essentially unheard? The worry that this question imposes an exclusive choice between two foci of loyalty, that one must turn one's back on tradition in order to be heard by the educated public at large (and vice versa), has turned many theologians into methodologists. But preoccupation with method is like clearing your throat: it can go on for only so long before you lose your audience. Theologians who dwell too long on matters of method can easily suffer both kinds of alienation they fear.[24]

In other words, discussions about theology and theological method might paralyse, rather than advance, constructive theological work. To

[24] Jeffrey Stout, *Ethics After Babel: The Languages of Morals and Their Discontents*, Boston: Beacon Press, 1988, p. 163.

paraphrase Bernard Shaw's cutting aphorism about teachers, 'those who can, do; those who can't, discuss method'.[25]

The task of agreeing a coherent programme for theology seems therefore to be caught in a trilemma – live by truces established in the past, create a free market which is supposed to result in 'theology', or begin a paralysing discussion about what constitutes theological method.

UNCERTAINTIES AMONGST THEOLOGIANS

The practices in university departments of theology which we have been reviewing seem to reflect more fundamental uncertainties about how responsibility for theology should be exercised. These deserve further consideration.

I recall the difficulty we had, while interviewing candidates for a post teaching New Testament at the University of Durham a few years ago, in finding anyone who would address theological issues in New Testament theology as such. One applicant compared the faith of New Testament writers with a fortress on a high hill. For his part, he said, he did not presume to approach the fortress itself; he was content to till the fields below the walls. He concerned himself with employing the many different methods available today for understanding the circumstances in which the authors wrote, setting aside the central convictions which motivated them to write.

Why are academics so often inattentive to such central convictions? One reason is that they seek for the approval of their professional colleagues. In their wish to be approved as full-blooded 'academics', many of those who work in theology have internalized the objections which might possibly be made against them by others. In the process, these objections are frequently magnified considerably, to such an extent that the challenges are seen as more severe than any which are actually applicable today. In other words, theologians react more to imagined criticisms than real ones, and retreat prematurely. The academics involved become the modern counterparts of those with a 'scrupulous conscience', people whose consciences became unreasonably severe, torturing them for imagined sins and forcing them constantly to declare their unworthiness.

With such scrupulous self-judgment, they are likely to agree – perhaps

---

[25] 'He who can, does. He who cannot, teaches.' G. B. Shaw, *Man and Superman: A Comedy and A Philosophy*, 'The Revolutionist's Handbook', New York: Dodd, Mead & Company, 1945, p. 230.

against their vocation as theologians – with those to whom their bad consciences make them beholden. Hence, for example, they may bend readily to public uninterest in – or ignorance of – matters theological, or to those who establish 'professional' standards for study in their field, and seek to find some common ground with them.

For example, a bad conscience about the acceptance of theology in public debate may lead to prolonged preoccupation with the publics to which theology should be commended, and strategies for commending it, during which relatively little attention is paid to the central impulses and configuration of theology itself.

The desire to be 'professional' may lead to sustained attempts to adhere to standards set by those perceived as the relevant professionals. The eventual outcome is seen where – as in the United States – it becomes commonplace for those who work in *theology* to accept the standards developed in the highly professionalized field *adjacent* to their own – *religious studies* in universities, whose objectives are quite different.[26] From them, the theologians inherit certain suppositions, that their business is primarily to *know* more about their fields of study in the ways deemed appropriate to the study of religion in American secular universities – 'sometimes quantitative, sometimes interpretive, sometimes philosophical, but always public and open to critical scrutiny.'[27]

Whether this kind of study (of religion) is what is best for, or all that is needed in, universities these days is another question. In the American context, more and more say 'no'. But within British universities the situation has been quite different; there is no apparent reason why the study conducted in university departments of religion or religious studies should be taken as normative for theological study – unless, of course, theology is assumed to be a branch of religious studies.

Preoccupation with the publics to which theology should be accountable and the pressures of academic respectability combine where the plurality of religions is concerned. Since the universal scope of Christian theology is no longer thought to be clear, and academic respectability favours restriction of all study to limited domains, there is a widespread predisposition to confine each 'theology' to a particular sphere of reference. 'Christendom' is therefore seen as presumptuous, a politico-theological attempt to define Christianity *into* universality; the response is to define it *out* of universality. It is said that assertions of truth are no more than those particular to certain people or their institutions – *'your views'*

---

[26] It is a curious fact that, while the majority of higher-degree candidates in theology in the United States are educated in *theological* institutions, those who teach them accept the standards applicable in *universities*, where the objectives in the study of religion are quite different – and perfectly legitimate given the constraints which operate in such places.

[27] Ivan Strenski, 'Lessons for Religious Studies in Waco?' in the *Journal of the American Academy of Religion*, Fall 1993, Volume LXI, Number Three, p. 567.

or *'our claims'* – and neither more nor less valuable than the claims of other religions. The only legitimate contenders to truth, therefore, are those assertions which are agreeable to all faiths.

The result is reminiscent of the strategy advocated by those who sought peace amidst the wars of religion in Europe; these – 'deists' as they came to be called – subsumed all special religious claims within generalities which would be nondivisive and offend no one. Today, the notion of 'religious toleration' functions comparably, but not normally with the hypothesis of an overarching 'religion'. It is used as a rule for civilized society instead, a rule for holding all religions in a position of putative equality. While often deferred to by theological scholars, the 'rule' is not unproblematic, since it is a rule *external* to each religion: 'you must not say or do things which appear to conflict with the claims of other religions'. By abiding by the rule, they consent – perhaps with too quick a humility – to the view that theirs is but one form of religion, one no more important because they hold it.[28]

There are, of course, ways of avoiding these problems while still being dedicated to the special value of one tradition. The way most often chosen is to study it in the forms in which it has occurred in the past, considering its meaning in contexts far from (or in some cases not so far from) the present. Of course, like the 'neutral' study of religions which is proper to universities where positive views of the value of faith are disallowed, this is essential to institutions where faith is thought to be taken seriously. But there are two problems with it.

One is that it supposes the value-in-itself of the period which is studied, relying perhaps on residual convictions of the centrality of the period to the history of particular traditions. The other is that the study is divorced from the theological value of history – as the circumstance for the continuing economy of God's work – which requires the interpretation of the past for the present.[29] In historical-theological study, it is attractive to affiliate oneself with an historical period in theology, while avoiding the task implicit in theological history, of showing how and why it makes sense to affirm such historical views as important in the present.

These strategies, which are widespread in the world of theological scholarship, leave a problematic vacuum in theology. The combination of inattention to the central issues of faith, the desire for acceptance by

---

[28] This is not the only strategy open to them. A more directly theological response would be to recognize that toleration is part of the fundamental configuration of theology, and included within compassion as its minimal form, a possibility which allows that the implications of Christianity *might be* universal – depending on their outworking.

[29] A professor once told me, 'I am a fourth-century Trinitarian.' As to what that meant today, he could not say. To take such a position, affirming a belief as understood within a certain context with no attempt to discover its continuing value, overlooks the requirements of history as theologically significant.

wider publics and professionals, complicity in the de-universalizing of their tradition, and the readiness to confine both the scope of theology and their own field of study: all of these interfere substantially with the exercise of their responsibilities for theology. Under these circumstances, there is a serious possibility that *theology* disappears in a busy market-place of alternatives.

FINDING THE AGENDA FOR THEOLOGY

As it operates now, the 'feedback loop' of religious education, religious people and institutions and those with responsibility for theology is not an encouraging one. While peopled by those of good intentions and high motivations, the practices we have observed suggest that they are overtaken by the recasting of religion as culture, a new pragmatism amongst religious people and institutions, and various ways of avoiding directly theological tasks amongst those thought to be responsible for theology.

To provide a cumulative account of the difficulties present in religion and theology is not to argue for a return to the ideas and practices which prevailed previously. It is rather to identify the areas and intersections which should become the *agenda for a combined effort* in religious education, religious institutions and places where the study of theology is provided, through which the primary motives and configurations of religious belief and life can be invigorated. In other words, we have been tracing the agenda which needs now to be addressed by those respon-sible, an agenda which will require vastly increased efforts by all those who are concerned for the future of religion in a coherent response to the needs now evident.

During the foregoing analysis, there have been many allusions to the fundamental determinants which affect both religious subjectivity and objectivity, or those elements to which they are 'preconformed' (Coler-idge) or configured. These refer to the worthship which forms the heart of religion.

Worship designates worth or positive value, the honor or dignity which is inherent in the one in whom (or which) it is found. In the case of divine worship, worth-ship designates one in whom there is maximum value by virtue of the occurrence of the highest form of the fundamental 'transcendental notes' – unity, truth, goodness and beauty – which mark being as such. Hence, in such worship, supremely positive value inheres in one God infinitely transcending lesser forms of unity, truth, goodness and beauty whether visible or not, in such a way that there is no basis of comparison between this God and them.[30] This is because all worth is God's, and all honour of the kind given by human beings derives from the worth of God. Hence honour or glory is God's, and only derivatively in the one who does honour to God.

Insofar as anything is distinct from this God, God – as the ultimately defining reality – is the source by which it and all other reality is established, and its value constituted. Its differentiation as 'other' from God is one constituted by God, and the nature of its independence is established by God. For example, 'creation' is constituted as distinct, but even this distinctness is one maintained as the expression of God's positive valuation.[31] The same applies to the distinctions which are brought about in creation by God. The existence and nature of the otherness of things from each other is constituted by God, and they are thereby proportioned to achieve their fullest, while not overreaching themselves.

Therefore, the distinction of a created reality, and the establishment of differentiations within it, is the result of the ultimately defining worth which God is. But the positive value of unity which inheres in God also constitutes a unity between God and creation, and between the differentiated elements of creation. It is not an inert unity, but an energetic, dynamic one through which creation and its elements are attracted – both themselves and their relations – to their fulfilment. Likewise, the truth, goodness and beauty which inhere in God also constitute God's active relations with creation and its distinct elements, through which they are brought to their fullest, 'sanctified in truth' (John 17.17).

The determinants of at least Christianity lie within relation to this worthship, its holiness, the conferral of holiness in the configuration of all thought and life, and the dynamics by which they are energized toward eschatological completion. (These are properly seen in Trinitarian terms which delineate the movements of holiness toward humanity in world-history.) The dynamics which we have observed in conceptions of culture in religion, in the pragmatics through which religious people and institutions arrive at a sense of common purpose,[32] and in achieving a common purpose for theology are all to be seen as *rooted*, *sustained* and *extended* through the configurations established in worthship.

---

[30] Hence, contrary to many modern translations, the appropriate expression of such worship is not ascriptions such as 'give honour to' or 'glory be to', but 'honoured be' or 'glory in' (e.g., '*Gloria in excelsis Deo*').

[31] Alternatively, if creation takes possession of its distinctness, a possibility which inheres in it by virtue of the fact that it is given genuine distinctness by God, it may bring divine judgment upon itself.

[32] There is as yet no theology capable of incorporating the dynamics of different positions in a deeper and more genuinely pragmatic synthesis which is informed by the worship of God and the fundamental determinants of Christian understanding and practice. It would be possible, however, to develop a theology informed by the insights of pragmatic idealism, a philosophy 'deeply rooted in the practical impetus to create a habitable place for ourselves

Against their 'inversion' as forms of purely human consciousness and action, therefore, culture, pragmatics and theology must struggle to uncover their transcendent origin, sustenance and goal.[33] The possibility which they have for the realization of the 'transcendental notes' of unity, truth, goodness and beauty – as traceable to the worthship of which we have been speaking – must be uncovered.

Such a struggle will raise basic issues of faith in their most acute form. These are the issues of the very *identity of God* and the *character of God's life in the world*, and how they are constitutive for the *world and human life*. Such issues go deeply into the nature and action of God – into the features of the life of God, and how this life is so rich and abundant as to be the source, sustenance and completion of the world – its nature, history, societies, human rationality and behaviour, expressions of meaning, and religions – and in turn how they are raised to their full stature by being reoriented to the worthship of God. These are the dimensions of the task in which religious education, religious institutions and university theology must combine their efforts today.

---

in a world in which we rational beings cannot comfortably live in a state of incomprehension and cognitive dissonance ... [with] an indelibly idealistic aspect, for it sees philosophy as a matter of coming to intellectual terms with the deliverances of our experience.' Nicholas Rescher, *A System of Pragmatic Idealism*, Princeton: Princeton University Press, 1994, Volume III, p. xv.

[33] 'Such are the problems that press upon any conscientious observer of our situation today. They can no longer be ignored. It is imperative that the existential rediscovery of philosophic-Christian truth be unfolded within society and history. Having struggled against its inverted opposite, Christianity can once again provide the authoritative public foundation of order.' David Walsh, *After Ideology: Rediscovering the Spiritual Foundations of Freedom*, San Francisco: HarperSanFrancisco, 1990, p. 183.

18

Reshaping Faculties of Theology in Europe[1]

INTRODUCTION: THE SCOPE OF THE QUESTIONS

AFTER centuries of involvement with religious life and theology, and less often mission, the faculties and departments in European universities which are dedicated to these matters present an extraordinarily complex picture. The task of considering their future shape is demanding in itself. And in a world whose complexity also grows exponentially, the responsibility of charting their future is even more daunting. But there can be no retreat from the breadth and complexity of these tasks, and we must attempt to consider the priorities by which the future of the faculties and departments of religious studies and theology may be reshaped.

The significance of mission for religious studies and theology, furthermore, raises difficult and fundamental questions about their nature and purpose. Is mission, for example, one further strand in what can at times be an uneasy relationship between the others; or do all three need to consider what kind of study they are, and how they are intrinsically – as distinct from extrinsically – related, and on what terms they are so related?

In order to address the significance of *mission* for theology and religious studies in this reshaping, we shall therefore need to keep in mind a few very far-reaching questions: *What is the nature and scope* of religious studies, theology and mission, severally and together? *What* formative factors are manifest in the present shaping of the faculties which deal with these things? *To what* are they to be reshaped?

But these issues cannot be addressed as if these three – religious studies, theology and mission – were self-contained, each one subsuming the other two (which is often taken to be the case), or the three together isolated from wider movements of thought and life (which is even more common in practice). That is why we must begin within a fuller conception of the dynamics of human life in the history of Europe.

[1] Address to the Conference, 'Searching for God in Europe and Africa: The Interplay of Mission, Theology and Religious Studies', Centre for Advanced Religious and Theological Studies, Faculty of Divinity, University of Cambridge, 26–29 March 1995, held with the support of the Pew Charitable Trusts.

The Search for Vitality in Europe

Common perceptions of theology, religious studies and mission are strongly shaped by the situations and traditions in which we find ourselves, within which our understanding and practices have been formed. But there is a more *primary vitality* in which these – and not only they – are implicated. All 'coherent activities'[2] of thought and practice mediate the most powerful forces shaping human understanding and life. They reflect such powers as existing human beings have available to deal with understanding and life, and the purpose of rendering them coherent as activities is to sustain these powers, focus them and increase their efficacy. Of course, these 'coherent activities' can be turned in on themselves and taken as self-important, but this reduces their true significance as enhancing the capabilities with which human life itself is undertaken.

In Europe over the centuries, the configuration of such 'coherent activities', and religion, theology and mission amidst them, have – within each alone and in their interplay – undergone successive changes, some of which we will review in a moment. This is not simply accidental, or ideologically motivated, as is often claimed, but motivated by a search for effective ways to mediate the ordered energies of life and understanding, even if such ways differ widely in their suppositions as to the source from which these ordered energies derive, how they are furthered, and what purpose they serve. They can all be seen as 'energy operations'.[3]

The search for the primary vitality of life and understanding which is pursued through the changing configuration of and between disciplines is not only a search for efficacy, however. Although this is easily overlooked or forgotten in a society whose fabric is maintained through a combination of scientific achievement, stable social institutions, personal character, homogeneous culture and common religion, the fabric of life and understanding – and the primary vitality which it mediates – is a moral one, and morally precious. The issue in the changing configuration of the activities of life and understanding, therefore, is not that they are competitors on a neutral field. The jostling of these activities of life and understanding exemplifies contending attempts not only to mediate the primary vitality of life, but also to manifest what is considered its morally beneficial character.

The searching for this vitality and its moral benefits is central to Christian theology, of course, where it coincides directly with what is described by St Paul:

[2] While the term 'disciplines' would be appropriate here, we reserve it for the special sense in which it came to be used in the nineteenth century, discussed later.
[3] The term is drawn from Richard Newbold Adams, *The Eighth Day: Social Evolution as the Self-Organization of Energy*, Austin: University of Texas Press, 1988, p. 5.

As it is written, 'What no eye has seen, nor ear heard,nor the heart of man conceived, what God has prepared for those who love him,' God has revealed to us through the Spirit. For the Spirit searches everything, even the depths of God. For what person knows a man's thoughts except the spirit of the man which is in him? So also no one comprehends the thoughts of God except the Spirit of God. ... This is how one should regard us, as servants of Christ and stewards of the mysteries of God. Moreover it is required of stewards that they be found trustworthy.[4]

The text speaks eloquently of how the very Spirit who searches all, even the depths of God, reveals the mysteries of God to those who are animated by the love of God through their service of Christ. The Spirit which searches the depths of its own Source is the self-same Spirit which gives vitality to those morally transformed by it.

What is the relation between these two, the search for the vitality and morality by which life and understanding are given their deepest resources, and the very Spirit understood by Christians to search and reveal the mysteries of the Triune God in the spirit of ordered human life? Through most of the history of Europe, there was a profound convergence between them, as each was to a degree involved with – or fed by – the other. But recognition of this convergence has markedly diminished.

The convergence was mediated in major fields of human activity through which human life and understanding were formed in Europe, in the knowing of God and the world, in the ordering of human society, in the formation of human character, in cultural expression, and in *religio* (the 'binding back or reattachment of fallen humanity to God'[5]). Likewise, the decline of the convergence came where these mediations were separated from reference to the Spirit of God active in them. At the risk of grotesque oversimplification, we can identify three stages in this. Certainly, through European history to the eighteenth century, there was a marked convergence between religion and other agencies of moral vitality in the process of 'feeding' the intellectual and social structure through which ordered human life was maintained in Europe, in England, as 'an elastic and all-embracing hegemonic order'[6]. The activity of

---

[4] 1 Corinthians 2.9–11; 4.1–2.
[5] Richard A. Muller, *Dictionary of Latin and Greek Theological Terms*, Grand Rapids: Baker Book House, 1985, p. 262.
[6] Perry Anderson, *English Questions*, London: Verso Books, 1992, p. 30. He continues:

Hegemony was defined by Gramsci as the dominance of one social bloc over another, not simply by means of force or wealth, but by a wider authority whose ultimate resource is cultural. This is an imperative order that not merely sets limits to the aims and actions of the subordinated bloc, but shapes its internal vision of itself and the world, imposing contingent historical facts as necessary co-ordinates of social life

God was accepted as integral to the ways and institutions by which those in charge of 'civilization' were formed, but – as this activity came to be seen as fixed and therefore manifest preeminently in the stability of worldly order – it was in due course outstripped by the changing forms of knowledge and life, seen in the sciences, history, societal development, the arts, etc. The vitality of the Spirit had been transformed into rules of behaviour, and was left aside in the vitalities of new forms of understanding and life. As F. M. Cornford wrote in *Microcosmographia Academica*, a 1908 satire on Cambridge University politics,

> The principle of Discipline (including Religion) is that *'there must be some rules.'* If you inquire the reason, you will find that the object of rules is to relieve the younger men of the burdensome feeling of moral or religious obligation. If their energies are to be left unimpaired for the pursuit of athletics, it is clearly necessary to protect them against the weakness of their own characters. They must never be troubled with having to think whether this or that ought to be done or not: it should be settled by rules. The most valuable rules are those which ordain attendance at lectures and at religious worship. If these were not enforced, young men would begin too early to take learning and religion too seriously; and that is well known to be bad form.[7]

Here religion is taken as equivalent to stability.

Second, the convergence between a searchingly active Spirit of God and other forms of the search for vitality (and its attendant morality) began to suffer as attention was transferred to the possibilities inherent in the disciplined activities of human beings – in the sciences, social order, personal character, human expression, etc. While these other forms were in evidence very early, at least from the onset of the European Renaissance, they were only alienated from the Spirit of God by degrees, as religious people proved themselves unable to respond to them – and their progenitors in turn turned away from religious conceptions. That took place over centuries.

One important climax, however, came with the advent of the modern universities in the nineteenth century – or the move from the 'Don of the Old School' to the 'Don of the New School' in the ancient universities of England – when the hold of religion on education was loosened. The

---

itself ... Such tranquil and unchallenged sovereignty is a relatively rare historical phenomenon. In England, however, the unparalleled temporal continuity of the dominant class has produced a striking example of it.

[7] Gordon Johnson, *University Politics: F. M. Cornford's Cambridge and his advice to the young academic politician*, Cambridge: Cambridge University Press, 1994, p. 100.

'ecclesiastical monopoly' was ended, and religion had to justify its position in universities.[8] In its place emerged a university system organized in disciplines which provided careers for a new breed of professional academics. These disciplines were justified in terms of their value in forming a new intellectual elite capable of guiding the society then emerging.[9]

The significance of these changes was that they licensed a variety of attempts, corresponding to different aspects of human understanding and life, to uncover the vitality of human understanding and life. Each discipline, with its own 'priesthood' of professionals, was self-governing, while universities pressed for excellence in these terms – free of religious tests. The overt convergence of religion with the new sources and mediums of vitality (moral and otherwise) largely disappeared; and the transcendent reference – particularly as understood by Christians – of the new sources of vitality was lost. Divinity retreated to the position of one faculty of disciplines amongst others, preparing for what was now seen as a profession, and only one such amongst more and more others, most of them seen as more efficacious. Where religion had previously brought some measure of coherence, the new form of coherence – such as it was – was rational and organizational, dedicated to the organization of teaching and the elevation of professional standards.

Third, alongside the free mediation of the vitalities of human understanding and life in the variety of university disciplines, there was another of potentially greater influence still. The emergence of commerce in the nineteenth century showed the power which could be unleashed through the growth of disciplines focused on the production of material goods. What emerged were new ways by which to concentrate human understanding and life for the purpose of production and marketing – thereby linking raw materials (and the different sources from which they came), productive processes and markets – and wealth creation. Here again, the overt connection between these manifestations of vitality and any intrinsic connection to transcendent sources of vitality was lost.

It could be claimed by Christians that, in each of the three cases, the ordering energy of the Spirit is transposed into a special form – an

---

[8] A. J. Engel, *From Clergyman to Don: The Rise of the Academic Profession in Nineteenth-Century Oxford*, Oxford: Clarendon Press, 1983, p. 78. The development of the modern university in Germany, as in Berlin, tells a similar story.

[9] 'With a clear sense of their mission, Oxford and Cambridge were remarkably successful in turning out graduates who monopolized the dominant positions in public and private life in Britain and throughout its empire. One explanation for that success is that the universities conferred a new authority on ideas. The newly modern universities took competing concepts from within the university and from the outside world, subjected them to prevailing standards of acceptance, and dispatched them to the various agencies of influence.' Reba N. Soffer, *Discipline and Power: The University, History, and the Making of an English Elite, 1870–1930*, Stanford: Stanford University Press, 1994, pp. 1–3.

hegemonic social structure, an intellectual elite and a commercial world. For them, it might seem that a vitality which in itself is essentially religious is transposed into mediate forms which come to marginalize their own religious basis. But such a view would not be readily credible to those actually involved, for which these forms of understanding and life were only that – vital ways. Furthermore, as we will see, religious – and Christian – people are carried along by this very process.

If this account, even if sketchy, is correct, it presents us with one overarching issue, *how to recover a true convergence between the animating vitalities of life and the Christian vision of the Spirit.* It is important, of course, to discover a better shaping for faculties of theology and religious studies today, but to what end? It seems to me crucial that they be reshaped in such a way as to recover the full religious, theological and missiological dynamic of all human understanding and life. This is the issue which we must bear in mind as we pursue the questions mentioned at the outset.

WHAT ARE RELIGIOUS STUDIES, THEOLOGY AND MISSION?

Before proceeding to examine the ways in which they are presently studied, we need at least to arrive at preliminary notions of what religious studies, theology and mission are. To some extent, it is artificial to attempt such notional definitions, because they cannot be separated from the different ways in which they are pursued, which we must afterwards discuss. But not to have at least some indications of what they are would lead to an unmanageable discussion.

If we recall the previous consideration of the vitalities of life and understanding, including a moral impulse and content, and remember that coherent human activities may reflect these, focus them and give them additional effect, *religions* can be called comprehensive and disciplined human activities which manifest these vitalities and thereby give them efficacy in human life in the world. By nature, they are comprehensive – reaching and vitalizing all aspects of life. To consider them 'cultures' tells only part of the story: they involve all aspects of understanding and life, theology, ontology, cosmology, sociality, human character, culture and symbols – all coordinated in a stable, complex whole. And, in thus mediating the vitalities in such varying and complex ways, religions not only manifest what is the case, but also operate performatively – incorporating these vitalities in the dynamic shaping and reshaping of human life and understanding through history.

Although one is tempted to call them comprehensive transpositions of the vitalities to which we have referred, they are more fundamental than that. From the standpoint of religions, other coherent human activities (including alternative religions) which mediate the vitalities are transpositions from religion. When earlier we outlined some of the main stages of the history of Europe, what we saw were transpositions from – rather than in – religion.

Where religions manifest the vitalities in such a way as to give them enhanced effect, *theology* is more specific in its dealing with them. While it has become common to consider theology as reflection on religion, posterior to it as a secondary activity, I believe this to be misleading. Theology attempts to know the character, configuration and dynamics of the vitality itself, and to configure thought and practice – whatever their object – to follow this order and dynamics. By the nature of the case, the vitality recedes from full view, and is therefore mysterious, but it is also present in the ordered energies of human understandingg and life in the world, and so can be known and followed.

Theology, therefore, is the thinking of the dynamic 'architecture' of the constancy of the reality of the living God, as the vital and moral source of the ordered energies of the world and human life in all the rich variety with which cosmology, ontology, sociality, human character, cultures, symbols and religions exemplify. From its point of view, all these others – if taken as self-important – are transpositions from theology.

Missions emerge in the processes by which connections are made between local forms of religion and theology and between the mediations through which they are manifest. They are the translocalization of religions, projected or hoped-for, and manifestations of the catholicity which is intrinsic to theology. As religions are brought into new regions, or the catholicity of theology is realized in fresh areas, there are collisions with the mediations of vitality which are antecedently present in these localities. What is made of these collisions will vary with the ways in which religion and theology are construed – a matter which we will need to consider presently.

It is no surprise, of course, that history itself, the history of each place, mediates the vitalities differently; there is no simple coordinated movement forward through history, by which all people and places, or all forms of understanding and life, march together to a single tune. It would be more surprising than not if the movements of religion and theology in history were not asynchronous. This gives rise to one of the most interesting features of mission, its diachronous and 'dispatial' agenda, one of connecting differently manifested religions and theologies and the different mediums through which they are manifest in different places and times – all within the sense of the vital economy of God's work. At the very least, that agenda threatens to disrupt oversimplified views of religion and theology. How is the searching of the Spirit – the primary vitality of which we have been speaking – present in the variously 'timed' and 'spaced' searchings of human hearts and minds – in their 'space-times'?

STRATEGIC PRACTICES OF RELIGIOUS STUDIES AND THEOLOGY

One important way of describing religious studies, theology and mission is that they are disciplines developed within the searching of the Spirit in 'the spirit of the man which is in him' – that is, in the ordered energies of human life and understanding. Insofar as they follow this Spirit in the world, they furnish distinct understandings of the source and character of this vitality and its correlative morality, and find ways to mediate it which are appropriate to it. But there are several identifiable strategies by which they do so, which affect all three, religious studies, theology and mission – as well as their capacity to find the Spirit *in the world*.

Strategy One: The intensity with which they (the practitioners of religious studies, theology and mission) study the vitality of the Spirit in the forms with which they are specially familiar may lead them to draw sharp boundaries around what is presumed to be central to this vitality, as if it were necessarily dissociated from other ways either derivative from it or disjoined from it. Karl Barth's cry (in his *Commentary on Romans*) 'Let God be God!' was one such boundary-drawing.

But there are many examples. On the one hand, religious studies, theology or mission – or indeed any of their subdisciplines – can draw sharp boundaries around itself, implicitly denying independent value to the others. On the other hand, any of them can draw its boundaries in such a way as to deny vitality to the natural world, social life, human beings, cultural life or even religious forms. In this case, there is a steadfast insistence that what is central to religion or theology or mission is sharply distinct in its subject matter, and not adequately conceivable with categories of thought drawn from elsewhere. At best, the relation between any one of these three, the others and other forms of vitality, is considered problematic; and dualistic, paradoxical and dialectical/contrastive forms of thought are prominent. This presumes a predefined or sharp boundary-line between the vitality which they know and others.

The same strategy is often found, in practice if not in principle, in places where the three (religious studies, theology and mission) are studied. Historically, the roots of this strategy are in the intertwining of the conception of a special subject-matter (of religion/theology/mission) with the emergence of separate disciplines, with correlative standards of professionality, in nineteenth-century universities. There, as we have seen, religion was rapidly losing ground as the dominant influence in university structure. And the resultant attitude could easily be defensive: retreat to those resources – Scripture and decisive forms of belief (early doctrine in England, classic confessions elsewhere) and practice which were peculiar to Christian faith. The strategy also deeply permeated the internal organization of the disciplines involved in such study, and most of the sharp distinctions and perceived impasses between the subdisciplines of divinity – Old Testament, New Testament, Doctrine, Church History – are traceable to their emergence as separate disciplines and professions.

Yet, there were ways in which these subdisciplines closed ranks when confronted with wider issues. As in 'the nineteenth- and twentieth-century belief in history [was] evidence of national rectitude'[10], so religion in its Christian form was seen within national situations. In the case of England, it was believed to exemplify 'moral values, ethical behavior, and God's beneficent purposes revealed in English history'. The same could be said of other European universities; awareness of a divine commission special to the nation was merged with the conception of the subject-matter to be studied, and the disciplines through which it was to be studied in its classical form. Why therefore study *religions*, or indeed *missions*? Their position was extrinsic, where the agreed disciplines were intrinsic to the special character of divinity.

Strategy Two: If, by comparison, there is greater concern for the activity of the Spirit *in the spirit of ordered human life in the world*, however, another strategy results. In this case, boundaries are seen differently, as permeable and capable therefore of receiving what is of value 'outside' or allowing interaction with what lies beyond. This is not to suggest that there are no boundaries, or that there is less firmness of conception about the activity of the Spirit, but that allowance is made for a symbiotic relation with other conceptions of the vitality present in the world.

But here these wider vitalities are *imported* into the primary field of inquiry, 'domesticated' (as it were) for their value in illuminating that primary field. 'God is not only interested in this field,' they might say, 'but that is where God is most fully found.'

It is important to pause at this point to recognize the degree to which types of study have been imported from elsewhere into religious studies, theology and mission. The very conception of each as a 'discipline', with professional standards, was in fact imported into the study of religion and theology during the development of the modern university. Not that alone, however, but the principal means of identifying the subject-matter

---

[10] Reba N. Soffer, *op. cit.*, p. 9.

of the discipline were drawn from adjacent disciplines; and those not used were considered too 'unfriendly' to use.[11]

Consider for a moment the devices which were imported into the study of religion and theology. There was 'textualization', whereby 'text-like' conceptions and practices were drawn from literary pursuits to identify what kind of material Scripture was, as well as the methods appropriate to its study. There was 'periodization', drawn from historical study to identify significant eras of history, by which pivotal periods were established. There was 'topicalization', drawn from philosophical study to identify the concepts of particular significance for theological study, by which the *loci* of doctrinal theology were set. There was 'culturation', drawn from the social studies, by which all the subject-matter of religion and theology was seen as cultural products. And, more broadly, there was 'methodization', drawn from the disciplinary preoccupations of the modern university, by which professional standards were maintained. No doubt there were others, but these were major ones. And they were only the beginning, as their source-disciplines developed sub-specialties, which also 'slid' into religion and theology.

It must not be overlooked that these new devices, when imported into religion and theology, refreshed and excited existing research. They allowed this research to fasten on and understand materials whose significance was very great – and continue to do so. For the materials, which were mediations in which the vitality of the tradition remained powerful, emerged with new fascination for those who studied them with these devices. But the fact remained that their reflection, focusing and regeneration of the vitality of the tradition was inherently limited by these devices. After all, is Scripture like any other book?

More broadly, much of the renewal of religious studies and theology in modern European universities has resulted from the use of this strategy. To no small extent, it reflects the place of religious studies and theology in the public domain in European universities – where their rightful place is allowed even if the value of their contribution is not well understood. To a large extent, this frees them from the defensiveness which marks such study in American universities.[12]

Strategy Three: The strategy we have just been considering, which allows the study of religion and theology to be refreshed by methods of study drawn from other disciplines which are imported and domesticated for the purpose, is potentially dangerous – in that it may allow the

---

[11] Speaking of the religious value of history in nineteenth-century universities, Reba Soffer has this to say: 'Unlike the sciences, which competed with religion by revealing an essentially rational and self-explanatory world, history provided an accommodating bridge between secular and religious convictions.' *Op. cit.*, p. 9.

[12] This is not to suggest that faculties of religious studies or theology can easily justify new appointments, given the functional considerations which now inform university financing.

assimilation of these subjects to the disciplines from which these devices are drawn. That can happen in a variety of ways, where religion and theology are seen as disciplines like others (which occurs, for example, where they are treated as 'cultures' or 'world-views'), or where their texts are equated with the literature studied elsewhere, or where their history is assimilated to world-history, or where their discernments of the vitalities of understanding and life are identified and analysed as philosophical 'topics'. Indeed, every disciplinary or subdisciplinary device may be dangerous, not because it is used for religion and theology, but where this use is expanded to the point of providing a full account of aspects of religion and theology.

We can distinguish between two ways in which these devices are used. One is to assist with the study of religion and theology, providing new ways by which subject-matter can be identified and studied; as such their value is *descriptive* for such aspects of the subject-matter as are like the disciplines from which they were drawn. The other is where they come to exercise fascination for their users, and are seen as fully determining the subject-matter and the ways it should be studied; in this case, what had been partially descriptive comes to be fully descriptive and normative. In such cases, they are like a 'Trojan horse' in religion and theology, taking over the 'city' into which they have come. Once they have been ceded such influence, these devices continue to feed the study of religion and theology with the growth of these techniques as it occurs outside, in their originating discipline. The 'Trojan horse' has a secret supply route.

What distinguishes this strategy from the Strategy Two? It is that here the independent value of religion and theology as mediating the primary vitality (and moral content) of human life and understanding has been lost, as the generic notion of 'discipline' – and particular disciplinary devices like 'text', 'history', 'topics', 'culture' and 'method' – have been introduced into religion and theology. There they are used as a 'sieve' through which the vitality of religion and theology *must* pass. But the 'mesh' of the sieve is so fine – and each wire so much tooled by the preoccupations of the disciplines responsible for it – that nothing of the original vitality of religion and theology remains. In other words, the position of these disciplines and sub-disciplines has been expanded to the point that religion and theology are nothing but what can be seen thereby.

In the case of this strategy, there is a willingness to assimilate the vital content of religion and theology to different forms of disciplinary understanding and practice, and to allow it to be conditioned by them without remainder. Hence, religious and theological life and understanding is dispersed into the subject-matter and methods of other disciplines and sub-disciplines, and maintained only as a 'religious' or 'theological' instance of what is found more widely.

Here, then, are three strategies by which the study of religion and theology proceeds. Each, in fact, identifies the vitality of religion and theology differently, one by intense and boundaried preoccupation with the vitality and its mediating forms, the second willing to introduce other disciplines for their descriptive illumination, and the third expanding the use of these disciplines in religion and theology to such a degree as to transfer attention from religious and theological vitality to the disciplines (drawn from elsewhere) through which religion and theology are understood. Exclusivity at the one extreme yields – via a moderate position – to dissipation.

The study of religion and the study of theology are each, in theory and practice, varied – varied in their concern for, and analysis of, the vitality with which these forms of life and understanding are laden.

THE INTERDEPENDENCE OF RELIGIOUS STUDIES AND THEOLOGY

So much were religious studies and theology polarized by the most prominent proponents of religious studies only a few years ago, that integrating them seemed impossible. They were set against each other as opposing disciplines, the one an empathetic but non-evaluative study and therefore suitable for universities, the other a form of special pleading, evaluative and confessional and therefore suitable only for church institutions.[13] From the perspective which has been emerging here, they are much closer. Indeed, to call them separate 'disciplines' with different 'methods' may reflect the use of a category generated by the internal politics of nineteenth-century universities.

While from a 'disciplinary' standpoint they would appear at most as complementary, their relationship is more profound – as distinct but mutually illuminating mediations of the source and character of the primary vitality of human life and understanding. As such, they should be turned toward each other more than they are in European universities today. But *how* turned toward each other?

All of the strategic practices which we have reviewed come into play in their interrelation. Quite rightly, there are those who would draw sharp boundaries around the special configurations which both religions and theologies employ to focus what is deemed central to the vitality which

---

[13] It is notable that this polarization was imported to England from the USA, where it had been employed as a defence for the establishment of departments of religious studies in universities where, because of the separation of church and state, the teaching of religion had not been permitted.

they mediate. There are also those who conscientiously regard elements developed through study of other forms – disciplines, texts, histories, topics, cultures, methods – to be illuminating for these special configurations, and employ them for their descriptive and analytic value. Others will go still farther, and treat these elements from elsewhere as transformative for those religions or theologies to which they are brought. In many respects, for religions and theologies to take both their own central configurations and each other seriously in these ways is more likely to enrich their capacity to focus the primary vitalities of the Spirit than if they assimilate themselves to sceptical forms of understanding which have decisively distanced themselves from the 'searching of the Spirit'. In effect, therefore, all of the strategic practices which we saw in Strategies One, Two and Three are legitimate and important in the interrelating of religious studies and theology.

But even they are not enough. There is another form of strategic practice through which religious studies and theology should be related. This, which we shall call *Strategy Four*, is an active attempt to integrate them. By this strategy, the religions and theologies are allowed to 'pass through' each other, and through doing so to reform themselves in such a way as to manifest their capacity to mediate the primary vitality of life and understanding – that is, to manifest their capacity to integrate that through which they have passed into their truth. Such a strategy – rarely found today – reflects a high commitment to the capacity of a given religion or theology to mediate the dynamic work of God in and through the various religions and theologies found in the world today.

Given the cool, dispassionate way in which religious studies and theology proceed in academic contexts today – which is probably evidence of their greater loyalty to 'discipline' and 'professionality' than to the task of mediating the primary vitality of human life and understanding – Strategy Four looks risky. One way of seeing it is to liken it to the refraction (properly 'dispersion') of light into bands of colour as it passes through a glass prism. If each religion or theology, with its mediation of the primary vitality of which we have been speaking, passes through the 'prisms' of others, the issue for each is then how its truth (its capacity to mediate the vitality) is to be sustained with the possibilities opened by this refractive process.

Let us be clear about how this compares with the other strategic practices we have discussed. Such a strategy neither resists contact with other religions and theologies (Strategy One), nor simply imports others into itself for purposes of illumination (Strategy Two), nor dissipates a religion or theology into another (Strategy Three). All of these may contribute to maintaining a distinct identity, illuminating it or translating it into other forms of understanding or life. But Strategy Four allows the refraction of a religion or theology through another while also seeking to fulfil its capacity to reflect, focus and enhance the primary vitality of human life and understanding in the world – in theological terms, to embrace their vitality within God's vitality. Indeed, anything less – the other strategies – in the end does a disservice to the truth of the vitality of God.

The strategy (Strategy Four) is easily resisted, resistance which arises from the habits of modern 'disciplinary' practices combined with ignorance and fear. In the first place, for religions and theologies to be refracted through each other refracts them into unfamiliar forms; and this is worrying to those whose understanding of them rests on familiar landmarks.

In the second place, there have been too many instances in the past, and are today, where they have simply been assimilated to other disciplines and sub-disciplines which have been claimed as having normative authority over them – often at the hands of people whose primary allegiance is elsewhere. Passing through the sausage factory of other disciplines, they emerge as the appropriate 'sausage' or 'mini-sausage'. We are all familiar with the disappearance of central elements of religions and theologies in textual, historical, topical, cultural or methodical preoccupations.

But it is mistaken to confuse these problems with what Strategy Four attempts, as if they necessarily lead to it. This, in effect, is to confuse refraction (Strategy Four) with dissipation (Strategy Three). Doing so, of course, confirms the cautious strategies (One and Two): 'I told you interreligious or intertheological studies are dangerous! Now you can see where they lead! Come back home!'

Such problems arise from a misunderstanding of the position of Strategy Four. It allows a *refraction* of a religion or theology in another, by which it is spread (as it were) as a band of colour, into terms familiar to those participants in the other. But although it sometimes dazzles people, the refraction is not the goal. The goal in Strategy Four is to discover a fuller way of reflecting, focusing and forwarding the primary vitality of human life and understanding *in* this 'band of colour' and *from* it. The problems which arise, therefore, do so because of the incomplete realization of this vitality in and from the refraction which occurs through engagement with other forms of understanding.

Under some circumstances, this incompleteness is compelled. This occurs where the forms of understanding through which the refraction occurs are inflated – often through being combined with the disciplinary devices of modern university study – and made unlimited in their implications. In such cases, their refraction is reductive, subsuming the vitality within a limiting refraction. This is what occurs in Strategy Three. There the refractive process is radically displaced, and the emergence of a fuller focusing of the primary vitality blocked altogether. These situations present important tests for Strategy Four, and must be confronted through anti-reductive questioning – opening their closure – rather than contradicting them by reference to alternative authorities, that is by techniques appropriate to Strategy Four rather than those of Strategy One.

What provides the basis for such questioning is the inherited tradition of religious or theological truth so carefully safeguarded by Strategy One. This is not simply left behind as it is refracted through interdisciplinary study. It remains necessary to the further focusing and forwarding of the vitality which is sought; but it is treated neither as the final deposit of the religion or theology nor as sufficient to the vitality which will emerge following the refractive process. While it is possible to correlate this 'necessary' with what is later discovered as 'sufficient' through apparently timeless conceptions (religious or theological ones), they are abstract and rule-like by comparison with the flow which is actually involved in the refocusing of the primary vitality following the refraction.

> This love that is forever is in motion,
> a coiling stream of now and now and now.
> Remember, remember a wistful time,
> sunlit age, upstream and long ago,
> a paradise of past when all is well -
> how things have changed! Or tomorrow you say,
> tomorrow, maybe downstream soon and hilly
> in the green far-away, if only when,
> if only then you say – but it is now
> a world of happening forever is in motion,
> now and here nothing will stand still
> our point of departure the actual; though
> we search for footholds in what was or will be
> or with a god's eye view attempt detachment
> to minimize our risks, human and fallible we
> trust the love that is surrender to the flow.[14]

THE PLACE OF MISSION IN RELIGIOUS AND THEOLOGICAL STUDY

In the discussion just undertaken, it may have been obvious that it is the nature of mission which is at stake. To consider mission as a discipline,

[14] Micheal O'Siadhail, 'Rhapsody: Flow' in *Hail! Madam Jazz*, Newcastle: Bloodaxe Books, 1992, p. 151.

with its own set of sub-disciplines, is as problematic as treating religious studies and theology as disciplines. Furthermore, it begets false separations of the sort which have plagued the relations between religious studies and theology.

Mission is better treated as 'inter-mission', a 'sending between' of religious studies and theology, and between them and wider spheres of life and understanding. For example, mission can take the understanding of religions which is provided in religious studies and generate interaction with theology, and vice versa. But more is involved: the 'sending between' religious studies and theology is not only for the mutual interaction of two disciplines, but one which invests this interaction with the vitalities of life and understanding found more widely in the world. It is from these 'refractions' that new understanding of the purposes of God for religious studies, theology and mission will arise.

There are two respects in which this is particularly demanding. One arises from the richness of the ways in which the primary vitality of God in the world is mediated. This mediation occurs in many ways – through ontology, sociality, character, culture, symbols – and these have become embedded in religious and theological traditions through texts, histories, beliefs, moralities, liturgies, etc. Given this, the discovery of the primary vitality of God in the refractions of human life and understanding which is sought in mission is an extraordinarily difficult task.

The difficulty is magnified if we recall what was said earlier about missions as recognizing the differences of mediations of the primary vitality which occur in different localities, and at different paces of history. The recognition of such differences and complexities is only appropriate to the reality of the world as we find it. Mission, therefore, does not simply deal with the 'sending between' religious studies and theology as if these were singular disciplines or studied simple religions or theology. It encourages the refraction of religions and theologies through each other in all the complexity of their difference by place and time – precisely in order to bring the fuller manifestation of the primary vitality which should result from such a refractive process.

In Christian terms, as we saw at the beginning, such a task invokes the same Spirit which 'searches everything, even the depths of God', in searching the thoughts and lives of human beings as they appear in different forms of religion and theology in different places and times. This is the searching of the Spirit through the refractive process we have been discussing. The goal is to uncover still more the true vitality of the Spirit, as that manifests the very character of God and the ordering of human life and understanding by Christ – for all, in all places and times. Seen still more fully, it is the opening of the diversity of religions and theology to the fuller manifestation of the Spirit of God, and thereby to the work of the Triune God. It is this to which – in the world of religious studies and theology – mission calls us, and of which it requires us to be stewards, trustworthy stewards of the mysteries of God and servants of Christ.

> This is how one should regard us, as servants of Christ and stewards of the mysteries of God. Moreover it is required of stewards that they be found trustworthy.[15]

---

[15] 1 Corinthians 4.1–2.

Part Five: Sermons for the Christian Year

19
Advent

As I was returning from London one evening not long ago, just as the train was about to pull out of King's Cross station, a man had a heart attack and died in the carriage in which I was sitting, at the opposite end. It happened quickly, and was dealt with by railway personnel and a doctor and nurse on the train, and afterwards with police and ambulance attendants; they did so with efficiency and concern, as others looked on with curiosity. After a delay of about thirty minutes, the train moved away; no further mention was made of the incident, apart from the conventional apologies for lateness – 'due to the illness of a passenger'.

The reaction to the event set me thinking. How private an event this was! Any meaning that the man's life might have had was strictly his own, and died with him, though it would have been shared by his family if he had one. As I said, he was treated with quiet efficiency, but in no sense did anyone feel diminished by the man's death. You remember the often-quoted words of John Donne: 'No man is an island ... Never send to see for whom the bell tolls. It tolls for thee.' In this case, there was no hint of loss, no hint that this man's death meant anything at all for those around him in that railway carriage. To put it another way, this man's history was his own – an anonymous man sitting alone in a railway carriage, his life coming to an end amongst people whose life histories had no connection with his. None of us in that carriage had any sense of a common history in which we were participating – no common time-frame in which we were living together. The only things that supplied any common history were railway carriages on a train moving northward, clocks and the guard's announcements.

Nor was this very strange. In a sense, it was a microcosm of the world in which we live. Ours is a world with *an empty time-frame*, one without a common sense of the meaning of the history in which we are all involved. That is not to say that we do not each fill our life with a myriad of meanings through what we know and do and hope for, and that we do not share these meanings with those around us. But this is like creating pools of light in what is otherwise darkness.

This has astonishing effects. It leads to the splintering of the history of the world into a myriad of small local histories which make no contact with each other: mine splintered from yours, each of ours from those of others around us, and from those more distant. It is only a step from this to simply not caring at all what happens to other people near and far. Worse even than this, the supposition of a world with an empty time-

331

frame can lead to the splintering of the history of each one of us, so that our lives have no continuity except what, by our own efforts, we can give them. And that is only a small step away from not caring about the course of our lives at all, to meaningless lives which make no sense.

All these things seem to result from the fact that we have no sense that history has a common meaning in which we are all involved. As I said, we live in an empty time-frame. And that's a dangerous state of affairs: empty places invite trouble. You remember Jesus' words:

> When an evil spirit comes out of a man, it goes through arid places seeking rest and does not find it. Then it says, 'I will return to the house I left.' When it arrives, it finds the house unoccupied, swept clean and put in order. Then it goes and takes with it seven other spirits more wicked than itself, and they go in and live there. And the final condition of that man is worse than the first. That is how it will be with this wicked generation.[1]

So it is with our understanding of our history. With no sense of a common history in which we are all involved, we are likely to be beset by a variety of ills. Any notion of what is thought to be progress, however ill-considered, can be thrust upon us. And quickly we can be surrounded by a whole mythology of the meaning of history.

And that is what has happened. In our day, we have been drawn into just such a situation. As the old understanding of the meaning of our common history has gradually disappeared, human beings and nations have come to resign themselves to forces which they think are largely beyond their control. The most glaring example of this is what happens when human beings allow themselves or their nation to be sorted out by the competitive forces of life in the world, in a universal market economy. Then, the possibility of a common history takes on a very ominous shape; history is competition in the market-place – and the 'great people' are those with the power to determine the market forces, the supermen of history, whether in government or business. Of course, given the new idea of history, people gird themselves up to make the best of it, and there is no shortage of aspiring supermen or superwomen nowadays. But even their success is very fragile. The market-place can undo them just as fast as it can make them.

The surprising thing is how readily we accept all this, supposing that history – whether our own or that of our nation – just runs on and on, shifted from this to that by market forces, by those who have the opportunity – through advantage or power – to do something about it. It seems that, in our day, the 'market-place' has become the great myth which tells

[1] Matthew 12.43–45.

us the meaning of our history, and which is allowed unquestioningly to sort us all out. It is in fact a new kind of fatalism: the frenetic activity which it produces only conceals a fate – called the 'market-place' – which determines all.

It is not that all of this is very obvious. But we all know that our own lives are being drawn more and more into a competitive race. Unless an individual has a very firm sense of vocation, he or she can easily be drawn into a life swung wildly about by the jobs available or by the whims of the moment. And perhaps he or she has no choice to do otherwise: what good is it to talk of having a firm sense of vocation if there is no way to fulfil your vocation and stay alive while doing it? Things are not different on the large scale, either. Unless a nation – or a Church or a university or any institution – has a firm sense of its future, it can easily be swung about by those who have the power to dictate its progress. And perhaps, under the great myth of the market-place, there is no choice to do otherwise: what good is it to have a firm sense of the future if history is simply a great competition in which the strongest wins? Underlying this, though largely unrecognized, is a kind of fatalism.

It seems that once the traditional view of the meaning of history has been swept out of the house, new myths – like those evil spirits to which Jesus referred – have come to take their place. And the last state is worse than the first. It is very much the situation of which Paul was writing to Timothy:[2]

> For the time will come when men will not put up with sound doctrine. Instead, to suit their own desires, they will gather around them a great number of teachers to say what their itching ears want to hear. They will turn their ears away from the truth and turn aside to myths.

That statement comes after a call from Paul to:

> continue in what you have learned ..., because ... from infancy you have known the holy Scriptures, which are able to make you wise for salvation through Christ Jesus.

As we well know, the Scriptures to which Paul was pointing were what we call the Old Testament. We might well ask why we should pay such attention to them.

There is one reason which stands out. What the Old Testament shows is that we do not exist in an empty time-frame after all, and that history itself has a meaning which is given in the action of God with his people.

[2] 2 Timothy 4.3–4.

Underneath all the details, that is the constant concern of those who speak in the Old Testament. Throughout the Old Testament, and in fact the whole Bible, we find that those who know God find that he is the master of time and therefore of history. Time comes into being as God creates, continues in his good pleasure, and ends when he wants it to end. So the very existence of time is God's work. It is only with such confidence, when it is known that time has an order which is provided by God himself, that someone can say 'there will be a time for every activity, a time for every deed'.[3] And when this orderliness is apparent, we already know that time is not emptily running on and on, as others would have been inclined to say – or as people now suppose.

And the Bible does not leave it simply at that. Because it is clear that God is with his people in their history. 'For the Lord is gracious, his mercy is everlasting: and his truth endureth from generation to generation.'[4] For that reason, whatever happens does not simply have its meaning in itself, as did the life of that man on the train; it has its own meaning, but that meaning arises from what God does with his people. The whole Bible is the showing forth of the meaning of history as the sphere of God's activity with human beings. The consequences are enormous, for the whole of life is seen as the sphere of God's activity: 'For none of us lives to himself alone and none of us dies to himself alone. If we live, we live to the Lord; and if we die, we die to the Lord. So, whether we live or die, we belong to the Lord.'[5] It matters infinitely how we live and die, because our life and death belong to God.

So the meaning which is to be found in every moment of the history of the Jews is its meaning in relation to God. And that is what gives life its excitement. If each thing which we are or do has its meaning in relation to God, it has an infinite meaning; it is no longer private to us, and it is not simply a momentary fragment of meaning. For this reason, there is a passionate concern with the meaning of each bit of life in this time-frame. Excitement doesn't have to be artificially induced; there is no need for 'hyping' people up through advertising, because everything that happens is deeply, excitingly significant.

> Listen, listen to me, and eat what is good, and your soul will delight in the richest of fare.[6]

Time and history have their meaning from God, and therein is the excitement of life. But what kind of meaning is it that they have?

---

[3] Ecclesiastes 3.17.
[4] Psalm 100.4.
[5] Romans 14.7–8.
[6] Isaiah 55.2b.

As the Old Testament understands it, there is a demand laid upon them from the God who is their origin and the judge of their meaning. The love and faithfulness which he shows them requires love and faithfulness in return, shown not only to him but to each other. This in effect 'sorts' them out into those who do not respond and those who do – into those who are with him and those who are not. Those who do not respond are those for whom time and history lose their meaning from God; these are the ancestors of all those today who find life and history empty except for the meaning which they inject into them. Those who do respond are those for whom time and history gain their meaning from God; they are the ancestors of those today – few as they are – who use time and history with the realization that they are the vehicles of God's mercy and truth.

As Paul recognized, the meaning which time and history are seen to have through the Old Testament comes to a focus in Jesus Christ: the Scriptures are able to make us wise for salvation through Christ Jesus. The New Testament is based on a stark announcement from Jesus, 'the time has come; the kingdom of God is near. Repent and believe the good news!' And that message echoes into the future: 'I am coming soon ... I am coming soon ... I am coming soon.'[7] It is clear that, for all the years of time which had gone before, in a sense time had just begun again, and so had the meaning of history. Time itself was concentrated in Jesus, and the meaning of history was receiving its proper shape through what he did and said. What had gone before was simply preparation.

What is remarkable about all this is the kind of meaning which is provided for history in this Jesus. Whereas history before had received its meaning from God, now the origin of all time and the meaning of history was within history itself, illuminating it from within so to speak. People have often spoken of this as God determining history, manipulating all that human beings do and all that happens to them like a puppeteer. But I think that is mistaken; it is another kind of fatalism. Instead, in Jesus Christ God lifts time and history from within, not by moulding it but by setting it free. More than that, by promising to 'come soon', he gives it its hope. So he broods over it, cajoles it, shows it how to direct itself, but does not determine it; then he waits for it to find itself. As the poet G. M. Hopkins put it so well:

> And for all this, nature is never spent;
> There lives the dearest freshness deep down things; ...
> Because the Holy Ghost over the bent
> World broods with warm breast and with ah! bright wings.[8]

[7] Revelation 22.
[8] 'God's Grandeur' in *Poems and Prose of Gerard Manley Hopkins*, ed. W. H. Gardner, London: Penguin Books, 1953, p. 27.

But, as I said, he waits for it to find itself. He leaves the end in suspension, so to speak, while history is lifted from underneath and within itself. His intentions for it are made public in Jesus. They are no secret – that is why at the end of the New Testament, the words of the prophecy of the Book of Revelation are not to be sealed up. But he does not enforce them; he broods and waits, very much as a father or mother waits for a child to come to his senses. But there is impatience, too: the time is short, 'I am coming soon ... I am coming soon.' Sort yourselves out. And that is the origin of the excitement of bringing in the kingdom of God.

That is the history in which we are bound together, all of us, our nation and others, we and the whole world. At no time has this common history been under greater threat than today. We have the capacity to make endless substitutes for it, as we are doing today; but they are all cheap and damaging, if not downright decadent. Our task as Christians, however, is to find again and proclaim the hope for a common history which we all share as God's people. Amen.

20

Christmas[1]

DURING Advent, we have been trying to learn to think as Christians about the movement of history. That is necessary if we are to take responsibility for the course of history, and shape it for the coming kingdom of God by bringing the compassion amongst human beings which will fulfil them. Preparing for the kingdom by 'creating oases of caring' is our defence against the many people and groups who manipulate the course of history for their own benefit. Today we must ask ourselves more directly about *how* God himself is involved in our task of preparing for the kingdom.

This is the day of the year when people contrive their *private* New Year's resolutions, a recipe of good intentions to guide them, at least for a while, in the year to come. And as we are about to enter a new decade, and the last decade of this millennium, the leaders of our particular *society* – the nation – are doing much the same, and much more publicly. They are all laying claim to the achievements of the past ten years, and putting themselves forward as the best leaders for the coming decade. Still more widely, people in Europe have been busy for some time with what we might call the *public* future of Europe, by setting up 'mega-resolutions' for the whole ten years – the goals which will guide Europe into its new identity as a Community, much more than the Common Market it has been so far. It is peculiar that virtually no one talks about the *universal* future with which Christian faith is concerned, the kingdom of God. Without this, however, the others – private, national and inter-European – lose their proper significance.

These different kinds of future bear a very uncertain connection with the calendar; calendar dates in themselves are not very important. Occasionally, we find advertisements which offer us the chance to buy a newspaper published on the day of our birth. That misses the point: what is important about our birthday is that we were born, that our own era began, not what else happened then. Strictly speaking, we have our own new calendar, the one which we observe each anniversary of our birth. And the resolutions which we might make for the New Year are really our own, and feature only in our private calendar. In like fashion, the future of the nation and of Europe have little connection with the calendar; they proceed by their own timetable. It is the same for the universal future. When people remade the calendar to count the years

[1] Durham Cathedral, 1989.

from the beginning of a new era with the birth-date of Christ, they did so in order to show that the future began from the birth of Christ. But in practice that is forgotten. Nowadays, we simply use the same neutral dating system. And it is fairly arbitrary to think that the first of January, New Year's Day, is the day on which we enter a new era.

The real issue which underlies all these different kinds of concern for the future – private, national, inter-European, universal – is the wish to embark on a new era. We all know that there *are* times when we seem to cross a divide and enter a new era, but we know much less about how to achieve the new era we long for. That, perhaps, is why we trump up occasions such as the New Year or New Decade, or 1992. We know that new eras do not automatically coincide with the beginning of a calendar year, or of a decade or a century, or even the beginning of a millennium. We know – or should know – that there is nothing so special about the rather artificial dates by which history is marked out into periods, beyond the fact that the arrival of each new period may be used as a symbol of the leaving behind of the old and the arrival of bright new possibilities so far unspoiled. By itself, a new year – and all the celebration which goes with it – is simply a rather empty possibility. Just how do we achieve a new era?

How do new eras begin? What really makes a new era is what has been called a 'knot of history' in which the strands of life are gathered and knotted together to form a new beginning for all the features of life. When this happens, there is a new awareness of the end or purpose of history, and of the possibilities already built into history from the beginning. The 'new beginning' also seems to bring a new energy to move forward.

With the new beginning, the 'old time' – the time of each of the strands of life before the knot – takes on a new character, to some extent out of phase with the time before. A good analogy for this is what happens with the lives of a man and a woman who marry. They 'tie the knot', as the old saying goes; and that describes it well. For thereafter, two independent strands of life, his and hers, are knotted together, two hitherto-independent histories woven together to form the beginning of one history; each lives with and from the other, each free with and from the other. They begin a new era with each other, and continue in it.

Such knots of history can be of many kinds: private, national, international or universal. They are always encompassing events which give people the sense of a new beginning. But they are not always for the best. And in general, it is the attempt to restrict the benefits of the new beginning which undo them.

Let me use the European Community as an example. Some say that the arrival of the European Community in 1992 will be such a turning-point in history. Others, and I include myself among them, question whether it is anything so grand; perhaps it is simply the enlargement of a very questionable society which exists already. As things stand, Western Europe – like the United States – lives as a self-satisfied, narcissistic society which is largely concerned with preserving pride of place for powerful people. This was well described recently by a Mexican writer:

> Now that she lives and is so admirable in so many things, does not Europe ... sweep too many things she would rather not see beneath the sumptuous carpet of her new prosperity? Does Europe not hide her undesirables too easily from sight? North American society, for example, has nowhere to send its poor blacks, its abandoned old folk, its homeless city-dwellers ... The failings of a too self-satisfied, depoliticized, narcissistic society are glaringly obvious on the streets of New York, Detroit, Miami. Europe is cleverer at disguising her poor ... and hide[s] a feeling of lassitude, of spiritual sloth.[2]

Will the transformation of the other half of Europe which we have been seeing recently bring anything better? The same Mexican said:

> Western Europe must see this [transformation] as something more than an opportunity for ... subsuming them under the logic of consumption. What is happening in Central Europe is more than the undoing of forty years of Stalinism. It is also the fruit of forty years of sacrifice, experience and reflection on the riches of an ideal form of society and community hoped for there despite all the obstacles erected against it in its own name ... Central Europe has no wish to free itself from a barbarous communism only to fall into a barbarous capitalism.

But what this might be, and whether it can be achieved without falling victim to a new kind of domination which marginalizes the poor, at home and abroad, is still far from clear.

The deepest dilemma which will confront Europe in 1992 is whether its benefits will be restricted to those who are privileged. If so, its prosperity will continue to be achieved at the expense of an 'underclass' within and beyond its borders, and by creating an underhistory, the history of those who 'lose out' at home and abroad. That is why those remarks by a Mexican are so important. He sees the possibility that European homogeneity – the very communality which European leaders seek – will be achieved by excluding the third world beyond Europe, or the second world within Europe. To achieve its true humanity, Europe must face and care for the different peoples within it and beyond it,

[2] Carlos Fuentes, *Liber* 2, 20.

including the multicultural, multiracial histories which are to be found there within it and beyond it.

Of course, it may be that the vicious circle of ecumenical capitalism will swallow up the circle of poly-cultural and multiracial societies that we want to build between Mexico and Argentina. Perhaps. But if that happens then Europe will have once again sacrificed a project of liberation.

So if 1992 is to be a true knot of history, Europe must search for a more universal history than it now envisages. But how is such a thing possible?

As we saw before, what really makes a new era is what can be called a 'knot of history' in which the strands of life are gathered and knotted together to form a new beginning for all the features of life. Such a 'new beginning' brings a new awareness of ultimate goals, coupled with the energy to move toward them.

There is another kind of knot in history which is more important and far-reaching than those we form for ourselves, whether as individuals, nations or regional communities (like the European Community). This is one which knots together all the ultimate features of life and thereby starts a new history. We get a hint of that in the story about Jesus and his parents in Luke 2, in which his life seems to take a new beginning. While his parents were returning home, Jesus remained behind in the temple, and they had to return to Jerusalem to search for him. Eventually they found him, 'sitting among the teachers, listening to them and asking them questions, [with] everyone who heard him ... amazed at his understanding and answers'.[3] This was not simply a matter of Jesus showing his wisdom and devotion, or his independence from his parents. It was an event in which he showed his maturity by starting to operate on a different time-scale; and they simply could not understand. As with all 'knots' of history, the normal movement of history was thrown out of phase, its strands knotted together to form a new beginning.

What we see from that story about Jesus is not simply that he had decided to operate on a different time-scale, but that the time-scale into which he came was one which derived from his relationship with God: 'Why were you searching for me? Didn't you know that I had to be involved in my Father's affairs?'[4] His new time-scale came from his involvement with God's life, and the responsibility for other people which that conferred on Jesus. If we take the widest view, we see that the strands of God's own life are knotted together with those of human beings in Jesus, and that this knot begins a new history. God's own

[3] Luke 2.46.
[4] Luke 2.49.

history is thereafter knotted together with the history of human beings. This begins a new era, a new history with humankind, in which God's own history is also the history of his life fully interacting with the lives of human beings.

What is particularly important about this is that this – the knotting of God's history with that of human beings – confers the possibility of a history in which all people are bound together in the life of God, a life which brings them fulfilment. In this, no part of God's own life is left aside, and that is a life which accepts responsibility for everything: the knotting of God's history with that of human beings encompasses every aspect of the lives and actions of human beings, whether in life or in death. It is the infolding into a knot of all that is – God himself, all kinds of people, holy and sinners, rich and poor, religious and nonreligious. And it embraces all their actions, in life and in death. No one is excluded, and nothing is excluded. And, through all this, there is a new outpouring of life.

If a new era is begun at the point where God's own history is knotted together with the history of humankind in Jesus, it is continued by living it out. It must be *lived into being*, so to speak. And it was first lived into being in Jesus; through the history of his life and the suffering of his death, it permeated his being. Through his life with others, and their life from him, it came to permeate them. There is a simple, but vastly important, lesson in that: 'it takes time' for a history to be embedded in the history of the world. Changes *take time* to become real changes, to permeate the being of those involved. The more pervasive way of stating it is to say that a new history must be realized historically.

That is not a comfortable lesson. We would much prefer to rest on accomplished facts. We habitually think of Jesus as simply the accomplished fact of God in man, easily dropping into the habit of thinking that the eternal perfection of God simply arrives as Jesus, instantaneously changing all of the history of the world. Perhaps this is an excuse for ourselves, for then we only need to believe this as fact and live it out in faith, because all the essential work has been done already. But it is not so: the knot of history joining the history of God's life to ours was lived into being in Jesus Christ; and that must be lived into being by us.

How should we live it into being? Primarily, we follow the pattern which Jesus followed. As Jesus himself drew deeply on the life of God as he lived it into being himself for others, so we draw deeply on the life of God in Jesus. And that draws us out of ourselves, out of self-serving, into concern for all humankind. As Jesus said, 'I, when I am lifted up, will draw all men to myself'. And insofar as we share in the pattern of his life, we will be drawn to care for all humankind. And that is surely the future to which we should look forward in the 1990s and beyond, even to the coming of the kingdom of God. Amen.

21

Epiphany[1]

ALL this week, we have been praying for unity amongst the Churches. Before the opportunity passes, we should stop to reflect a little about where we ourselves are – and what we should be doing – about Church unity. We need to look at the past, the present and the future.

THE PAST

Although I am an American, during my 26 years in England I have always admired the fact that the Church of England recognizes its responsibility to be everywhere, for there to be a parish church in every place, which is responsible – alongside other churches – for the Christian life of every person in the land. It seems admirable that it has always been the stated task of the Church to be *the Church* in England, to be an inclusive, all-embracing community of Christians in which all Christians in the land are united. Properly speaking, the Church of England is an attempt to create a united church for the English nation, an ecumenical church as we would now call it, one in which all Christians in this land should be joined.

This is very different from the situation in the United States, where the churches draw their people from the places where they are, and only hold themselves responsible for looking after those people who choose to come. They are sometimes called 'optional churches', and that's a fair description. From here, we look across the ocean and are impressed by the numbers of people thronging the churches. But what's the good of that if these people lack a sense of responsibility for those around them in the town, and are concerned only for their own well-being and uplift?

But some years ago, I realized that the Church of England was not really what it claimed to be. It had settled in practice for something very much less than the ideal which it held out for itself. It had moved decisively in the American direction, each of its parishes becoming optional churches for those who chose to come to them. And in doing so, they had lost their sense of responsibility in three ways: in the *first* place, they had forgotten the needs of those around them and were concentrating instead on looking after those who chose to come; *secondly*, they had forgotten their obligation to other Christians – those in other churches,

[1] St John's Church, Durham, 1988.

342

whether Anglican or others; and *thirdly* they had lost their sense of responsibility for the communication of the Gospel in the world near and far. These things were easy to see in the practice of church life. *Firstly,* ministry was to touch only those who wanted it. *Secondly,* the churches forgot about each other, and often competed with each other, each presenting itself as somehow superior to the others. *Thirdly,* people no longer found it natural to speak of their faith in ordinary life or to make it possible for the Gospel to be communicated where it had not been heard, in foreign lands for example. These *wider* responsibilities which should mark the Church of England were left to the enthusiasts, those who cared about those things. At the best, a parish church might have some people who recognized these responsibilities, or who had the responsibilities given to them; but they would usually be left to get on with it themselves.

Of course, these things are not only true of the Church of England; they are as true of the other churches – Methodist, United Reformed, Baptist, Roman Catholic. They too have been caught in these things. They too have largely lost their sense of responsibility to other churches and the wider world. It seems to be true of all the churches. Is it of this one? Obviously, I don't know. But it would be surprising if at least some of these things were not true here.

The truth is that in many ways the complexities of the world have overtaken the churches, and they have retreated from their wider responsibilities in order to survive and to succeed. We might see it as a natural response to the complexities of the modern world, to concentrate on a specialist job for a special group, and to leave other things aside. So, instead of being a church for all Christians, concentrate on the people who want to participate. Instead of working with other churches, concentrate on one's own. Instead of being concerned with the world, be concerned with the 'spiritual' and the salvation of souls. Stick to your own business: strictly personal, strictly local, strictly specialized. Then we will *succeed* – and, what is considered just as important – *see* our success.

If we think back over the last 200 years, we will find that they have been the years when the churches have moved in the direction I have been describing – becoming ever more concerned with the personal, the local and the spiritual, more and more excluding other things. Furthermore, they have been the years when the churches were concerned more and more with success measured in these terms.

THE PRESENT

It's time we came to our senses. The Gospel of Jesus Christ offers far more to the world, demands far more of us, and measures success by quite different standards.

Look at the story of the feeding of the five thousand. There are a lot of lessons for the churches in what Jesus did. First of all, he was confronted by a throng of ordinary people who happened to be there; and he was immediately concerned for all of them, not just his disciples. This was no simply private gathering intended for those who chose to come. Secondly, he was concerned for their physical well-being, not simply with saving them spiritually; he showed them what he wanted to show them through what he did for their physical well-being. Thirdly, what he did provided for them abundantly, giving them all they needed; and even then there was more than anyone could eat. This was the real mark of success, not in doing something rather special for a special group, but in providing abundantly for all according to their need. And the response was one appropriate to what had happened: 'Surely this must be the prophet that was to come into the world.' In other words, 'Surely this is one who truly shows the ways of God for the world.'[2]

Then look at what Paul said in the other reading:

It was good of you to share in my hardships ... No other church helped me with gifts of money. You were the only ones; and twice since my stay in Thessalonica you have sent me what I needed. It is not your gift that I value; what is valuable to me is what you are given credit for ... the sacrifice which you make and God finds pleasing.[3]

As in the case of the feeding of the five thousand, what is important is the abundance which comes in sharing. This is no private faith which is only concerned with helping those who come with their spiritual needs. It is a reaching out, and a giving to meet the needs of others. And it is a giving to meet material needs. And with that God is well-pleased.

In both readings, we find a picture of the Church quite different from the one to which we have become accustomed. A church is not to be cut off, either from other churches or from the unchurched around it. Nor is it to be concerned only with the spiritual needs of those who choose to come to it; it is to be concerned with all the needs of all the people, and with all the churches. When it is widely concerned with these things, it makes itself pleasing to God.

[2] John 6.1–14.
[3] Philippians 4.10–20, rearranged.

THE FUTURE

There are signs that the churches are beginning to learn these lessons, even after all those years of being isolated from each other, suspicious of each other and even hating each other. There was a conference of delegates from the churches held at Swanwick in Derbyshire early last September. About 350 leaders of the various Christian denominations – what was called 'the widest spectrum of Christians ever' – came together after several years of consultations, intending to find a way forward. Relations between the churches have made little progress for some years now, despite the good will and efforts of many people. One of the biggest problems was that some of the churches, including the Roman Catholic Church, had refused to join the British Council of Churches, so there was no institution which could carry forward the work of bringing the churches together and working for all of them on wider issues. But before the Swanwick conference all the officers of the British Council of Churches had offered their resignations. That made for an air of expectancy: it was possible that the Conference could prove a turning-point, producing a new initiative.

And it did. The declaration made by Cardinal Hume, Archbishop of Westminster, made it clear that those who were attending the Conference from the Roman Catholic Church were prepared to recommend that their Church and people be involved in a new initiative to bring the churches together. They were prepared to 'move quite deliberately from a situation of co-operation to one of commitment to each other'.

> We should have in view a moving, in God's time, to full communion, or communion that is both visible and organic. We must not lose sight of this ultimate aim of our ecumenical prayer and endeavour.

It was in those terms that the Conference sent out a call to all the churches.

> Our churches must now move from *co-operation* to clear *commitment* to each other, in search of the *unity for which Christ prayed and in common evangelism and service of the world*. We urge Church leaders and representatives to take all necessary steps to present as soon as possible, to our Church authorities, assemblies and congregations, the report of this conference, together with developed proposals for ecumenical instruments to help the Churches of these Islands to move ahead together.

From co-operation to commitment to each other to unity in evangelism and service of the world: these were the steps called for. And, as Cardinal Hume suggested, they might, in God's time, bring a full communion between the churches which is both visible and organic. We might put it very simply: 'join hands and face the world!'

Why are these such important steps? It is simply because, at long last, they are steps in opening the churches to the sharing in which God's abundance is found, a sharing in the meeting of the needs of each other and of the world. And it will be these possibilities, and how they are handled, which will determine whether this new move will be any better than all the earlier efforts. These things are very significant. Let me try to say why.

What does it mean to 'join hands', to be *committed to each other*? It is not some rather romantic dream of togetherness – like 'we're off to see the Wizard, the wonderful Wizard of Oz'. It is preparedness to give and share in the way that we saw in the feeding of the 5000, and in the Philippians' gifts to the apostle Paul, the *giving and sharing which is well-pleasing to God and in which his abundance is known*. It means being deeply involved with others, to such a degree that all are interdependent, inextricably linked to one another. That is why the churches must learn sharing, not simply sharing things external to themselves but sharing *themselves*.

Being committed to each other means giving and sharing all that you have to give and share, including the most important parts of yourself. But it does not mean imposing yourself and your ways on other people. Through the centuries, and very naturally, churches have become different. That difference is not simply to be lost in some 'superchurch'. On the contrary, the differences are to be affirmed as valuable, not simply rejected.

There is an important lesson here for the Church of England, and of course for all the other churches as well. No church can put itself forward as the all-embracing church, and reject the others until they meekly agree to abide by the rules. No longer can any one church pretend itself to be the all-embracing church, the right one. Try to see the new film *Cry Freedom*, about Steve Biko and those who seek freedom for the blacks in South Africa. He says at one point to a white South African, 'We will not be what you tell us to be in our country.' So it is with the churches. Any church is right to say to another, 'We will not be what you tell us to be in Christian life.' And the only basis upon which the churches can come together is respect for each other's differentness. If the Church of England wishes to be the Church of *England*, it can be this only in respecting and enhancing the freedom and dignity of other churches, and in freely sharing with them in the deepest interdependence with them.

This *commitment to each other* has a purpose beyond itself. The goal is not to 'balance' each other in some ideal equilibrium, 'round and round the mulberry bush', so to speak. The commitment is directed beyond ourselves, to practical goals in the world. 'Join hands *and face the world.*' We are to move to *unity in evangelism and service of the world.* Here again, the feeding of the 5000 is relevant. Jesus faced the ordinary people in the world, and gave them the conditions for their life, food as well as himself, and did so with overflowing abundance. 'In him was life', and at no point in his life did he do less than give life abundantly to others; consistently he gave himself in order to give them life. This is the gift which the churches may share in giving to the world. They may not only *serve* ordinary people by bringing this life to them; they may *tell* of the one from whom this life comes – 'O taste and see how gracious the Lord is!' His concern is with the total well-being of people; so the churches also must be concerned with the total well-being of people in the world.

As I said, there are signs that the churches are learning the lessons which God has to teach them. But it remains a question, for this church as well as for the others, whether the seed thus sown will fall on good ground or on rocks. The future is an open question. And the responsibility rests with us. Amen.

22

Lent I[1]

THERE is no more fundamental testimony to the abundant goodness of God than life itself. The very fact that there is a 'here', that we are here, full of life, testifies to the overflowing goodness of God. If you want evidence of the existence and goodness of God, you need look no further than that, to the 'lifefulness' of life. That is why we should not bemoan the means by which people show their lifefulness – all their desirings and all the activities by which they put their desires into motion. For life enacts itself through our desires, and desires become concrete in our actions. Even when we are not aware of wanting anything, or when we are not doing anything, we still find opportunities to show what is most natural to us – our lifefulness.

But there is another side of life which also testifies to the abundant goodness of God. That is the integrity of life, which is the means by which life becomes definite, particular and consistent, by which we are ourselves and remain ourselves. It needs to be as deeply rooted in us as life itself, providing the means for harnessing those desirings and actions by which life is expressed. Without integrity life loses its lifefulness, dissipating life rather than gaining it.

There was a sentence introduced in the Alternative Service Book with which it took me years to come to terms. The preface before 'Lift up your hearts' at the beginning of the Eucharistic Prayer in Holy Communion, which was suggested for Lent, was: 'And now we give you thanks because through him you have given us the spirit of discipline, that we may triumph over evil and grow in grace.' No doubt it doesn't seem offensive, but I associated it with the idea that Jesus had provided a new law; and I thought that English people were too much inclined to be moralistic anyway. It seemed to me that people tended to think of Christianity as a set of principles or commandments by which to restrict life. There is the old story about a man who was not very well, and asked his doctor's advice. The doctor instructed him to give up smoking, to give up drinking and to give up womanizing. He asked the doctor whether this would really make him live longer. 'Not really,' said the doctor, 'but it will *seem* a lot longer!'

But at a much more fundamental level, the prayer for 'the spirit of discipline' is right. Life itself, or 'spirit' in the words of the prayer, requires a kind of integrity or constancy by which to be life; anything less

[1] Durham Cathedral, 1988.

dissipates life. Our desirings, and the actions by which they become concrete, require an inner consistency or discipline; without it they turn into kinds of poison. And it is only when they achieve that kind of consistency that we really *live*. Living with such an inner consistency is not at all the same as living by a lot of imposed rules and regulations. It is more like relaxing and being ourselves. And most of us hardly know how to do that.

Both these things, life and the constancy or integrity by which life is most fully lifeful, are signs of the abundance of God. And, at its deepest, finding integrity of life is closely tied up with finding the abundance of God. As the Psalmist says, 'With you, O Lord, is the fountain of life; in your light we see light.'[2] Again, it is not that God simply hands down the rules for living life, or even that he gives direct personal guidance for the living of life. Life is much more free than that, and in our freedom we must find the life and integrity which God gives. Life is like an experiment in which three things are bound up together in such a way that you can only find the truth about each when you find the truth about the others. Think, for example, of the great formula by which Einstein explained energy: $E = mc^2$. I won't try to say what it means, but only point out that energy could only be explained in terms of mass and light. So, you might say, God can only be found through referring to life and integrity together; and conversely, each of the others – life and integrity can only be found in the presence of each other and God. And, as I said, life is an experiment in which the true character of life – which means integrity and God – must be found.

Life is an experiment in another way. Our integrity is not a fixed quantity, the same throughout our life. Since it is not an unchanging thing, it grows or diminishes as the complexities of life meet us. And it must continue to grow if it is to provide the note of firmness by which we remain ourselves. And this is where we find ourselves in particular difficulties nowadays. Life is so complex that most of the time what is outside us in the world pulls us away from such consistency of life as we have found; the world just seems too confusing and complex for us to lead a consistent life. It is beyond what we can incorporate within the pattern of life we have developed. Of course, with time we might develop a consistency of life which could make sense of all this complexity. But we are constantly 'overloaded'; the fuses in our integrity blow, so to speak, and contradictions develop where we just cannot hold the pattern that we have developed together with the complexities of life which surround us. So we resort to 'getting along' instead, pretending that we do not need consistency of life, or at least not much.

Here is where we might help each other a lot, but we often don't. There was an interesting article by Bernard Levin some while ago, in which he discussed the case of a London schoolteacher accused of taking sexual advantage of a schoolgirl. The man pleaded that there was no law against such a thing. Bernard Levin's comment was: 'The girl might be presumed not to know [that it was wrong], but if so, that is precisely the point, for the adult would be expected to make up any deficiency in her understanding with the surplus of his presumed responsibility.'[3] That in fact is just the point: we are constantly taking away from or adding to other people's integrity – it's the fundamental business of life.

That life is an experiment in which we are constantly adding to or losing our integrity is made very clear in the two readings for today, about the trials of Job and of Jesus. One way of living life is presented in the figure of Satan in the Book of Job; he is a figure of restlessness, one who comes before God 'from roaming through the earth and going to and fro in it'. In other words, his very nature is arbitrariness or 'getting along'. And God immediately holds up the constancy of Job as a contrast:

> Have you considered my servant Job? There is no one on earth like him; he is blameless and upright, a man who fears God and shuns evil. And he still maintains his integrity.

Job is one whose life is full not only because of its integrity but because he finds the integrity of his life in his fear of God. But Satan is convinced that Job can be undone; he thinks that, like anyone, Job will be more interested in having life than in integrity of life or God: if Job's life is threatened, he will lose his integrity *and* curse God. Simply to preserve his life, he will sacrifice his integrity and his faith, and thereby lose the very bases of full life. Human beings will, so he thinks, save their lives by losing their souls, and end up like him, prepared simply to 'get along'.

And the long trial begins. What kind of a trial it is is shown right at the beginning, after Job is covered with sores, when he is immediately teased by his wife: 'Are you still holding onto your integrity? Curse God and die!' That is the real issue. Will Job cease to 'fear God and shun evil'? In other words, will he lose his integrity and his faith in God, and thereby lose the real meaning of his life, or not? Far from losing integrity and faith, however, he grows in them. That is not to say that he understands the reasons.

Despite the mystery of his suffering, Job comes to see it as a trial, and his integrity and faith grow through his suffering; he wails and complains, but becomes ever more committed to constancy in the goodness of his life:

[3] *Taking Sides*, London: Penguin Books, 1988, p. 27.

When he has tested me, I shall come forth as gold. My feet have closely followed his steps; I have kept to his way without turning aside . . .[4]

Till I die, I will not deny my integrity. I will maintain my righteousness and never let go of it; my conscience will not reproach me as long as I live.[5]

Strangely enough, in view of all that is usually said about Job, his sufferings strengthen the integrity of his life, and his determination to draw upon the life of God. And in the end, he is overwhelmed by the sheer richness of God's life.

The trial of Jesus in the palace of the high priest is also a trial of life, constancy and faith. Unlike Job, whose friends stay with him disputing the meaning of his sufferings, Jesus is abandoned and alone; all the disciples had fled. Like Satan in the case of Job, the chief priests and the Sanhedrin are looking for a way to undermine the integrity of Jesus and the life he had spent, and for a reason for what they already decided to do, putting him to death. And in their view, they succeed; they manage to find some witnesses who recall Jesus' claim to be able to destroy the temple of God and rebuild it in three days. Jesus keeps his silence, so they ask him directly: 'under oath by the living God: tell us if you are the Christ, the Son of God'. That is like asking him directly if he is the one who brings life from God. And he responds:

Yes, it is as you say. But I say to all of you: in the future you will see the Son of Man sitting at the right hand of the Mighty One and coming on the clouds of heaven.

This 'blasphemy' in their view justifies his persecution and death.

But why is this blasphemy? This was no simple statement identifying Jesus with God. On the contrary, it is a statement of the constancy of his desire for the integrity of the life of God in him. The very One who is so different from him is the One he desires to be in him, and to become the constant integrity of his life. And by this, as he recognizes, he is brought into the inmost constancy of God for all future time.

The trial which Jesus underwent was therefore the culmination of his lifelong devotion to God, a struggle to bring his own integrity – and therefore his life – to its fullest, by allowing his weakness before the chief priest to be filled with the constancy of God. And that is exactly why he is so important to us, because he brings our weakness to be filled with the

[4] Job 23.11.
[5] Job 27.5, 6.

constant integrity of God, adding infinitely to the deficiency of our integrity. As one whose integrity is entirely formed by the constancy of God in him, he provides us with the greatest possibility of life.

May his lifefulness, seen in the constancy of God in him, be ours. Amen.

23

Lent II[1]

ONE good reason for a Church Year in which we follow the life of Jesus is that it confronts us with important questions which we might otherwise avoid. So it is that today we find ourselves reading of the trial of Jesus before the Sanhedrin. And that requires of us that we face the question of *why* he was condemned to death.

What makes a man worthy of death? There is a long-standing tradition in some countries, the UK included, which says, 'Nothing: nothing can make someone worthy of death.' In such places, there is such a strong idea of the worth of the life of a person that the death penalty simply cannot be used: since society is given its power by individuals, its power can be used to restrict individuals from doing wrong, but can never be used to deprive individuals of their life.

The answer would be different in other countries. In many, if not most, countries of the world, another tradition prevails, where the prime consideration is the well-being of society itself, and the interests of individuals are secondary. Society is intrinsically communal, and people are defined by their relationship to each other, not by their independence from each other. And in such a society, if someone sufficiently disrupts the well-being of the community, to the point of destroying it, he or she is worthy of death.

From the viewpoint of those committed to the overriding value of the lives of individuals, this other view of society looks rather like totalitarianism. But it isn't. A society can as easily be benevolent and compassionate as totalitarian and evil. We like to think that our society is benevolent and compassionate. That is why such importance is placed on such institutions as the National Health Service for example; for us it symbolizes a society that is benevolent and compassionate. And people expect the same of the Church; it too should behave as a benevolent and compassionate society.

It is true that things can go badly wrong, but this can happen whether individuals or societies are in control. But the reasons which people find for them going wrong are different. Where everything is centred on individuals, when things go right or wrong, it is because of this or that individual; the praise or blame is not given to society. 'It's Mrs. Thatcher', they will say, 'she's the trouble!' Where more emphasis is given to society itself, when things go right or wrong, it's because some-

[1] Durham Cathedral, 1990.

thing has gone right or wrong in society itself. Of course, the leaders of society might not want to admit that; and they may very well look for someone to blame it on, a scapegoat. That's rather handy: it takes the pressure off when there is someone on whom to blame the trouble. Furthermore, executing a scapegoat can actually build up a society; he or she becomes like a victim sacrificed as a ritual purification of the society, eliminating what is alien in it.

That's how the execution this week of Farzad Barzoft, the *Observer* journalist in Iraq, needs to be seen. It misses the point to see him as an individual, whether tainted by past crimes or not, who was victimized for a personal crime, whether he committed it or not. He was executed for a crime against the Iraqi social order, in a nation preoccupied with its existence as a society. He could well have been used as a scapegoat by the Iraqi leaders, and his execution as a ritual purification of the nation from foreign impurities, a ritual act which would actually raise the nation to its true stature. And I suppose that the efforts of England to secure his release were seen as an invasion of Iraqi sovereignty too, a further crime against the social order.

Though Barzoft's death is not to be compared with the death of Jesus, there is one way in which it casts interesting light on the trial of Jesus. Much as we tend to read the trial and death of Jesus as a personal matter, in which the individual man Jesus was on trial for his personal behaviour and views, and was put to death for his claims about himself, they were not. What made this Jesus worthy of death? It was an offence against the social order, one which actually undermined it, threatened it with extinction. So he was on trial for a crime against the social order, and was put to death in order to purify the social order. Those who crucified him could easily have seen his death as one which would purify the social order of this impurity – Jesus himself and his teachings – which had intruded itself into it, rendering it unclean.

Tried and executed for an offence against the social order, in order to reaffirm – and even build up – the value of the old social order? That was how the leaders of the Jews would have seen his trial. And Jesus himself would have recognized this. But for him, the trial was a trial of the old social order itself, and his death the means by which the old social order was replaced by a new one. The result of his trial and death was not the return to an old social order, as was hoped by those who tried him, but the establishment of a new foundation for our society, a new covenant. For this reason, it is not to be seen as the purification of the sins of individuals; it is for the purification and refounding of our society.

Look at what happened. Jesus was brought to the Sanhedrin for 'trial'. There were three groups involved in the trial, the priests of the Temple represented by Caiaphas (the high priest), the teachers of the Law and the elders, who were the focal point of the community – through the ages, they, the sages, judges or wise men of the community had maintained it, and resolved its problems. So far as there was Jewish society under the alien Roman Empire, these three groups co-operated in maintaining it; and the officials of these groups were there at this 'trial' of Jesus. You might call them the three pillars of Jewish society, the priests of the Temple, the teachers of Law and the Wise Men of society. When I say 'the pillars' of Jewish society, I mean that seriously: the cultic practices of the Temple, the regulation of social behaviour by the Law and the advice of the Wise were the *fabric* of Jewish society, which actually held it together – the more so under Roman rule. What they did was not simply human: they were in charge of the three main ways by which God sanctified the bonds of society. To fail to observe the Law, to fail to engage in cultic practices or not to follow the Sages was to fail to be *God's people*. And the trial of Jesus was to be conducted by those who were responsible for the Law, the Temple and society itself.

For a while, the trial of Jesus seemed to be a non-starter. No evidence could be found. Things only started to move when two things happened. And they were highly disturbing. One was the report that, 'This fellow said, "I am able to destroy the temple of God and rebuild it in three days." '

That would have unsettled at least two of the three groups involved in the trial. Suppose someone were to claim that he could destroy and rebuild in three days this great Cathedral of Durham, forty years in its first building and many more in various changes, the symbolic centre of the North East of England and a thousand years of Christian history. The shock of anyone claiming power over such a deep symbol of Christian life gives a hint, but only a small one, of the shock the Jews must have felt when it was thought that Jesus claimed power over the central symbol of Jewish faith over 1000 years, the place spoken of in the Psalm:

> How lovely are thy tabernacles, O Lord of hosts!
> My soul longeth, yea, even fainteth for the courts of the Lord ...
> For a day in thy courts is better than a thousand.[2]

But the Temple was more than a symbol. The people of Israel were a people more deeply tied to their land than we can imagine, and both Jerusalem and its Temple were the centre of their land, the place where God's heaven and the earth came together. A claim from anyone to have power over the Temple would deeply disturb both the priests and the wise men present at the trial: this was a threat to the cultic life of the people, and a threat to the heart of Jewish society. Even more distressing,

[2] Psalm 84.

it set up human power over the very power of God in the place where God met his people.

But the charge was only hearsay, of course, and Jesus remained silent. Then something rather strange happened. The chief priest addressed Jesus directly: 'By the living God I charge you to tell us: are you the Messiah, the Son of God?'

Where before they were ready to accept any false evidence, here in effect, the chief priest is precluding any falsity – exorcizing, expelling the evil from the encounter. It is much more than putting Jesus on oath to tell the truth. It is putting the living God between them, so that no evil can enter between them, and only truth can be spoken.

The words are extremely powerful: 'By God, are you the Son of God?' And Jesus gives an astonishing reply. He does not give the direct answer which many Christians would like to hear; he does not say, 'I am'. Instead, he turns the chief priest's *question* into an *affirmation*, and says, 'The words are yours.' 'You have said it.' This puzzling reply is significant in two ways: In effect, it is saying, 'By God, you know that I am the Son of God.' Jesus places the responsibility for recognizing him as the Son of God on the priest, implying that he is Son of God when the high priest recognizes him as such. But, given that this is a trial for offences against the social order of Israel, this assumes a much broader significance. Jesus is placing the responsibility on Israel itself for recognizing him as Son of God. It is when Jesus is recognized by those groups represented by the high priest, the teachers of the Law and the Wise Men, that he is Son of God. He, Jesus, is Son of God when all Israel recognizes him as such. Of course, that was no conclusive evidence against Jesus. To say, 'I am king when you recognize me as king', is no criminal offence.

The more important words come after: 'But I tell you this: from now on you will see the Son of Man seated at the right hand of the power [the Almighty] and coming on the clouds of heaven.'

These words seem mild enough. But I suspect that those who were trying him saw in them a direct invocation of the name of the most holy God. How? Remember the way in which God identified himself to the Israelites. As told in the Book of Exodus, Moses went over to the burning bush, and God called him from the midst of the bush:

He said, Moses! Moses!
Pull off your shoes from your feet, for the place on which you are standing is sanctifying ground.
And he said, I am your father's God ...

And he called Moses to lead Israel out of Egypt. But Moses said,

Who am I that I should lead the sons of Israel out of Egypt?

But he said, Surely I will be there with you.[3]

As Moses discovered, the name of God designates the presence of God. And that presence is both present and future: whenever God is mentioned, it is an invocation of the presence and future of God. He is invoked as I AM THAT I AM and as I WILL BE THERE WITH YOU. Thereafter, through their whole history, the Israelites lived not only with the presence of God but with his promised coming.

And here, at his trial, Jesus seemed to be expecting them to recognize not only the presence of God in him – I AM THAT I AM. That would have been bad enough. But he now invoked the coming of the kingdom of God, coming on the clouds of heaven – I WILL BE THERE WITH YOU. Something clearly happened when he spoke in this fashion. Suddenly, they caught a glimpse of the power in him, the same power that he had exercised before which of course they themselves denied. And it must have been evident that he himself was indwelt by the I AM THAT I AM, and could therefore speak with power of the I WILL BE THERE WITH YOU, of the coming of the kingdom. What else could have made them so suddenly agree: 'This is blasphemy! Do we need further witnesses? You have just heard the blasphemy ... He is guilty; he should die.'

Remember that he was under trial by the groups which formed the pillars of society for a crime against society. And what they saw particularly threatening in him was not simply his personal power, but a power to reconstitute society itself. It was accepted by all of them that their society and its social order were from God, and the Temple, the Law and the Wisdom of their leadership were the means by which the righteousness of God was realized in their social order. And they also saw that this Jesus was a trouble-maker, not so much because of all the small disruptions he had caused – healing people in breach of the laws about Sabbath observance, and so on – but because he stood for a different way of ordering the relations of human beings, which placed compassion above the requirements of the law. That, after all, was why they had taken such pains to bring him to trial.

But what actually appeared in the trial was astonishing and frightening. For here was a man in whom shone the power to reconstitute society itself. Furthermore, he showed them that a fully reconstituted society was on the way, for which he had laid the preparations. And that was scary; it is no wonder that they thought him worthy of death. For it was a new social order which would displace the one to which they themselves were dedicated, a new covenant to replace the old. So his trial was really a trial about what was the will of God, and how it was to be shown in human society. The priests of the Temple, the teachers of the Law and the Wise

[3] Exodus 3.

Men, all of them already knew the will of God; and it had already been fully institutionalized in Temple worship, the Law and current social practices. It was all reasonably manageable if you behaved yourself and did the right things. If anyone challenged it, he was worthy of death. And it would actually help build up the social order to have him killed – the more publicly the better.

But for Jesus the will of God lay beyond all these, and yet refounded the whole order of society. What was the will of God, and what did it call upon human beings to do? What was this new social order? It rested fundamentally on the indwelling in it of God's grace and righteousness, and was to be found in such virtues as 'love, joy, peace, patience, kindness, goodness, faithfulness, gentleness and self-control'.[4] And if this new social order required his death, it would be well worth it. That is the irony: the very death by which the old order was to have been rendered safe could be the means of building up the new order.

But the new social order which Jesus died to bring still remains a promise. And it will be by the fostering of such humane gifts that we will know the presence of God now amongst human beings, and the first dawning of the kingdom of God. Amen.

---

[4] Galatians 5.22–23.

24
Maundy Thursday[1]

THERE is a qualitative difference between the events of these next few days – Maundy Thursday, Good Friday, Easter Even and Easter itself – and the events of the rest of the Church's Year. It reflects the difference between Jesus' ministry of preaching, teaching and healing and the events at the close of his life. The difference is one of depth and intensity; these are events in which all the rest is concentrated, and in which his life and work are brought to their climax.

The circumstances were important. It was clear by then that Jesus' life was at risk, and that enabled him to bring the central meaning of his life into focus and to move decisively forward with what was his to do. An American mother facing great danger in El Salvador wrote this to her daughter:

> The reason why so many people are being killed is quite complicated, yet there are some clear, simple strands. One is that many people have found a meaning to live, to sacrifice, to struggle and even to die and whether their life spans sixteen years, sixty or ninety, for them their life has had a purpose. In many ways they are fortunate people. Brooklyn is not passing through the drama of El Salvador, but some things hold true wherever one is, and at whatever age. What I am saying is that I hope you can come to find that which gives life a deep meaning for you, something that energizes you, enthuses you, enables you to keep moving ahead.[2]

And the prospect of his death evoked in Jesus a deep need to consolidate and communicate what his life had been about, and moreover to carry it to its conclusion. But what was most important about the events of Maundy Thursday was that on it Jesus drew others into what he was doing. Since his life was always spent with and for others, the completing of his work meant drawing them fully into what he was doing.

There are clear phases in this focusing and completing of Jesus' life and work. The phase which concerns us this evening is Jesus' move to complete the incorporation of his fellow human beings into his life and work – to gather them and us into the death which was to follow. It was not the only 'gathering' which occurred, of course, because his descent into

[1] All Saints' Church, Princeton, New Jersey, 1993.
[2] Sheila Cassidy, *Good Friday People*, Maryknoll: Orbis Books, 1991, p. 62.

death was also the means by which he gathered the dead into his life and work; but that is a matter for discussion two days from now, on Holy Saturday.

But the 'gathering' on the night before his crucifixion, the incorporation of his fellow human beings into his life and work, is pivotal for what occurred thereafter. One of the early Fathers of the Church said, 'the unassumed is the unhealed' – meaning that whatever characteristic of human life Jesus did not share he did not save. But that is true in a much broader sense: those whom Jesus did not incorporate into his work were unaffected by what he did. And his move to draw his fellow human beings into what he was doing was therefore profoundly important. And the lesson for us is that we are unlikely to appreciate fully what happens on Good Friday and Holy Saturday unless we are now drawn into him. What Jesus did was done as our representative – as One in whom we are present, in whose action we participate.

By drawing us into him, he drew us into a struggle which goes far deeper than we realize. What he did was not limited to what we can understand, or to what is of immediate benefit to us.

We make a mistake if we emphasize too much the visible, human events and their significance for us in our living now. In an age when human beings are so much concerned with what is relevant to them, and what can directly help them live their lives, there is a tendency to restrict these events – Maundy Thursday to Easter Day – to their obvious significance for human beings. Difficult as it is to enlarge our vision to wider and deeper issues, we must come to understand that what is at stake is the very nature of the world, its history and life itself. And the questions are not simply practical ones of how we – and the world – live, but also issues of goodness and truth, and how they are rebuilt amidst evil and falsehood. Great cosmic conflicts are present, and resolved, in these events. That is exactly why they are so important for the living of life, because they address the deepest issues and problems of life – not because they give easy guidance for practical living.

> Again this need to mend a world's mistakes.
> For short-term gain,
> Our fouled up shoreline, clogged lakes.
> And sister earth is fretted: forest, air
> A waterflow, a breeze, a rain,
> Intricate fragile web and net. A young
> Man rages 'Greed and waste
> Unravel nests we share.'[3]

[3] Micheal O'Siadhail, 'Feedback' (Stanza 1) in *Hail! Madam Jazz*, Newcastle: Bloodaxe Books, 1992, p. 146.

And these dilemmas are met exactly because it is *God's* work and life which are being worked and lived in what happens in these events – Maundy Thursday to Easter Day. Jesus brings into focus not only the world's great problems but God's action. He focuses the divine work itself, with what consequences we shall have to see.

As I said, Maundy Thursday is the first phase of what happens in these few days, and has to do with how Jesus completes the incorporation of his fellow human beings into his work, and gathers them (and us) into what is about to happen. The manner in which Jesus does this incorporation is highly important, not only for our understanding of his work but also for our conception of God's action, how God's work and life are worked and lived in relation to the deepest problems of the world and human life.

Most of us, I suppose, expect to be gathered into the benefits of his work without being much changed in the process. But the secret of what he does is that we are drawn into him by being completely changed. The way in which we are human, and practise our humanity, are changed. The pattern for the meaning we are to find in life changes. And it is as changed that we are lifted up to God in his death on the cross. His death signals the end of human life as it is usually lived, and the coming of another kind of life.

The best way to try to understand this change is to look carefully at the deceptively simple actions of Jesus with his disciples, narrated in the readings but also performed this evening. Look first at the exchange between Jesus and Simon Peter as Jesus came to wash Peter's feet. Peter resists in his usual, headstrong way: 'Lord, do you wash my feet?' 'You shall never wash my feet.' And in that simple resistance, we see how it is that human beings are usually themselves: they constitute themselves as a field of power, claiming the right to do as they wish and to control those around them, particularly where others infringe on the zone which they control. By the nature of the case, this isolates them; others can come close only insofar as they are allowed to, on the condition that they submit or lose the power by which *they* are *them*selves. So those in the controlling position build up their power by avoiding or reducing the power of others.

This is the way in which we normally exist. And human beings are not different from other beings in these matters: all beings in the world are like force-fields – in which they generate and sustain themselves as a field of power, the power to be themselves by controlling others. But we hardly notice this because what we do does not seem dangerous; our fields of power are restricted by the society in which we live. We are not allowed to control or damage each other except in sharply circumscribed ways. But the same social constraints also allow some people to have far greater power than others. Some people (or groups) control more resources, perform important activities upon which others depend, control more decisions, and can reward (or punish) others by conferring (or withholding) recognition. Our societies rationalize the distribution of power, often producing gross inequalities; and few question why some are more in control, and have more influence, than others.

But civilization is a very delicate and fragile thing. And moral inhibitions against damaging others are easily eroded. In 'normal' circumstances, restricting, controlling and sapping others is an unintentional by-product of building oneself up; it is very common in our self-interested society, and is actually rationalized in our social system. But let civilizing social restrictions slip, and soon it becomes conceivable intentionally to destroy others in the process of building and maintaining oneself or one's society. Suddenly, accepted authorities seem to authorize violence, while at the same time the others are seen as less than human and not worth preserving; that is as clearly seen in the trial and death of Jesus as it is in the tortures which are so widespread in the world today, or in the 'ethnic cleansing' now taking place in Bosnia. We avoid thinking about these things, but they are deeply rooted in the very way by which human beings practise their humanity. It is deeply troubling how little there is to distinguish between what we accept as normal self-building and such instances of outright evil.

If we really watch what Jesus does on Maundy Thursday, there is a clear lesson: we misunderstand the theory and practice of human life. That seems to be the implication of Jesus' response to Peter. To Peter's resistance ('You shall never wash my feet'), he responds, 'If I do not wash you, you have no part in me.' And Peter, finally getting the point, gushes enthusiastically, 'Lord, not my feet only but also my hands and my head!'

The implication is that treating oneself as a field of power is no way to be a human being. The basis on which Jesus approaches his disciples is different: it establishes a different kind of bond, one not based on the exercise of power, on domination and the requirement to submit, but one based on deep affirmation of others and the energy by which to raise others through devotion. Jesus not only taught this, but also enacted it by what he did – hand-washing the disciples' feet and drying them with a towel also wrapped around him, as personal an act of devotion as one could imagine. What it signified, and enacted, was the closest bond between human beings.

With our habit of thinking of ourselves as separate fields of power, such a close bond as Jesus established is nearly inconceivable even as a bond of devotion. But there is a great deal more involved. It was not simply an act of human solidarity on Jesus' part, but something which arose directly from the action of God in him: 'knowing that the Father had given all things into his hands, and that he had come from God and was going to God'. The bond with the disciples which Jesus established arose from God's life and action in him, and was the means by which God restored them to unity with him. As Jesus later said,

> the glory which thou hast given me I have given to them, that they may be one even as we are one, I in them and thou in me, that they may become perfectly one, so that the world may know that thou hast sent me and hast loved them even as thou hast loved me.[4]

Now let us make no mistake. This, God's deepest love, is intended as a different basis for human life and action, one which reconstitutes the nature of human life. If human beings are force-fields, it is inevitable that others are disempowered. But they are not. Instead, human beings are those through whom God's glory is given to others, by which others are built up through the gift of love. And there is an inexhaustible supply of this glory and love for those who live in the love of God conferred in Jesus.

We were asking ourselves how – through such a simple act as washing his disciples' feet – Jesus completed the incorporation of human beings into his life and work. What was performed in that act was a transformation of human life. It enacted a different conception of human life, one which was nourished by God's life and work in Jesus. And insofar as human beings now live this new life, they are indeed incorporated into Jesus' work and the healing which it brought: 'If I then, your Lord and Teacher, have washed your feet, you also ought to wash one another's feet – you also should do as I have done to you.'

What this brought, and enacted, was a different conception of the goal of life. Instead of our habitual preoccupation with building ourselves up through our natural power, the goal of life is to live from and in the goodness which is constituted by the gift of God. Likewise, the means by which we attain this goal are different: instead of getting and keeping in order to establish and maintain ourselves, we give to others.

It is that new humanity which we perform tonight in an act of thanksgiving to God for reconstituting it. We perform Jesus' words:

> My little children,
> I shall not be with you much longer ...
> I give you a new commandment:
> love one another;
> just as I have loved you,
> you must also love one another.
> By this love you have for one another,

---

[4] John 17.22–23.

everyone will know that you are my disciples.

By this love – a love by which we meet our fellow human beings in humility and seek to raise them – we are joined to the life and work of God in the death and resurrection of Jesus. Amen.

25

Good Friday[1]

HUMAN beings never seem to realize, never mind catch up with, what God does for them. But that does not mean that God is therefore prevented from doing what is necessary: fortunately for us, for God to do what is necessary does not need to wait for us to catch up, or agree with, what he does – although we still have to for our own sakes.

On Maundy Thursday, yesterday, we recalled – called again upon – those events in which Jesus embraced and included us in what he was to do. In the footwashing by which he showed that he *served* those who followed him, and in the Last Supper by which he *took them into* what he was to do, we too were served by, and included in, what was to follow – his capture, trial, sentencing and death on the Cross.

What followed was actually done *for us* and *with us*, and not only for and with us but for and with the whole world. So we are *served* by him and are *embraced* in his capture, trial, sentence and death. Of course, like Peter, we don't quite realize – or catch up with – what he did. And if he had or we did, it would be very dangerous, for what was going on was a trial which went to the depths of what is evil and what it is to be human. Where Jesus was straightforward, unambivalent about what he was doing and fully aware of what was happening, we lag behind, are ambivalent and unaware of the magnitude of what was going on – just never quite 'there'. So part of what we are about tonight is to catch up with what went on – to learn to be wholeheartedly with him who is already wholeheartedly with us, and no longer to be ambivalent.

We will need to move from being *uncomprehending spectators* to *learning followers and participants* (for to learn and follow are what it means to be 'disciples') in this which happened between those who tried Jesus and Jesus – and between Jesus and God. That is no small change. And it is a *real change* we need to undergo, not only a *feeling* of being moved by impressive events, a feeling which we can leave behind as we leave here.

Much more important, however, is to try to understand – as well as live in – what happened. We are to recall – call again upon – what happened, and find ourselves illuminated and changed by it. What was at stake in his trial? And what happened between Jesus and God that day? And how are we illuminated and changed by it?

What was at stake in Jesus' trial was bewilderingly great. Part of the

[1] All Saints' Church, Princeton, New Jersey, 1995.

reason we have such difficulty in seeing what was involved is that the issues are so much our own problems. The things which led to the trial and crucifixion of Jesus are as much present in us as they were in those responsible for his death. Were we in their position and someone like Jesus came along, we would be as threatened as they, and as anxious to find a way of focusing the problems on this man and ridding ourselves of them. Don't suppose that the same problems are not present in us, or underestimate their range and magnitude. There, in the successive stages of the trial of Jesus, he was accused of secret plotting, overthrowing the law and thereby the recognized basis of society itself, usurping the place of the rightful leaders, aspiring to ultimate power (making himself the Son of God), false prophesying (bearing false witness to the truth) and bargaining with God (priestly acts). Can we honestly say that these are not our problems?

Any one of these would have been enough. But Jesus was seen as directly challenging *all* the 'powers that be', and undermining all that was held without question by the people of his place and time. Don't suppose that the issues at stake were primarily 'the Jews' or 'religious', or 'other people'; the problems touched every aspect of life, the whole system of life. Those rivers (or sewers) run in us, even if we'd like to pretend otherwise. And they were magnified by the power game which was being played out amongst the people and their leaders, and between them and the higher powers (in this case, the Roman governors). Jesus became a pawn in this power game, a way by which each humiliated the other – and that magnified all the problems still further, and caused extra embarrassment.

In other words, the trial showed the *corruption* of each and every element in the society of the day: the trial of this innocent man – although he was anything but innocent from the vantage-point of those who accused him – focused light on the decay in each of those who accused him, much as it reveals the corruption in each of us. But they were far from acknowledging any problem in them, just as we are. Amongst them, ironically, only Judas – the disciple who betrayed Jesus and afterward killed himself for it – acknowledged his fault. And the problems are as great today, fifty years after the freeing of the prisoners at Belsen and a year after the massive genocide (mostly by people who called themselves Christian) in Rwanda.

So Jesus bore a many-sided burden: he was the one upon whom all the systemic evils of human life were focused. Every aspect of life as it decays in all of us, whether then or now – singly or together – were embraced in him. And yet he was in no way responsible for these very wrongs which came to be focused upon him. He had done nothing to promote them: his presence, words and actions only revealed them. It was because he had attempted to redress them, and to redirect the tendencies which led to them, that such wrath came to be focused on him. There is no sign of wrongdoing in what we see of him. He was the innocent victim of the many who managed to agree in condemning him – where they could agree on little else; he was the victim of their unacknowledged guilt.

As comprehensive as were all these issues of corruption, they were not all that was at issue there on the Cross. Underlying all of this is the simple question of life itself. Since Adam and Eve, death had been regarded as the penalty for sin: sin led to death, and death was the only future for human beings. Could death ever be anything more than that? Could it ever be more than the ultimate punishment for sin? Could it ever become the gateway to anything beyond? We have to remember that the whole of life and its corruption were focused in this trial and death, but not only those, but the very possibility of a hope through and beyond death.

Huge issues – there could be none more enormous – were at stake on the Cross. What was really at issue was *what was to become of life and its decay, and of death itself.* In the last analysis, however, all of these rest on what happens *between Jesus and God* on the Cross. Could there be a resolution of the fundamental dilemma of life – death? Could there be a healing – a salvation – of the corruption of life?

As viewed from the history of creation, the fundamental issue in these matters was always *what God would do,* not whether there were some quick and clever panaceas. What the Cross signifies is the point where the value of all human remedies – whether to the decay of life, or to death – is at an end. Jesus does not in fact defend himself during his trial and crucifixion, for there is no remedy available to human beings for death and the decay of life. He simply suffers and dies, and dies the death of a sinner – as if he was actually guilty of all the offences of which he was accused. And there is no easy way out, no removal of the cup of suffering, no reduction of the suffering, no avoidance of the death. That is why Jesus does not respond when he is mocked – 'He trusts in God; let God deliver him now, if he wants to; for he said "I am God's Son."' And that is why Jesus cried out in the words at the beginning of Psalm 22, 'My God, my God, why have you forsaken me?'

WHAT WOULD GOD DO?

What could God do? God had constituted the world in a certain way, and that did not permit him to interfere, as if by magic, to put things right. At the foundation of the world, a covenant of promise had been made by God: he had conferred upon the world its otherness, its exist- ence as separate from him, and promised its fulfilment. It was in that gift that human beings received themselves from God, and received their freedom – on the understanding (for this was part of the covenant) that they would return thanks, use their existence and freedom to return glory to the One who had been so abundant and generous in his gifts.

It was only when they refused to do so, and pretended to be self-sufficient, that things went so badly amiss, and they were consigned to self-extinction in death. It was only when they used their existence and their freedom outside the terms of the covenant that life went bad on them, and death became the end of life.

But look what happened with Jesus. He bore the multiple burden of the corruption of the lives of others, and – quite naturally – was consigned to death. What else was there?

But there was a striking and all-important difference: there on the Cross, where he was an innocent person upon whom was focused all the corruption and evil of the world, he nonetheless offered *himself* to God – willingly embracing the very people who had either abandoned him (his disciples) or put him to death (all the rest). Despite all the 'mud' clinging to him, this was a pure self-offering for those mired in the evil of the world. But this was by no means all: he offered not only his *life* but also his *death*. It is all in those simple words: 'the Son of man came not to be served but to serve, and to *give* his life as a ransom for many'.[2]

But the real significance of these things was more far-reaching: *Jesus completed what was due under the covenant of promise.* His self-offering, embracing the corruption of human life and the death which naturally accompanied it, completed the return of creation to the One who had given it the very otherness of its being. He became the one man in whom the covenant with God was fulfilled, for he fulfilled the obligation due under the terms of the covenant. *And God, in fulfilment of his covenant, accepted what Jesus had done.* At least in Jesus, the corruption of life was ended, and the hopelessness of death was ended.

All of this took place through the only medium where it makes any sense, the mode of life itself. What had been given by God in the covenant was life itself and the promise of its fulfilment. With the corruption of life – because human beings refused to return thanks and glory to God – the promise was lost, and death became the only end of life. But in Jesus, in the very one upon whom all of the decay of life was concentrated, and upon whom suffering and death were imposed, *in this very man thanks and glory were returned to God.* And life, both full life in this world and life beyond death, were returned. Creation was finally put to rights.

The truth of Good Friday is in the end, not the beginning, of the Psalm which was on Jesus' lips as he died. You remember it began, 'My God, my God, why have you forsaken me? and are so far from my cry and from the words of my distress?' It ends:

[2] Matthew 20.28.

To him alone all who sleep in the earth bow down in worship;
all who go down to the dust fall before him.
My soul shall live for him;
my descendants shall serve him;
they shall be known as the Lord's for ever.
They shall come and make known to a people yet unborn
the saving deeds that he has done.[3]

It is at that Cross that we now stand, where – for all the sins of others which he bore – thanks and glory to God are returned, and where God restores to us the promise of fulfilment in life and death. *Face it, and look upon it in hope – your own hope, our hope, for life and for death – on this Good Day.* Amen.

[3] Psalm 22.28–30.

26

Easter[1]

ONE of the things that always surprised me in England was that people were simply unable to preach Easter and its message. Apart from talking fairly straightforwardly about the events narrated in the gospels, or the necessity of believing in them, or even rather grandly of their relevance for the life of the world, there seemed little to say on Easter. 'Here they are!' 'You must believe them if you are to be Christian, you know!' 'Look how relevant they are for life today!' There seemed little else to be said. People did go on repeating, 'Christ is risen! He is risen indeed!', and there were persistent reminders that we were still in the Easter Season. But as to what Easter really meant, the whole matter was quickly left behind in favour of things more easily understood, and presumably more relevant. Perhaps there are the same problems here. I was rather stunned to be talking with someone the other day – a lifelong churchgoer – who simply didn't believe in the Resurrection of Jesus, or that it was in any way important for anything else in Christian faith.

It is difficult to comprehend the real truth of Easter, but urgent that we seek to understand it, even while believing it. People sometimes imagine that the Resurrection is simply one of the many issues of Christian faith, as if it were one small branch on the great tree of faith. But it is not; it is more like the tap-root of the tree, from which it draws its nourishment. Cut that away, and the tree is weakened to the point of death, in its trunk and top-most branches. It may stand, apparently sound, for years; but this is a pretence of health: eventually it will topple.

On the face of it, the Resurrection seems simply to be an historical question: did it happen, or did it not? And, by supposing that we were all involved in the Resurrection of Jesus from the dead, the answer to the historical question might tell us whether or not we can hope for Resurrection ourselves. The Resurrection of Jesus is the basis for our hope for eternal life. As we will see, such a self-interested way of approaching the Resurrection completely undermines its deepest meaning.

The truth of the Resurrection is not so simple; it is not just the historical event by which we have access to life eternal. It is knit into the most fundamental matters, into the whole structure of Christian faith. The whole efficacy of the salvation wrought by Jesus depends on it; apart from the Resurrection, Jesus would have been no more than one in a long line of prophets and teachers. Even more, it tells of the very being and

[1] All Saints' Church, Princeton, New Jersey, 1991.

activity of the God whom we find in the salvation wrought by Jesus, and of the character of all his work everywhere. For that reason, its meaning is of an infinite depth which reaches far beyond the surface questions of what actually happened on the Third Day. To use that same image of the tree and its tap-root, the nourishment given by this tap-root makes the tree of Christian faith possible, with all its other roots and branches; and it is the whole tree of faith which is comprehensively important, in life and in death.

It is for those reasons that belief in the Resurrection is so important, not because it is the miraculous pin-point on which our own eternal life rests. And belief in the Resurrection is a testing ground for our capacity to understand God and his ways with us; if we are unable to believe this, then something has gone wrong with all our perception of God and his works. There is much more to be said about this, but there is no time to go into it at the moment.

When we see that the Resurrection leads into the mystery of Christian faith in God, that changes the importance of the actual historical event, the raising of Jesus on the Third Day. For then we see that this event points backwards and forwards, backwards to the events of the life and death of Jesus, and forwards to the future of the Christian community right up to the Last Day. People are sometimes inclined to say that belief in the historical event of the Resurrection is all that Christian faith rests on. But if we really do see the Resurrection as leading into the whole 'tree' of Christian faith, all that had led up to it, and all that follows from it, are also the basis of Christian faith. The Resurrection is not to be considered the sole 'verification' of Christian faith.

We need to look much more carefully now at how the Resurrection leads us into Christian faith. Let's look at three things: How is it that the Resurrection leads us into the character of God's activity? What does it show about the character of God? And what does it show us about the kind of life which we are now to lead?

HOW IS IT THAT THE RESURRECTION LEADS US INTO THE CHARACTER OF GOD'S ACTIVITY?

Looked at from the standpoint of knowledge, it is, in a sense, the opening up of a remarkable insight into God through the guidance of God himself, the Holy Spirit. That is what becomes clear as we think about the lesson from the Acts of the Apostles this morning.[2] For there was

[2] Acts 8.26–40.

Philip, told by an angel to go out to the Gaza Road outside of Jerusalem, and told by the Spirit to go up to the chariot in which the Ethiopian eunuch was returning from worship at Jerusalem. Philip answered the Ethiopian's perplexity about a passage from the Book of Isaiah by showing him that it spoke of the humiliating sacrifice of Jesus and the new life which came from it for those who followed him. The eunuch immediately asked to be baptized – and afterward 'went on his way rejoicing'. As scanty as the story is, it is clear that God himself, the Spirit, through Philip, gives the eunuch that remarkable insight into God which is contained in the narrative of the silent suffering of Jesus, the denial of a just trial, his death and his being taken up from the earth. And what becomes clear is not a lot of information about what had happened, and how important it is, but what we could call the *generativity* of it. The experience of the eunuch is that it is still happening, through the Spirit, as others are drawn into that suffering, death and resurrection. The generation of the Jesus who suffered, died and was raised is those who come after and, in the Spirit, are drawn into what had happened. The baptism of the eunuch enacts, implants it, in his very being, and he goes on his way in joy, the joy of Easter.

So that apparently simple story tells us how, following after the Resurrection we are led into God's activity. It happens this way: through the witness of the Spirit, we – like the eunuch – are led into the suffering of Jesus, his death and his resurrection, and the activity of God's Spirit is confirmed in us so that we too may go on our way rejoicing.

WHAT DOES THIS SHOW ABOUT THE CHARACTER OF GOD?

What sort of remarkable insight into God does this bring?

One answer is that this is simply a drama into which we enter, which shows rather indirectly the righteous love of God. There are those who would have us think that it is only this, a drama in which we 'project ourselves onto an ultimate plane that gives meaning, and thus we are given ourselves ... surrender[ing] ourselves to something that transcends and gives meaning to the limited horizon of everyday life.'[3] And in such a drama as the suffering, death and resurrection of Jesus, they see a demonstration of God's righteous love – a righteous love which somehow stands apart from the drama itself. In other words, God is the author and producer of this drama of righteous love, where we are the

[3] Hans Urs Von Balthasar, *Theo-Drama*, San Francisco: Ignatius Press, 1988, Vol. I, p. 309.

actors. The author and producer have gone away, leaving us this power-ful drama by which we may recover ourselves.

I think that considerably understates the righteous love of God, and its implications for the way in which God draws us to himself. In our very individualistic society, we are well accustomed to the habit of declaring our concern for others while also standing back from them. In our early days in Princeton, my wife and I learned with what readiness and frien-dliness people will say, 'how very nice to meet you; we must get together for lunch – we'll be in touch with you this week!' The only problem is that the call never arrives, and there is no further meeting – unless we ourselves initiate it. This is not very much different from the supposition that God affirms his people with a resounding 'yes!' while at the same time staying distant from them. Nor is it far different from the idea that God sets in motion a drama of righteous love, played out in Jesus and those who follow him, while himself standing apart. But suppose God is involved in the suffering death and resurrection of Jesus in a different way.

Let me quote the words of a love poem, published just recently, of a marvellous Irish poet, Micheal O'Siadhail:

> Nothing can explain this adventure – let's say a quirk
> of fortune steered us together – we made our covenants,
> began this odyssey of ours, by hunch and guesswork,
> a blind date where foolish love consented in advance.
> No my beloved, neither knew what lay behind the frontiers.
> You told me once you hesitated: a needle can waver,
> then fix on its pole; I am still after many years
> baffled that the needle's gift dipped in my favour.
> Should I dare to be so lucky? Is this a dream?
> Suddenly in the commonplace that first amazement seizes
> me all over again – a freak twist to the theme,
> subtle jazz of the new familiar, trip of surprises.
> Gratuitous, beyond our fathom, both binding and freeing,
> this love re-invades us, shifts the boundaries of our being.[4]

'This love re-invades us, shifts the boundaries of our being', is the line on which to fasten.

Let us pause and think about that in relation to our own love for the one closest to us. For us who have such love, love means that we are not selves in the way we were before, nor need we be withdrawn and self-protective in the way we have come to consider normal. The boundaries of our being are shifted, and go on being shifted, as our love draws us

---

[4] 'Out of the Blue', *The Chosen Garden*, Dublin: The Dedalus Press, 1990, p. 71.

more and more deeply together, more and more profoundly with each other, limited only by the quality of the love which gives us freedom to love. We are free thereby, in all the extremities of life, to love and cherish each other.

If love does shift the boundaries of our being, can it be any the less so with God? Can we really suppose that the drama of the suffering, death and resurrection of Jesus into which we are brought (like the eunuch) by the Spirit is a drama from which God stands apart? The truth is that the boundaries of being between God and us shift with each new expression of his love. And God himself is *most* with us in the drama of the suffering death and resurrection of Jesus as we are drawn into it by the Spirit. The Holy Spirit does not simply draw us into the drama of Jesus. He draws us into the drama in which God's love is most deeply present, and in which God is closest to us. The only limiting factor is the degree to which we are prepared to respond in love. It is, therefore, *we* who insist that God is distant, and *we* who erect a barrier which keeps God in his heaven and leaves us alone here on earth. Far from this, he is most himself where in the utmost love he enters most deeply into our life, in the suffering death and resurrection of Jesus into which we are drawn by the Holy Spirit. There, he lives through the extremities of our life – our sin and self-isolation from him, and our death – and is still most near to us. Not even the boundaries which we erect to separate ourselves from him are barriers to his love; his love shifts all such boundaries.

WHAT DOES ALL THIS SHOW US ABOUT THE KIND OF LIFE WHICH WE ARE NOW TO LEAD?

Recall the words from the First Letter of John:

We know that we have passed out of death into life, because we love the brethren. He who does not love abides in death. Any one who hates his brother is a murderer, and you know that no murderer has eternal life abiding in him. By this we know love, that he laid down his life for us; and we ought to lay down our lives for the brethren ... Little children, let us not love in word or speech but in deed and in truth.[5]

When we are drawn by the Holy Spirit into the suffering death and

[5] 1 John 3.14–18.

resurrection of Jesus, and thus drawn into the love of God, the chief mark of what has happened to us is to be found in our 'love for the brethren'.

Three things are very directly connected here, the love of God, the manner in which the love of God is present for us, and the way in which these are shown in our love for each other. As we saw before, God's love for us actually shifts the boundaries between him and us in the suffering death and resurrection of Jesus; and we are drawn into that by the Spirit, drawn into the close embrace of God's love. The suffering death and resurrection of Jesus were not simply a drama illustrating the principle of God's love.

And the suffering death and resurrection of Jesus are not simply the illustration of some kind of ideal which should vaguely inform our actions toward others. When we are drawn by the Spirit into the suffering death and resurrection of Jesus, we are drawn into a new kind of life with each other. That may seem scary. Sacrifice for each other usually frightens us because it seems death-like, wasting ourselves for the sake of someone else; and we usually rationalize ourselves into believing that no one else could be worth such sacrificial wasting of ourselves. And for that reason, we usually turn the suffering death of Jesus into a vague ideal for a kind of love which isn't really expected of us.

But we are wrong, both in thinking of this as a vague ideal for love and in treating it as scary. Far from being informed of a vague ideal, we are actually drawn by the Spirit into 'the truth', the awesome dynamic of God's love, and it is in the dynamic of that love that we love each other. Following that dynamic, we 'lay down our lives for the brethren', not in fear but in the realization that in such sacrifice God meets us most closely and – in our very loss – raises us up. As we lose ourselves for the brethren, so we will win ourselves. This is the mark that the Spirit has drawn us into the suffering death and resurrection of Jesus.

Only one thing more need be said. The dynamic of this love transforms the way in which we are with each other. It is 'gratuitous, beyond our fathom, both binding and freeing ... [it] re-invades us, shifts the boundaries of our being'. We can embrace others, and be embraced, in ways quite beyond our imagining – and there continue to be enlarged by the nearness of God's love. This is the way in which the love of God is continued amongst us. Amen.

27

Pentecost[1]

A great French philosopher once said, 'The trouble with the English is that they always have to *see* things to understand them.' The same is probably true of the Americans as well. After 29 years spent in England, one of the things which has struck me very much about life here in the USA is that people here are content to go entirely by appearances, and not to think more deeply about what they mean. Whether or not that is so, it seems that most people cannot get beyond the strongly visual imagery of the narratives about what happened to Jesus Christ: there he was, and he rose upwards to heaven; and then afterward the disciples had a strange experience of new life at Pentecost. I can remember hearing tales about a church in Philadelphia years ago, whose rector made the most of portraying everything graphically; not only did he always have a live ass in church on Palm Sunday, he also had a figure of Christ which 'ascended' through the ceiling of the church every Ascension Day. Such ideas tell us more about where Christ went than why this happened.

There are other images for the Ascension and Pentecost which seem even more widespread, that Christ went up to heaven as a declaration of his majesty, that in ascending he went – as it were – to the palace of the King, there to share in God's reign for ever, to return when this reign is complete and God is sovereign over all other powers. Then a messenger was sent out from the palace to tell us of his place with God, and to share his accomplishment with us, and to bring us to the palace, where we too can share in the reign of God and Christ. Those are images which tells us more about Christ's status, his Lordship over all powers on or beyond the earth, and that we must submit to his Lordship. They tell us little about what actually occurred at Pentecost, and it is no wonder that people have such a hard time understanding the Holy Spirit, and how the Holy Spirit figures in the work of Christ.

It seems to me that there is a great deal more in what is said about Christ's ascension and the events of Pentecost than we normally can see, and that we need to take a much wider and deeper view of what happened than we usually do. The most important things, which are there in the stories, are difficult to portray; that's why we cling to visual images. One way of approaching the real meaning of those events, Ascension and Pentecost, is to ask *why* and *how* the followers of Jesus were so encouraged by them.

[1] All Saints' Church, Princeton, New Jersey, 1991.

The first thing to *see* is *that* the disciples were enormously affected by the ascension of Jesus and still more so by what happened at Pentecost. It is said that they were full of joy afterward: 'They worshipped him and then went back to Jerusalem full of joy; and they were continually in the temple praising God.'

We need to contrast that with the desperation which they felt after his crucifixion, and how it shut them off from the world.

There is a very impressive book which was written by a father after the tragic, unexpected death of his son. Two of the feelings which he very movingly describes were the 'neverness' and the feeling of being at a distance from the world:

> Never again to be here with us – never to sit with us at table, never to travel with us, never to laugh with us, never to cry with us, never to embrace us as he leaves for school, never to see his brother and sister marry.[2]

The result was not simply a personal grief; it was something which did damage to the father's life in the world: 'I've become an alien in the world, shyly touching it as if it's not mine. I don't belong anymore. When someone loved leaves home, home becomes mere house.'

But the two things which Jesus' followers felt after his ascension and Pentecost were exactly the reverse. In place of the 'never again' of the Crucifixion, they found an 'always again', that he was always with them, again and again and again. That is one of the interesting things about the comings of Jesus ('appearances' is not a good word for us today: it seems to suggest intangible visions). There were so many of them, to so many people, and under so many different circumstances. It really did seem that he was 'always with them'.

And instead of finding themselves alien in their world, it was just the reverse. After the Ascension, they went back into the *centre* of things – to Jerusalem and the Temple, which for Jews were the centre of the world. If they had not had such a thing happen to them, they would probably have tried to disappear into the obscurity of the countryside, where their false hopes would be forgotten. But they went back to 'the centre', Jerusalem. And at Pentecost, they – who after all were all Jews, speaking but one language – began to speak in all the languages of the world, and were understood by people of all languages. These two things were the fulfilment of what Jesus had told them before ascending, 'repentance for the forgiveness of sins would be preached to all the nations, beginning from Jerusalem. You are [to be] witnesses to this.' And there they were, back at Jerusalem and already started on their appointed task.

[2] Nicholas Wolterstorff, *Lament for a Son*, London: Hodder & Stoughton, 1989, p.15.

But *why* exactly were they so much transformed by what happened? To answer that we must look carefully at a level of the story of Jesus which people rarely notice. We must remember that the birth of Jesus is announced to Mary by an angel, that when Jesus comes to be baptized the Holy Spirit descends on him, and when he fasts in the desert and is tempted by Satan, the angels minister to him. All of these incidents refer to *life* which he is given. The Holy Spirit doesn't appear only at Pentecost, but is a constant presence, not only through the history of Israel but in Jesus' own life as well, giving and sustaining his life.

When Jesus appeared to the disciples after the Resurrection, they discovered that Jesus had escaped death, that he himself had triumphed over death. Now that was great news. They now had him back with them. But the part which astonished them was not simply that he was not dead, but that he was in some sense *more full of life* than he had been before. That is difficult to understand: isn't life just, well, life? We must remember that, in Jesus' death, he had actually carried life itself into death. And his resurrection was not simply life popping up again, so to speak, but a new concentration, a new explosion of life. It was a fullness of life – a new *kind of life* – which had not been seen before, the completion of the coming of God's life into the world. So there in Jesus' resurrection and ascension was an astonishing new life.

But still, at the Ascension, he seemed to be again departing from them, in this case permanently. Why were they not as desolate as before, when he had been crucified? Why were they not again mourning the fact that they would 'never again' enjoy him? And why were they not again as 'aliens in the world'?

The answer lies in what they now discovered. We must remember that the fact that Jesus was raised from the dead, that he himself had triumphed over death, and had even brought a new kind of life, says precisely nothing about his ability to *give life* to others. He was ascending to the Father, not simply to show that he would share in the majesty of God, but to share in the favour which it is the Father's to give, and to fill the whole universe with the favour of God. As Paul puts it, 'he ... ascended higher than all the heavens, so that he might fill the whole universe.'[3]

With what did he fill it? If we go beyond the rather abstract answer that he filled the whole universe with the favour of God, and ask in what God's favour consists, the answer is: *life*. That is what the disciples found Jesus giving them as he ascended from them:

Then he took them out as far as the outskirts of Bethany, and lifting

---

[3] Ephesians. 4.10.

up his hands he blessed them. Now as he blessed them, he withdrew from them and was carried up to heaven.

The blessing which he conferred on them was not simply a gift of his good wishes. That would certainly not have compensated them for leaving them bereft again. His blessing actually *transferred* something to them from God, something which is of the very essence of what God is. Above all, he is life; and the blessing which Jesus gave, gave his followers the very life of God. So the Ascension marks what the Resurrection does not, the giving of life by God to his people.

It is this which filled them with joy. For they found themselves full of the life which Jesus bestowed. And they were transformed, energized, by that life, even if they could see him no longer. The signs of that are found in what they did. They worshipped him; that is, they responded to his blessing by blessing him, and returned to Jerusalem and 'were continually in the temple blessing God'. Imagine the possibility of sharing fully in the life which God gives. That is the promise which is given us in the Ascension of Christ, and the promise is fulfilled in the blessing which we find here and now as we bless God in Jesus Christ once again.

But there is a condition attached. At Pentecost, the disciples discovered that they could not simply enjoy the fullness of God's blessing in blessing God. The kind of life which God gives is more than that. Just as the Resurrection is an explosion of new life, so the fullness of God's life is known, not through keeping it to ourselves, but in an explosion which brings life into all the world. That may happen in many ways – varieties of gifts:

> To each is given the manifestation of the Spirit for the common good. To one is given through the Spirit the utterance of wisdom, and to another the utterance of knowledge by the same Spirit, to another faith by the same Spirit ...

The Spirit is known in the giving of life to others, or – in other language – ministering life to others. And this, by the way, is not giving them life with which to 'do their own thing', but 'for the common good'. We cannot be withdrawn and impersonal with each other, for we are building the Body of Christ amongst us. As we here, in different ways, give life to each other, we build the common good, the Body of Christ here. But we must do more than that. We must bring this life to the world around us in ways which it can understand, and build it too in the Body of Christ.

As we do, we will make an astonishing discovery. *In receiving* life through giving life to others, and *in giving* life to others in ways which free them, you will discover that Jesus is the *Lord of life itself, yours and theirs* (in technical language, an *a posteriori* Lordship). And in that we will know that neither heights nor depths can separate us from the love of God. We will find that the Spirit of Christ is always with us, again and again and again, even to eternity. Amen.

28

Trinity Sunday[1]

THE Church, or its clergy anyway, give three kinds of impression about the Trinity. One is that the Trinity is dull. The second is that it is complicated. The third is that it is probably unnecessary to think about it anyway. Each Spring, I have become accustomed as a theologian to being invited to churches – ones which might never have invited me otherwise – to preach on Trinity Sunday. I suppose there were several kinds of challenge implicit in these invitations: (1) Can he keep it from being dull? (2) Since the Vicar can't figure the Trinity out, can he? (3) And can he show that it has anything to do with, say, the Bible and the rest of what we do? I suppose people felt that having a theologian to preach was in some way a good thing, even if it didn't accomplish anything: he probably wouldn't be able to show that it wasn't dull or complicated or that it was very important, but having him there would show somehow that it *should* be important. Then, having shown that it should be important, they could go on through 'all those interminable Sundays after Trinity' (as I heard them called the other day) as if nothing had happened.

Let me be completely straightforward. Trinity Sunday is the most exciting day of the year, because it celebrates the simple heart of Christian faith, and wraps up all the excitement of the other great festivals of the Church's year into one sunburst of a celebration. But there is also a sense in which this excitingly simple heart of Christian faith is an open heart; and for that reason it cannot be wrapped up. That is important too.

A lot of the difficulties which people feel with the Trinity are tied up with what they think it is. People have fallen into the habit of thinking that it is only a doctrine, only a teaching about God. But that tames it, domesticates it, by turning it from something real and powerful into ideas. You may remember the technique used by soldiers in the First World War, when shells fell into the trenches unexploded. They would give the bombs familiar names, 'Old Harry' or whatever, treating them as old friends. In effect, this 'domesticated' them, eliminating the terrible awareness that they might blow up at any moment. For many people, calling the Trinity a 'doctrine' has just that effect; it's a way of domesticating it, allowing them to take it less seriously by treating it as only human ideas about God. This technique is used very widely nowadays

---

[1] Durham Cathedral, 1987.

amongst Christians. As I was walking by a city library one day several years ago, I was stopped by a very earnest young man who pressed into my hand a tract with the title 'the Doctrine of the Trinity', all about how the Trinity was not to be found in the New Testament at all, and was therefore not a Christian view at all. It was a way of telling me that I need not take it very seriously.

But while some of the ideas we have about God may be only our ideas, the Trinity itself is what you could call the very shape of God; it is the way in which God is. Just as someone who knows me knows what kind of person I am, and how to respond to me, so those who know God know what sort of God God is, and how to respond to him. 'God' is not just a name for an empty space; the very reality of God has a certain kind of shape, and it is the shape of a Trinity.

The best way to begin to understand that shape, is to sense something of the abundance of God, and then to try to see that the very abundance of God happens in a certain way – and therefore has a certain kind of shape. We can see these things running through the Bible. When Moses was called by God up onto Mount Sinai, 'the Lord came down in the cloud and stood there with him and proclaimed his name, the Lord', and proclaimed his nature: 'compassionate, gracious, slow to anger, abounding in love and faithfulness, maintaining love to thousands, and forgiving wickedness, rebellion and sin'.[2] That was a glimpse of the kind of God that God is; his nature was one of abundant fullness, complete well-being – or glory if you like. But you notice that this God is a God of compassion, the mark of whose faithfulness is to pour out his grace, love and forgiveness on his people – not simply a heavenly monarch content to remain shut up in himself. His abundance has a shape; it takes the form of lovingkindness for his people.

For the early Christians it was much the same: as St Paul said, 'God fills everything in every way.'[3] Because he is fullness and well-being itself – is abundance itself – he fills everything with whatever reality, fullness and well-being it has. There is no other conceivable source of fullness and well-being than God; and everything which has them has them from God himself. There are many words for such fullness: truth, nobility, integrity, justice, purity, beauty. These are the marks of full well-being as this is found in God, and they are found in the world only because they arise there from the fullness of God.

One way to respond to this fullness is simply to affirm it, to enjoy it, to live in the boundless fullness of God. And whenever our hearts and voices are full of the praise of God, not only in himself but also in the fullness he provides for the world, we do just that. But, quickly following from that,

[2] Exodus 34.5–6.
[3] Ephesians 1.23.

comes the awareness that affirming it in praise, and living in it, brings a certain kind of responsibility: we must be faithful to the fullness of God in our world. That is what Paul was suggesting in the advice he gives in Philippians: 'Whatever is true, whatever is noble, whatever is right, whatever is pure, whatever is lovely, whatever is admirable – if anything is excellent or praiseworthy – think about such things ... and put them into practice. And [then] the God of peace – the source of well-being – will be with you.'[4] In other words, we must locate what is the fullness of God and be faithful to it in our world.

That leads to a most important thing, the attempt to appreciate – in the simplest and deepest terms – what is the well-being of God, how it comes to us, and how it returns to God through us. This is the attempt to appreciate the shape of God in his relation to us, which is also the shape of our relation to God. And it turns out to be the shape of a Trinity.

It is quite possible to do it in the way which we read in the Acts of the Apostles just now – by telling of Jesus of Nazareth, 'handed over by God's set purpose and foreknowledge', put to death on the cross, raised by God from the dead to life. 'Exalted to the right hand of God, he has received from the Father the promised Holy Spirit and has poured out what you now see and hear.'[5] In one way, that is as good a statement of the movement of God's fullness to us and through us as you could want. It tells how, to use St Paul's words, 'In Christ all the fullness of God lives in bodily form, and by him we are given fullness in Christ, who is the head over every power and authority.'[6] Of course, it is Trinitarian in form, showing how the fullness of God comes to us in Christ, and through him by the Holy Spirit.

But that kind of summary of the shape of God, of the movement of God's fullness to us and through us, is not really enough. For one thing, it doesn't say as much as it might; for another, it is not enough help in being faithful to the fullness of God in our own world. A really simple statement of the movement of God to us and through us will inform us fully about what that movement really is; and it will also help us discover how to live in this movement.

That is why people went on from the Bible to try to provide better summaries of this movement. They were not simply providing a description to tell curious people about it; they were opening their hearts and minds to the movement of God toward us in Christ and by the Holy Spirit so that they could be carried by that same movement toward God. And this meant that they had two tasks. One was to tell us more about the well-being of God, how it comes to us in its fullness, and how it

[4] Philippians 4.8–9.
[5] Acts 2.23–33.
[6] Colossians 2.9.

returns to God through us. The second was to provide us with a practical way to live in the fullness of God, and allow it to return us to God.

It comes to something very simple. There is a funny way of describing the way in which man and woman fall in love: 'he chased her and she caught him'. So we think that we search for God, but it happens because he has already provided every means by which we do so. So we must learn how he does, so that we may actually find him.

As these tasks are confronted, the movement of God's fullness to us and through us is astonishingly simple. He who is in himself the most complete well-being, lives amongst us in Christ; and 'from the fullness of his grace [in the Holy Spirit] confers on us one blessing after another'.[7] And that fullness, evident in constant blessing, expands us and moves us towards God. Put even more simply, he whose nature it is to affirm affirms us unendingly, and so opens us to himself. What could be more exciting, or more practical, than that? It is the story, and the power, of life itself.

One thing more needs to be said. The circle which I have been describing, of the movement of God to us by which we move to God, is an open circle, open to things new or different – and even very puzzling – which happen in the world. They need to be drawn into this circle of movement. And that will always be true for us; the movement will never stop. For the movement of God to us and through us looks forward to the coming kingdom of God; and it is only then that we will live fully in the movement of God's fullness to us and through us – only then that we will 'know as we are known'. We make a big mistake not connecting Trinity Season with Advent, as far off as it is. The season of Trinity looks forward to Advent and the coming of the Last and Great Day, and so it should. There is hardly enough time during the many Sundays between now and Advent to complete the movement of God which has been begun in us. Amen.

[7] Cf. John 1.16.

29

Mission[1]

ST Willibrord (658–739) was from Northumbria, that beautiful region of England far to the northeast. Unlike his near-contemporary St Cuthbert, who came from Scotland as a missionary to bring Christianity to Northumbria, and eventually became Bishop of Lindisfarne, Willibrord went out from Northumbria. After training in the monastery of Ripon (now in Yorkshire), he went first to Ireland, and then as a missionary priest to Western Frisia, eventually to become Bishop of Utrecht (now in Holland). It is difficult for us to imagine such a time, when these parts of the world were still unchristianized and would have remained so, were it not for people like Cuthbert and Willibrord. For theirs was a kind of Christian commitment which, by its very nature, was missionary in focus. Why else would they have done such things?

Such Christian commitment contrasts strongly with the rather domesticated version with which we are familiar, in which the Church has a set of formal responsibilities which include concern for something often called 'outreach' – almost always left on the fringes of the main task of the Church. The kind of commitment we find in a Willibrord is *essentially centred on those who are beyond the Church* and on *giving compassionately to them*. Not only that, it is centred on giving to them the very essence of compassion, giving the compassion of God in Jesus to those who – in the words of an old bidding prayer – 'know not the Lord Jesus or love him not'.

Such a Christian faith is the reversal of the usual kinds of interest, and is focused on the true well-being of the other – neither building up the giver nor building up the self-interest of the other, but a passionate dedication to free the other person in turn to become passionately dedicated to the freeing of others for dedication. In that sense, Christian faith is a continuous act of giving, by God to this person for that person, and by God to that person for still others. It is therefore about engaging people's compassion, in order to deepen it by the compassion of God in Jesus Christ.

If that is the case, Christian faith is about self-dispossession, not self-possession, even when it carries you into an alien land or adverse circumstances. And the joy is that even in such circumstances, where compassion is brought to life in other people, your call will be confirmed. Recall what the prophet Jeremiah said to the people whom the Lord had

[1] The General Theological Seminary, New York, 1995.

sent into exile in Babylon: 'Seek the welfare of the city where I have sent you into exile, and pray to the Lord on its behalf, for in its welfare you will find your welfare.'[2]

Even in exile, where you are an alien, by seeking the welfare of those amongst whom you are, you will find your welfare.

God, it seems to me, set exactly this pattern for himself in creation and redemption, giving only for the good which others may do to each other and then – undaunted by the misuse of his gift – re-giving for the good which they may do to each other. Hence his gift ultimately undoes all attempts to distort and minimize it – even where they are at their most extreme.[3] God is an astonishing giver of good, one who provides a wonderful abundance. That abundance is in fact the most challenging aspect of Christian faith, a giving which calls us to goodness rendered to each other without the limitations of our self-interest or those of others. It is a 'freshness' constantly given us with which to give to others.

It is this form of Christian faith which we see in the readings for today. There, we see that the God embedded in Jesus is a *sender*, not only a giver but a sender of compassion – one who sends people to each other. This is not a sending to people to bring them what they do not have, 'missionaries' to the 'heathen' – as if those who are sent are the possessors of a stockpile of goodness which they bring when they go. It is not as if there has already been a harvest here 'at home' and its fruits need to be brought to those who have nothing (or worse, are in darkness). It is instead a sending *to the harvest* elsewhere, to gather in *the plenty already there*. That is a pattern which runs through the life of the early Christians like a golden thread; the 'sending' is a *going to find* what is already there and awaiting harvest. That is what Paul and the others always did: they went to *find* Christ amongst all the peoples to whom they went.

In what sense is it there? Recall Jesus' commissioning of the seventy:

> Whatever house you enter, first say, 'Peace to this house!' And if anyone is there who shares in peace, your peace will rest on that person; but if not, it will return to you. Remain in the same house, eating and drinking whatever they provide, for the labourer deserves to be paid. Do not move about from house to house.[4]

'When someone is there who shares in peace, your peace will rest on that person, but if not, it will return to you.' What springs up between the two

[2] Jeremiah 29.7.
[3] So farewell hope, and with hope farewell fear,
　Farewell remorse: all good to me is lost;
　Evil, be thou my good. (Milton, *Paradise Lost*, l. 108)
[4] Luke 10.5–7.

is a deep accord – a *sharing of the peace of the kingdom of God*. This is far more than simply sharing 'interests' which they may have. It is an awakening in them – in the sent and in those who receive them – of the mutual compassion which is the peace of the kingdom of God, the fulfilment of the *true purpose of all life*.

This springing into being of the peace of the kingdom of God is extraordinarily difficult to express, especially where people are as suspicious of each other as most of us have learned to be. It is hinted at in this poem written by a fine Irish poet, who likens it to a dance in which we weave a 'fragile city':

> So tables aside! Any dance at all.
> I'd loved our flight from the formal.
> Our broken observance. Rock and Roll.
> The Twist. Disco. Sweet and manic.
> Our blare of rapture. Alone. Freelance.
> But I yearn again for ritual, organic
> Patterns, circlings, the whorled dance.
>
> Openness. Again and again to realign.
> Another face and the moves begin
> Anew. And we unfold into our design.
> I want to dance for ever. A veil
> Shakes between now-ness and infinity.
> Touch of hands. Communal and frail.
> Our courtesies weave a fragile city.[5]

Why can't we envisage the sharing of the peace of the kingdom of God? It seems to me that the problem is not only our separateness or our mutual suspicion, but that we have rationalized ourselves out of the possibility of the full sharing of the peace of the kingdom of God. Let me explain.

Many years ago, while I was teaching in Birmingham, England and knew the then-Bishop very well, he said something which rather shocked me, which I have remembered ever since: 'In proclaiming Christian faith, you must appeal to people's self-interest.' There is a sense in which that is true: you must *engage people as they are*, and enter deeply into their awareness if you are to ever to share the peace with them; that is a very demanding task, requiring all the love, listening and understanding which we can muster.

But he also seemed to be suggesting that the communication of Chris-

[5] Micheal O'Saidhail, 'Weaving' in *A Fragile City*, Newcastle: Bloodaxe Books, 1995, stanzas 1 and 5.

tian faith is one 'interest' meeting another 'interest' – in dialogue, so to speak. And that misses the real point. For to say 'Peace to this house!' is to offer the compassion of God. And – at least in those open to it – that may cause the compassion of God to arise in them, transforming them into sharers of peace. And so, the peace which you offer can be transformative of the other. If not, 'it will return to you', as if it had never been spoken.

The problem, of course, is in supposing that these are simply 'interests' with which people confront each other and vie for superiority. It reminds me of the story of the meeting of two great players of the music of J. S. Bach, Wanda Landowska and Rosalyn Tureck. Landowska the harpsichordist had heard of Tureck the pianist, and greeted her icily, 'Ah, my dear, how lovely to meet you. I understand that we both play Bach – you in your way, and I in his!' Of course, when 'peace' is seen as an 'interest' offered to another with his 'interest', there is no full engagement with the other, no offering of the self-giving compassion of God and little of the transformative effect which such compassion brings.

The problems do not end there. If the Gospel of the transformative compassion of God in Jesus Christ is translated into 'interests', we soon find ourselves mired in the swamp of problems which have afflicted the Church since the first years of my ministry, which I have spent a lifetime addressing. It was nicely put by Flannery O'Connor:

> One of the effects of modern liberal Protestantism has been gradually to turn religion into poetry and therapy, to make truth vaguer and vaguer and more and more relative, to banish intellectual distinctions, to depend on feeling instead of thought, and gradually to come to believe that God has no real power, that he cannot communicate with us, cannot reveal himself to us, indeed has not done so and that religion is our own sweet invention.[6]

So Christianity has become enmired in the facets of human 'interests'. Should it have been *assimilated* to them?

One of the conclusions to which you come when the Church is assimilated to people's interests is that there is no good reason to engage with others. Yes, there is reason to elicit support for what might be called a 'dead poets' society', but not to engage seriously with people with the compassion of God. And after a while, the Church abandons its apostolic task. Instead, it rests content with the preservation of the *status quo*. That, indeed, is one of the most frightening signs of the Episcopal Church

---

[6] *Women's Wisdom Through the Ages: Timeless Quotations on Life and Faith*, New York: Farrar, Strauss & Giroux, 1988.

today. The Church here tacitly accepts that it will not grow, and has little responsibility apart from perpetuating its present state.

But we are about something different: the offering of peace, that is the offering of the transformative compassion of God. That is why when we come together here, as those sent to each other in self-giving compassion, we offer peace and anticipate that it will transform the other – and so bring the sharing of peace which is the mark of the presence of the kingdom of God amongst us.

It is also clear from the story of the Sending of the Seventy what should follow from such a transformative sharing of the peace: 'Remain in the same house, eating and drinking whatever they provide, for the labourer deserves to be paid. Do not move about from house to house.'[7]

The sharing of the peace brings stability, existing patiently with each other, and benefiting from each other. The sending and giving becomes mutual, and each has nourishment to give to the other – and the other is to receive it gladly.

This has vast implications for what it is for us to be together as the Church. It shows how we are to stay together, as those whom the Lord has sent to be together, how we are to give to each other from the gifts (material *and* spiritual) which God has given us, and how we are to heal each other through the love we tender each other. We here stay together, living in the constant interplay between us of the peace and love of the kingdom of God in the Body of Christ. That is what the Church is.

But it is unreal to suppose that it all happens so easily – anywhere, whether here or in the world to which we are sent. There is still the rampant, proliferated self-interest with which we and our world are infected.

Go on your way. See, I am sending you out like lambs into the midst of wolves ... whenever you enter a town and they do not welcome you, go out into its streets and say, 'Even the dust of your town that clings to our feet, we wipe off in protest against you. Yet know this: the kingdom of God has come near.' I tell you, on that day it will be more tolerable for Sodom than for that town.

Remember what this is all about. The giving, sending God sends us on our way to give to others: we are thrust outward in a yearning of the Spirit to join with others in the harvest of the kingdom of God. The only thing which should stop us is if this is not reciprocated by those to whom we go, if our offer of the compassionate, transformative peace of God meets with no response. And we cannot assume that *will* happen until it

[7] Luke 10.7.

does. And we need to be sure – truly sure – that we are offering the right thing – genuinely offering the peace which is of the kingdom of God and not simply a clever substitute. It is the *peace of the Kingdom of God* which we are sent to find.

God's peace finds people where they are, and challenges their self-interest.

Indeed, the word of God is living and active, sharper than any two-edged sword, piercing until it divides soul from spirit, joints from marrow; it is able to judge the thoughts and intentions of the heart.[8]

We have only to recall the death of Prime Minister Yitzhak Rabin of Israel, last Saturday to understand that. I heard the news on the car radio as I was returning to Princeton from Kennedy Airport. As shocking as the news itself was the comment from a Chief Rabbi here that this assassination was unquestionably the work of God, an act fully justified for one who was an apostate undoing the divine gift of the land to the Jewish people – not even deserving of a Jewish burial.

When it is expressed, God's peace shows the ramifications of self-interest in sharp relief. The strategies of self-interest suddenly appear for what they are, the very reversal of the selfless giving of good by God. The neglect of other people, the willingness to use them for one's own purposes, the institutionalizing of a kind of life which is damaging for all concerned: these are some of the marks. Taken to the extreme – as could be seen in the remarks of that Rabbi – they are poisonous, unforgiving, punitive and manipulative. Worst of all, they show an incapacity for God's peace and the struggle which is necessary if that is to be made effective in the world.

Whenever and wherever we are sent to find the kingdom of God, this incapacity for God's peace is what we will find, in one degree or another. And there will be occasions when it is useless to confront it; those involved are too much hardened. But we must not allow their hardness to harden us, so that we are deterred from the more fundamental task of awakening a transformative peace in others and ourselves. The struggle to remain in that transformative process is the way of the God who sends us to find his kingdom.

It is confidence in the compassionate, transformative way of peace – which is confidence in the gift by God of himself – which sends us onwards, in full confidence of sharing the peace of the kingdom with

[8] Hebrews 4.12.

others. And when that sharing happens, the peace which is in them will match and enlarge the peace in us, releasing a new outpouring of the Spirit of God. That is the only reward we should expect; it is a foretaste of the kingdom of heaven. Amen.

30

Remembrance Sunday[1]

'ARE the windows open?' I heard someone ask. 'Yes, the windows are open', was my friend's reply. This man had been with his wife for over twenty years, as her mental illness grew worse and worse. During all that time, but increasingly, she blamed all her own troubles on her husband and her son, while drawing her own strength from them. It was an utterly repressive household, which left deep scars on both her husband and her son. But the symptom of her illness which was most obvious to outsiders was that she would never allow the windows to be opened. Eventually, she left her husband and son, and they could begin to be free again. Hence my friend's reply, 'Yes, the windows are open now.'

The woman dominated her family, oppressing them by the means that are standard to such situations, isolating them, twisting their relationships with each other and with those outside, and holding them captive by her power over them. And in loyalty to her, they remained with her, despite her domination, trying and trying to win her back to health through intimate care, even though it was at the cost of great suffering to them. These days that is remarkable. The wisdom which would more usually be offered now is: 'Why don't you just walk away from her? Leave her to sort out her own problems' 'Or better still, why don't you see if you can have her institutionalized, put away somewhere where she can do no more harm?'

I tell that true story because it is a perfect example of why wars get started. They always begin with domination, where people are repressed by those who are in power. It easily happens, even where people think they are free. We can see this by the events of the past few days in East Germany. With hindsight, we can see that the very freedom which was won for Germany by World War II was actually the beginning of a new repression. The seeds for a new form of repression in East Germany were quickly sown, and it grew stronger and stronger. Like the illness of the woman I have just mentioned, the symptom was a closing of the windows, the building of the Berlin Wall. And behind the windows, there was a confined and restrictive life, which will have left its scars on all those who lived there. It was not a matter of how prosperous they were. Even if today they were as prosperous as the West Germans, they would still have lived as repressed, as unfree.

But, remembering the case of the woman and her family tells us that

[1] Durham Cathedral, 1989.

there is more than one way of dealing with repression. One way, the way adopted by her husband and son, is constructive loyalty, as they tried to win her back to health through simply loving her, even though it was at the cost of great suffering to them. There is nothing happy or clean about this way; it involves trying to heal her from within, by understanding her, by respecting her, by loving her, even as she disrespects them, misunderstands them, hates them. It takes a lot of faith and endurance – purity, justice, meekness, mercy and peacemaking – where they are met with persecution; you remember, these were all the virtues mentioned in the reading from Jesus' Sermon on the Mount.

That way, incidentally, was the way followed by the East German people. It is not to be mistaken for 'Communist sympathizing'; it is, or at least it can be, the way of suffering love. And you have to admire them for it. It can work. And it is honoured by God. They have at least won the right to 'open the windows' there, now that the Wall has been opened, and that is the beginning of freedom. It is only a first step, and no one should think that in itself it guarantees freedom, any more than did the winning of World War II.

Ideally it should always be possible to meet domination through constructive loyalty, following the steps outlined in the Sermon on the Mount, as the pacifists insist. But what *should* be so is not *necessarily* so. The blunt fact, which is shown by history time and time again, is that domination cannot always be met through constructive loyalty, even when pursued through suffering love. Domination can in fact destroy every effort to heal it, even through many years of loyal love; that was what was shown by the life of that couple I mentioned. It is still more difficult where the lives of whole nations are at stake, and nations must overcome the domination of nations. People of good will can struggle for years to limit the efforts of repressive nations to extend their domination to other nations. That was the enormously sad truth which could be seen in the attempts of the Prime Minister at the time, Neville Chamberlain, to limit the expansion of Nazi repression. In the end, the peaceful effort to undo domination *may* come to nothing. And that is a tragedy, the tragic failure of constructive loyalty to transform domination. Let us never forget that it is a tragedy.

Is one simply to live in that tragedy? It is the dilemma to which one of the great speeches of Shakespeare's *Hamlet* refers:

> To be, or not to be – that is the question;
> Whether 'tis nobler in the mind to suffer
> The slings and arrows of outrageous fortune,
> Or to take arms against a sea of troubles,
> And by opposing end them?[2]

² *Hamlet*, Act III, Scene 1.

Often, there is no choice. Unless you, and others like you, are to be swallowed up by the forces of domination, you must resist. And that is equally true wherever, and however, there is such domination. Terrorism is one of the many masks of domination.

The forces of domination seek to overwhelm others, war breaks out, and we must meet force with force. Yes, by our actions, we are – in a sense – speaking the truth, telling the world that this domination must end once and for all. That is why we must, in our hearts, believe that 'we fight to end this war'; we are telling the world that this domination must be brought to an end. That should be the only reason we have for engaging in war.

But when we begin to resist, 'take arms against a sea of troubles', we are in mortal danger. For we have begun to use the very same tactics as are used by those whose domination we seek to resist. It is a war *upon* the warfare of those who seek to dominate us, but it is still *us conducting war*. It is the attempt to bring down those who would dominate us, but the means we use is to dominate them. There is no other way: conducting war against war is still war; bringing those who dominate into subjection is still domination. That is why it is wrong to glorify war, the machinery of war, or the people who must conduct war. War not only begins in tragedy; it is a tragedy. And we today are remembering that tragedy, and those who have been its victims, whoever they are, *not* – as some misunderstand us – glorying in war.

Anyone who engages in war is steeped in tragedy, even in the times of triumph. For we must engage in war to end the war which has been made upon us, dominate others to end their domination of us. How can it be otherwise? There is only one way it can be different. And that is to use war, to use the domination required in war, as a *means to freedom*, a means to freedom for all those who need to be freed from domination.

It is only when the goal for war is freedom, when the goal for the means of domination which goes with war is freedom from domination, that war and domination can be transformed. In themselves war and domination can never be holy, but their *end* can be holy. The goal of freedom is the only goal which justifies such a tragic means of achieving it. And it is the only goal which justifies the enormous cost which it brings in suffering and death. It is the only goal which makes such sacrifice worthwhile. And strangely enough, when it is the way to freedom, war can be merciful, just, and a means of peacemaking.

The difficulty is holding to such a goal amidst all the temptations which the power of war brings. As a boy in my early teens during World War II, I can still remember the excitement evoked by reports of this breakthrough or that triumph, as I followed the advances day by day with flags pinned to a map of Europe. That simply missed the point. How much more difficult would it be to hold fast to a *moral purpose* for war in the day-to-day struggle and tragedy of war, hold fast to the conviction that it was *for freedom*. The greatest struggle would not be to stay alive, or even to succeed militarily, but the struggle to achieve freedom for those under domination. One man, one who struggled loyally to heal Germany from within during World War II, put it in these words:

> If you set out to seek freedom, then learn before all things
> to govern your soul and your senses, for fear that your passions and
> longing may lead you away from the path you should follow.
> Chaste be your mind and your body, and both in subjection,
> obediently, steadfastly seeking the aim set before them;
> only through discipline may a man learn to be free.[3]

The goal is always freedom, and war and domination – as well as all the machinery and personnel of an army – should serve that goal. If they do not, war and the means of war will brutalize all those who are involved, turning all participants into animals tearing at each other.

The greatest difference in those who take part in war is not in who and what they were. Ranks and tasks are not the real difference, nor should we differentiate between those who died in combat and those who lived on. The greatest difference is between those who held fast to the moral purpose of war, that it was for freedom. These are the true heroes, for they were not destroyed by war, whether they died or not. The true heroes, whether long dead or alive to this day, are those who served to bring others freedom from domination. Fortunately, perhaps, who they are is known only to God.

Far beyond what any human being can dream, God is the one who brings freedom, who brought freedom from domination in Jesus Christ. Those who have served freedom have unquestionably served the purposes of God; as that same German said shortly before his own death:

> Freedom, how long have we served thee . . .;
> dying, we may now behold thee revealed in the Lord.[4]

We remember them, all those who served freedom, whoever and whatever they were, and we honour them. Their victory is the Lord's victory, in the way to freedom for humanity. They opened the windows, and brought the beginning of freedom. Amen.

---

[3] Dietrich Bonhoeffer, *Letters and Papers from Prison*, London: SCM Press, 1953, pp. 370–1.
[4] *Ibid.*

31

Sermon at a Marriage[1]

WE are here this afternoon to participate in one of the true joys of human life, the marriage of two people – Kate and Frans – with the blessing of God. The marriage is not just between them, or between them and God. We are essential to it, for we witness their marriage, and also recognize and rejoice in – and thereby spread – the blessing of God which arises in their joining together for lifelong union.

As you will know, Kate and Frans were married in August in a civil ceremony. By doing so, they undertook marriage solemnly, in a way which we here do not overlook. But their marriage then was within the laws and customs which are normal in a secular society – a contract seriously entered into but undertaken with the kind of expectations which are normal in modern society, which are different from those of Christians in the Church. By making their vows now here in this Church, in the presence of other Christians, they undertake something else. Our part in their marriage is also different, and throughout the marriage we here invoke the presence and blessing of God. That is why this service repeats some of the features of their civil marriage, but with a different understanding of what is happening and what is essential to marriage.

Given the circumstances of modern life, marriage – in the full sense of the word – is extremely difficult to understand and maintain. Most of the tendencies of modern understanding, as well as the fragmentation we see at every level of social life, combine to produce a low view of the need for – and the possibility of – marriage. Rarely is marriage seen for what it is, a covenant, a clear but intangible relationship based on promises given and faithfully fulfilled; these promises are the manifestations of a bond of trust which is formed between two people. That makes marriage a relationship of the same sort as that established between the Lord God and the people of Israel, a relationship of radical self-giving which is most fully manifest in Jesus Christ and perpetuated even now in the community of the Church. Indeed, it is a relationship of the same sort as occurs whenever promises are given and kept.

Covenants are a primary means by which relationships are constituted. In marriage, they are the way in which a particular kind of relationship between two parties is set up, in which the dynamics of two lives are interwoven. There are so many things involved: (1) the meaning of each person as given by the other partner (as himself or herself), (2) how in

[1] All Saints' Church, Princeton, New Jersey, 1994.

their otherness they are present for and with each other, (3) how the dynamics of their lives are meshed, (4) how this enfolds other relationships and unfolds into the rest of life, and (5) what makes all of these possible.

The heart of a covenant, however, is a *promise*. A promising is a 'sending forth' of yourself, a bestowing of yourself on another person. This takes the form of a declaration that you will do certain things for the other person. The self-bestowal which takes place in marriage is the declaration that each will take, have, hold, honour, keep, love, cherish and comfort the other – will be for this other one as for no others, and will be with him or her under all circumstances and through all of life.

It is very important to understand the character of this sending-forth of oneself, this self-bestowal. It is, for one thing, an objective act of self-giving. It is therefore a *commitment to shape one's feelings in a certain way*, and the commitment should override the feelings one may have from time to time. I remember my own marriage as if it were yesterday. After the wedding, I felt the enormity of the act of self-giving which was involved. But it took some time before my feelings caught up. There was something very important about that. Marriage – whether at the beginning or later on – is not dependent on one's feelings; it is a commitment to shape one's feelings in a certain way. Feelings follow the commitment made; the commitment does not follow from the feelings one may have.

Second, this self-giving is an objective *declaration of one's being* toward another. This is easily confused with the acceptance of a set of obligations, where the meaning of taking, having, holding, and so on, is translated by one party into certain definite responsibilities which the other comes to take as expectations. The implications of marriage, worked out day by day, are definite, but they are not the marriage itself. The overriding issue in the marriage is the self-dedication of one's whole being to be for the other, a dedication in which all activities are to be incorporated.

In the long run of marriage, it is easy for this dedication to be replaced by a series of binding conventions. Let me explain. I recall the story of the one-time President of Princeton Theological Seminary, a Texan by birth, acquiring a tract of land on Mount Lucas Road here in Princeton. When the bank which owned the land contacted him to ask whether the Seminary was interested, he visited it with some bank officials. On the spot, he concluded that the price was good, and shook hands on the deal. Overnight, the bank officials had second thoughts – it was surely worth more than they had asked – and called him to renegotiate the price. He responded, 'my word is my bond; when we shook hands, the deal was made. Where I come from, people who break their word are found dead in ditches.' What we see in that episode was a series of conventions guaranteeing certain actions.

While many marriages become conventions for the purpose of companionable living, marriage itself is a constancy of dedication, the dedication of one's being toward another. The obligations and conventions which two people develop in marriage must be rooted in the continuing renewal of a profound self-dedication between the two. Much more primary than these conventions is the self-renewing dedication on which they are founded – one which is manifest in their giving to each other of respect, dignity and hope, even worship.

There will be times in any marriage when the conventions which the two people have worked out will collapse; and it may even seem that their dedication itself has disappeared. But that does not mean that their marriage has collapsed. For they are sustained within their original declaration – the declaration of their being toward each other – and the life which it shapes. In this way, their covenant with each other is very like the covenant seen in the Book of Deuteronomy: even the waywardness and exile of the people of Israel was within the covenant which God had established with his people, and they would return and be forgiven, 'for the Lord your God is a compassionate God; he will not ... destroy you; he will not forget the covenant that he made ... with your fathers.'[2]

Third, the self-giving in marriage is genuinely a *giving* to the other person. It is not the imposition of one on another, but the opening of possibility by one for the other. This is easily confused with power, when each in effect says to the other: you are what I tell you you are, and will do what I tell you to do. That converts giving into power, in which one has the power to impose certain possibilities on the other, implicitly confining the other person to what he or she allows. The giving in marriage is a matter of *honour*: one granting to the other respect and dignity – recognizing the other as one of intrinsic worth – and elevating him or her to true worth. This giving is a declaration of hope, looking forward to a lifetime in which the other is raised to true worth, and oneself is raised by the other.

Fourth, the self-giving is *capacious*, a readiness actually to take-hold-honour-keep-love-cherish-and-comfort under all circumstances for all life. In this sense, it is like opening up an unlimited space for the other person to flourish. By the nature of the case, therefore, it has *no bounds* – no limitations of circumstance or time. And there is no circumstance or time when it is finished: there is no 'out', expressed or implied, no 'but I won't if he or she doesn't', no 'that's the last straw'.

But however do these things happen? What can bring people into marriage, and sustain them there?

The beginning and continuing of marriage is a remarkable thing. Mar-

---

[2] Deuteronomy 4.31.

riage is always the sending forth – by two people toward each other – of profound *trust*. There are no guarantees except the anticipation of like trust from the other. Even if many people treat it as a legal contract, it is not binding in the way that a contract is; it is trust given in the expectation of trust. And trust given, responded to with trust, is the most secure, durable and expansive of all relationships – as you will quickly find from the history of God with humankind.

What basis do they have for their trust? One answer is that they have been prepared for it by all the communities – families, churches, neighbourhoods, and so forth – in which they have learned to trust others. And, by our participation in their marriage, we promise to uphold them in it.

But that rests on something still deeper – a deep bond of community between all human beings, a commonness of life which God made as a fact of life for all human beings. That ultimately is the basis on which a promise between two people is built: it goes back as far as the creative act by which God created mankind as male and female, yet one with each other and therefore with God. The promise between two people is not so fragile as it seems: it is a new realization of the creative act of God, a renewal of the communities from which these two people learned that it was possible to make promises and keep them, and the beginning of a family in which trust will be learned.

But nothing which they have learned will quite prepare them for the adventure which their marriage will be, and how thoroughly it will transform them. This poem expresses it well:

> Nothing can explain this adventure – let's say a quirk
> of fortune steered us together – we made our covenants,
> began this odyssey of ours, by hunch and guesswork,
> a blind date where foolish love consented in advance.
> No my beloved, neither knew what lay behind the frontiers.
> You told me once you hesitated: *A needle can waver,*
> *then fix on its pole*; I am still after many years
> baffled that the needle's gift dipped in my favour.
> Should I dare to be so lucky? Is this a dream?
> Suddenly in the commonplace that first amazement seizes
> me all over again – a freak twist to the theme,
> subtle jazz of the new familiar, trip of surprises.
> Gratuitous, beyond our fathom, both binding and freeing,
> this love re-invades us, shifts the boundaries of our being.[3]

---

[3] Micheal O'Siadhail, 'Out of the Blue' in *Hail! Madam Jazz*, Newcastle: Bloodaxe Books, 1992, p. 118.

The trust of marriage is as fortuitous and surprising as that even in its firmness. And it is so immense in its effect that the very being of the two is constantly altered, and the boundaries between them constantly 'shifted'.

What stands beneath the enduring trust in their marriage is the very being and activity of God. In effect, God says to them, 'Why do you not trust? I have.' Their covenant of trust is the outworking in them of the radical act of trust which God has made in making and redeeming the world; it is the expression of the blessing and enrichment of the world by God. That is why we here can declare God's blessing on this marriage; we do not simply 'drop' God's blessing on them, but find it there already and – by expressing it – magnify it. The same blessing which has brought them together is what we here celebrate; it will sustain them in their dedication to each other if their hearts are always open to it. Their trust will be upheld by God's blessing given in trust.

The effects will be seen in the very texture of their marriage. The benefits of this blessing are extraordinary: the giving and receiving of promises brings new structure and energy to the lives of those who are joined together – a kind of stability and energy provided by nothing else in life to such a degree. And those are the marks of the presence of God's blessing in their marriage. And they spread to all who are around them, to give new vitality to the trust which is the foundation of human society itself.

Kate and Frans, we pray that you, and we all, will draw constantly on the vitality of God's promise of life and blessing in the life which you are now beginning with each other. Amen.

Index of Names

Index of Subjects

23–26 *passim*, 377–378, 383, entropy and, 99–100, 126, eschatology, 154, 155, 250, and kingdom of God, 390, 394, 395, and meaning, 331, 334, 341, 351, 353, 354, 357, 358, reconstitution of, 251, 253, Chapters 25 and 26 *passim*

demarcation, absolute, 97, information-theoretical, 126–129, methodological, 115, 116, 118, 119, 123–124, *see also* boundaries, periodization

density, 139, of wisdom, 237, 245, 247, of information, 129–131

Deuteronomy, 398

direction, of attention, 96–97, 106, in creation and eschatology, Chapter 9 *passim*, of God, 25, 26, 30, of human knowledge, 238, 247, 252, 255, 256, 262, 274, 279, 285, 292, 304, 342, 343, of life, 2, 5–7, 13, 235, order in, 136, of society, 189, through theology, 41–43, 69, set by worship, 15, *see also* orientation

disciplines, 1, interdisciplinary study, 303, 304, Chapter 18 *passim*, variety, 70, 71, 153, 154, 221, 256, 257, worship and, 5, 7, 15

discipline, 229, discipleship, 365, and freedom, 395, and integrity, 348, 349

disorder, 99, 126, *see also* entropy

distribution, economic, 204, 205, of matter, 148, 176, 182, rationalizing, 362, of responsibilities and benefits, 73, 222

diversity, in contextuality, 75, in human thought, 109, of language, 65, of life, 206–208, ontological, 78, 79, 82, 86, religious, 326, social, 85, 185, 186

division, contextual, 24, 34, 70, 80, of formed, 196–197, of wisdom, 256, *see also* closure

dualism, 32, 194, 235, 239–241, 249, 256, 318

dynamic,
of Church, Chapters 12, 13 and 21 *passim*
of cognition and ethics, Chapter 2 *passim*
of contexts, Chapter 5 *passim*
of cosmos, Chapter 8 *passim*
of creation, Chapter 7 *passim*
of creation and eschatology, Chapter 9 *passim*
of cultures, Chapter 3 *passim*
in English theology, Chapter 16 *passim*
of history, Chapter 15 *passim*
of humanity, Chapter 6 *passim*
of language, Chapter 4 *passim*
of religion, theology and mission, Chapters 17 and 18 *passim*
of society, Chapters 10 and 11 *passim*
of wisdom and knowledge, Chapter 14 *passim*

Easter, 45, 359, 360, 361, Chapter 26 *passim*

Ecclesiastes, 334

ecology, 29, 34, 73, 153, 203, ecosystem, 86, 101–102, 106

economy, economics, 73, 204, 205, 218, 251, 252, 332, of history, 57–58, of language, 61, 65, of salvation, 112, 138, 307, 317, of theories, 123, 130, 256, of Trinity, 80, 87, 131, and universals, 248, in worship, 246

ecumenics, Chapter 21 *passim*

education, 179, Chapter 12 *passim*, 220, 239, Chapters 17 and 18 *passim*

empiricism, 9, 10, 70, 71, 192, 203, 231, 263

energy, contingent, 277, entropy and negentropy, 95, 99, 126–130, 232, of human well-being, 28–30, mass and, 263, in new, 338, 340, in raising others, 362, of reason, 234, 235, in shaping of universe, 140,

public, 208, 337–340, social, 49,
85, 173, 174, time, 58, universities,
212

generativity, God's, 16, 28, 60, 82,
130, 147, 334, human, 285, 361,
of life, 75–78, 102, 126, 128, of
Resurrection, 45–50, 372, of social
order, 197, 202, of wisdom, 243,
245, see also blessing, vitalities
Genesis, 94, 97, 194
gift, churches', 344, 346–347,
covenant, 368, 399, creation, 147,
162, God's, 65, 87, 161–165, 167,
169, 201, 363, 386, 390, life, 367,
368, 379, love, 373, 389, ministry,
219, 222, social, 358
glory, God's, 163–169, 189, 282,
kingdom of God, 23, 255, 357, in
language, 62, in love, 363, mystery
of, 19, 20, as well-being, 30, 382,
in worship, 21–23, 165, 169, 309,
368, 369
goals, for churches, 346–347, of
creation, 163, contingency of, 110,
289, human, 17, 21, 34, 103–105,
363, new, 340, rational, 118, 232,
236–237, social, 175–176, 180,
337, for theology, 40, 303, 310,
324, 326, for universities, 213, in
war, 394–395
God, passim
Good Friday, Chapter 25 passim
goodness, 21, 360, abundance of, 64,
created, 37, 164, God's, 162, 309,
Jesus', 64, 249, of life, 348, 350,
363, noetic, 123, 241, social, 163,
195, 300, 386, transcendental, 190,
308, virtue, 358, in wisdom, 43, in
worship, 15, 165, 167, 236, 237,
310, see also truth
gospel, 10, 20, 32, 64, 124, 343,
388
government, 160, 168, 173, 174,
178–179, 184, 223, 332
grace, 46, 57, 159, 234, 290
gravity, 34, 66, 263

healing, 225, 253, 255, 357, 359,
363, 367
Hebrews, Letter to, 22, 64
heuristics, 41, 70
historians, 266–269, 272–275, 277
history, church, 217, conceptions of,
Chapter 15 passim, as condition,
16, confusion with God, 194,
contingency, 53, 57, 108,
covenantal, 151, as discipline,
311–321, 324, economy, 58,
eschatology, Chapter 9 passim,
evolutionary, 101, Judaeo-
Christian, 254–256, God's actions
in, 61, 63, 67, 113, 128, 131, 357,
360, 367, 370, 371, 378, meaning,
117, 255, Chapters 19 and 20
passim, normative, 39, 71, 102,
198, origin, 91, particularity, 66,
83, of rationality, 232, 236,
256–259, self-referential, 116–119,
121, 196, social, 178, 179, 183,
188, 203–205, theology and,
132–135, 287, 290, 291, 296–297,
303–304, 307, 310, 326, time and,
126, and truth, 8–11, universal,
107–110, wisdom and, 238,
240–248, world, 152, 154,
worship and, 5
holiness, 16, 166, 169, 186, 200, 219,
220–224, 309
Holocaust, 254
honour, Christ's, 62, God's, 42, 308,
309, of life, 169, in marriage,
397–398, of prodigal, 64, of
suffering, 393, 395
humanism, 107, 195, historical, 264,
266, 268, 270, 271, 273–275
humanity, Chapter 6 passim, 216,
autonomous, 53, 114, 189, 256,
267, 280–291, complexity, 184,
created, 114–115, 229–234, and
culture(s), 35, 68, 293–295, and
eschatology, Chapter 9 passim,
evolution, 34, 98, 100–102, 106,
107, 193, 198, 274, 290, features
of, 17, 73, 143, 149, God's action
in, 15–16, 20–22, 26, 61, 130,